Relative Deprivation

Specification, Development, and Integration

The relative deprivation construct has been widely used in the social sciences to explain different types of phenomena from experiencing psychosomatic stress to participating in urban riots. It is currently a hot topic of research, being used primarily to understand the processes of social identity and the responses to disadvantage by both disadvantaged minorities and privileged majorities. This book assembles chapters by the world's leading relative deprivation researchers in order to present a synthesis of the current knowledge in the field. Featuring cutting-edge integrative theoretical and empirical work from social psychology, sociology, and psychology, the book will be a standard reference work for relative deprivation researchers for years to come. It is relevant to researchers in intergroup relations, prejudice, racism, social identity, group processes, social comparison, collective behavior, and social movements. This book is suited for use as a text in both graduate-level and advanced undergraduate-level courses.

Iain Walker is an Associate Professor in the School of Psychology at Murdoch University in Perth, Western Australia. He co-authored *Social Cognition: An Integrated Introduction* (1995) and has published in journals such as *British Journal of Social Psychology, European Journal of Social Psychology, Personality and Social Psychology Bulletin, Journal of Community and Applied Social Psychology, Journal for the Theory of Social Behaviour, Theory and Psychology,* and *Australian Journal of Psychology.*

Heather J. Smith is an Assistant Professor in the Psychology Department at Sonoma State University in Rohnert Park, California. She co-authored *Social Justice in a Diverse Society* (1997) and has published in journals such as *Journal of Personality and Social Psychology, Psychological Science, Personality and Social Psychology Bulletin, European Journal of Social Psychology, Journal of Non-verbal Behavior,* and *Journal of Experimental Social Psychology.*

Relative Deprivation

Specification, Development, and Integration

Edited by

Iain Walker
Murdoch University

Heather J. Smith
Sonoma State University

CAMBRIDGE
UNIVERSITY PRESS

CAMBRIDGE UNIVERSITY PRESS
Cambridge, New York, Melbourne, Madrid, Cape Town, Singapore,
São Paulo, Delhi, Dubai, Tokyo, Mexico City

Cambridge University Press
The Edinburgh Building, Cambridge CB2 8RU, UK

Published in the United States of America by Cambridge University Press, New York

www.cambridge.org
Information on this title: www.cambridge.org/9780521180696

First published 2002
First paperback edition 2010

A catalogue record for this publication is available from the British Library

Library of Congress Cataloguing in Publication data

Relative deprivation: specification, development, and integration / edited by
     Iain Walker, Heather J. Smith
          p. cm.
     Includes bibliographical references and index.
     ISBN 0-521-80132-X (hardback)
          1. Social psychology. 2. Deprivation (Psychology) 3. Intergroup relations.
     4. Social perception. 5. Collective behavior. I. Walker, Iain, 1960– II. Smith, Heather J.
     (Heather Jean), 1962–

HM1033.R45 2001
302 – dc21   2001018437

ISBN 978-0-521-80132-4 Hardback
ISBN 978-0-521-18069-6 Paperback

Contents

List of Contributors

Ann M. Beaton
Departement de Psychologie
Universite de Moncton
Moncton
Nouveau Brunswick, E1A 3E9
Canada

Matthew Crosby
The University of Tokyo
   International Lodge K208
Tokyo 153-0041
Japan

Faye Crosby
Psychology Department
University of California
   at Santa Cruz
Santa Cruz, California 95064
USA

John Duckitt
Psychology Department
University of Auckland
Auckland
New Zealand

Naomi Ellemers
Department of Social and
   Organizational Psychology
Leiden University
2300 RD Leiden
Netherlands

C. David Gartrell
Department of Sociology
University of Victoria
Victoria, BC V8W 3P5
Canada

Colin Ho
Department of Psychological
   Sciences
Purdue University
West Lafayette, Indiana 47907-1364
USA

Etsuko Hoshino-Browne
Department of Psychology
University of Waterloo
Waterloo, Ontario N2L 3G1
Canada

Aarti Iyer
Department of Psychology
University of California at
    Santa Cruz
Santa Cruz, California 95064
USA

Kerry Kretzschmar
School of Psychology
Murdoch University
Murdoch, WA 6150
Australia

Colin Wayne Leach
Department of Psychology
University of California
    at Santa Cruz
Santa Cruz, California 95064
USA

E. Allan Lind
Fuqua School of Business
Duke University
Durham, North Carolina 27708
USA

Thobi Mphuthing
Department of Psychology
University of the Witwatersrand
WITS, 2050
South Africa

James M. Olson
Department of Psychology
University of Western Ontario
London
Ontario N6A 5C2
Canada

Daniel J. Ortiz
Department of Psychology
University of California,
    Los Angeles
Los Angeles, California 90095
USA

Kazuho Ozawa
Parsons School of Design
New School University
New York, New York 10011
USA

Thomas F. Pettigrew
Department of Psychology
University of California
    at Santa Cruz
Santa Cruz, California 95064
USA

Neal J. Roese
Department of Psychology
Northwestern University
Evanston, Illinois 60208
USA

Michael Ross
Department of Psychology
University of Waterloo
Waterloo, Ontario N2L 3G1
Canada

Eliot R. Smith
Department of Psychological
    Sciences
Purdue University
West Lafayette, Indiana 47907
USA

Heather J. Smith
Department of Psychology
Sonoma State University
Rohnert Park, California 94928
USA

Nastia Snider
Department of Anthropology
University of Pennsylvania
Philadelphia, Pennsylvania 19104
USA

Marylee C. Taylor
Department of Sociology
Pennsylvania State University
University Park, Pennsylvania
16802
USA

Francine Tougas
Ecole de Psychologie
Université d'Ottawa
C.P. 450, Succ. A
Ottawa
Ontario K1N 6N5
Canada

Linda R. Tropp
Department of Psychology
Boston College
Chestnut Hill, Massachussets 02467
USA

Tom R. Tyler
Psychology Department
New York University
New York, New York 10003
USA

Iain Walker
School of Psychology
Murdoch University
Murdoch, WA 6150
Australia

Anne Wilson
Department of Psychology
University of Waterloo
Waterloo, Ontario N2L 3G1
Canada

Ngai Kin Wong
School of Psychology
Murdoch University
Murdoch, WA 6150
Australia

Stephen C. Wright
Department of Psychology
University of California at
Santa Cruz
Santa Cruz, California 95064
USA

ONE

Fifty Years of Relative Deprivation Research

Iain Walker and Heather J. Smith

The relative deprivation (RD) construct has been extensively used in social psychology, sociology, and other social sciences for more than half a century. This popularity reflects RD's usefulness for explaining numerous paradoxes (Tyler, Boeckmann, Smith, & Huo, 1997). Why were African American soldiers stationed in the southern United States more satisfied than African American soldiers stationed in the northern United States during World War II (Stouffer, Suchman, DeVinney, Star, & Williams, 1949)? Why did the 1960s urban riots in the United States occur when they did (Miller, Bolce, & Halligan, 1977)? Why aren't working women who earn less than their male colleagues more angry (Crosby, 1982)? The list could continue. The common theme among the answers to these questions is that people's reactions to objective circumstances depend on their subjective comparisons. African American soldiers compared their situation with the situation for local African Americans (a situation much worse in the South than in the North). The urban riots followed a period of economic and political gain for minorities that ironically created a discrepancy between their expectations and a reality that was not improving quickly enough. And, most working women compare their situation with other working women, not with their male colleagues.

Obviously, a concept that can explain so many different phenomena is one worth having in the armory of the social sciences. However, research on RD has progressed only fitfully. The construct of RD was first articulated by Stouffer and his colleagues (Stouffer et al., 1949) to explain a series of unexpected relationships between feelings of satisfaction and one's position in the army. The seductive nature of RD as a post hoc explanation led to a wide range of applications and definitions. Unfortunately, many attempts to test the concept directly were less successful (e.g., Gaskell & Smith, 1984; Thompson, 1989). For example, in the area of social movement research, RD was once commonly used as an explanatory vehicle (e.g., Abeles, 1976; Geschwender & Geschwender, 1973; Gurr, 1970). However, by the 1980s, the construct fell into disfavor and disrepute, partly because of devastating reviews by McPhail (1971) and Gurney and Tierney (1982). Subsequent social movement research relied almost exclusively on concepts such as resource mobilization to explain when and why people engage in collective behavior. The 1990s, though, saw the rediscovery of RD and its integration into theories of collective behavior. The ways in which people interpret grievance – central to RD – are now recognized as essential to a full under-standing of social movement participation (e.g., Kelly & Breinlinger, 1996; Klandermans, 1997; Simon et al., 1998; Tyler & Smith, 1998).

Over the past ten years, RD researchers have elaborated the distinction between feeling deprived as a unique individual and feeling deprived as a representative group member, and have integrated RD theory with other related theories such as social identity theory, social comparison theory, and distributive justice theory. The purpose of this book is to summarize recent developments in RD research and to help steer research in the coming years. We approached leading researchers from around the world and asked them to describe their recent work. Different authors have, as their work dictates, focused on different aspects of RD. We have organized each of their chapters into one of the three broad categories of specification, development, and integration. Of course, each chapter pertains to all three categories in one way or another.

SPECIFICATION

One risk of having a concept such as RD ranging as widely as it does is that it becomes too wide and ends up explaining nothing. Central to the task of precise specification of any construct is the delineation of what it is *not* as much as what it is, and of where it does *not* apply as much as where it does. Theoretical work by Crosby (1976, 1982), Folger (1984, 1986), and others has led to clarification of the nature and number of preconditions necessary to the experience of RD. Cook, Crosby, and Hennigan (1977) clearly articulated the contradictory positions regarding preconditions, especially the notion of feasibility, taken by earlier researchers. Subsequent research by Crosby (1982) and others pared the number of preconditions to just two: wanting what one does not have, and feeling that one deserves whatever it is one wants but does not have. The four chapters in the first section of the book continue, directly or indirectly, to specify more precisely the RD construct and its range of applicability.

Taylor's chapter begins the book by showing how a close reading of three perspectives on white racism – Runciman's fraternal deprivation, Blumer's collective threat, and Kinder and Sanders' racial resentment – reveals more similarities than differences. She supports her theoretical conclusions with analyses of data from the 1990 and 1994 U.S. General Social Surveys. Taylor uses the convergence of these three perspectives to suggest new questions for research – how are intergroup boundaries maintained and how do stratification systems define groups' interests?

Taylor draws on an important and frequently used distinction in the RD literature between egoistic (or personal) and fraternalistic (or group) RD. The former normally refers to RD experiences produced through intrapersonal or interpersonal social comparisons; the latter to RD experiences produced through intergroup comparisons. In their chapter, Tyler and Lind propose extending to the intergroup level the distinction between procedural and distributive justice that has been important at the interpersonal level. Across three studies, Tyler and Lind show that disadvantaged comparisons based on *treatment* consistently explain more variance in people's reactions than disadvantaged comparisons based on *outcomes*.

The transition in South Africa from apartheid to a majority Black government provides the political backdrop to the study reported in the chapter by Duckitt and Mphuthing. In their research, Black South African participants completed measures of cognitive and affective RD and reported their attitudes toward Afrikaans and English Whites before and after the transition. Although ratings of RD and illegitimacy changed from pre- to post-transition, these changes were not accompanied by any notable changes in intergroup attitudes. This research is particularly remarkable because it combines a longitudinal design with a charged political context – both rare events in social psychological research.

The final chapter in this section on the further specification of the RD construct is by Smith and Ortiz. RD theory initially promised to explain, among other things, participation in collective behavior, but some claim this promise has not been realized. Smith and Ortiz explore several important theoretical distinctions within RD theory that help account for this failure, and then present meta-analytic evidence to support these distinctions. The meta-analysis suggests clearly that group and affective measures of RD *do* predict relevant social behaviors, so long as the measures directly tap RD and do not infer it from comparisons of responses to different items. The second part of the chapter extends the meta-analysis by incorporating aspects of social identity theory into an explanation and test of reasons for the differential effects of personal and group RD.

DEVELOPMENT

As important as clear specification of theoretical constructs is, a theory on which only specification work was done would quickly pass away. Theories need to be developed in many ways if they are to continue to have currency in the academic community. The five chapters in this section illustrate some of the important theoretical and empirical developments over the past decade.

In the first chapter, Tougas and Beaton examine three types of relative deprivation: personal, group, and deprivation experienced on behalf of others. The vicarious experience of RD is an especially underresearched area, but the phenomenon of advantaged group members acting for the interests of a disadvantaged group (and against their personal and group interests) is surely common enough to be worthy of more attention. Tougas and Beaton summarize several studies demonstrating the importance of temporal and social comparisons to all three types of RD, and showing the differential impacts of the three types on social behaviors. Finally, the chapter proposes an integrative approach to the relationships between social identity, self-esteem, and relative deprivation. This model systematizes existing knowledge and points the way for future research in this area.

Whereas Tougas and Beaton explore the possibility that majority group members might feel deprived on behalf of a disadvantaged group, Leach, Iyer and Snider explore the psychology of the advantaged more completely, including the more common tendency for the advantaged to ignore or minimize their disadvantage. Drawing on material from many different disciplines, Leach and his colleagues present an innovative, integrative model of reactions to relative advantage. They propose three broad classes of reactions to advantage (taking advantage for granted, minimizing advantage, and acknowledging advantage) that each contain several different ways of experiencing advantage. Finally, they examine the implications of different reactions for promoting or inhibiting social change.

Social comparisons between people (as individuals or as groups) are at the heart of relative deprivation. A perennial problem in relative deprivation theory is the inability to specify a priori who compares with whom. Gartrell argues forcefully that a main reason for the continuation of this problem lies in psychologists' assumption that individuals are free agents to engage in whichever social comparisons they choose. Instead, Gartrell argues, social comparisons are embedded in social networks that largely dictate comparison others. Elaborating a model of embedded social comparisons, Gartrell then presents evidence that treating social comparisons as patterns of ties in a social network affords a powerful new understanding of the nature and meaning of social comparisons.

Gender discrimination in the workplace is a global problem, and affirmative action policies are one of the most common and effective tools used to attack discriminatory practices. Crosby, Ozawa, and Crosby reason that reactions to gender discrimination and to affirmative action policies are likely to vary across nations and cultures. In particular, they propose that responses may depend on whether the focus is on how practices affect either an individual or a group. They suggest that Americans, being predominantly individualistic, are likely to favor remedies to the problem of gender discrimination that focus on individuals, whereas Japanese, being more collectivistic, will favor categorical remedies. After presenting data from Japan and America testing these ideas, the authors consider the implications of cross-cultural research work for relative deprivation research.

There are many different possible responses to the perception of relative deprivation or disadvantage, ranging from collective action to doing nothing. In the final chapter of this section, Wright and Tropp incorporate (1) insights from social identity theory and self-categorization theory, (2) the distinction between personal and group relative deprivation, and (3) the distinction between cognitive and affective relative deprivation to build an impressive model of responses to disadvantage. Their model and its supporting research especially helps us understand why it is that grievance so often fails to result in collective action.

INTEGRATION

Much of the current integrative work was presaged by a seminal contribution to the Nebraska Symposium on Motivation series by Tom Pettigrew in 1967. In that chapter, Pettigrew integrated research from social psychology, sociology, anthropology, and education into a single focus on "social evaluation." Following this tradition, the last decade or so has seen considerable work integrating the construct into other, related frameworks. Notable in this regard has been work relating RD to social identity theory (SIT). Tajfel (1981, 1982) and subsequently Tajfel's students and colleagues (e.g., Hogg & Abrams, 1988; Tajfel & Turner, 1979; Turner, Hogg, Oakes,

Reicher, & Wetherell, 1987) developed SIT partly in response to the over-whelmingly individualistic emphasis of North American social psychology at the time. SIT is a broad theory of social behavior, and now occupies a position of international prominence. Tajfel early on saw the links between RD and social identity (e.g., Tajfel, 1981, pp. 259–267).

Following Tajfel's lead, several chapters in this section, as well as in the other sections, employ social identity theory to help explain or further explicate relative deprivation effects and conundrums. The chapter by Ellemers tackles the relationship between social identity and relative deprivation theories directly and systematically. Ellemers outlines an integrative model linking the antecedents and consequences of social identification with behavioral and social consequences. Resonating with the theoretical and empirical perspective presented in the chapter by Wright and Tropp, this model neatly draws together two different research traditions into a single framework and ought to serve as a guide for research for some time.

Relative deprivation theory typically asserts that social and/or temporal comparisons are an essential component in assessing whether one is deprived. Olson and Roese argue that both these comparisons can be subsumed within the more general process of counterfactual comparisons between one's current outcomes and the outcomes that might have been. Olson and Roese enumerate principles of research on counterfactual thinking, and apply each principle to relative deprivation. The product is a clear research agenda for examining the cognitive processes involved in constituting relative deprivation, as well as greater theoretical integrativeness, breadth, and depth.

The chapter by Walker, Wong, and Kretzschmar attempts to delineate a theoretical integration of principles from attribution theory into relative deprivation theory, and provides a series of testable hypotheses derived from this integration. Two studies are described, each designed to address some of the attributional processes linking grievance interpretation to social action. The first, of members of environmental groups, leads to the conclusion that relative deprivation principles may not apply to all kinds of protest action. The second, of personal and group relative deprivation in a sample of working women, suggests that attributional style exerts a predictable and significant influence in the mediation between grievance and action.

Relative deprivation theorists rarely take a developmental approach to the study of relative deprivation. Similarly, they rarely study naturally occurring in situ comparisons leading to perceived injustice. The chapter by Wilson, Hoshino-Browne, and Ross documents a study of naturally occurring social comparisons in the narratives children provide about conflicts involving them and their siblings. The number of comparisons made increased with age, but even the younger children made comparisons (at ages younger than the literature suggests). The children mostly made social, not temporal, comparisons. Moreover, children seemed satisfied with the way conflicts about perceived inequalities between themselves and their siblings were resolved. The chapter exemplifies how relative deprivation research can be researched in situ, focusing on naturally occurring conflicts of practical interest and importance, and also furthers the integration of principles from social comparison theory into relative deprivation theory.

Smith's (1993) reconceptualization of prejudice as intergroup emotion presented a significant turn in the understanding of prejudice. The prejudice-as-emotion model is used in his chapter with Ho to provide a framework within which linkages to relative deprivation and social comparison are developed. These linkages make group relative deprivation a significant precursor of prejudice. The model is then used to explain the paradoxical finding that positive stereotypes of Asian Americans can lead to negative emotions (prejudice) toward the same group.

THE CONTRIBUTIONS OF THOMAS F. PETTIGREW

The RD construct recently (1999) celebrated its fiftieth birthday. When we developed the idea for this book, and when we approached potential authors, the field was celebrating another anniversary – the thirtieth anniversary of a landmark publication by Tom Pettigrew (1967). Pettigrew's 1967 chapter is a landmark in many ways. It demonstrates clearly the broad, multidisciplinary nature of RD, drawing examples from theory and research in psychology, social psychology, sociology, education, economics, and political science – a rare feat in a single publication, especially a single-authored publication. The chapter also was notable in its application of sometimes esoteric social scientific theory and research to significant social problems. In many ways, Pettigrew's chapter is a prototype of the sort of social psychology that significant pioneers of social psychology such as Kurt Lewin envisaged.

It is significant, and certainly no accident, that both of us, and many of the contributors to this volume, have been students and/or colleagues of Pettigrew. His influence in social psychology generally, and on RD work particularly, has been widespread and lasting. It is rare in social psychology that a publication exerts significant influence more than thirty years on. The present volume provides testimony to Pettigrew's lasting influence on the field, as well as to the significant personal influence he has had on many of the authors within the present volume. We are lucky indeed that Pettigrew agreed to write a concluding chapter (his "old man" chapter, as he calls it) to the book, addressing each of the chapters within it, as well as the area of RD overall.

In his chapter, Pettigrew encapsulates what he sees as eight prominent themes from across the chapters in the book, and puts them neatly into historical and theoretical perspective. Typically unable to resist pushing ideas further, he develops a few hypotheses from these themes, and goes on to test them with one of his all-time favorite data sets – the 1988 Euro-barometer Survey (Reif & Melich, 1991). In this and other ways, Pettigrew's concluding chapter is typical of his contributions to the field over almost four decades.

We hope that the chapters in this book will foster the progression of RD from a provocative post hoc explanation of unexpected findings to a fleshed out theory of social justice.

REFERENCES

Abeles, R. P. (1976). Relative deprivation, rising expectations, and Black militancy. *Journal of Social Issues, 32,* 119–137.

Cook, T. D., Crosby, F. J., & Hennigan, K. M. (1977). The construct validity of relative deprivation. In J. M. Suls & R. L. Miller (Eds.), *Social comparison processes: Theoretical and empirical perspectives* (pp. 307–333). Washington, DC: Hemisphere.

Crosby, F. J. (1976). A model of egoistical relative deprivation. *Psychological Review, 83,* 85–113.

Crosby, F. J. (1982). *Relative deprivation and working women.* New York: Oxford University Press.

Folger, R. (1984). Perceived injustice, referent cognitions, and the concept of comparison level. *Representative Research in Social Psychology, 14,* 88–108.

Folger, R. (1986). A referent cognitions theory of relative deprivation. In J. M. Olson, C. P. Herman, & M. P. Zanna (Eds.), *Relative deprivation and social comparison: The Ontario symposium* (Vol. 4, pp. 217–242). Hillsdale, NJ: Lawrence Erlbaum.

Gaskell, G., & Smith, P. (1984). Relative deprivation in Black and White youth: An empirical investigation. *British Journal of Social Psychology, 23,* 121–131.

Geschwender, B. A., & Geschwender, J. A. (1973). Relative deprivation and participation in the civil rights movement. *Social Science Quarterly, 54,* 405–411.

Gurney, P., & Tierney, K. (1982). Relative deprivation and social movements: A critical look at twenty years of theory and research. *Sociological Quarterly, 23,* 33–47.

Gurr, T. R. (1970). *Why men rebel.* Princeton, NJ: Princeton University Press.

Hogg, M. A., & Abrams, D. (1988). *Social identifications: A social psychology of intergroup relations and group processes.* London: Routledge.

Kelly, C., & Breinlinger, S. (1996). *The social psychology of collective action: Identity, injustice, and gender.* Washington, DC: Taylor & Francis.

Klandermans, B. (1997). *The social psychology of protest.* Oxford: Blackwell.

McPhail, C. (1971). Civil disorder participation: A critical examination of recent research. *American Sociological Review, 36,* 1058–1073.

Miller, A. H., Bolce, L. H., & Halligan, M. (1977). The J-curve and the Black urban riots: An empirical test of progressive relative deprivation theory. *American Political Science Review, 70,* 964–982.

Pettigrew, T. F. (1967). Social evaluation theory: Convergences and applications. In D. Levine (Ed.), *Nebraska symposium on motivation* (Vol. 15, pp. 241–311). Lincoln: University of Nebraska Press.

Reif, K., & Melich, A. (1991). *Euro-barometer 30: Immigrants and outgroups in Western Europe, October–November 1988.* (ICPSR 9321). Ann Arbor, MI: Interuniversity Consortium for Political and Social Research.

Simon, B., Loewy, M., Sturmer, S., Weber, U., Freytag, P. Habig, C., Kaupmeier, C., & Spahlinger, D. (1998). Collective identification and social movement participation. *Journal of Personality and Social Psychology, 74,* 646–658.

Smith, E. R. (1993). Social identity and social emotions: Towards new conceptualizations of prejudice. In D. Mackie & D. Hamilton (Eds.), *Affect, cognition, and stereotyping* (pp. 297–315). San Diego, CA: Academic Press.

Stouffer, S. A., Suchman, E. A., DeVinney, L. C., Starr, S. A., & Williams, R. M. (1949). *The American soldier: Adjustment to army life* (Vol. 1). Princeton, NJ: Princeton University Press.

Tajfel, H. (1981). *Human groups and social categories: Studies in social psychology.* Cambridge: Cambridge University Press.

Tajfel, H. (1982). *Social identity and intergroup relations.* Cambridge: Cambridge University Press.

Tajfel, H., & Turner, J. C. (1979). An integrative theory of intergroup conflict. In W. G. Austin & S. Worchel (Eds.), *The social psychology of intergroup relations* (pp. 33–48). Monterey, CA: Brooks/Cole.

Thompson, J. L. (1989). Deprivation and political violence in Northern Ireland, 1922–1985. *Journal of Conflict Resolution, 33,* 676–699.

Turner, J. C., Hogg, M. A., Oakes, P. J., Reicher, S. D., & Wetherell, M. S. (1987). *Rediscovering the social group: A self-categorization theory.* New York: Blackwell.

Tyler, T. R., Boeckmann, R. J., Smith, H. J., & Huo, Y. (1997). *Social justice in a diverse society.* Boulder, CO: Westview Press.

Tyler, T. R., & Smith, H. J. (1998). Social justice and social movements. In D. Gilbert, S. T. Fiske, & G. Lindzey (Eds.), *Handbook of social psychology* (4th ed., Vol. 2, pp. 595–629). New York: McGraw-Hill.

PART ONE

SPECIFICATION

TWO

Fraternal Deprivation, Collective Threat, and Racial Resentment

Perspective on White Racism

Marylee C. Taylor

"Fraternalist" relative deprivation (Runciman, 1966) was spotlighted in Thomas F. Pettigrew's (1967) integrative outline of social comparison processes. Vanneman and Pettigrew's (1972) subsequent study examined survey data from White residents of four cities for evidence that fraternalist but not egoistic deprivation predicted "competitive racism," characterized as opposition to structural change. More recently, Pettigrew and Meertens (1995) assessed the impact of fraternalist deprivation on blatant and subtle prejudice toward minorities in four European countries.

This chapter compares Runciman's fraternal deprivation with two perspectives that have very different roots: from the symbolic interactionist school of sociology, Blumer's (1958) "collective threat," and from political psychology, Kinder and Sanders' (1996) "racial resentment," along with its close cousins "symbolic racism" and "modern racism." We assess the overlap of these perspectives as conceptualized and as measured. Points made about the operationalization of fraternal deprivation, collective threat, and racial resentment are illustrated with data from the 1990 and 1994 U.S. General Social Surveys.

RUNCIMAN'S CONCEPT OF FRATERNAL DEPRIVATION

The concept of fraternalist deprivation was formally introduced into the sociology literature by Runciman in 1966. Focusing on class, status, and power hierarchies in Britain, Runciman asked when inequality is translated into grievance and why so often it is not. His focus was the attitudes of subordinate groups vis-à-vis the respective superordinate group in a hierarchy, for example, the attitudes of manual toward white-collar workers.

In the subordinate group, the sense of grievance labeled relative deprivation (Merton & Kitt, 1950; Stouffer et al., 1949) is said to be motivated by the desire to rise in the hierarchy of class, status, or power. Formally, "A is relatively deprived of X when (i) he does not have X, (ii) he sees some other person or persons, which may include himself at some previous or expected time, as having X (whether or not this is or will be in fact the case), (iii) he wants X, and (iv) he sees it as feasible that he should have X" (Runciman, 1966, p. 10).

Entitlement

Runciman's use of "feasible" in this list of conditions left considerable ambiguity (Olson & Hazlewood, 1986): Feasibility has sometimes been interpreted simply as future likelihood or past occurrence, sometimes as sense of entitlement.

Indeed, entitlement has received considerable attention in the literature as a defining characteristic of relative deprivation (e.g., Gurr, 1970). Pettigrew describes relative deprivation "in the basic case" as feelings of "unfairness" as well as deprivation (1967, pp. 262–263) and later speaks of "unfair exchange" and "injustice" as "essentially a recasting of 'relative deprivation'" (1967, p. 266). Williams similarly stresses the importance of perceived entitlement as foundation for experienced relative deprivation – perceived entitlement that may be promoted by universalistic norms (1975, p. 364) and rapid social change (1975, p. 370).

After earlier outlining six factors involved in relative deprivation, Crosby came to focus on two: "frustrated wants and violated entitlements" (1984, p. 51). In her important empirical project, Crosby identified sense of deservingness as "probably most important of all in accounting for the differential frequencies of group and personal deprivation among working women" (1982, p. 95).[1]

Affect

Relative deprivation may entail perceptual comparison, but as the term "deprivation" implies, affect is central to the phenomenon as well. Some writers explicitly acknowledge an affective as well as a cognitive component. Thus Dube and Guimond (1986, p. 207) identify "perceptions of intergroup inequality" and "feelings of group discontent" as elements forming a causal chain that leads to social protest (see also Veilleux & Tougas, 1989, p. 486). But even when the presence of affect is not explicitly noted, terms used to characterize relative deprivation clearly signify the affective dimension. Runciman often uses "resentment" in describing the experience of fraternalist deprivation (for an example, see 1966, p. 33). Crosby measured group relative deprivation among working women by asking whether they "felt 'bitter or resentful'" (1982, p. 80). More recently, Tyler and Smith described relative deprivation as a judgment "linked to feelings of anger and frustration" (1998, p. 597).

The Fraternalist/Egoistic Distinction

What distinguishes fraternalist from egoistic deprivation? In Runciman's words: "Did he [sic] want to rise out of his membership group or with it? If the first, then he was dissatisfied with his position as a member of what he saw as his group; if the second, then he was dissatisfied with the position of what he saw as his group relative to other groups in the larger system" (1966, p. 31). The distinction is important because fraternalist deprivation uniquely generates agitation for or against structural change.

According to Runciman, the key factor promoting fraternalist deprivation is "lateral solidarity," a sense of kinship with other members of one's membership group (1966, p. 34). Here reference group theory becomes useful, particularly the distinction between comparative and normative functions of reference groups (Hyman, 1942; Kelley, 1952). For Runciman, whereas any form of relative deprivation represents the *comparative* influence of reference groups, the lateral solidarity that channels deprivation into fraternalist forms may represent the *normative* influence of reference groups, as when norms of working-class solidarity channel grievance into fraternalist deprivation.[2]

Subsequent analysts have echoed and elaborated on Runciman's outline. Vanneman and Pettigrew (1972) affirm the formative role of "ingroup solidarity" in channeling grievance into fraternalist deprivation. Williams (1975, p. 368) identifies "closure of intimate social interaction ... barriers against social locomotion out of the category ... (and) attachments" as factors promoting fraternal rather than individual deprivation.

Recalling Tajfel's (1982) insights, Dube and Guimond (1986, p. 212) remind readers that social categorization itself must be recognized as the foundation of any ingroup/outgroup comparisons. Social identity theory offers expanded understanding of this process: Individuals' investment in their membership group and the salience of group boundaries increase the likelihood that relative deprivation will be experienced in its fraternalist form (Tyler & Smith, 1998, p. 598). Runciman's (1966) discussion of solidary norms within the working class serves as a reminder that investment and salience are not determined solely by individual characteristics or transitory situational factors.

Runciman's typology clearly rang true to other social scientists. The fraternalist/egoistic distinction has figured in a long list of conceptual treatments and empirical reports: To name a few: Crosby (1976); Martin (1981); Meertens and Pettigrew (1997); Pettigrew (1967); Pettigrew and Meertens (1995); Pettigrew (2000); Taylor (1980); Tyler and Smith (1998); Vanneman and Pettigrew (1972); Walker and Pettigrew (1984); Williams (1975).[3]

Instead of the original "egoistic" and "fraternalist" forms labeled by Runciman, recent literature is more likely to distinguish between "individual" or "personal" and "group" deprivation (e.g., Pettigrew & Meertens, 1995; Tyler & Smith, 1998); "collective" is sometimes the label for the second category (e.g., Major, 1994). Crosby (1984, pp. 77–78) offered a more elaborate terminological scheme. To the conventional set of personal (egoistic) and "in-group" (fraternal) deprivation, she added: "ideological deprivation," sympathizing with the plight of a group other than one's own (here Crosby cites Hennigan [1977]); and "backlash," resenting the gains of an outgroup. In subsequent literature, the ideological deprivation notion seems rarely considered a form of relative deprivation (but, for one exception, see Veilleux & Tougas, 1989). Crosby's final "backlash" label did not stick, but the phenomenon has been widely analyzed as group relative deprivation based on downward comparison by members of the dominant group. This phenomenon is the central focus here and the topic to which we now turn.

Downward Group Comparisons
Translation of *in*equality into grievance is not Runciman's (1966) only concern. As Runciman's illustrations unfold, we learn that translation of *equality* into grievance is at issue as well: When lower nonmanual workers in mid-twentieth-century England responded with relative deprivation to manual workers' gains, the root was the nonmanual workers' desire to maintain a relatively privileged position, in Runciman's words "to maintain a diminishing difference" (1966, p. 93). Thus relative deprivation based on dominant group members' comparisons with subordinate groups comes in to the picture.

In the absence of a well-developed conceptual outline, downward relative deprivation must be understood by extrapolation from the dynamics of upward relative deprivation. If the fraternal deprivation experienced by subordinate groups allows for the pursuit of ambition while maintaining strong fraternal ties, presumably lateral solidarity also underlies the fraternal deprivation experienced by dominant groups anxious to preserve for their group a "diminishing difference."

Vanneman and Pettigrew (1972) captured the spirit of Runciman's downward comparison discussion when they identified White Americans' reactions to Black advances as a form of relative deprivation. In survey data from four American cities, these researchers examined the relationship of fraternal deprivation with "contact" and "competitive" racism, concluding that competitive racism, which they characterized as opposition to structural change, is uniquely linked to fraternal deprivation (but see Taylor, 1980).

Although application of the relative deprivation construct to upward comparisons is more common, Vanneman and Pettigrew (1972) were not alone in treating dominant group reactions to encroachment by a subordinate group as relative deprivation (e.g., Pettigrew & Meertens, 1995; Taylor, 1980; Veilleux & Tougas, 1989). As Tyler and Smith (1998, p. 599) note, some analysts (Crosby, 1984; Kahneman, 1992; Williams, 1975) have suggested that losses may be more psychologically poignant than blocked gains, so that in Williams's words: "A narrowing of differentials between Ego and those just below him are more salient and consequential than widening of differentials between Ego and those above his position" (1975, p. 368).

Thus fraternal deprivation on the part of a dominant group vis-à-vis a subordinate group may be a particularly powerful phenomenon. Compiling the themes previously summarized, just what characterizes this form of fraternal deprivation? The experience of deprivation encompasses frustration, anger, and resentment; fraternal deprivation flows from a sense of entitlement; it may entail the perception that norms of fairness and justice have been violated; it is a manifestation of group solidarity, salient intergroup boundaries, and investment in ingroup identity, encouraged not only by personal and situational factors but by prevailing norms.[4]

MEASURING FRATERNAL DEPRIVATION

How has fraternal deprivation been assessed? Runciman measured the sense of fraternal class deprivation by asking his 1962 British and Welsh respondents whether manual workers were doing much better than white-collar workers and whether manual workers "ought to do as well as they are doing," comparatively speaking (1966, p. 302).

Among subsequent examinations of downward group relative deprivation, Vanneman and Pettigrew's (1972) study is prominent. Vanneman and Pettigrew (1972) relied on respondents' assessments of their personal economic gains over the past five years in relation to their ingroup on the one hand, and to their outgroup on the other; White respondents reporting that they kept apace of Whites but fell behind Blacks were considered fraternally deprived. Taylor (1980) employed the Vanneman and Pettigrew "economic gains" questions to measure fraternal deprivation among Whites, and also used the difference in respondents' placements of Blacks and Whites on a ladder representing rank in American society.

To assess European respondents' "group relative deprivation" vis-à-vis minorities, Pettigrew and Meertens (1995) relied on a question asking whether over the past five years "people like yourself in (the nation)" have been better or worse off than "most (minority group) living here" (1995, p. 67).

These operationalizations of fraternal deprivation among the dominant group have not featured the affective component of fraternal deprivation spotlighted when Crosby asked female respondents how "bitter or resentful" they were about various aspects of "women's employment situation" (1982, p. 80). Affect did receive attention, however, when Veilleux and Tougas (1989) represented collective relative deprivation among men as the product of the men's assessments of the disadvantage affirmative action brings their group and their reported levels of dissatisfaction with that disadvantage. Also, Dube and Guimond (1986) explicitly acknowledged affect when they examined perceptions of inequality as one precursor of group discontent, which then motivates social protest.

HERBERT BLUMER'S "SENSE OF GROUP POSITION" AND "COMPETITIVE THREAT"

At first glance, Herbert Blumer's (1958) perspective on social stratification and intergroup relations may seem diametrically opposite from that of Runciman. For one thing, although portrayals of fraternal deprivation often emphasize structural factors that have common influence on similarly situated individuals (Runciman, 1966; Vanneman & Pettigrew, 1972), empirical work typically focuses on individual differences among members of the focal group (e.g., Pettigrew & Meertens, 1995; Vanneman & Pettigrew, 1972). Herbert Blumer (1958) denies interest in individual differences, calling attention instead to the collective definitions groups construct of themselves, of outgroups, and of the relations between them. Social psychologists in other traditions (e.g., Pettigrew, 1991) might say Blumer's concern is with norms rather than attitudes.

Attention to collective definitions rather than to individual differences is not the only point of contrast between Runciman (1966) and Blumer (1958).

Where Runciman (1966) looked at relative deprivation along the dimensions of class, status, and power, Herbert Blumer's (1958) concern was the racial divide. And where Runciman's study emphasized upward comparison, Blumer's influential essay was explicitly confined to downward comparison, to the perspective of the dominant group vis-à-vis subordinate groups.

Between Runciman and Blumer, however, there are also many points of contact, as revealed by looking closely at Blumer's powerful essay on "prejudice as sense of group position."

For Blumer, precisely what is the sense of group position? "The sense of group position is the very heart of the relation of the dominant to the subordinate group. It supplies the dominant group with its framework of perception, its standard of judgment, its patterns of sensitivity, and its emotional proclivities" (1958, p. 4). "Sociologically it is not a mere reflection of the objective relations between racial groups. Rather, it stands for 'what ought to be' rather than for 'what is.' It is a sense of where the two racial groups *belong*" (1958, p. 5).

For Blumer, race prejudice entails such a collective definition held by the dominant group vis-à-vis a subordinate group. It contains four elements: (1) feeling of superiority; (2) feeling of differentiation; (3) feeling of "proprietary claim to certain areas of privilege and advantage"; and (4) sense that those privileges and advantages are threatened by the subordinate group. It is the fourth element that fully activates Blumer's race prejudice. "Race prejudice is a defensive reaction to such challenging of the sense of group position. It consists of the disturbed feelings, usually of marked hostility, that are thereby aroused. As such, race prejudice is a protective device. It functions, however short-sightedly, to preserve the integrity and the position of the dominant group" (1958, p. 5).

More needs to be said about Blumer's notion of collective definition. He tells us: "Race prejudice presupposes, necessarily, that racially prejudiced individuals think of themselves as belonging to a given racial group. It means, also, that they assign to other racial groups those against whom they are prejudiced. Thus, logically and actually, a scheme of racial identification is necessary as a framework for racial prejudice. Moreover, such identification involves the formation of an image or a conception of one's own racial group and of another racial group, inevitably in terms of the relationship of such groups" (1958, p. 3).

Blumer goes on to emphasize that racial identification is forged through a complex collective process.

First, the process of definition occurs obviously through complex interaction and communication between the members of the dominant group. Leaders, prestige bearers, officials, group agents, dominant individuals and ordinary laymen present to one another characterizations of the subordinate group and express their feelings and ideas on the relations. Through talk, tales, stories, gossip, anecdotes, messages, pronouncements, news accounts, orations, sermons, preachments and the like definitions are presented and feelings are expressed. In this usually vast and complex interaction separate views run against one another, influence one another, modify each other, incite one another and fuse together in new forms.... Currents of view and currents of feeling come into being; sweeping along to positions of dominance and serving as polar points for the organization of thought and sentiment. If the interaction becomes increasingly circular and reinforcing, devoid of serious inner opposition, such currents grow, fuse and become strengthened. It is through such a process that a collective image of the subordinate group is formed and a sense of group position is set. The evidence of such a process is glaring when one reviews the history of any racial arrangement marked by prejudice (1958, pp. 5–6).

Finally, this collective definition may override understandings borne of individual experience. "Thus, even though given individual members may have personal views and feelings different from the sense of group position, they will have to conjure with the sense of position held by their racial group. If the sense of position is strong, to act contrary to it is to risk a feeling of self-alienation and to face the possibility of ostracism" (1958, p. 5).

It should be emphasized that the form and power of the sense of group position is determined in an inegalitarian fashion, not through coalescence of individual perspectives but "in those areas where the dominant group as such is characterizing the subordinate group as such ... in the 'public arena' wherein the spokesmen appear as representatives and agents of the dominant group ... legislative assemblies, public meetings, conventions, the press, and the printed word" (1958, p. 6). Disproportionate influence is "exercised by individuals and groups who have the public ear and who are felt to have standing, prestige, authority and power" (1958, p. 6). Strong interest groups may play a pivotal role, vigorously "seeking to manufacture events to attract public attention and to set lines of issue in such a way as to predetermine interpretations favorable to their interests" (1958, p. 6).

It would be a mistake to read Blumer's description to imply that racism in the United States is inevitable. His perspective implies that shifting conditions such as migration, political realignment and international events may set change in motion. But emphasis should be placed on the "may." Blumer leaves room for variability not only over time but in the match between perceived racial threat and actual material contingencies. His primary attention is directed not at economic or political realities but at the agents that serve as mediators and moderators in the production of collective definitions – the media and political leaders.

Finally, Blumer concludes that

> race prejudice has ... (a) variable and intermittent career.... The sense of group position dissolves and race prejudice declines when the process of running definition does not keep abreast of major shifts in the social order. When events touching on relations are not treated as 'big events' and hence do not set crucial issues in the area of public discussion; or when the elite leaders or spokesmen do not define such big events vehemently or adversely; or where they define them in the direction of racial harmony; or when there is a paucity of strong interest groups seeking to build up a strong adverse image for special advantage – under such conditions the sense of group position recedes and race prejudice declines (1958, p. 7).[5]

Measuring Collective Threat

Operationalizing Blumer's (1958, 1965) perspective is a daunting task. Taken literally, his viewpoint would seem to require tracing changes in norms over time or differences across societies. However, social psychologists are wedded to the study of individual differences, and a number of researchers have attempted to represent Blumer's perspective in their individual-level analyses, assessing the impact of "group conflict," "group threat," or "group interest" on racial views. In Bobo and Kluegel (1993), Whites' racial group self-interest was said to be reflected in unaccounted-for White/Black differences in racial policy views. Earlier, Bobo (1983) found evidence of "realistic group conflict" in the fact that Whites' dislike of Black political efforts and of government action on behalf of Blacks predicted opposition to busing. A few years later, Bobo (1988) similarly found support for the group conflict model in the pattern of White and Black reactions to Black political efforts.

Bobo's recent research attempts more direct representation of Blumer's "group-position model." In Bobo and Hutchings (1996), "competitive threat" is represented by the self-reported belief that zero-sum conditions pertain to the outcomes achievable by various ethnic groups. Jackman (1994) measured perceived group interests in a similar fashion, looking for evidence of zero-sum thinking in respondents' assessments that specific policies would help or harm the dominant group on the one hand, the subordinate group on the other. In Bobo and Zubrinsky, because "it is ideas and beliefs about the relative group positions that constitute the psychological core of prejudice, not merely in-group attachment or out-group aversion," Blumer's group position model is represented by an "affective differentiation" measure – the difference in thermometer ratings assigned Whites and minorities (1996, p. 892).

A different empirical approach – contextual analysis – has also been employed to represent Blumer's ideas and theories of collective threat and competition. When Taylor (1998) and Fossett and Kiecolt (1989) found that local Black population share affects White residents' attitudes, the pattern was interpreted as a possible manifestation of racial threat. (Taylor [1998] also attempted more direct assessment of threat, examining the possible mediational role played by opinions that Whites are losing out to equally or less-qualified Blacks in the labor market, and that Whites have too little and Blacks too much influence on American life and politics.) Quillian (1996) used regional per capita income as well as population proportions as indicators of racial threat.

KINDER AND SANDERS'S "RACIAL RESENTMENT"

"Racial resentment" is introduced into Kinder and Sanders's *Divided by Color: Racial Politics and Democratic Ideals* in this fashion: "A new form of prejudice has come to prominence, one that is preoccupied with matters of moral character, informed by the virtues associated with the traditions of individualism. At its center are the contentions that Blacks do not try hard enough to overcome the difficulties they face and that they take what they have not earned. Today, we say, prejudice is expressed in the language of American individualism" (1996, pp. 105–106). But also, more broadly, the authors say that racial resentment "distinguishes between those Whites who are sympathetic toward Blacks and those who are generally unsympathetic" (1996, p. 106).

Kinder and Sanders (1996) acknowledge a close relationship between the racial resentment construct and other conceptualizations of "new racism" in America. "Symbolic racism," claimed by Sears and Kinder (1971) to drive the suburban White vote in the 1969 Bradley/Yorty mayoral campaign in Los Angeles, is "racial animosity of a particular sort, one emphasizing abstract, moralistic racial resentments: Blacks were too pushy, they were getting more than they were entitled to, Blacks on welfare were lazy and didn't need the help, they were receiving attention from government that they didn't deserve" (Kinder & Sanders, 1996, p. 291). "Disconnected from the experiences of everyday life," Kinder and Sanders say, "symbolic racism appeared to be an expression of a moral code, a sense of how people should behave and society should work" (1996, p. 291). And later, we learn, Kinder and Sears (1981) defined symbolic racism as "'a blend of antiblack affect and the kind of traditional American values embodied in the Protestant Ethic … based … in deep-seated feelings of social morality and propriety and in early-learned racial fears and stereotypes'" (Kinder & Sanders, 1996, p. 291).

Sears's writings reiterate these themes. Sears and Allen (1984) summarize the meaning of symbolic racism using the Kinder and Sears (1981) phrasing: The new racism is a blend of antiblack affect with traditional American values. Sears and Allen also identify the "content of symbolic racism … (as falling) … into three categories: (1) a denial that discrimination continues against Blacks … (2) resentment about special favors for Blacks … and (3) antagonism toward Blacks' 'pushing too hard' and moving too fast" (1984, p. 133).

Another form of American new racism, acknowledged by Kinder and Sanders as a close cousin to racial resentment, is McConahay's "modern racism" (McConahay, 1982; McConahay & Hough, 1976), which "derives from 'the feeling that Blacks are violating cherished values or making illegitimate demands for changes in the racial status quo' … (with) essential tenets … that 'discrimination is a thing of the past, Blacks are pushing too hard, they are getting too much attention and sympathy from the nation's elites, and that Blacks gains and demands are no longer justified'" (1996, p. 292).

Communalities seen by Kinder and Sanders among symbolic racism, modern racism, and "subtle racism" (Pettigrew & Meertens, 1995) lie in their shared insistence "that racism is the *conjunction* of prejudice and values" (1996, p. 292). (Pettigrew and Meertens' subtle racism is not treated in this chapter as a member of the racial resentment/symbolic racism/modern racism family because of important distinctions outlined later.)

In most respects, Kinder and Sanders reportedly intend racial resentment to "take on the characteristics normally attributed to symbolic racism … like symbolic racism, racial resentment is thought to be the conjunction of Whites' feelings toward Blacks and their support for American values, particularly secularized versions of the Protestant ethic" (1996, p. 293). But also, importantly, "Like symbolic racism, racial resentment features indignation as a central emotional theme, one provoked by the sense that Black Americans are getting and taking more than their fair share" (Kinder & Sanders, 1996, p. 293).

Kinder and Sanders join Sears, McConahay, and their colleagues in attempting to demonstrate that this new form of racism is a particularly powerful predictor of important policy opinions. But Kinder and Sanders offer a distinctive contribution by focusing on the societal context of the growth in White racial resentment, making an "effort to specify how racial ideology is shaped by alterations in intellectual currents, changes in economic arrangements, and eruptions of political crisis" (1996, p. 294).

Measuring Racial Resentment, Symbolic Racism, and Modern Racism

Operationalizations of symbolic racism have fluctuated over the years, a fact that has not gone unnoticed by critics. Whites' opinions taken in the original Sears and Kinder (1971) paper to represent symbolic racism are these: Local officials pay less attention to Whites than Blacks; Blacks receiving welfare could get along without it; Blacks have recently gained more than they are entitled to; and Blacks shouldn't push themselves where they are not wanted (1971, p. 365). Opinions representing symbolic racism in Kinder and Sears (1981) included these early four, together with a second statement that Blacks get more than they deserve, opposition to quotas in college admission, and denial that Blacks face discrimination in employment. Most recently, Sears, Henry, and Kosterman (2000) describe survey measures of symbolic racism as falling in four categories: Opinion that Blacks receive undeserved advantage (three items); denial of continuing discrimination (three items); opinion that Blacks make excessive demands (two items); and opinion that Blacks violate the work ethic (three items).

McConahay's (1982) research combined the following into an index of modern racism: Opinion that government and media have been showing Blacks more respect than they deserve; opinion that Blacks have been getting more economically than they deserve; opinion that Blacks are too demanding in their push for equality; lack of understanding of Black anger; and denial of antiblack discrimination in jobs or housing (two items). A subsequent, widely adopted operationalization of modern racism (McConahay, 1986) collapses the two denial of discrimination items into one and adds opinion that Blacks have more influence on school desegregation than they ought, together with a second reaction against Black pushing.

How has racial resentment been operationalized? Originally, it represented opinion that Blacks could get along without welfare if they tried; claims that Blacks have gotten more than they deserve; denial that government officials pay less attention to Blacks; denial that the legacy of slavery and discrimination makes it hard for Blacks to work their way up the social class ladder; affirmation that Blacks should work their way up without special favors; and opinion that Blacks could do as well as Whites if they just tried harder (Kinder & Sanders, 1996). More recently, Kinder and Mendelberg (2000) rely on four U.S. General Social Survey items to measure racial resentment: affirmation that Blacks should work their way up without special favors; attribution of racial inequality to Blacks' lack of motivation; denial that racial inequality is attributable to discrimination; and opinion that Blacks get more attention from government than they deserve.

FRATERNAL DEPRIVATION, COLLECTIVE THREAT, AND RACIAL RESENTMENT – IN THEORY

What is the relationship among the concepts of Runciman, Blumer, and Kinder and Sanders? The preceding discussion alluded to some points of contrast. Runciman focused on class, status, and power. Blumer, as well as Kinder and his associates, analyzed the racial divide. Runciman's primary interest was in those groups that are relatively deprived in some observable sense – subordinate groups in a hierarchy – with limited acknowledgment of dominant groups' reactions when their advantage shrinks. Those dominant group reactions are the focus of Blumer, as well as Kinder and Sanders. Without denying the influence of societal conditions and norms, Runciman's concern, shared by Kinder and his collaborators, was individuals' views. Blumer focused on collective definitions or norms, not individuals. Here we have another point of contrast.

Even when the three frameworks are applied to the same phenomenon – White Americans' individual views on race – a central semantic distinction exists. Runciman's fraternal deprivation is envisioned as a precursor to prejudice and racism: For example, as construed by Vanneman and Pettigrew (1972), fraternal deprivation among Whites – the feeling that Blacks are pulling ahead vis-à-vis Whites – is an intermediate construct, putatively mediating structural influences on competitive racism. In contrast, Blumer's 1958 title "Prejudice as a Sense of Group Position" reveals his view that the collective definition and reaction he describes is itself the essence of prejudice. Blumer might say: Egoistic deprivation based on perceived status differentials doesn't lead to status envy, it *is* status envy; fraternal deprivation on the part of blue-collar workers vis-à-vis white-collar workers doesn't lead to a sense of class competition, it *is* a sense of class competition; and fraternal deprivation felt by Whites vis-à-vis Blacks doesn't lead to racism, it *is* racism. Like Blumer's collective threat, Kinder and Sanders' racial resentment is itself a form of racism or prejudice.

The semantic distinction notwithstanding, when both are applied to the orientation of Whites vis-à-vis minorities, Runciman's fraternal deprivation is strikingly similar to Blumer's sense of group position. The foundation of both phenomena is said to be salient racial identity and solidarity that entails perceived entitlement to position and privilege. When minority group gains diminish the intergroup difference that "ought" to exist (Runciman) or threaten the group position of Whites (Blumer), those gains are perceived to be unjust and thus evoke the resentment and hostility called fraternal deprivation by Runciman and prejudice by Blumer.

What of racial resentment and the sister concepts symbolic racism and modern racism? How distinct are they from the constructs of Runciman and Blumer? That depends on which definitional statements are taken most seriously and, more important, how definitional themes are seen to intersect.

The insistence by Kinder and his associates that individualism, along with antiblack affect, is a key element of racial resentment, symbolic racism, and modern racism would seem to distinguish this new form of American racism from fraternal deprivation and collective threat.

However, other themes are present in definitions of the new racism as well. Recall Sears and Kinder (1971) saying that symbolic racism is "racial animosity of a particular sort, one emphasizing abstract, moralistic racial resentments: Blacks were too pushy, they were getting more than they were entitled to, Blacks on welfare were lazy and didn't need the help, they were receiving attention from government that they didn't deserve" (Kinder & Sanders, 1996, p. 291). As noted earlier, modern racism is said to derive from "'the feeling that Blacks are violating cherished values *or* making illegitimate demands for changes in the racial status quo'... (with) essential tenets ... that 'discrimination is a thing of the past, Blacks are pushing too hard, they are getting too much attention and sympathy from the nation's elites, and that Blacks gains and demands are no longer justified'" (1996, p. 292, emphasis added). And as for racial resentment? Again recall an earlier-quoted passage: "Like symbolic racism, racial resentment features indignation as a central emotional theme, one provoked by the sense that Black Americans are getting and taking more than their fair share" (Kinder & Sanders, 1996, p. 293).

How do these broader themes fit with the individualism element in formal definitions of racial resentment/symbolic racism/modern racism?

Gains made by Black Americans over the past several decades have been due, in substantial measure, to government action (see, e.g., Farley [1996]). Calls for continuation of such intervention are supported by claims that past and present discrimination fetter even the most worthy African Americans. Opposition to continued official action on behalf of Blacks is justified by denying discrimination as a barrier and by blaming current racial inequality on Blacks' alleged failure of effort and enterprise. The point made by Bobo, Kluegel, and Smith's (1997) "laissez faire racism" label for the racial perspective prevalent today is this: In the current context, to say that discrimination has disappeared, that there is no need for further intervention on behalf of Blacks, that Blacks can and should pull themselves up by individual effort – that is, to advocate laissez-faire policy – is to seek a halt in movement toward racial equality.

So, shall individualism be viewed as a root of opposition to efforts that would continue Black gains? If so, racial resentment and its cousins are clearly differentiated from fraternal deprivation and collective threat. But insistence on the sanctity of individualism may more often be a rationale for the call to stop the train of Black progress, justification for opposing Black encroachment on areas of White privilege. If the role of individualism in expressions of the new racism is thus construed, we are left with indignation at purportedly illegitimate Black demands and gains as the core of the new racism. And the gulf that divides this form of racism from fraternal deprivation and collective threat recedes.

Implicit acknowledgment of convergence among the fraternal deprivation, collective threat, and racial resentment/symbolic racism/modern racism constructs can sometimes be seen in the language of analysts working within the respective frameworks. Thus, for example, Veilleux and Tougas (1989) considered the collective "self-interest" that may lead men to oppose affirmative action is an example of Runciman's "collective relative deprivation." Vanneman and Pettigrew found that Runciman's "fraternalistic deprivation offered a way to conceptualize" the possibility that "status and economic threat" are involved in the racism of skilled White workers (1972, p. 469). Dube and Guimond (1986, p. 210) draw a parallel between: (a) their conclusion that group relative deprivation is more important than individual relative deprivation in predicting protest; and (b) Sears's claims that "abstract and moralistic resentment" are more important than direct individual threat in predicting Whites' racial policy opinions.

FRATERNAL DEPRIVATION, COLLECTIVE THREAT, AND RACIAL RESENTMENT – AS MEASURED

Fraternal Deprivation

Operationalizations of fraternal deprivation more often represent the perceptual/cognitive facet of the phenomenon – the comparison itself – than the fuller and more heated reaction of injustice, resentment, anger, and frustration depicted in conceptual treatments. (For examples of "cool"

Table 2.1. *Pearson Correlation Coefficients Relating Alternate Measures of Fraternal Deprivation to Policy Opinion Scales*[a]

	Policy Opinion	
Measures of Fraternal Deprivation	**Affirmative Action**	**Government Action**
Relative wealth	.007	.055
	(1145)	(1091)
Relative trends	.132***	.156***
	(748)	(731)
Blacks displacing Whites	.228***	.281***
	(1141)	(1091)
Undeserved government attention	.321***	.398***
	(1126)	(1078)

[a] Data come from the 1994 General Social Survey. *N*s are presented in parentheses.

* $p < .05$ **$p < .01$ ***$p < .001$

measures, see Pettigrew & Meertens, 1995; Taylor, 1980; Vanneman & Pettigrew, 1972.) For this reason, fraternal deprivation as measured is more sharply distinguished from collective threat and racial resentment than is fraternal deprivation in theory.

But if the cognitive operationalizations serve to make fraternal deprivation measures distinctive, they also fail to capture an important dimension of the phenomenon, a point made by Walker and Pettigrew (1984). By implication, "cool" measures probably underestimate the impact of fraternal deprivation.

The effect estimates reported in Table 2.1 illustrate this point. Analyses were performed on data from the 1994 General Social Survey, administered to a probability sample of households in the continental United States (Davis & Smith, 1994).

Two scales of policy opinion served as outcomes: Affirmative Action represents responses to two questions about preferential hiring and promotion; Government Action represents opinions about government spending for Blacks, governmental responsibility to redress antiblack discrimination, and busing. For both policy scales, opposition was scored high.

Four measures of fraternal deprivation were featured. Relative Wealth is similar to the Cantril ladder: It is the difference in respondents' placement of "Whites in general" and Blacks on a seven-point scale ranging from rich to poor. Relative Trends is the difference between respondents' estimates of the trend in conditions for Blacks over the past few years and the trend in the nation's economy over the past year (both standardized). Blacks Displacing Whites is a scale built from four questions about how often Blacks are given preference over equally or better-qualified Whites in the labor market and college admissions. Undeserved Government Attention is the difference in answers to questions about whether Blacks on the one hand, Whites on the other, get more or less attention than they deserve from the government. For all four fraternal deprivation measures, views that Blacks are relatively advantaged were scored high.[6]

The four fraternal deprivation predictors vary in the extent to which they refer to entitlement and thereby presumptively tap reactions of anger or resentment. The Relative Wealth and Relative Trend measures are entirely "cool," reflecting straightforward assessments of Black/White economic status and trends. Given the meritocratic norms that prevail in American society, Blacks Displacing Whites, with its specification that the Blacks getting the jobs instead of Whites are less or at best equally qualified, does raise the issue of entitlement, though without explicitly measuring White respondents' reactions. It is intermediate on the cool/warm continuum. Undeserved Government Attention, explicitly tapping respondents' reactions as well as their perceptions, lies at the warm end of the continuum.

The estimates reported in Table 2.1 are Pearson correlation coefficients representing the impact of each fraternal deprivation measure on the two policy opinion scales. (The correlations differ minimally from standardized regression coefficients produced by multivariate analyses in which age, gender, education, occupational prestige, work status, and region [South vs. non-South] served as controls.)

The strength of the estimated effects of fraternal deprivation increases as the warmth of the fraternal deprivation measure rises. Relative Wealth has a near-zero and nonsignificant effect on the policy outcomes. In line with the widespread observation that changing conditions are more potent instigators of relative deprivation than static differences, Relative Trends does show a significant effect on both policy opinion scales, but these effects are modest in size. The estimated effects of fraternal deprivation are notably stronger when Blacks Displacing Whites is the measure, as its intermediate position on the cool/warm continuum would suggest. And the effects are strongest for Undeserved Government Attention, the fraternal deprivation measure that explicitly taps respondents' reactions as well as their perceptions of Black and White outcomes.

The 1990 General Social Survey contained fewer items reasonably construed as measures of fraternal deprivation, but it was possible to construct three scales representing cool, intermediate, and warm points on the continuum of fraternal deprivation measures: a Relative Wealth scale identical to the 1994 scale; a Blacks Displacing Whites measure based on a single question about preferential hiring; and an Undeserved Socio/Political Influence measure built from a pair of questions asking whether Blacks on the one hand, Whites on the other, have more or less influence than they deserve on American life and politics. The policy opinion outcome was a Government Action scale parallel to that used in the analysis of 1994 General Social Survey data.[7] Results (not shown) closely parallel those reported in Table 2.1. The estimated impact of Relative Wealth on policy opinions was near zero and nonsignificant. The estimated impact of Blacks Displacing Whites was significant and intermediate in size (Pearson r = .259, p < .001). The estimated impact of fraternal deprivation measured with the warm Undeserved Socio/Political Influence scale was not only significant but substantial (Pearson r = .437, p < .001).

To recap, though the theory is "warm," the most commonly used measures of fraternal deprivation have been "cool." Not surprisingly, the warmth of the measure makes a difference. If results from our modest empirical exploration of General Social Survey data are to be believed, measures that capture Whites' reactions to the relative outcomes of Blacks and Whites are considerably stronger predictors of racial policy opinion than cool measures of fraternal deprivation. Smith and Pettigrew's (2001) meta-analysis leads them to the same conclusion. Importantly, the warmer and more potent measures of fraternal deprivation advocated by Walker and Pettigrew (1984) look very much like some operationalizations of competitive threat and racial resentment.

Collective Threat

Individual-level measures of collective threat cover quite a range, from belief in a zero-sum reality (Bobo & Hutchings, 1996); to expression of resentment at Black political efforts (Bobo, 1983, 1988) and sociopolitical advantages (Bobo, 1983; Taylor, 1998); to relative affective orientation toward Blacks and Whites (Bobo & Zubrinski, 1996).

As noted earlier, contextual analyses arguably model Blumer's ideas more closely than individual-level analyses. One form of contextual analysis assesses main effects of such demographic patterns as racial proportions (Fossett & Kiecolt, 1989; Quillian, 1995, 1996; Taylor, 1998), but there are other possibilities as well. For example, Blumer would have researchers chart public discourse in order to trace changes in collective definitions or norms. Where localities are being compared, such investigations might focus on local media and political debate, as suggested in Taylor (1998).

An alternative approach picks up on Blumer's statement that prejudice declines where issues once seen in racial terms are no longer defined as racial. We know that levels of prejudice, opposition to race targeting, and progressive policy-related beliefs are more prevalent where Blacks are a greater share of the population, as are subjective expressions of racial threat or competition (Taylor, 1998). But in heavily Black localities, evidence that race is important in public debate might also be seen in elevated effects of traditional prejudice and subjective racial threat on explicitly racial policy opinion and on opinion in policy arenas like welfare and crime, not racial on their face but often linked to race in public discourse and presumably in individual thinking.

This approach to studying collective threat is represented in Kinder and Mendelberg's (1994) assessment of the interaction of prejudice and "racial isolation" in affecting racial policy opinion and views about welfare, crime, and aid to cities. Competitive threat theories imply that prejudice should be more closely tied to policy opinion among Whites in racially diverse contexts than among Whites who are racially isolated. Using individuals' reports of interracial contact as the measure of racial isolation, the earlier researchers found just the opposite: Prejudice had more impact on policy opinion among Whites who were racially isolated, a pattern interpreted to reflect the benefits of intergroup contact on Whites' attitudes.

Illustrative analyses performed for this chapter also examined the interaction of racial context and individual attitudes in affecting policy opinion, but with an important difference: Kinder and Mendelberg's (1994) measure of racial context was survey respondents' reports of personal interracial contact, behavior that arguably suffers from being a potential outcome as well as cause of racial attitudes. The analysis reported here employed a data file that links responses to the 1990 General Social Survey with 1990 census-based descriptors of the respondents' localities. Thus our contextual measures come from official statistics for the area rather than respondents' self-reports of volitional behavior.

Our focus is correlations of traditional prejudice and subjective racial threat with policy opinion that is either explicitly racial or potentially racially linked. The question is whether these correlations differ across localities as a function of Black population share.

A Traditional Prejudice scale was built from 18 General Social Survey items that assess racial stereotyping, aversion to interracial contact, and opposition to racial equality in principle (for details, see Taylor, 1998). The

Racial Threat scale represents questions about how often Whites lose out on jobs to equally or less qualified Blacks and whether Whites and Blacks, respectively, have too much or too little influence on American life and politics. The Race-Targeting policy scale represents opinions about governmental responsibility and spending; enterprise zones, educational programs, and scholarships, and busing (see Taylor, 1998). The Welfare scale represents evaluations of spending levels, subsidy amounts, and work requirements. The Punish Crime scale reflects opinion on capital punishment, leniency by the courts, and the relative importance of protecting innocent accusees versus convicting the guilty.[8] High scores reveal prejudice, threat, and conservative policy opinions.

Correlations of Traditional Prejudice and Racial Threat with the Race Targeting, Welfare, and Punish Crime policy opinion scales are presented in Table 2.2, first for White residents of localities where the Black population share was low, then for Whites living in areas with proportionately larger Black populations. The pattern is uniform: In each case, the correlation is stronger among White residents of localities with large proportions of Black residents – as competitive threat notions suggest.

A qualifying note should be quickly added. Multivariate analyses were performed, with age, gender, education, work status, occupational pres-

Table 2.2. *Correlation Coefficients Relating Traditional Prejudice and Racial Threat to Race Targeting, Welfare, and Punish Crime Policy Opinion Scales, for Localities Where the Black Population Share is Low and High.[a]*

	Race Targeting	Welfare	Punish Crime
Low Black Population Share			
Traditional prejudice	.333***	.196***	.110*
	(186)	(444)	(432)
Racial threat	.393***	.192***	.093*
	(216)	(548)	(528)
High Black Population Share			
Traditional prejudice	.422***	.242***	.181*
	(215)	(498)	(486)
Racial threat	.434***	.264***	.189***
	(239)	(571)	(560)

[a] Data come from the 1990 General Social Survey. Ns are presented in parentheses.

* $p < .05$ ** $p < .01$ *** $p < .001$

tige, city size, and region serving as controls. The interaction of Black population share with Traditional Prejudice and Racial Threat was always in the direction revealed in the bivariate correlations, but none of the six interaction effects was statistically significant. Thus these analyses do not provide strong support for predictions derived from competitive threat theories. It is nonetheless interesting that interactions observed here run in the direction opposite from those observed in Kinder and Mendelberg (1994). The discrepancy testifies to the differing role of individual interracial contact, often voluntary, and an aggregate racial context that lies beyond individual control. More broadly, these analyses illustrate an approach that brings individual-level and contextual data together to represent Blumerian notions about competitive threat.

Racial Resentment

The dictionary defines "resent" as follows: "To feel or show displeasure and indignation ... [at (some act, remark, etc.) or toward (a person),] from a sense of being injured or offended."

As revealed in the earlier discussion, this definition aptly describes most of the survey items used over the years to measure symbolic racism, modern racism, and racial resentment. In fact, the entire modern racism scale, probably the most common means of measuring ideas represented under this trio of labels, fits neatly under the dictionary definition of resentment.

Generally speaking, the individualism theme found in definitions of these related constructs is explicitly represented by a minority of items in symbolic racism scales, in no items of the modern racism scale, and in several of the "racial resentment" items.

By implication, empirical support that new racism is important in the United States has been marshalled using operationalizations of these constructs in which racial resentment is arguably dominant and commitment to individualism explicitly represented only occasionally. It is ironic that with the newest, "racial resentment" variant, we gain a label more descriptive than "symbolic" or "modern racism" of the symbolic and modern racism scales, while the items composing the racial resentment measure focus less uniformly on resentment and more on individualism.

Is it more appropriate to designate individualism and antiblack affect as the twin engines of the new racism? Or, as the newest "racial resentment" label suggests, is resentment the core of the new racism, with denial of discrimination and affirmation of individualism serving as supporting justifications?

A strategy for assessing these alternate constructions is to decompose the new racism scales, asking which items are carrying the biggest load, most strongly predicting policy opinions. Data limitations allow only a tentative and sketchy illustration of this approach here.

Table 2.3 presents two sets of bivariate correlations from the 1990 and 1994 General Social Surveys, respectively. Individual items that are identical or similar to those included in scales of racial resentment/symbolic racism/modern racism serve as racial attitude predictors. For the 1990 data, the Race Targeting policy scale represented in Table 2.2 and described in the preceding section serves as the policy opinion outcome measure represented in Table 2.3. For the 1994 data, the Government Action policy scale represented in Table 2.1 and described in the text for that section serves as the Table 2.3 policy opinion outcome. Because interpretation of the attitudinal predictors is the issue here, the table presents the full question wording.

All correlations in Table 2.3 run in the predicted direction, new racism attitudes predicting the nonprogressive racial policy position. Readers may not concur in every case about whether a given predictor primarily represents an affirmation of individualism or the expression of racial resentment; however, the character of some predictors seems clear. In the 1990 and the 1994 data, the attribution of racial inequality to Blacks' lack of effort and motivation makes the most explicit reference to individualistic norms. And in both surveys, this is the weakest predictor of policy opinions. On the other side, the items that make no explicit or implicit reference to individualism can easily be identified – for the 1990 data, the statement that Blacks have too much influence on American life and politics; and for the 1994 data, that Blacks get attention they don't deserve from government. These purest representatives of the racial resentment notion are relatively strong predictors of racial policy opinions in the respective surveys, one of the two strongest predictors in the 1990 data and by a substantial margin the strongest predictor in the 1994 data. (Of the remaining items, as a group showing intermediate relationships with policy opinion, four of the five are assessments of discrimination.)

As acknowledged earlier, this evidence cannot support strong claims about a particular interpretation of racial resentment/symbolic racism/modern racism scales. However, the analysis suggests a strategy for pursuing the interpretational question. And the item-by-item examination of the 1990 and 1994 GSS data does provide tentative support for the suggestion that racial resentment may be a more relevant ingredient in the new racism than individualistic values.

Table 2.3. *Correlation Coefficients Relating New Racism Scale Items to 1990 Government Action and 1994 Race Targeting Policy Scales[a]*

1990 General Social Survey	Race Targeting
On the average Blacks have worse jobs, income, and housing than White people. Do you think these differences are…	
Because most Blacks just don't have the motivation or will power to pull themselves up out of poverty?	.300*** (430)
Mainly due to discrimination?	.398*** (437)
How much discrimination is there that hurts the chances of (Blacks) to get good paying jobs? Would you say there is a lot, some, only a little, or none at all?	.341*** (444)
How much discrimination is there that makes it hard for (Blacks) to buy or rent housing wherever they want?	.317*** (443)
Some people think that certain groups have too much influence in American life and politics, while other people feel that certain groups don't have as much influence as they deserve. On this card are three statements about how much influence a group might have. (1. Too much influence, 2. Just about the right amount of influence, 3. Too little influence). For each group … just tell me the number of the statement that best says how you feel … Blacks	.394*** (433)

1994 General Social Survey	Government Action
On the average Blacks have worse jobs, income, and housing than White people. Do you think these differences are…	
Because most Blacks just don't have the motivation or will power to pull themselves up out of poverty?	.159*** (712)
Mainly due to discrimination?	.263*** (711)

(continued)

Table 2.3 *(continued)*

1994 General Social Survey	Government Action
Do you agree strongly, agree somewhat, neither agree nor disagree, disagree somewhat, or disagree strongly with the following statement: Irish, Italians, Jewish and many other minorities overcame prejudice and worked their way up. Blacks should do the same without any special favors.	.272*** (745)
Do you think that Blacks get more attention from government than they deserve? Would you answer much more attention from government than they deserve, more attention than they deserve, about the right amount of attention, less attention than they deserve, or much less attention than they deserve?	.385*** (1089)

[a] Data come from the 1990 and 1994 General Social Surveys. Ns are presented in parentheses.

$*p < .05$ $**p < .01$ $***p < .001$

By now it should be clear why this chapter omits Pettigrew and Meerten's (1995) "subtle racism" from the racial resentment/symbolic racism/modern racism family of constructs and measures. As their label suggests, Pettigrew and Meertens' emphasis is on the covertness of their "subtle" scale, its capacity to detect racism among those who seek to avoid appearing racist to themselves or others. The analysts explicitly place racial threat on the other side of the fence, an aspect of "blatant" racism, in contrast to "subtle." The affective facet of subtle racism is the withholding of sympathy and admiration – quite different from resentment. Thus subtle racism is described as "cool, distant, and indirect," where blatant racism is "hot, close, and direct" (Meertens & Pettigrew, 1997, p. 54). The apparent point of contact between subtle racism and the racial resentment/symbolic racism/modern racism scales is that defense of "traditional values" is one of the three subtle racism subscales. Two of the four items in the traditional values subscale of the subtle racism measure explicitly refer to the virtues of effort and self-reliance (Meertens & Pettigrew, 1997), the heart of "traditions of individualism" as described by Kinder and Sanders (1996, pp. 105–106). But the argument I advanced previously suggests that hot, close, and direct racial resentment may be more central than the traditional value of individualism to the racial resentment/symbolic racism/modern racism scales.

CONCLUSION

The purpose of this chapter has been to assess the overlap and the distinctiveness of three frameworks used to understand White racism, frameworks having very different roots – Walter Runciman's (1966) fraternal deprivation, Herbert Blumer's (1958) collective threat, and David Kinder and Lynn Sanders's (1996) racial resentment.

Our conclusion is that the overlap is a great deal more extensive than treatments of these concepts generally acknowledge. Many apparent points of distinction turn on semantic choices. Others disappear in application. Among the three sets of concepts and measures, it is difficult to identify consistent points of distinction.

Comparison of intergroup outcomes is central in the label "fraternal relative deprivation," more implicit in discussions of collective threat and racial resentment. But when the goal is to "maintain a diminishing difference" in favor of Whites, when Whites feel entitled to superior position and are angry at encroachment, the fraternal deprivation perspective comes to look very similar to collective threat and racial resentment.

The prejudice described by Blumer as "a sense of group position" is a collectively developed and understood phenomenon, a "norm" in the language of others. But most recent empirical work relying on Blumer examines individual differences, erasing level of analysis as a differentiating feature of the collective threat perspective.

In formal definitions, racial resentment and other forms of new racism operationalized with American data are typically differentiated from old-fashioned racism, with which they share antiblack affect, by the emphasis on defense of traditional values, particularly individualism. However, the originators of the new racism scales also often describe the phenomenon they assess in terms aptly summarized by the "racial resentment" label, making it look very much like downward fraternal deprivation and collective threat.

Recognizing the convergence among these perspectives raises some questions about their application to the study of racism among Whites. For one thing, is downward fraternal deprivation most usefully portrayed as a mediating variable, a precursor of prejudice, or might it more aptly be viewed as a form of racism itself? Also, how appropriate is it to pit collective threat and new racism perspectives against each other in empirical studies?

Overall, however, recognizing convergence among the three perspectives does not so much suggest limits or changes as identify opportunities to expand and synthesize psychological, sociological, and political insights.

Although not Runciman's emphasis, recent treatments of fraternal relative deprivation underline the need to better understand ingroup identification and the maintenance of intergroup boundaries (Brewer, 1991; Tajfel, 1982; Turner et al., 1987). Understanding these phenomena is no less important for analysts grounding their work in Blumer's concept of collective threat or in some variant of new racism theory than for relative deprivation theorists.

Blumer's outline of prejudice as sense of group position calls attention to societal history and to the stratification system that defines group interests. Also, Blumer reminds us of one simple and straightforward reality – the power of the status quo, recalling the insistence of Williams (1975), Crosby (1984), and Kahneman (1992) that losing ground is more painful than failure to gain.

But Blumer also points to a more complicated reality of race relations – the coexistence of collective definitions and pressures with individual inclinations. Recognition of this coexistence undergirds insights of sociologists like Merton (1949) as he depicts fair-weather liberals, and psychologists like Devine (1989) as she discusses automatic and controlled components of prejudice. This coexistence bears on the challenging task of encouraging generalization from positive cross-race experiences of individuals to judgments about groups (Cook, 1984; Pettigrew & Martin, 1987). Tracing the intersection of normative patterns and personal proclivities remains a crucial challenge.

When Blumer discusses the importance of opinion leaders and lobbying groups, he calls attention to political processes. Fleshing out this crucial part of the picture, analyzing recent patterns of racial discourse in terms of party politics and media portrayals, is a major contribution of Kinder and Sanders.

In short, the convergence of these three perspectives underlines the need for analyses of race relations to be enriched with multidisciplinary understandings.

As this chapter noted points of conceptual overlap and convergence, it also made several empirical suggestions. "Warmer" measures of fraternal deprivation, explicitly tapping perceived entitlement and affect, increase the overlap of this construct with collective threat and racial resentment, but they also represent fraternal deprivation theory more faithfully and relate more powerfully to other racial attitude measures. Contextual analysis offers opportunities to examine Blumer's ideas at the collective level he intended. Such examination need not be confined to main effects of context: Assessing the interaction between context and individual attitudes is one strategy for understanding the intersection of the two levels. As for racial resentment and its cousins symbolic and modern racism, more detailed correlational analysis of specific survey questions may increase our understanding of just what constitutes the new racism.

There is no shortage of conceptual and empirical challenges.

NOTES

1. Later, in 1986, Crosby expresses disappointment in the performance of both the six-factor and the two-factor formulations and suggests treating relative deprivation as a concept rather than a model.
2. The fraternalist/egoist distinction was approached in an earlier exposition by Davis (1959), which was spotlighted in Pettigrew (1967). After describing the outcome of comparisons between "ego" and "alter," Davis turns to comparisons with outgroup alters that generate feelings "toward alter's group," feelings of "relative subordination" or "relative superiority," in either case "social distance." In the same vein, Williams notes that "when comparisons deal with groups or categories as such, the relative *gratification* of the individual becomes the relative *superiority* of a collectivity; the phenomenon is vividly illustrated in countless forms of invidious distinctions" (1975, p. 363).
3. For a discussion of the construct validity of egoistic deprivation, see Cook, Crosby, and Hennigan (1977). The earlier authors saw a need for considerable work refining the relative deprivation concept, although their suggested approach was quite different from that offered here.
4. If the related points made by Davis (1959) and Williams (1975) are brought into the picture, the phenomenon entails an effort by dominant group members to increase social distance and maintain a sense of relative superiority.
5. If writing this passage ten years later, Blumer might well have given greater attention to the influence of political efforts on the part of the subordinate group.
6. 1994 GSS variables encompassed in Table 2.1 measures are as follows:
    Affirmative Action – JOBAFF, AFFRMACT
    Government Action – NATRACE, NATRACEY, HELPBLK, BUSING
    Relative Wealth – WLTHBLKS, WLTHWHTS
    Relative Trends – BLKSIMP, ECONPDWN
    Blacks Displacing Whites – DISCAFF, DISCAFFY, COLAFF, COLAFFY
    Undeserved Government Attention – BLKGOVT, WHTGOVT
7. 1990 GSS variables encompassed in measures used for supplementary analyses are as follows:
    Government Action – NATRACE, NATRACEY, HELPBLK, BUSING
    Relative Wealth – WLTHBLKS, WLTHWHTS

Blacks Displacing Whites – DISCAFF
Undeserved Socio/Political Influence – INFLUBLK, INFLUWHT
8. 1990 GSS variables encompassed in Table 2.2 measures are as follows:
Traditional Prejudice – INTLBLKS, INTLWHTS, WORKBLKS, WORKWHTS, FAREBLKS, FAREWHTS, VIOLBLKS, VIOLWHTS, PATRBLKS, PATR-WHTS, MARBLK, LIVEBLKS, RACFEW, RACHAF, RACMOST, RACPRES, RACSEG, RACMAR
Racial Threat – DISCAFF, INFLUBLK, INFLUWHT
Race Targeting – NATRACE, NATRACEY, HELPBLK, BLKZONE, BLKSCHS, BLKCOL, BUSING
Welfare – NATFARE, LESSFARE, WORKFARE
Punish Crime – CAPPUN, COURTS, VERDICT

REFERENCES

Blumer, H. (1958). Race prejudice as a sense of group position. *Pacific Sociological Review, 1,* 3–7.
Blumer, H. (1965). The future of the color line. In J. C. McKinney & E. T. Thompson (Eds.), *The South in continuity and change* (pp. 322–336). Durham, NC: Seeman.
Bobo, L. (1983). Whites' opposition to busing: Symbolic racism or realistic group conflict? *Journal of Personality and Social Psychology, 45,* 1196–1210.
Bobo, L. (1988). Attitudes toward the Black political movement: Trends, meaning and effects on racial policy preferences. *Social Psychology Quarterly, 51,* 287–302.
Bobo, L., & Hutchings, V. L. (1996). Perceptions of racial group competition: Extending Blumer's theory of group position to a multiracial social context. *American Sociological Review, 61,* 951–972.
Bobo, L., & Kluegel, J. R. (1993). Opposition to race-targeting: Self-interest, stratification ideology, or racial attitudes? *American Sociological Review, 58,* 443–464.
Bobo, L., Kluegel, J. R., & Smith, R. A. (1997). Laissez faire racism: The crystalliza-tion of a 'kinder, gentler' anti-black ideology. In S. A. Tuch & J. K. Martin (Eds.), *Racial attitudes in the 1990s: Continuity and Change.* Greenwood, CT: Praeger.
Bobo, L., & Zubrinsky, C. L. (1996). Attitudes on residential integration: Perceived status differences, mere in-group preference, or racial prejudice? *Social Forces, 74,* 883–909.
Brewer, M. B. (1991). The social self: On being the same and different at the same time. *Personality and Social Psychology Bulletin, 17,* 475–482.
Cook, S. W. (1984). Cooperative interaction in multiethnic contexts. In N. Miller & M. B. Brewer (Eds.), *Groups in contact: The psychology of desegregation* (pp. 155–185). New York: Academic Press.
Cook, T. D., Crosby, F. J., & Hennigan, K. M. . (1977). The construct validity of relative deprivation. In J. M. Suls & R. Miller (Eds.), *Social comparison processes: Theoretical and empirical perspectives* (pp. 307–333). New York: John Wiley.
Crosby, F. J. (1976). A model of egoistical relative deprivation. *Psychological Review, 83,* 85–113.

Crosby, F. J. (1982). *Relative deprivation and working women.* New York: Oxford University Press.

Crosby, F. J. (1984). Relative deprivation in organizational settings. *Research in Organizational Behavior, 6,* 51–93.

Crosby, F. J., Muehrer, P., & Loewenstein, G. (1986). Relative deprivation and explanation: Models and concepts. In J. M. Olson, C. P. Herman, & M. P. Zanna (Eds.), *Relative deprivation and social comparison: The Ontario symposium* (Vol. 4, pp. 17–32). Hillsdale, NJ: Lawrence Erlbaum.

Davis, J. A. (1959). A formal interpretation of the theory of relative deprivation. *Sociometry, 22,* 280–296.

Davis, J. A., & Smith, T. W. (1994). *General Social Surveys, 1972–1994: Cumulative Codebook.* Chicago: NORC, University of Chicago.

Devine, P. G. (1989). Stereotypes and prejudice: Their automatic and controlled components. *Journal of Personality and Social Psychology, 56,* 5–18.

Dube, L., & Guimond, S. (1986). Relative deprivation and social protest: The personal-group issue. In J. M. Olson, C. P. Herman, & M. P. Zanna (Eds.), *Relative deprivation and social comparison: The Ontario symposium* (Vol. 4, pp. 201–216). Hillsdale, NJ: Lawrence Erlbaum.

Farley, R. (1996). *The new American reality: Who we are, how we got here, where we are going.* New York: Russell Sage.

Fossett, M. A., & Kiecolt, K. J. (1989). The relative size of minority populations and white racial attitudes. *Social Science Quarterly, 70,* 820–835.

Gurr, T. R. (1970). *Why men rebel.* Princeton, NJ: Princeton University Press.

Hennigan, K. M. (1977). *The construct validity of relative deprivation: Conceptual and empirical analyses.* Unpublished doctoral dissertation, Northwestern University.

Hyman, H. H. (1942). The psychology of status. *Archives of Psychology.* No. 269.

Hyman, H. H. (1960). Reflections on reference groups. *Public Opinion Quarterly, 24,* 383–396.

Jackman, M. R. (1994). *The velvet glove: Paternalism and conflict in gender, class, and race relations.* Los Angeles: University of California Press.

Kahneman, D. (1992). Reference points, anchors, norms, and mixed feelings. *Organizational Behavior and Human Decision Processes, 51,* 296–312.

Kelley, H. H. (1952). Two functions of reference groups. In G. E. Swanson, T. M. Newcomb, & E. L. Hartley (Eds.), *Readings in social psychology* (2nd ed., pp. 410–414). New York: Holt.

Kinder, D. R., & Mendelberg, T. (2000). Individualism reconsidered: Principles and prejudice in contemporary American opinion. In D. O. Sears, J. Sidanius, & L. Bobo (Eds.), *Racialized politics: The debate about racism in America* (pp. 44–74). Chicago: University of Chicago Press.

Kinder, D. R., & Mendelberg, T. (1995). Cracks in American apartheid: The political impact of prejudice among desegregated whites. *The Journal of Politics, 57,* 402–24.

Kinder, D. R., & Sanders, L. M. (1996). *Divided by color: Racial politics and democratic ideals.* Chicago: University of Chicago Press.

Kinder, D. R., & Sears, D. O. (1981). Prejudice and politics: Symbolic racism versus racial threats to the good life. *Journal of Personality and Social Psychology, 40,* 414–431.

Major, B. (1994). From social inequality to personal entitlement: The role of social comparisons, legitimacy appraisals and group membership. *Advances in Experimental Social Psychology, 26,* 293–355.

Martin, J. (1981). Relative deprivation: A theory of distributive justice for an era of shrinking resources. In L. L. Cummings & B. M. Straw (Eds.), *Research in Organizational Behavior* (Vol. 3, pp. 53–107). Greenwich, CT: JAI Press.

McConahay, J. B. (1982). Self-interest versus racial attitudes as correlates of anti-busing attitudes in Louisville. *Journal of Politics, 44,* 692–720.

McConahay, J. B. (1986). Modern racism ambivalence, and the modern racism scale. In J. F. Dovidio & S. L. Gaertner (Eds.), *Prejudice, discrimination, and racism: Theory and research.* New York: Academic Press.

McConahay, J. B., & Hough, J. C. (1976). Symbolic racism. *Journal of Social Issues, 32,* 23–46.

Meertens, R. W., & Pettigrew, T. F. (1997). Is subtle prejudice really prejudice? *Public Opinion Quarterly, 61,* 54–71.

Merton, R. K. (1949). Discrimination and the American creed. In R. M. MacIver (Ed.), *Discrimination and national welfare* (pp. 99–126). New York: Harper.

Merton, R. K., & Kitt, A. S. (1950). Contributions to the theory of reference group behavior. In R. K. Merton & P. F. Lazarsfeld (Eds.), *Continuities in social research: Studies in the scope and method of "The American Soldier"* (p. 40–105). Glencoe, IL: Free Press.

Olson, J. M., & Hazlewood, J. D. (1986). Relative deprivation and social comparison: An integrative perspective. In J. M. Olson, C. P. Herman, & M. P. Zanna (Eds.), *Relative deprivation and social comparison: The Ontario symposium* (Vol. 4, pp. 1–16). Hillsdale, NJ: Lawrence Erlbaum.

Pettigrew, T. F. (1967). Social evaluation theory. In D. Levine (Ed.), *Nebraska Symposium on Motivation* (Vol. 15, pp. 241–315). Lincoln: University of Nebraska Press.

Pettigrew, T. F. (1991). Normative theory in intergroup relations: Explaining both harmony and conflict. *Psychology and Developing Societies, 3,* 3–16.

Pettigrew, T. F. (2000). Systematizing the predictors of prejudice. In D. O. Sears, J. Sidanius, & L. Bobo (Eds.), *Racialized politics: The debate about racism in America* (pp. 280–301). Chicago: University of Chicago Press.

Pettigrew, T. F., & Martin, J. (1987). Shaping the organizational context for black American inclusion. *Journal of Social Issues, 43,* 41–78.

Pettigrew, T. F., & Meertens, R. W. (1995). Subtle and blatant prejudice in western Europe. *European Journal of Social Psychology, 25,* 57–75.

Quillian, L. (1995). Prejudice as a response to perceived group threat: Population composition and anti-immigrant and racial prejudice in Europe. *American Sociological Review, 60,* 586–611.

Quillian, L. (1996). Group threat and regional change in attitudes toward African-Americans. *American Journal of Sociology, 3,* 816–860.

Runciman, W. G. (1966). *Relative deprivation and social justice.* Berkeley: University of California Press.

Sears, D. O. Symbolic racism. In P. Katz & D. A. Taylor (Eds.), *Eliminating racism: Profiles in controversy* (pp. 53–84). New York: Plenum.

Sears, D. O., & Allen, H. M. Jr. (1984). The trajectory of local desegregation controversies and whites' opposition to busing. In N. Miller & M. Brewer (Eds.), *Groups in contact: The psychology of desegregation* (pp. 123–151). New York: Academic Press.

Sears, D. O., & Kinder, D. R. (1971). Racial tensions and voting in Los Angeles. In W. Z. Hirsch (Ed.), *Los Angeles: Viability and prospects for metropolitan leadership.* New York: Praeger.

Sears, D. O., Henry, P. J., & Kosterman, R. (2000). Egalitarian values and contemporary racial politics. In D. O. Sears, J. Sidanius, & L. Bobo (Eds.), *Racialized politics: The debate about racism in America* (pp. 75–117). Chicago: University of Chicago Press.

Smith, H. J., & Pettigrew, T. F. (2001). *Relative deprivation: A critique and meta-analysis.* Unpublished paper, University of California, Santa Cruz, CA.

Stouffer, S. A., Suchman, E. A., DeVinney, L. C., Star, S. A., and Williams, R. A., Jr. (1949). *The American soldier: Adjustments during army life* (Vol. 1). Princeton, NJ: Princeton University Press.

Tajfel, H. (1982). *Human groups and social categories.* New York: Cambridge University Press.

Taylor, M. C. (1980). Fraternal deprivation and competitive racism: A second look. *Sociology and Social Research, 65,* 37–55.

Taylor, M. C. (1998). How white attitudes vary with the racial composition of local populations: Numbers count. *American Sociological Review, 63,* 512–535.

Turner, J. C., Hogg, M. A., Oakes, P. J., Reicher, S., & Wetherell, M. S. (1987). *Rediscovering the social group: A self-categorisation theory.* Oxford: Blackwell.

Tyler, T. R., & Smith, H. J. (1998). Social justice and social movements. In D. T. Gilbert, S. T. Fiske, and G. Lindzey (Eds.), *Handbook of social psychology* (4th ed., Vol. 2, pp. 595–629). New York: McGraw-Hill.

Vanneman, R. D., & Pettigrew, T. F. (1972). Race and relative deprivation. *Race, 13,* 461–486.

Veilleux, F., & Tougas, F. (1989). Male acceptance of affirmative action programs for women: The results of altruistic or egotistical motives? *International Journal of Psychology, 24,* 485–496.

Walker, I., & Mann, L. (1987). Unemployment, relative deprivation, and social protest. *Personality and Social Psychology Bulletin, 13,* 275–283.

Walker, I., & Pettigrew, T. F. (1984). Relative deprivation theory: An overview and conceptual critique. *British Journal of Social Psychology, 23,* 301–310.

Williams, R. M. Jr. (1975). Relative deprivation. In L. A. Coser (Ed.), *The idea of social structure: Papers in honor of Robert K. Merton* (pp. 355–378). New York: Harcourt Brace Jovanovich.

THREE

Understanding the Nature of Fraternalistic Deprivation

Does Group-based Deprivation Involve Fair Outcomes or Fair Treatment?

Tom R. Tyler and E. Allan Lind

The development of relative deprivation theory is one of the most important advances of social science theory during the twentieth century (Tyler, Boeckmann, Smith, & Huo, 1997; Tyler & Smith, 1997). The importance of relative deprivation theory and research is that it makes clear that people's feelings and behaviors are not simply a reflection of their objective situation. Instead, people interpret their experience, judging it against internal standards. Because people exercise control over the choice of the standards against which they make comparisons, feelings of satisfaction and dissatisfaction are strongly influenced by people's decisions about the alternatives to which their objective situation ought to be compared. A particular situation might be viewed as reflecting relative deprivation if people compare their situation to that of the people around them, while if compared to their past situation, the same situation might seem satisfactory or even overabundant.

Hence, the subjective interpretation of personal experiences is central to the personal and social consequences of those experiences. This key insight of relative deprivation theory suggests the importance of the study of the interpretation of experience, which has become a core aspect of social psychology. This recognition lays the groundwork for the development of theories of social justice, theories that argue that people use principles of justice to identify the feelings of entitlement that shape people's reactions to their outcomes. In other words, when people compare their outcomes to those of others or to their own outcomes at other points in time, they need some set of principles to tell them what they deserve ("equal" outcomes; "proportional" outcomes; etc.). The principles that people use often involve their sense of moral correctness or justice. People use their sense of what ought to be when judging what is.

One of the most important conceptual distinctions to emerge from the literature on relative deprivation is the distinction between egoistic and fraternalistic deprivation. Egoistic deprivation refers to feelings of deprivation that develop out of a comparison of one's own situation to the situation of other people. Fraternalistic deprivation refers to feelings of deprivation that develop out of a comparison of the situation of one's group relative to the situation of another group. If I think, for example, that I am paid too little, relative to my colleagues, I am feeling egoistic deprivation. If I feel that college professors are paid too little relative to lawyers, I am feeling fraternalistic deprivation.

The classic study of egoistic versus fraternalistic deprivation is a study based on a sample of English citizens. The study was conducted by Runciman (1966). In this study, egoistic deprivation was assessed by asking respondents if they thought that there were other people "doing noticeably better at the moment than you and your family." Fraternalistic deprivation was determined by asking respondents whether, for example, "manual workers are doing much better nowadays than white-collar workers." These questions asked respondents to compare a reference group (as determined by Runciman) they felt they belonged to some other group.

This conceptual distinction is important because subsequent studies suggest that egoistic and fraternalistic comparisons have different behavioral consequences. If people feel that they are not doing well relative to other people, they react in individualistic ways. If they think change is possible, they might go to school or work harder. If they think change is not possible, they might drink or use drugs. In either case, they respond to feelings of deprivation by taking individual actions. They react as a person.

In contrast, if people feel that their group is deprived relative to other groups, they are more likely to become involved in actions that focus on changing the situation of their group. It is of particular interest if they engage in collective behavior such as joining a political movement, participating in a strike, or acting in some other way that is expected to change the situation of their group (Dion, 1986; Dube & Guimond, 1986; Hafer & Olson, 1993; Vanneman & Pettigrew, 1972; Walker & Mann, 1987). Runciman suggests that "in general, relative deprivations [of a fraternalistic type] are those which play the largest part in the transformations of an existing structure of social inequalities" (Runciman, 1966, p. 34).

Several studies support the suggestion that egoistic and fraternalistic deprivation have differing behavioral consequences (see Dion, 1986, for a review). Vanneman and Pettigrew (1972) studied White support for African American mayoral candidates in the late 1960s and 1970s. They

found that those Whites who felt that there were differences in the economic situations of Whites and African Americans, with African
Americans gaining more economically than Whites (fraternalistic deprivation), were less supportive of minority political candidates. Abeles (1976)
studied African Americans and found that fraternalistic beliefs about economic inequality led to Black militancy. Guimond and Dube-Simard
(1983) similarly found that among French-speaking Canadians in the
province of Quebec, fraternalistic deprivation predicted nationalistic attitudes and support for political autonomy for the province. Finally, Walker
and Mann (1987) found that among a sample of unemployed Australians,
fraternalistic deprivation predicted people's orientations toward social
protest.

The egoistic/fraternalistic distinction is important because it suggests
the centrality of the interpretation of experience in mediating people's
reactions to events. People potentially can interpret their experiences as
reflecting the consequences of their personal decisions and actions. For
example, the American workers studied by Lane (1962) interpreted their
economic situation as due to their own personal choices, such as failing to
stay in school. If people think about themselves, and interpret their experience, in personal terms, then they will make comparisons to other people
and experience egoistic deprivation. On the other hand, people can think
of themselves as members of social groups – that is, as being Black, female,
and so on. If they think of themselves in this way, they will interpret their
social experience as reflecting their group situation. This will lead to group
comparisons and feelings of fraternalistic deprivation.

The importance of the manner in which people conceptualize themselves has subsequently been developed within theories of social identity
(Hogg & Abrams, 1988). Those theories recognize that people's sense of
self is composed of a *personal self* that reflects idiosyncratic personal characteristics, and a *social self* that reflects the characteristics of the groups to
which one belongs.

Social identity theory demonstrates that people differ in the degree to
which their self is dominated by personal or social components. To the
degree that people think of themselves in terms of the groups to which
they belong (i.e., have self-definitions dominated by their social self as
opposed to their personal self), they tend to interpret their experiences as
reflecting their treatment as members of groups. To the degree that people
think of themselves in personal terms, they interpret their experience as
reflecting their unique characteristics and behaviors. Hence, people with
strong social selves will be more likely to interpret their behavior in frater-

nalistic terms and to engage in collective behavior (Abrams, 1990; Kelly & Kelly, 1994; Lalonde & Silverman, 1994; Simon, Loewy, Sturmer, Weber, Freytag, Habig, Kampmeier, & Spahlinger, 1998).

Our goal in this discussion is not to explore the relationship between egoistic and fraternalistic deprivation. Instead we will accept the research evidence that indicates the importance of feelings of fraternalistic deprivation, particularly in the development of collective behavior. In this discussion, we will suggest a broader theoretical framework for understanding feelings of fraternal deprivation. Our concern is with understanding the type of group-based deprivations that lead to discontent. We want to argue that there has been too little attention paid to the issue of which types of fraternalistic deprivation are important to people.

In this discussion we will distinguish between two types of fraternalistic deprivation: outcome deprivation and procedural deprivation. Our argument is that prior discussions of fraternalistic deprivation have implicitly assumed that people's concerns, whether individual or group-based, were about the failure to receive fair or favorable outcome distributions – that is, about distributive justice. We would like to argue that, in fact, people are more concerned about whether their group receives fair treatment – that is, experiences of procedural justice – than they are about the outcomes they receive from society.

To understand this distinction, consider two sets of concerns that might lead to discontent. One set focuses on the outcomes received by one's group. For example, minority citizens might become upset because minorities receive lower incomes and have fewer assets than Whites do (Tyler, Boeckmann, Smith, & Huo, 1997). This focus would be on an outcome-based view of deprivation. On the other hand, minorities might be upset because they feel their group is exposed to unfair, disrespectful, and demeaning treatment from society and social authorities.

A concrete example can be found in the minority group discontent with the police that has recently surfaced in New York City. One reason that minorities might potentially be unhappy with the police is that they feel the police fail to provide minority communities with adequate police protection. Alternatively, they might feel that minority citizens are more likely to be arrested and incarcerated for crimes. In these two examples, they would be focusing on the unfavorable outcomes received by minorities relative to Whites. However, interviews with minority group members suggest that minorities are focused on other issues. They mentioned feeling humiliated and demeaned by the police. Interestingly, these feelings center around the feeling that minorities are not respected, rather than on complaints about poor outcomes. These anecdotal findings frame the central concern of this analysis: the degree to which fraternalistic grievances are centered on poor outcomes and the degree to which they focus on poor quality treatment.

Building on the prevailing thinking about social justice at the time, Runciman (1966) focused on the fraternal deprivation of outcomes. His argument was that people are concerned about the poor outcomes received by the members of the groups to which they belong, relative to their own group, as well as being concerned about the poor outcomes that they personally received, relative to the outcomes received by others.

The outcome focus used by Runciman led naturally into a connection between relative deprivation and the literature on distributive justice and equity – which also focuses on people's outcomes. Like the literature on relative deprivation, the equity literature demonstrates that people's feelings and behaviors are shaped by their judgments about the outcomes they have received relative to others (Tyler, Boeckmann, Smith, & Huo, 1997).

More recently, a parallel literature on feelings of personal deprivation has emerged – the literature on procedural justice. This literature demonstrates that people care about the procedures by which outcomes are allocated, distinct from their concerns about those outcomes themselves (Thibaut & Walker, 1975). In other words, people are concerned about experiencing unfair procedures, as well as about receiving unfair outcomes. People can feel deprived when decisions are not made following the procedures that they judge to be fair and/or when they are treated in ways that they regard as unfair.

Research on procedural justice has repeatedly indicated that people's feelings and behaviors are affected by their assessments of the fairness of decision-making procedures (Lind & Tyler, 1988; Tyler et al., 1997; Tyler & Smith, 1997). In fact, such procedural justice judgments are often found to be more important than are judgments of outcome favorability or outcome fairness.

Although there is an extensive literature on procedural justice, the fraternalistic deprivation literature has not developed in the area of procedural justice. In procedural justice studies, people are typically asked whether they received a fair or an unfair procedure. However, they are not typically asked whether or not Blacks, or women, generally receive fair procedures. In other words, people have been asked to focus on their own personal treatment and to judge its fairness.

Our goal in this analysis is to define a fraternalistic version of procedural justice, and to contrast its effects to those of fraternalistic outcome deprivation. We will do so using two types of data. The first type

Table 3.1. *Types of Fraternalistic Judgments*

	Group Level Judgment	Individual Interpretation of Experience
Outcome	My group gets lower outcomes than other groups.	I get bad outcomes because of my group membership.
Procedure	My groups gets worse treatment than other groups.	I get bad treatment because of my group membership.

addresses the concern identified by Runciman: judgments about a person's own group relative to others. Our concern will be with the comparative importance of judgments about relative outcomes and about relative treatment (see Table 3.1). From this traditional perspective, the key issue is whether people feel that their group, as a group, is deprived relative to other groups. This issue will be addressed in study one.

We will also extend the idea of fraternalistic deprivation to an issue more consistent with the recent concerns identified by social identity theory. That issue is people's interpretation of their own experience. Here our concern is with whether people feel that their personal experience of deprivation occurs because of their group membership. Again, we will make the distinction between unfair outcomes and unfair treatment. However, in this case, our concern is with how the people involved interpret their personal experience. People have to decide why the deprivation they experienced occurred: was it due to their personality, the other people involved, or the idiosyncratic aspects of the situation; or was it due to their group memberships. If they decide that their experience occurred because of their group memberships, then they have experienced fraternalistic deprivation.

Consider the case of the police, which we have already outlined. If a minority group member has a personal encounter with the police, they experience a process that leads to an outcome. For example, some type of procedure will be used to decide whether to give a person a ticket when they are stopped by the police. People might feel that the process is unfair and/or that the outcome is unfair. Our concern is with people's views about what it is that is unfair. Were they treated unfairly because they are a woman or a minority group member? Did they receive an unfair outcome because they are a woman or a minority group member? If people feel that the unfairness they experienced occurred due to their group memberships, then they have experienced injustice that is fraternal in character. Studies two and three address the issue of fraternalistic deprivation on this level.

STUDY ONE: GENERAL JUDGMENTS ABOUT GROUP OUTCOMES

The first study focuses on general judgments about the situation of one's group. It uses a sample of White and African American citizens to examine their views about their outcomes and the procedures used to arrive at them.

This study considered people's interpretations of the economic marketplace in the United States. Studies of American society often highlight the highly unequal distribution of wealth across ethnic groups. In fact, group-based inequality is greater within the United States than it is within any other advanced industrial society (Tyler et al., 1997). Therefore, to the degree that fraternalistic deprivation is an important motivational force, we might expect that there would be considerable social unrest within American society. And, in fact, there have been eras during which collective unrest linked to group-based concerns has been an important force within American society. Those include the race riots of the 1960s, as well as the more recent Los Angeles riot. Sometimes fraternalistic concerns have an important motivating impact.

Despite these clear instances of the motivating power of group-based deprivation, the general finding of social scientists within the United States has been that minorities view the existing social system as generally legitimate. Studies suggest that Americans, both White and minority, generally regard the market system as a reasonable and fair way to allocate economic status within American society (Kluegal & Smith, 1986). However, that does not mean that people might not recognize problems with such a market system.

As previously noted, one type of problem that people might recognize with the American market system is the striking disparity in the economic well-being of the members of different ethnic and racial groups (Tyler et al., 1997). In objective terms, there is clearly economic deprivation associated with being a member of a minority ethnic group. However, people may or may not interpret this objective pattern of deprivation as reflecting on the appropriateness of using the market system for allocating economic outcomes. And, as noted, they typically do not view markets as unfair.

The first study we will consider defines fraternalistic deprivation using the outcome-based conceptual framework established by Runciman (1966) and used by later researchers. That approach asks fraternalistic deprivation questions as general questions about groups and their outcomes. For example, Hafer and Olson (1993) asked: "To what extent are you satisfied or dissatisfied with the job situation of women generally?" and "Do you feel resentful about the job situation of women as a group?" Guimond and Dube-Simard (1983) asked if respondents felt "frustration or dissatis-faction towards the way the salaries are distributed between Francophiles and Anglophiles in Quebec." These questions ask for general evaluations of the situation of a particular group.

This study also asks people to make general judgments about the situation of a particular group. In this study, White and African American respondents are each asked to judge the situation of their own group. They are then asked to judge the situation of the other group. Our concern is with the potential motivational impact of perceived discrepancies between the two group's situations. This type of fraternalistic deprivation involves judgments about whether the market distributes outcomes to the members of different ethnic groups fairly or unfairly (fraternalistic deprivation–outcomes).

We contrast this outcome-based view of deprivation to one that argues that the procedures of the marketplace are unfair because they use unfair procedures, which discriminate against the members of some ethnic groups (fraternalistic deprivation–procedures). Discrimination is a judgment of unfair process that indicates a particular group is being treated unfairly.

The first judgment of outcome unfairness directly addresses the question of whether the respondent feels that different groups receive different levels of outcomes. The second judgment speaks directly to the process. Is it fair, or is it biased and discriminatory?

Each of the two judgments of group-based deprivation that have been outlined might be made separately from the other, or they might be related. In other words, we might expect that people who believe that groups are discriminated against (i.e., that the market is not a neutral and unbiased allocation procedure) would believe that minority groups would have poorer outcomes (i.e., that there would be group-based outcome deprivation). However, this analysis treats the relationship between these two types of judgment as an empirical questions.

In this analysis we will examine the extent to which each form of frater-nalistic deprivation – outcome based and procedure based – influences feelings of willingness to support government intervention into markets. Such feelings that government ought to intervene are an issue of political support for government action, like the political support and action that have been the focus of past fraternalistic deprivation studies.

As we have noted, Americans typically like and support the market system of economic allocation. However, the members of minority groups might be expected to be less supportive, given evidence that minority groups, on average, do considerably worse in the marketplace than do

Whites. Hence, we might expect minorities to feel deprived when asked about the results of the market. We might also expect minorities to question the neutrality of market procedures, indicating that the outcomes that people receive from markets are shaped by discrimination. Our concern is with whether either deprivation shapes political judgments.

Method

We will examine this issue using a sample of citizens from the northern California area around San Francisco. Random digit telephone sampling was used to contact San Francisco Bay area residents between January and June 1992 (see Smith & Tyler, 1966, for more detailed sampling information). The sample of 502 was composed of two groups. First, English-speaking adults who identified themselves as White. Of those eligible for interviews, a completed interview was obtained with 352 respondents. Second, English-speaking adults who identified themselves as African American. This sample was created by combining two subsamples. The first subsample was of 45 African Americans identified in the random sample that produced the 352 Whites. In order to obtain an adequate African American sample, a second subsample was created by telephoning into calling areas with relatively large African American populations (Oakland and Richmond). In this subsample only African Americans were interviewed. This additional subsample yielded 105 respondents.

Respondents were asked two questions concerning the relative outcomes of Whites and African Americans: "Think about the pay most [members of own racial group] receive from their jobs. Generally speaking, do you think they receive – more than they deserve, less than they deserve, or is the amount of pay they receive just about right"; and "Think about the pay most [members of other racial group] receive from their jobs. Generally speaking, do you think they receive – more than they deserve, less than they deserve, or is the amount of pay they receive just about right?" Using these two items, we constructed four indices of fraternalistic relative deprivation linked to outcomes.

Two indices were abstract indices of group-based unfairness. Those indices measured whether people felt that group-based unfairness was occurring, irrespective of whom was experiencing it. The first index reflected *abstract deservingness*. Respondents were divided into two groups based on whether they indicated that both groups were receiving the outcomes they deserved (67% no, at least one group was experiencing unfair outcomes). A second index was constructed to measure *abstract unequal outcomes*. That index reflected whether or not people felt that one group was receiving more or less than the other. For example, if both groups get more than they deserve, that is an equal relative outcome. Using this index, 54% indicated that outcomes between group were unfair. This index is abstract in that it measures the occurrence of injustice without reference to whether or not the respondent's group is being unfairly treated.

Three other ways of thinking about unfairness link it to one's own group. First, people can simply indicate whether or not their own group receives too little. This reflects *own group deservedness*. In this sample 33% indicate that their group receives less than it deserves. Second, people can judge that their group receives less than the other group. In this case, the issue is not whether one group receives less than another does. The issue is whether one's own group receives less than the other group. This reflects *own group unequal outcomes*. In this sample, 12% indicated that their group receives less then the other group. Finally, *own group winning* reflects whether or not people think that their own group is doing better than the other group. In this sample 29% felt their group was winning, and 25% that their group was losing (29% thought there was a tie).

Respondents were asked four questions about the general fairness of market procedures *(procedural fairness)*. They were asked to agree–disagree with each statement on a four-point scale ranging from agree strongly to disagree strongly. The questions were: "Whites and African Americans have an equal opportunity to succeed in the workplace in America today?" "African Americans and Whites receive equal pay when they do equal work." "African Americans have as much chance as Whites to be successful in the workplace in America today"; and "In America today, African Americans are still discriminated against in the workplace (reverse scored)" (alpha = .80).

Respondents also were asked to agree or disagree that: "All things considered, the economic system in the United States is fair" *(general fairness)*. Forty-three percent of respondents described the system as fair, 57% as unfair. Nine items were used to evaluate each respondent's willingness to allow government to intervene in the marketplace *(policy support)*. Each item used four response alternatives, ranging from agree strongly to disagree strongly. The items were: "Congress should have the power to make laws about who is hired, fired, and promoted in private business." "Congress is doing too much to help African Americans (reversed)"; "Congress should make whatever laws are necessary to protect all people from discrimination in hiring and promotion." "When making laws, Congress should consider people as individuals, not as members of racial or ethnic groups (reversed)." "Do you favor laws to prevent job discrimination against members of different ethnic and racial groups?" "If a politician supported these laws, would you vote for them?" "Do you favor the government taking laws giving African Americans preferential treatment in hiring, firing, and promotion?" "Do you favor federal programs providing African Americans with additional training and education so they can compete for jobs?" and "Do you favor federal programs to provide people from poor families with additional training so they can compete for jobs" (alpha = .77).

Results

The relationship among the various forms of fraternalistic deprivation is shown in Table 3.2. On average, the correlation between judgments of outcome fairness and procedural fairness was 0.24. It is clear that the magnitude of the association depends on how we conceptualize outcome fairness. In general, people who see one form of deprivation are more likely to also see the other form of deprivation.

We used regression analysis to explore the impact of each form of fraternalistic deprivation on the dependent variables – overall fairness and policy support. The independent variables were the five judgments of outcome fairness, one judgment of procedural fairness, and a term reflecting the interaction of the two forms of deprivation. In addition, controls were included for judgments of the impact of the proposed policies on the respondent and the respondent's group. Feelings about Congress were also included as a control for general feelings about government. Finally, the respondent's race was included as a control variable.

The results of the regression analyses are shown in Table 3.3. They indicate that procedural issues dominate the influence of fraternalistic judg-

Table 3.2. *Intercorrelation of Indicators: Study One*

	1.	2.	3.	4.	5.	6.	7.
1. Abstract deservingness	—						
2. Abstract unequal outcomes	.80	—					
3. Own group deservingness	.49	.20	—				
4. Own group unequal outcomes	.26	−.30	.41	—			
5. Own group is winning	−.04	−.05	.70	.10	—		
6. Procedural fairness	.47	.42	.25	.09	.01	—	
7. General fairness	.20	.12	.16	.14	.06	.29	—
8. Policy support	.34	.29	.30	.09	.14	.47	.26

Note: Entries are Pearson correlations.

Table 3.3: *The Antecedents of Overall Fairness and Policy Views: Study One*

	Overall Fairness					Support for Intervention				
Fraternalistic outcome fairness:										
Abstract deservingness	.04					.12**				
Abstract unequal outcomes		-.03					.07			
Own group deservingness			.08					.07		
Own group unequal outcomes				.11*					.05	
Own group winning					-.06					.08
Fraternalistic procedural fairness	.21***	.24***	.22***	.22***	.24***	.32***	.34***	.36***	.36***	.36***
Interaction	-.10*	-.10*	-.09*	-.10*	-.11*	-.11*	-.12*	-.12*	-.12*	-.12*
Impact on respondent	.07	.07	.08	.08	.08	-.07	-.08	-.07	-.07	-.08
Impact on respondent's group	-.03	-.03	-.03	-.04	-.04	-.13*	-.13*	-.13*	-.13*	-.12*
Feelings about Congress	-.17***	-.18***	-.17***	-.17***	-.18**	.13*	.13**	.13*	.13*	.12**
Race	.10	.12*	.07	.11*	.07	.18***	.18***	.16**	.20***	.25***
Adjusted R-squared	12%	12%	12%	13%	12%	35%	34%	34%	34%	34%

Note: Entries are beta weights for an equation including all terms.

$*p < .05$ $**p < .01$ $***p < .001$

ments on both dependent variables. In the case of both overall fairness and support for government intervention in the marketplace, only procedural issues consistently have a significant influence. Irrespective of how outcome deprivation is operationalized, procedural deprivation is the key judgment that shapes fairness assessments and policy support.

In neither case were people influenced by their assessments of their own outcomes relative to those of the other group. However, views about Congress – the agency that would enact the policy – and the respondent's racial group consistently had an influence.

The nature of the interaction effects reported in Table 3.3 is indicated in Table 3.4. Table 3.4 shows the means for each level of procedural and outcome-based fraternalistic deprivation. For this analysis, abstract unequal outcomes was used as the index of outcome deprivation. This choice was made because that scale most evenly divides the respondents into two groups (54%/46%). However, the results shown in Table 3.3 make clear that similar results are obtained irrespective of which outcome index is used.

The results shown in Table 3.4 indicate that, in the case of overall fairness ratings of the market, the lack of discrimination in allocation procedures leads to higher ratings of overall fairness. In the case of support for policies in which the government influences the market, discrimination in allocation procedures similarly leads to greater support for government intervention.

The analysis reported in Table 3.3 also includes covariates to reflect self-interest and views about Congress. Interestingly, self-interest has no signifi-

Table 3.4. *Mean Values of the Dependent Variables: Study One*

		Overall Fairness of the Market		
		Fraternalistic Outcome Deprivation		
		No	**Yes**	**Average**
Fraternalistic procedural	No	3.82	4.16	3.96
Deprivation	Yes	4.64	4.93	4.82
	Average	4.11	4.60	

		Support for Policies in Which the Government Influences the Market		
Fraternalistic procedural	No	4.20	4.65	4.38
Deprivation	Yes	5.32	5.40	5.38
	Average	4.60	5.08	

Note: Entries are the mean ratings for each cell. High numbers indicate overall unfairness and support for policies.

cant influence on overall fairness judgments. However, people who felt that government intervention will hurt their group were less likely to support government intervention. Views about Congress influence all the dependent variables. Those who are more favorable toward Congress view markets as fairer and are more supportive of government intervention.

Discussion

The findings outlined support the argument that it is important to distinguish two questions. The first question is whether people are influenced by fraternalistic judgments. The findings reported here support those of earlier studies in suggesting that fraternalistic judgments have an important role in shaping political actions.

The second question is what type of fraternalistic deprivation people are concerned about. This study suggests that it is evidence of discrimination against one's group – a procedural deprivation that leads to denying people within the group equal treatment by the market – which is central to shaping people's feelings. Judgments of fraternalistic outcome deprivation – the denial of equal outcomes to different groups – has little direct impact.

If people feel that the market is procedurally unjust because it discriminates against the members of particular ethnic groups, they feel that it is generally unfair, and they support government intervention in markets to correct this unfairness. This influence of procedural judgments is stronger than the influence of distributive justice judgments about the degree to which outcomes are distributed unfairly across groups. Interestingly, this same conclusion emerges across five different operationalizations of outcome fairness.

Hence, these findings argue for the importance of changing our conception of the form of fraternalistic deprivation that shapes political policy support. It is deprivation of equal treatment, a procedural issue, which is key.

Of course, in objective terms we might argue that issues of outcome and procedure are inevitably intertwined. If there is discrimination (a procedural issue), then outcomes will be unequal (a distributive issue). However, the people interviewed in this study do not view these two issues as strongly correlated. Hence, subjectively, these two issues are distinct in the minds of the people being interviewed. Those individuals do not see the existence of discrimination as tightly linked to the occurrence of income inequality across groups. Hence, from a political psychology perspective, these two issues can be treated as distinct because they are distinct in the minds of those being studied.

Of course, it is important not to overstate the findings of this study. For one thing, this study does not look directly at political behavior. Instead, it looks at policy support. It is clear that further research is needed to examine the impact of fraternalistic judgments about procedures on political behaviors such as voting and engaging in collective actions.

STUDY TWO: THE EVALUATION OF PERSONAL EXPERIENCES

The second study examines people's interpretation of their personal experiences with authorities, in this case the police and the courts. When people deal with legal authorities, they receive some type of outcome. They also experience some degree of fair or unfair treatment during the process that leads to that outcome. Our concern is with people's interpretations about why these types of outcomes and treatment occur.

People can decide that the outcomes they receive and/or the way they are treated are the result of their group memberships. That is, they can think they result from their gender, their race, their age, or other ascribed personal characteristics associated with their group memberships. On the other hand, they can also think of them as reflecting characteristics of them as people (i.e., what they say and do in the situation; the nature of the situation they have placed themselves in, etc.). Our concern is with the impact of attributions for poor outcomes and poor procedures to the consequences of group membership upon reactions to experience.

The focus of this study is not the same as that of the Runciman work on fraternal deprivation. In this case, we are asking how group membership affects people when they believe that they are receiving poor outcomes and/or poor treatment because they are the members of a disadvantaged group.

In the original Runciman research, people were asked whether groups generally received unjust outcomes, but not whether they received unjust outcomes because they belonged to a group. However, the distinction between fraternalistic outcome deprivation and fraternalistic procedural deprivation remains the same within this new formulation of the issue. The difference is that people are not reacting to judgments about their group in general. They are reacting to judgments about a negative personal experience which they believe is due to group membership.

Method

This study utilized a sample of citizens discussing their personal experiences with the police and courts. The sample involved telephone interviews with a random sample of 1,575 citizens in Chicago during the spring of 1984. Of those interviewed, 652 reported a personal experience with the police or courts during the year prior to the interview. This analysis uses that subset of respondents. See Tyler (1990) for background on the nature of the sample.

Our concern is with responses to two questions. First, each respondent was asked about the quality of the outcome of their personal experience relative to what other people would have received in a similar situation. There were three possible responses: better, the same, or worse. Those individuals who indicated that their outcome was worse than others would have received in a similar situation were then asked whether this was due to their "race, sex, age, nationality, or some other characteristic of you as a person." Of those interviewed 24 (4%) indicated that they felt *fraternalistic outcome deprivation* – that is, they felt that they had received an inferior outcome because of their group characteristics.

Respondents were also asked about how they were treated by the police or courts. Again, people could indicate that they were treated better, the same, or worse than others would be treated in the same situation. Those who indicated that they were treated worse than others would be treated in a similar situation were then asked whether this was due to their "race, sex, age, nationality, or some other characteristic of you as a person." Of those interviewed 39 (6%) indicated that they felt *fraternalistic procedural deprivation* – that is, they felt that they had received inferior treatment due to their group characteristics.

Our concern is with the impact of these experiences of fraternalistic mistreatment on evaluations of the authorities involved. Interestingly, unlike the findings at the general level, at the personal level these two judgments of deprivation were more closely correlated ($r = .43$, $p < .001$). Those who felt they received poor outcomes due to their group characteristics also felt that they received poor treatment.

To examine the impact of these judgments, two dependent variables were created: (1) a measure of affect and (2) an overall evaluation of the legitimacy of the authorities. *Affect* was determined by asking respondents if they felt angry, frustrated, or happy (reverse scored). These items were combined into an overall index of feeling (alpha = 0.79). The *legitimacy* evaluation had three components: evaluation, obligation, and obedience. Evaluation was assessed using a four-item scale that evaluated the type of authority they had dealt with. Those who dealt with the police were asked to agree or disagree that: "I have a great deal of respect for the Chicago police"; "On the whole Chicago police officers are honest"; "I feel proud of the Chicago police"; and "I feel that I should support the Chicago police." For the courts the four items were: "The courts in Chicago generally guarantee everyone a fair trial"; "The basic rights of Chicago citizens are well protected in the courts"; "On the whole, Chicago judges are honest"; and "Court decisions in Chicago are almost always fair." Each respondent received the evaluation score appropriate for their personal experience. Obligation was assessed using a four-item scale: "People should obey the law even if it goes against what they think is right"; "I always try to follow the law even if I think it is wrong"; "Disobeying the law is seldom justified"; and "It is difficult to break the law and keep one's self-respect." Finally, asking respondents how frequently they violated six laws during their everyday lives assessed obedience. For example, how frequently did they speed, drive while intoxicated, or steal from stores? Responses to these three aspects of legitimacy were combined into an overall index of legitimacy (alpha = 0.72).

Of the 652 people interviewed, 82 indicated that they had either received a poor outcome and/or poor treatment. This group formed the sample analyzed. Of these respondents, 45 indicated receiving poor outcomes (24 due to group memberships and 21 not due to group memberships) and 64 indicated receiving poor treatment (39 due to group memberships and 25 not due to group memberships).

Results

As in the prior study, regression analysis was used to examine the impact of outcome and procedural judgments on the dependent variables (see Table 3.5). Consider first the case of affect. Both judging that one received a poor outcome due to group characteristics and judging that one received unfair treatment due to group characteristics influenced affect following the experience. However, the magnitude of fraternalistic procedural deprivation was greater (beta = .35 vs. beta = .23 for outcomes).

Further, in the case of impact on evaluations of the legitimacy of the authorities, only fraternalistic procedural deprivation mattered. People's

Table 3.5. *The Impact of Fraternalistic Judgments about Experience: Study Two*

	Positive Affect	Legitimacy of Authority
Fraternalistic outcome deprivation	.23**	.13
Fraternalistic procedural deprivation	.35***	.20***
Interaction	.17*	−.09
Adjusted R-squared	15%***	5%***

Note: Entries are beta weights for an equation with all terms entered at the same time.
$*p < .05$ $**p < .01$ $***p < .001$

Table 3.6. *Mean Values of the Dependent Variables across Condition: Study Two*

		Positive Affect		
		Fraternalistic Outcome Deprivation		
		No	**Yes**	**Average**
Fraternalistic procedural	No	1.71	1.21	1.70
Deprivation	Yes	1.17	1.11	1.15
	Average	1.69	1.13	
		Legitimacy of Authority		
Fraternalistic procedural	No	1.59	1.14	1.58
Deprivation	Yes	1.05	0.96	1.01
	Average	1.57	1.01	

Note: Entries are the mean rating for each cell. High numbers indicate positive feeling and high legitimacy (i.e., favorable evaluations, high obligation to obey; and high levels of actual obedience).

views about the legitimacy of the government authorities with whom they had dealt were not influenced by their judgments about whether they received poor outcomes due to group characteristics (beta = .13, n.s.). However, they were influenced by whether or not people felt that they received unfair treatment due to the groups to which they belonged (beta = .20, $p < .001$).

In the case of affect there is an interaction between outcome and procedural deprivation and the means shown in Table 3.6 make the nature of that interaction clear. People feel especially upset if they are in the double deprivation condition (mean affect = 1.11). The interaction term was not significant when legitimacy was the dependent variable.

Discussion
This second study approaches fraternalistic deprivation in a different way than it was originally conceptualized by Runciman. It examines the judgments people make about their own personal experiences, and why those experiences have gone badly. Those who received unfavorable outcomes and/or unfair treatment were each asked whether this was due to fraternalistic, (i.e., group-based), characteristics. In each case, some respondents said yes to one or both of these questions. Our concern is with this group of people. We want to determine which of these two

judgments had the most impact on views about the legitimacy of political authorities. The findings suggest clearly that, as in the prior study, procedural judgments dominate reactions to experiences. People were more influenced by feeling that they were treated poorly (i.e. denied fair decision-making procedures) because of their group characteristics than they were by believing that they received unfavorable outcomes due to their group characteristics.

STUDY THREE: A REPLICATION OF STUDY TWO

Method

Study three replicates the approach of study two, but uses a larger sample and a better designed questionnaire. The study examines the reactions of White and minority citizens to personal experiences with the police and courts. The sample is a stratified random sample of citizens in Oakland and Los Angeles. The sampling approach is designed to over sample minorities in both cities. The resulting sample consists of 1,656 respondents: 586 Whites, 561 African Americans, and 509 Hispanics. Each respondent reported a recent experience with the police or courts.[1]

Of the respondents, 267 reported that they received outcomes and/or treatment that were influenced by their "race, ethnicity, sex, or age." In this study, respondents were able to indicate that they received either better or worse outcomes/treatment due to these group-based factors. In the case of outcomes, 99 respondents indicated receiving better outcomes than others due to their group memberships, 28 that they received worse outcomes. With treatment, 99 respondents indicated receiving better treatment due to their group memberships, 115 receiving worse treatment.

Each person interviewed was asked about his or her most recent experience with the legal system. Three types of experience were reported: calling the police for help, being stopped by the police, and going to court. The analysis looks at the impact of experience-based judgments about outcomes and treatment during these experiences on the *willingness to accept the decision* and *evaluation of the authority*. Three items were used to assess willingness to accept decisions: "I willingly accepted the decisions made"; "In a similar situation in the future, I would like to see the situation handled in the same way"; and "He/she could have handled the situation better than he/she did (reversed)." (alpha = 0.80). Each person also rated the police officer or court official with whom they dealt. They were asked: "How much do you trust him/her?" "How much do you respect him/her?" "How much do you like him/her?" and "How much do you

fear him/her (reversed)." These were combined into an index of evaluation (alpha = 0.78).

To explore the influence of fraternalistic judgments, a regression analysis
was conducted using the 267 people who indicated that they were either
treated differently due to their group-based characteristics or that they
received a different outcome. In the initial analysis, an interaction term was
also included. However, no significant interactions were found, so the interaction terms were dropped from the analysis. Only main effects of the two
indices of group-based deprivation are presented. Finally, because of the
multiethnic nature of the sample, controls were included for ethnicity.

The examination of the impact of fraternalistic judgments about personal
experience on the willingness to accept decisions and evaluations of the
authority supports the conclusions of study two (see Table 3.7). With the
willingness to accept decisions, both forms of fraternalistic deprivation
influence willingness. The dominant influence comes from procedural judgments (beta = .39, $p < .001$), with a secondary influence of outcome judgments (beta = .24, $p < .001$). In the case of evaluations, only procedural
judgments have a significant influence (beta = .29, $p < .001$).

Because of the multicultural background of the people interviewed in
study three, it is possible to test the argument that members of minority
groups are more likely to view themselves as the victims of group-based discrimination. To do this a correlational analysis was conducted to look at the
impact of ethnicity [African American ($n = 561$) vs. White ($n = 586$)/Hispanic
($n = 509$) vs. White ($n = 586$)] on judgments about group-based discrimination. The results support our expectations. African Americans are more likely

Table 3.7. *The Influence of Fraternalistic Judgments about Personal Experience: Study Three*

	Willingness to Accept the Decision	Evaluation of the Authority
Fraternalistic relative outcome judgment	.24***	.13
Fraternalistic relative treatment judgment	.39***	.29***
African American (yes, no)	.06	−.02
Hispanic (yes, no)	−.05	−.03
Adjusted R-squared	30%***	11%***

Note: Entries are beta weights for an equation with all terms entered at the same time.
*$p < .05$ **$p < .01$ ***$p < .001$

to indicate receiving unequal treatment than are Whites ($r = .35, p < .001$), but not more likely to indicate receiving unequal outcomes. Hispanics are more likely to indicate that they receive both unequal outcomes ($r = .26, p < .001$) and unequal treatment ($r = .25, p < .001$) than are Whites. This pattern suggests that when ethnicity is a salient dimension of personal identity, people are more likely to see their outcomes in group-based terms.

Discussion

The findings of study three replicate those of study two using a better methodology. In study three, respondents can indicate that they received either better or worse outcomes and/or treatment than others due to their race, gender, or some other group-based characteristic. Still, the findings of this study support the argument that it is primarily judgments about procedural deprivation that shape reactions to personal experiences with authorities.

GENERAL DISCUSSION

At the time that Runciman originally distinguished the concept of fraternalistic deprivation from the concept of egoistic deprivation, justice theories were primarily focused on issues of the outcomes groups obtained, relative to the outcomes of other groups. Hence, Runciman assumed that fraternalistic deprivation focused on group-based judgments of outcome deprivation. He argued that the crucial issue is whether people feel that the groups to which they belong are deprived of fair levels of outcomes.

Subsequent justice research has suggested the importance of distinguishing between distributive or outcome-based justice and procedural justice (Lind & Tyler, 1988; Tyler & Smith, 1997). Studies of personal experiences with injustice suggest that people are affected by the fairness of the procedures they experience, independent of the fairness of the outcomes they receive (Lind & Tyler, 1988).

These findings argue for the importance of considering procedural issues on a fraternalistic level. Just as people may feel that their groups do not receive fair outcomes, they may feel that their groups do not receive fair treatment. And either of these feelings might provoke the political action that has been shown to flow from judgments of fraternalistic deprivation.

The suggestion that fraternalistic deprivation might be procedural in character makes sense in that studies have suggested that procedural justice has an especially important influence on the evaluations of authorities and on judgments about institutions and policies (Lind & Tyler, 1988; Tyler & Lind, 1992). Because, as has been noted, fraternalistic deprivation is especially strongly linked to issues of collective action such as political behavior and policy support, it makes sense that procedural judgments would be intertwined with fraternalistic evaluations.

And, in fact, the results of the first study outlined support the argument that fraternalistic deprivation is heavily procedural in character. People's political actions – in this case their willingness to support government intervention into economic markets – are shaped by their fraternalistic judgments. However, they are more strongly shaped by the belief that the members of different groups do not receive equal treatment in the market-place. The outcome based assessments that indicate whether different groups receive the same level of outcomes are not the central factor shaping political action.

Similar results are obtained when the same question was addressed using a very different methodology. In the second study, people were asked about their personal experience. They were asked whether fair outcomes were denied to them because of group membership and/or whether they were treated unfairly due to their group membership. As in study one, feeling unfairly treated due to group membership led people to lose their sense that the government authorities with which they are dealing were legitimate. Interestingly, feeling that they received poor outcomes due to the groups to which they belong had no independent influence on people's views about government.

Based on the findings of these two very different approaches to fraternalistic deprivation we suggest that fraternalistic procedural deprivation is an important new aspect of thinking about fraternalistic deprivation that needs to be considered when talking about group-based justice judgments. Both studies suggest that fraternalistic procedural deprivation is more important to individuals than fraternalistic outcome deprivation. In other words, people care more about the judgment that procedures hurt them or their group than they care about the judgments that they or their group are receiving poor outcomes due to group membership. Hence, we argue, the idea of fraternalistic deprivation needs to be reconceptualized to include the idea of fraternalistic procedural deprivation.

We have argued that issues of procedural justice are important because people rely on procedural justice as a cue to evaluate social situations (Lind, Kulik, Ambrose, & de Vera Park, 1993; Lind & Tyler, 1988). Simply put, we argue that people use the occurrence of procedural fairness as a shorthand method for evaluating their social situations. If they believe that the outcomes they are receiving develop from fair procedures, they evaluate those outcomes to be fair. Here we would like to argue that this logic could be extended to the fraternalistic level. In other words, people use their judgments about social procedures to evaluate broader societal mechanisms of allocation. Instead of looking to outcome fairness to evaluate society, people evaluate society through the fairness of its allocation procedures.

This argument accords well with the literature on "contest mobility" that has been used to explain why the American public accepts differences in the distribution of economic resources across individuals and groups (Kluegel & Smith, 1986). The argument is that people regard the procedures of the marketplace as fair. In other words, they believe that the market allocates resources to people in a neutral unbiased way, based on how hard they work and how intelligent and well educated they are. Because the procedures of the market are fair, people do not focus on whether individuals or groups in fact receive fair outcomes.

These findings help up to understand why the objective reality of widespread group-based inequality in American society does not lead to social discontent (Tyler et al., 1997). This seeming inconsistency occurs because people focus on procedures, not outcomes, when evaluating both economic markets and political authorities and institutions (Tyler & McGraw, 1986).

NOTES

1. Funding for study three was provided by the National Science Foundation and the Public Policy Institute of California. For more detailed sampling information, see Huo and Tyler (2000).

REFERENCES

Abeles, R. P. (1976). Relative deprivation, rising expectations, and black militancy. *Journal of Social Issues, 32,* 119–137.

Abrams, D. (1990). *Political identity: Relative deprivation, social identity, and the case of Scottish nationalism.* Economic and Social Research Council 16–19 Initiative Occasional Paper no. 24. Social Statistics Research Unit, City University, London.

Dion, K. L. (1986). Responses to perceived discrimination and relative deprivation. In J. M. Olson, C. P. Herman, & M. P. Zanna (Eds.), *Relative deprivation and social comparison: The Ontario symposium* (Vol. 4, pp. 159–179). Hillsdale, NJ: Lawrence Erlbaum.

Dube, L., & Guimond, S. (1986). Relative deprivation and social protest: The personal-group issue. In J. M. Olson, C. P. Herman, & M. P. Zanna (Eds.),

Relative deprivation and social comparison: The Ontario symposium (Vol. 4, pp. 201–216). Hillsdale, NJ: Lawrence Erlbaum.

Guimond, S., & Dube-Simard, L. (1983). Relative deprivation theory and the Quebec nationalist movement. *Journal of Personality and Social Psychology, 44,* 526–535.

Hafer, C. L., & Olson, J. M. (1993). Beliefs in a just world, discontent, and assertive actions by working women. *Personality and Social Psychology Bulletin, 19,* 30–38.

Hogg, M. A., & Abrams, D. (1988). *Social identifications: A social psychology of intergroup relations and group processes.* London: Routledge.

Huo, Y. J., & Tyler, T. R. (2000). *How different ethnic groups react to legal authority.* San Francisco: Public Policy Institute of California.

Kelly, C., & Kelly, J. (1994). Who gets involved in collective action? Social psychological determinants of individual participation in trade unions. *Human Relations, 47,* 63–88.

Kluegal, J. R., & Smith, E. R. (1986). *Beliefs about inequality: Americans' views of what is and what ought to be.* New York: Aldine.

Lalonde, R., & Silverman, R. A. (1994). Behavioral preferences in response to social injustice: The effects of group permeability and social identity salience. *Journal of Personality and Social Psychology, 66,* 78–85.

Lane, R. E. (1962). *Political ideology.* New York: Free Press.

Lind, E. A. Kulik, C., Ambrose, M., & de Vera Park, M. (1993). Individual and corporate dispute resolution: Using procedural fairness as a decision heuristic. *Administrative Science Quarterly, 38,* 224–251.

Lind, E. A., & Tyler, T. R. (1988). *The social psychology of procedural justice.* New York: Plenum.

Runciman, W. G. (1966). *Relative deprivation and social justice.* London: Routledge.

Simon, B., Loewy, M., Sturmer, S., Weber, U., Freytag, P., Habig, C., Kampmeier, C., & Spahlinger, P. (1998). Collective identification and social movement participation. *Journal of Personality and Social Psychology, 74,* 646–658.

Smith, H. J., & Tyler, T. R. (1996). Justice and power: Can justice motivations and superordinate categorizations encourage the advantaged to support policies which redistribute economic resources and encourage the disadvantaged to willingly obey the law? *European Journal of Social Psychology, 26,* 171–200.

Thibaut, J., & Walker, L. (1975). *Procedural justice.* Hillsdale, NJ: Lawrence Erlbaum.

Tyler, T. R. (1990). *Why people obey the law.* New Haven: Yale University Press.

Tyler, T. R. Boeckmann, R. J., Smith, H. J., & Huo, Y. J. (1997). *Social justice in a diverse society.* Boulder, CO: Westview.

Tyler, T. R., & Lind, E. A. (1992). A relational model of authority in groups. In M. Zanna (Ed.), *Advances in experimental social psychology* (Vol. 25, pp. 115–191). New York: Academic.

Tyler, T. R., & McGraw, K. (1986). Ideology and the interpretation of personal experience: Procedural justice and political quiescence. *Journal of Social Issues, 42,* 115–128.

Tyler, T. R., & Smith, H. J. (1997). Social justice and social movements. In D. Gilbert, S. Fiske, & G. Lindzey (Eds.), *Handbook of social psychology* (4th ed., Vol. 2, pp. 595–629). New York: McGraw Hill.

Vanneman, R. D., & Pettigrew, T. (1972). Race and relative deprivation in the urban United States. *Race, 13,* 461–486.

Walker, I., & Mann, L. (1987). Unemployment, relative deprivation, and social protest. *Personality and Social Psychology Bulletin, 13,* 275–283.

FOUR

Relative Deprivation and Intergroup Attitudes

South Africa before and after the Transition

John Duckitt and Thobi Mphuthing

In May 1994, South Africa's first democratic election marked a dramatic transfer of political power from the White minority to the long subjugated Black majority. This provided a unique opportunity to investigate several critical questions about the interaction of sociopolitical change and intergroup relations. In this chapter we report on one such set of questions: how this political transition influenced Africans' perceptions of relative deprivation to Whites, their attitudes to Whites and their ethnic ingroup, and whether changes in relative deprivation causally affected group attitudes, as relative deprivation theorists have long argued.

Prior to the transition in 1994, South Africa was characterized by massive and long standing socioeconomic inequalities between White and Black. From 1917 to 1980, the distribution of personal per capita income showed relatively little change, with Whites earning ten times more than Africans and four to five times more than the Apartheid-designated Asian and Coloured Black minorities. In 1978, South Africa was found to have the most unequal distribution of income of all 57 countries surveyed by the Second Carnegie Commission into Poverty and Development in South Africa, generating a Gini coefficient of no less than .66 (Gini coefficients can vary between 0, where incomes are perfectly evenly distributed, and 1, with most Western countries having coefficients between .20 and .35) (Odén, Ohlson, Davidson, Strand, Lundahl, & Moritz, 1994).

These inequalities, the oppression of the Black majority, and the conflict between Blacks and Whites over political power were predictably reflected in African attitudes to Whites prior to the transition. Research typically found strong perceptions and feelings of socioeconomic injustice, dissatisfaction, and relative deprivation and attitudes of hostility and mistrust toward Whites, with this hostility largely directed at the politically dominant White Afrikaaners, and not toward the numerically smaller English-speaking White group (Appelgryn & Bornman, 1996; Appelgryn & Nieuwoudt, 1988; Duckitt, 1994; Foster & Nel, 1991; McCrone, 1937; Nieuwoudt & Plug, 1983; Van den Berghe, 1962).

The successful democratic election of 1994, however, raised the question of what the impact of the transition from oppressed minority to empowered majority would be on African perceptions of relative deprivation to Whites and their attitudes to Whites. Over the period of the democratic transition, which culminated in the ANC and Afrikaner-dominated National Party joining forces in a government of national unity dedicated to the creation of a new united "rainbow nation," there certainly seemed to be an enormous change in the interracial climate – from an atmosphere of extreme distrust, hostility, and almost open conflict immediately before the election to one of racial reconciliation and goodwill afterward. Political commentators at the time almost universally interpreted this as indicating major changes in intergroup perceptions and attitudes through which South Africans began to discover a common identity that overrode racial differences – in Archbishop Desmond Tutu's terms, the forging of a "rainbow nation" (e.g., Sparks, 1995; cf. Guelke, 1996). An important theory of intergroup relations, Realistic Conflict Theory (RCT), has also proposed that "real threat" from outgroups determines attitudes to those outgroups (LeVine & Campbell, 1972). Because the loss of political power by Whites, and by Afrikaaners in particular, would markedly reduce their capacity to threaten African interests, RCT would expect the South African transition, all others things being equal, to ameliorate attitudes to Whites, and particularly to Afrikaaners. In this chapter we therefore report longitudinal data on African students' intergroup attitudes and perceptions from just before the transitional election to four months later to investigate how much change actually did occur over this period.

These data would also permit the evaluation of a relatively neglected theoretical hypothesis – that of the causal relationship between group relative deprivation and intergroup attitudes. Much research has examined the impact of personal relative deprivation on behavior or attitudes; however, as Walker and Pettigrew (1984) and others (cf. Brown, 1995; DeRidder, Schruijer, & Tripathi, 1992; Grant & Brown, 1995) have noted, personal relative deprivation involves only intraindividual and interindividual comparisons and therefore cannot explain intergroup phenomena adequately. Relatively few studies have investigated group relative deprivation and these have largely been concerned with its effect on intergroup behavioral outcomes, such as readiness to participate in protests or other collective actions, rather than group attitudes (Abeles, 1976; Caplan, 1970; Caplan & Paige, 1968; DeCarufel, 1981; Dubé-Simard & Guimond, 1986; Grant & Brown, 1995; Guimond & Dubé-Simard, 1983; Martin, Brickman, & Murray, 1984; McPhail, 1980; Vanneman & Pettigrew, 1972; Wright, Taylor, & Moghaddam, 1990).

The few experimental studies of the impact of group relative deprivation on intergroup outcomes have produced conflicting findings, with two finding significant effects (Grant & Brown, 1995; Wright et al., 1990) and one not (Martin et al., 1984). Only Grant and Brown (1995) examined intergroup attitudes as a dependant variable, and they did find significant effects of affective relative deprivation, but these effects could have been due to threat to social identity that was inextricably confounded with the manipulation of group relative deprivation in their study.

Non-experimental studies using real social groups in naturalistic contexts have more consistently found significant correlations between group relative deprivation and intergroup outcomes. However, the cross-sectional and correlational nature of these findings inevitably left the question of causality and its direction open. For example, in the case of group attitudes in particular, it seems just as feasible that nationalistic ingroup sentiments or negative attitudes to an outgroup could be causing feelings, perceptions, or evaluations of relative deprivation to the outgroup, as the reverse.

Although longitudinal data cannot definitively resolve issues of causality, they can provide much stronger tests of causal hypotheses than cross-sectional data. Thus, for the longitudinal two-wave panel data in the study reported here, causal impacts of relative deprivation on group attitudes would be indicated if the regression of relative deprivation at pre-election on group attitudes at post-election, with group attitudes at pre-election controlled, were significant (Plewis, 1985; Rogosa, 1979). Conversely, causal impacts of group attitudes on relative deprivation would be suggested if the regression of group attitudes at pre-election on relative deprivation at post-election, with relative deprivation at pre-election controlled, were significant.

Previous empirical research has also tended to neglect several critical conceptual distinctions concerning the nature of relative deprivation. For example, it has been argued that it is not just the perception of the degree or magnitude of deprivation relative to another group (cognitive relative deprivation) that is important, but the perceived illegitimacy or injustice of the degree of deprivation (cf. Grant & Brown, 1995; Kawakami & Dion, 1995). A further contrast is with affective relative deprivation – that is, the degree to which feelings of anger, upset, and outrage are elicited by a perception of relative deprivation to another group. For example, Guimond and Dubé-Simard (1983) reported that only affective relative deprivation was significantly correlated with nationalism in Francophone Québécois (cf. also Grant & Brown, 1995). In this research we therefore measured all three forms of relative deprivation in order to investigate any differences in their capacity to predict and causally affect group attitudes.

METHOD

Sample and Procedure

A self-administered questionnaire was used to collect data from African college and high school students on their perceptions of the socioeconomic standing of Africans, Afrikaans Whites, and English-speaking Whites, and on measures of group identification, intergroup attitudes, and intergroup trait evaluation. The questionnaire was administered to classes at a historically Black university and an inner city Black high school, both in Johannesburg, during normal teaching sessions one week before the transitional election in May 1994 and then again to exactly the same classes four months after the election. The few questionnaires completed by non-Africans were discarded prior to any analyses.

Satisfactorily completed questionnaires were obtained for 340 African participants before the election and 240 after the election. The reduced N at phase 2, which was later in the academic year, probably largely reflected the high level of academic attrition characterizing Black eduction at the time. The questionnaires were anonymous, but pre- and post-election questionnaires from the same participants could be matched using date of birth and demographic information. In this way 101 participants were satisfactorily matched, enabling longitudinal analyses. Most of the matched 101 participants were full-time college students (82%), with the remainder being part-time students (8%), or high school students (10%). A majority were female (77%).

The number of matched participants was less than had been expected, and much less than the post-election N of 240. It seemed that many participants, particularly those from rural backgrounds, may not have attached much cultural significance to knowing their exact date of birth.

Measures

Socioeconomic Perceptions and Relative Deprivation. Group socioeconomic perceptions were assessed using a version of the Cantril ladder with rungs from 1 to 10 in which the top rung represented the best possible socioeconomic situation for a group in the country and the bottom rung the worst. Socioeconomic situation was defined as follows: "The socioeconomic situation of people implies their general standard of living in this country as determined by their income, wealth, housing, educational level, and occupational level." Participants were asked to indicate on which rung of the ladder they felt Africans as a group, English Whites as a group, and Afrikaans Whites as a group were at present, then five years ago, then where they expected them to be five years in the future, and finally where they felt each group should stand if it were to have its fair and rightful share of the wealth of the country (the groups' "justice level").

These ladder ratings were used to compute indices of the perceived relative deprivation of Africans to English and Afrikaans Whites by subtracting the rating for where Africans stood at present from the same rating for each of the other two groups – a procedure that has been used in several previous studies to assess group relative deprivation (e.g., Appelgryn & Bornman, 1996; Appelgryn & Nieuwoudt, 1988; Finchilescu & de la Rey, 1991). This index is referred to as cognitive RD here because it does not involve any evaluation of the fairness or justice of the differential between groups.

An index of the illegitimacy of RD was constructed by subtracting each groups' present ladder position from its "justice level" position. This would indicate the degree to which each group was unjustly disadvantaged (as was typically the case for the rating of Africans), which would be reflected by positive scores, or unjustly advantaged (as was more usually the case for the two White groups), which would be reflected by negative scores. The difference between the degree of unjust disadvantage for Africans and of unjust advantage for each of the two White groups then provided the indices of illegitimacy of RD. The more Africans were disadvantaged and the White group advantaged the larger this score would be. If the White group was seen as being just as disadvantaged as Africans, the score would be zero, and in the less likely eventuality of a White group being seen as more disadvantaged than Africans, this score would be negative. The score thus provides an index of the relative degree of perceived injustice/justice of the socioeconomic differential between two groups.

The validity of this index of illegitimacy of RD was checked in the postelection questionnaire by the inclusion of a single five-point self-rating (from "not at all" to "exceptionally") of "how unjust or unfair" the socioeconomic differential was that the participant had indicated on the ladder between Africans and English or Afrikaans Whites. These single item validity ratings showed highly significant positive correlations with the indices of illegitimacy of RD ($r = .34$, $n = 234$, $p < .0001$, for Afrikaans Whites, and $r = .42$, $n = 235$, $p < .0001$, for English Whites).

Participant's affective outrage over the relative deprivation of Africans to English and Afrikaans Whites was assessed as the sum of two ratings (on five-point scales) of "how upset" and "how angry" participants felt about the difference between Africans' socioeconomic condition and that of each of the two White groups. These two ratings were highly correlated with each other (ranging between .71 and .80) justifying their combination into a single index of affective outrage over relative deprivation (affective RD).

Group Attitudes. Participants' ethnic identification as Black Africans was measured by a 10-item group identification scale developed and validated by Brown et al. (1986). The 10 items, which are potentially applicable to any group, consist of equal numbers of positive and negative statements designed to tap awareness of group membership, evaluation of that membership, and the affective investment in that membership. Examples of items are "I am a person who feels strong ties with Black African people" and "I am a person who feels held back by the Black African people." Participants rated agreement or disagreement with each item on a seven-point Likert scale ($+3$ to -3), so that the summed scores had a theoretical range from -30 to $+30$.

Attitudes to Afrikaans and English Whites were measured using 10-item Likert scales with five items expressing positive and five negative sentiments about the target group (Duckitt, 1995). Both scales used exactly the same 10 items with only the target group varied, making direct statistical comparisons between attitudes to these two groups possible. Examples of items are "White English-speaking/Afrikaans-speaking South Africans are basically a good and decent people" and "In general I don't really like White English-speaking/Afrikaans-speaking South Africans." Responses were on the same seven-point Likert rating scale ($+3$ to -3) as that used for the ethnic identification items, so that the theoretical range for the scale also varied from $+30$ to -30, with high (positive) scores indicating more negative attitudes.

Trait evaluation of Afrikaans and English Whites were measured by participants rating both these two groups on the same set of 14 trait adjectives, seven being evaluatively positive (e.g., "kind," "trustworthy") and seven being evaluatively negative (e.g., "dishonest," "unfair") (Duckitt, 1995). Responses were rated on a six-point scale ranging from "Not at all characteristic" to "Exceptionally characteristic." The use of exactly the same set of trait adjectives for both target groups once again made cross-group statistical comparisons possible. High scores again indicated a more negative evaluation.

The reliability and construct validity of these negative attitude and trait evaluation measures had been assessed and found to be satisfactory in a prior pilot study of 40 African college students (Buthelezi, 1995). For example, the alpha coefficients for the scales measuring ethnic identification, attitude to English Whites, attitude to Afrikaans Whites, and trait evaluations of English and Afrikaans Whites all matched or exceeded .75 in this pilot study and the scale intercorrelations were consistent with their construct validity.

RESULTS

Repeated measures analyses employing the longitudinal data set for matched participants were used in order to assess change in relative deprivation and group attitudes from pre- to post-election. The relationship between the indices of relative deprivation and intergroup negative attitudes and identification was assessed through uni- and multivariate correlational analyses on the full pre- and post-election samples separately, and then by cross-lagged partial regressions on the longitudinal data.

RD and Group Attitude Change from Pre- to Post-election

Table 4.1 shows the participants' mean scores on measures of relative deprivation and group attitudes for Afrikaans and English Whites at pre- and post-election. These means show substantial decreases for each of the indices of relative deprivation from pre- to post-election, with the main effect for pre- versus post-election highly significant in each case. There were also differences between level of relative deprivation to English and Afrikaans Whites, but the direction or pattern of difference varied for the different relative deprivation indices. Thus, the participants reported markedly more cognitive RD to English Whites than to Afrikaans Whites at both pre- and post-election with the difference becoming larger at post-election (as indicated by the interaction effect closely approaching significance, $p = .06$).

This English–Afrikaans difference for cognitive RD was, however, completely reversed for affective RD and partially reversed for illegitimacy of RD. Thus, the participants reported greater affective RD to Afrikaans Whites than to English Whites at both pre- and post-election, with this main effect highly significant. Although this difference decreased at post-

Table 4.1. *Pre- and Post-Election Means, Standard Deviations, and ANOVA Results for the Indices of Relative Deprivation and Group Attitudes*

	Pre-Election		Post-Election	
Variable	Mean	SD	Mean	SD
Cognitive RD				
Afrikaans	3.0	4.0	1.3	3.4
English	3.6	3.2	2.4	2.7
ANOVA: Group $F = 27.7^{**}$, Time $F = 14.9^{**}$, Interaction $F = 3.6$				
Illegitimacy				
Afrikaans	5.0	4.2	3.2	4.4
English	4.4	3.7	3.1	4.2
ANOVA: Group $F = 2.1$, Time $F = 12.9^{**}$, Interaction $F = 3.0$				
Affective RD				
Afrikaans	7.4	1.8	6.6	2.1
English	6.1	2.3	5.7	2.3
ANOVA: Group $F = 39.1^{**}$, Time $F = 10.5^{**}$, Interaction $F = 0.9$				
Anti-outgroup attitude				
Afrikaans	10.4	10.2	9.0	11.5
English	−6.1	12.1	−5.6	12.8
ANOVA: Group $F = 136.5^{**}$, Time $F = 0.9$, Interaction $F = 1.9$				
Anti-outgroup evaluation				
Afrikaans	58.1	12.1	59.0	12.0
English	45.8	11.4	46.8	12.0
ANOVA: Group $F = 61.9^{**}$, Time $F = 2.5$, Interaction $F = 0.3$				
Ethnic identification				
African	22.4	8.8	23.9	7.9
ANOVA: Time $F = 2.4$				

Note: Numerator *df* range from 66 to 97.

$^{*}p < .05$ $^{**}p < .01$

election, this decrease was relatively slight and the interaction was non-significant. This reversal of the pattern for cognitive RD was also partially evident for illegitimacy of RD. Perceived illegitimacy of RD at pre-election was greater to Afrikaans Whites than to English Whites, while at post-election the means for the two groups were virtually identical. Although the overall main effect for group was nonsignificant, the interaction approached significance ($p < .09$) and multiple comparison tests indicated that the Afrikaans-English difference was significant at pre-election (Newman-Keuls, $p = .02$) and not at post-election.

In contrast to the marked changes that occurred in relative deprivation, none of the means for the three indices of group attitude showed significant change from pre- to post-election. The means for ethnic identification were high in absolute terms since the theoretical range for the scale was from −30 to +30 with a midpoint of 0, but the change from pre- to post-election was not statistically significant. The mean attitude to and evaluation of Afrikaans Whites and English Whites scores showed little or no change from pre- to post-election, with no difference remotely approaching statistical significance. There were highly significant differences, however, between means for the two White groups. The means for attitude to and evaluation of Afrikaans Whites were far above the scale midpoints (indicating a very unfavorable attitude/evaluation), while those for English Whites were somewhat below the scale midpoints, suggesting a somewhat positive attitudinal and evaluative orientation.

To sum up, there were substantial declines on all three indices of relative deprivation to both White groups from pre- to post-election with greater cognitive RD to English Whites, but more affective RD and illegitimacy of RD to Afrikaans Whites (though, in the latter case, only at pre-election). There were high levels of African ethnic identification, and attitudes to and evaluations of Afrikaans Whites were very negative, while those of English Whites were far more favorable, with no change in any of these group attitude indices from pre- to post-election.

Correlational Analyses of RD and Group Attitudes

When the three indices of RD were intercorrelated, cognitive RD and illegitimacy were very highly correlated (r's varying between .71 and .76), which would have been at least partly due to the computation of both involving the same ladder rating ("present ladder position"). Cognitive and affective RD were weakly to moderately correlated (r's varying between .16 and .34), as were illegitimacy and affective RD (r's varying between .22 and .35). Table 4.2 shows the zero-order correlations of the three indices of relative deprivation with the three group attitude measures for Afrikaans and English Whites. Because of the relatively large sample sizes, the more stringent 1% level was used to test the significance of effects.

Cognitive RD showed relatively little association with attitudes, evaluation, and identification; the correlations were weak and only marginally significant in two cases out of twelve. Illegitimacy and affective RD, on the other hand, were consistently associated with more negative attitudes and

Table 4.2. *Correlations of Indices of Relative Deprivation with Group Attitudes*

RD Indices	Anti-outgroup Attitude	Anti-outgroup Evaluation	Identification
Pre-Election: Afrikaans Whites			
Cognitive RD	.12	.11	.17*
Illegit of RD	.30**	.27**	.19**
Affective RD	.23**	.09	.16*
Pre-Election: English Whites			
Cognitive RD	.08	.20*	−.02
Illegit of RD	.24**	.22**	.17*
Affective RD	.27**	.30**	.16*
Post-Election: Afrikaans Whites			
Cognitive RD	−.01	.05	.06
Illegit of RD	.15*	.26*	.20*
Affective RD	.19*	.17	.16
Post-Election: English Whites			
Cognitive RD	.16	.15	.06
Illegit of RD	.21**	.20*	.20*
Affective RD	.44**	.27**	.17*

Note: Pre-election n's vary from 237 to 318; post-election n's from 171 to 220.

*$p < .01$ **$p < .001$

trait evaluations of the corresponding White groups and higher ethnic identification, with 21 out of 24 of these correlations being significant and two others closely approaching significance ($p < .05$). However, despite their consistency, the effect sizes were weak, with the average correlations for illegitimacy and affective RD with the group attitude indices being only .21 and .22, respectively.

Canonical correlations were computed to indicate the multivariate association between the three indices of relative deprivation and the indices of group attitude. The canonical correlation would indicate the overall degree of association between those factors derived from each variable set that correlated maximally with each other. Each of the four canonical analyses produced only one statistically significant ($p < .01$) canonical variate (set of correlated factors) with canonical correlations of .40 (for Afrikaans Whites at pre-election, $n = 216$), .43 (for English Whites at pre-election, $n = 219$), .42 (for Afrikaans Whites at post-election, $n = 155$), and .50 (for English Whites at post-election, $n = 171$).

The standardized canonical weights and factor loadings for the two variable sets for each of four significant canonical variates are shown in Table 4.3. The factor loadings, which indicate the degree to which each variable in a variable set loads on the factor derived from that variable set, reveal that all three relative deprivation indices contributed positively to the overall relative deprivation factor, with illegitimacy and affective RD consistently having stronger loadings than cognitive RD. Similarly, all three group attitude indices contributed to the group attitude factor, although the loadings for outgroup attitude and evaluation tended to be stronger than those for ethnic identification.

The canonical weights, which are equivalent to partial regression weights (betas) for each variable (showing its impact on the other variable set factor with the remaining variables in its own set partialed out) showed that illegitimacy and affective RD independently predicted the group attitude factor, with illegitimacy being overall the stronger predictor. The canonical weights for cognitive RD were unexpected, however, not only in contributing independently to prediction in most cases, but in being *negatively* weighted, in complete contrast to its factor loadings, which had been positive. The negative canonical weights for cognitive RD indicated that once the effects of illegitimacy and affective RD had been partialed out, cognitive RD negatively predicted the outgroup attitude factor; that is, was associated with a more positive attitude to and evaluation of the corresponding White group and lower ethnic identification.

The canonical analysis also suggested that combined indices of both relative deprivation and group attitude could be created that could be used in the longitudinal analyses as multivariate composites. Composites were created by standardizing all variables to z scores and summing illegitimacy of RD, affective RD and cognitive RD (with the former two weighted positively and the latter weighted negatively, following the results for the canonical weights) to give a composite RD index for each White group. A composite group attitude index for each White group was obtained by summing the standardized measures of attitude to and evaluation of that group and ethnic identification; high scores on this composite therefore indicated more negative outgroup attitudes and lower ethnic identification.

Summing up, therefore, these cross-sectional correlational findings showed that illegitimacy of RD and affective RD were consistently and independently associated with more negative outgroup attitudes and evaluations and heightened ingroup identification. Cognitive RD showed little association with negative outgroup attitudes in univariate analyses, but in multi-

Table 4.3. *Canonical Correlation Coefficients for Illegitimacy of and Affective Outrage over Relative Deprivation with Measures of Intergroup Attitude and Identification*

| | Pre-election | | | | Post-election | | | |
| | Afrikaans | | English | | Afrikaans | | English | |
Variable	Weight	Loading	Weight	Loading	Weight	Loading	Weight	Loading
Variable Set 1								
Cognitive RD	-.45	.35	-.21	.51	-.89	.12	-.43	.37
Illegitimacy RD	1.05	.85	.75	.76	1.20	.72	.70	.67
Affective RD	.43	.61	.68	.80	.41	.59	.77	.90
Variable Set 2								
Anti-Afrik/Eng Att.	.72	.89	.57	.85	.50	.80	.65	.82
Anti-Afrik/Eng Eval.	.43	.70	.45	.78	.47	.83	.30	.67
Identification	.16	.34	.42	.44	.35	.59	.51	.53

variate analyses with illegitimacy and affective RD controlled proved to be associated with more positive outgroup attitudes. Finally, although these correlational relationships were highly consistent, at least for illegitimacy and affective RD with group attitudes, they were not strong, being weak in the univariate case, and only moderate in the multivariate case, where indices were being combined to mathematically maximize their association.

Cross-lagged Partial Regression Analyses
Cross-lagged partial regressions on the two-wave longitudinal pre- to post-election data were used to investigate whether pre-election variables appeared to be having significant causal impacts on post-election variables. The original use of cross-lagged panel correlations to test causal hypotheses from two-wave longitudinal data has been severely criticized by Rogosa (1979) and Plewis (1985), who have argued convincingly that cross-lagged partial regressions would be more appropriate. The standardized partial regression coefficients (betas) are shown in Table 4.4, with those in the upper half indicating the effects of the pre-election relative deprivation indices on post-election group attitude indices (with its corresponding pre-election group attitude indicator partialed out), and those in the lower half indicating the effects of pre-election group attitude indices on post-election indices of relative deprivation.

As would be expected from the correlational findings, there were no significant effects for pre-election cognitive RD on post-election group attitudes or reverse impacts of pre-election group attitudes on post-election cognitive RD. However, while the correlational findings had shown consistently significant relationships between illegitimacy of RD and group attitudes, none of the cross-lagged betas for pre-election illegitimacy of RD on post-election group attitudes were significant. The reverse effects of group attitudes on illegitimacy were also mostly nonsignificant, with the only significant effects being for pre-election identification on post-election illegitimacy (for both Afrikaans and English Whites). However, given the number of betas computed, this might have been due to chance, particularly because one of the two betas was only marginally significant. The overall effect for the group attitude composite on illegitimacy of RD was also nonsignificant for both Afrikaans and English Whites. These analyses, and particularly those for the composite group attitude measures as both predictor and outcome variables, thus suggest that the significant correlational relationship observed between illegitimacy of RD and group attitudes must be largely noncausal or spurious.

Table 4.4. *Beta Coefficients from the Partial Regression Analyses of Pre-election on Post-election Variables with Pre-election Equivalents Controlled (n's in Parentheses)*

Pre-election Relative Deprivation on Post-election Group Attitudes

Predictor	Anti-outgroup Attitude	Anti-outgroup Evaluation	Identi-fication	Composite Group Attitude
Cognitive RD				
Afrikaans	−.07 (83)	−.12 (65)	−.17 (91)	−.18 (52)
English	−.09 (92)	−.12 (73)	−.06 (91)	−.18 (65)
Illegitimacy of RD				
Afrikaans	.01 (80)	−.16 (63)	.08 (88)	−.09 (50)
English	−.16 (92)	−.18 (73)	.11 (91)	−.19 (65)
Affective RD				
Afrikaans	**.26** (83)	.18 (67)	**.34** (91)	**.25** (53)
English	**.23** (94)	.06 (75)	−.06 (93)	.08 (67)
Composite RD				
Afrikaans	**.23** (78)	.10 (62)	**.40** (86)	**.29** (49)
English	.13 (92)	.01 (72)	.08 (91)	.07 (62)

Pre-election Group Attitudes on Post-election Relative Deprivation

Predictor	Cognitive RD	Illegitimacy of RD	Affective RD	Composite
Anti-outgroup Attitude				
Afrikaans	−.08 (87)	.10 (84)	−.01 (97)	.11 (81)
English	.07 (93)	.19 (93)	**.27** (95)	**.31** (95)
Anti-outgroup Evaluation				
Afrikaans	−.07 (76)	.03 (73)	−.10 (77)	−.02 (72)
English	−.04 (77)	.06 (77)	**.28** (79)	**.27** (77)
Identification				
for Afrikaans RD	.08 (94)	**.22** (91)	−.01 (94)	.04 (89)
for English RD	.16 (94)	**.30** (94)	.09 (96)	.18 (94)
Composite Group Attitude				
for Afrikaans	−.10 (68)	.19 (65)	−.14 (69)	.02 (64)
for English	.05 (72)	.15 (72)	**.27** (74)	**.35** (72)

Note: Boldface coefficients are significant at $p < .05$.

There was considerably more evidence of causal impacts between affective RD and group attitudes. Thus, four of the five betas for pre-election affective RD on post-election group attitudes for Afrikaans Whites were significant (and the fifth closely approaching significance, $p = .07$). On the other hand only one of five betas for pre-election affective RD on group attitudes for English Whites was significant, suggesting causal impacts of affective RD on group attitudes for Afrikaans Whites but not for English Whites. The three significant betas for the composite RD indicator were overall no stronger than those for affective RD, suggesting that they merely reflected the effect for affective RD. Almost exactly the opposite was apparent for cross-lagged effects of group attitudes on affective RD. Three of the four betas for English Whites were significant, but none for Afrikaans Whites. The pattern of significant betas for group attitudes on composite RD exactly paralleled those for group attitudes on affective RD, suggesting that they merely reflected that effect.

Summing up, therefore, there was little evidence of any overall causal impacts of either cognitive RD and illegitimacy on group attitudes or the reverse, suggesting that the cross-sectional correlation of illegitimacy of RD and group attitudes must be largely spurious. Affective RD, however, seemed to have causal impacts on group attitudes, but only for Afrikaans Whites, while group attitudes seemed to have causal impacts on affective RD, but only for English Whites.

DISCUSSION

The findings revealed a high level of perceived relative deprivation of Africans to both the White groups, which is consistent with previous research in South Africa (Appelgryn & Bornman, 1996; Appelgryn & Nieuwoudt, 1988; Finchilescu & de la Rey, 1991; Foster & Nel, 1991; Van den Berghe, 1962). Cognitive RD – that is, the purely socioeconomic differential perceived – was greater to English than to Afrikaans Whites, reflecting the real overall socioeconomic differential between English and Afrikaans Whites (Hanf, Weiland, & Vierdag, 1981). This effect was partially reversed for illegitimacy of RD and wholly reversed for affective outrage over RD, which was greater to Afrikaaners than English Whites. English Whites' greater affluence thus appears to have been seen as somewhat less illegitimate than Afrikaaners, and as incurring less discontent and anger. Because attitudes to English Whites were far more favorable than to Afrikaaners, this reversal suggests that cognitive RD on its own, without any implication of illegitimacy and discontent, was unlikely to be causing negative outgroup attitudes. Indeed, when illegitimacy and affective RD were statistically removed, greater cognitive RD tended to be associated with more positive attitudes.

The post-election survey revealed marked shifts in relative deprivation. Cognitive RD, affective RD, and the illegitimacy of RD to both White groups decreased, with the decrease to Afrikaaners tending to be slightly more pronounced. What is interesting about these changes is that it is highly unlikely that any real socioeconomic changes occurred in these groups' relative conditions over the four-month period of the survey. These changes almost certainly therefore reflect shifts in perception and belief deriving directly from Africans' political empowerment, and Whites' effective loss of political dominance.

The findings for group attitudes at pre-election revealed high levels of African ethnic identification, and a major attitudinal differentiation between Afrikaans and English Whites, with the former viewed negatively and the latter somewhat positively. These findings are consistent with previous research on African attitudes in South Africa (cf. the comprehensive review by Foster & Nel, 1991). Africans therefore seem to have reacted to Apartheid and racism by selectively disliking and blaming Afrikaaners, and not English Whites. This does involve an element of irony, as Apartheid grew out of the segregationist policies of British colonial rule and the pre-1948 South African governments in which English Whites often played significant roles (cf. Thompson, 1995). Nevertheless, this attitudinal differentiation does have a number of important social and political bases: most notably perhaps the overwhelming support for the National Party and Apartheid policies by Afrikaaners, compared to English Whites' support for anti-Apartheid opposition political parties, and the empirically documented much higher levels of antiblack racism among Afrikaaner Whites than among English Whites (e.g., Duckitt, 1994; Foster & Nel, 1991; Nieuwoudt & Plug, 1983).

In contrast to the quite marked changes that occurred in relative deprivation, there were essentially no changes in inter-ethnic attitudes from before to after the election. This is clearly inconsistent with the proposition that group relative deprivation toward outgroups has a major causal impact on attitudes to those groups and in heightening ingroup identification, and suggests that any such causal effects would have to be quite weak; a conclusion that was broadly confirmed by the correlational findings and longitudinal analyses.

The cross-sectional analyses indicated reasonably consistent significant associations of illegitimacy of RD and affective RD to Afrikaans and

English Whites with the attitude to and evaluation of the corresponding groups, and ingroup ethnic identification. These cross-sectional associations are quite similar to those obtained in prior cross-sectional field studies (Abeles, 1976; Caplan, 1970; Caplan & Paige, 1968; Dubé-Simard & Guimond, 1986; Guimond & Dubé-Simard, 1983; Vanneman & Pettigrew, 1972), with the magnitude of the effects ranging from weak to moderate. Once again, this suggested that any causal effects between relative deprivation and group attitudes could only be relatively weak.

This was confirmed by the more rigorous test of causality provided by the longitudinal analyses. There was no evidence for causal impacts of illegitimacy of RD on group attitudes, or for reverse causal impacts of outgroup attitudes on illegitimacy of RD overall. This suggested that the consistent cross-sectional relationships between illegitimacy of RD and group attitudes were noncausal or spurious, reflecting the causal impacts of some third variable or variables on both.

Only the affective component of relative deprivation appeared to have consistently significant causal effects on intergroup attitudes and ethnic identification, and then only for Afrikaans Whites and not English Whites. Reverse causal effects of group attitudes on affective RD were also apparent, but only for English and not for Afrikaans Whites. This suggests that some other variable might be moderating the causality between affective RD and group attitudes. One possibility is the perceived degree of conflict or competitiveness between ingroup and outgroup. When an intergroup relationship is seen as highly competitive, as appears to be the case for Africans and Afrikaaners (cf. also Foster & Nel, 1991), affective discontent over socioeconomic advantages enjoyed by the competing outgroup might cause attitudes to that outgroup to become more negative, while discontent over socioeconomic advantages enjoyed by an outgroup seen as noncompetitive or cooperative, such as English Whites, might not translate directly into negative attitudes to that outgroup. On the other hand, when ingroup members generally see an outgroup, such as English Whites, as noncompetitive, only those ingroup members with negative attitudes to that outgroup may experience or come to experience affective RD about the socioeconomic advantages of that outgroup.

A general conclusion from these findings is that relative deprivation seems to have little effect on group attitudes, with this effect limited to the affective dimension and moderated by other variables, possibly outgroup competition and threat. In this research, the absence of notable causal effects of relative deprivation on group attitudes was most dramatically shown by the marked post-election declines in relative deprivation without any accompanying change in group attitudes.

It is possible that the weakness of the relationship between relative deprivation and outgroup attitudes in this study might be due to weaknesses of the research, rather than the theory. Broader and more comprehensive measures of relative deprivation might have produced stronger effects. Stronger effects may also have been obtained with a sample more representative of the general African community. However, there are no indications in the research literature that students seem to respond any differently to relative deprivation than the general population. Moreover, in South Africa, African students' relatively high levels of militancy, politicization, and awareness of socioeconomic inequity seem more likely to have accentuated effects rather than to have dampened them.

A third possibility is that the social context for the research was an unusual one marked by social turbulence and change. A causal relationship between relative deprivation and intergroup attitudes might be time lagged, with changes in relative deprivation taking a long period, perhaps years, to affect intergroup attitudes. If so, clear associations between relative deprivation and group attitudes would be observable in stable historical and social contexts, but could be weakened or even eliminated in turbulent historical periods such as the one during which this study was conducted. Although we cannot exclude this possibility, there is one finding that does seem to militate against it: the cross-sectional relationships between relative deprivation and outgroup attitudes obtained in the study were consistently significant and similar to those obtained in prior research, which would have been mostly done in periods of stability (e.g., Abeles, 1976; Caplan, 1970; Caplan & Paige, 1968; Dubé-Simard & Guimond, 1986; Guimond & Dubé-Simard, 1983; Vanneman & Pettigrew, 1972).

The sharp post-election declines in relative deprivation without any accompanying change in group attitudes not only confounded relative deprivation theory, but another important and related theory of intergroup relations as well: Realistic Conflict Theory (RCT). According to LeVine and Campbell (1972), RCT suggests that Whites', and particularly Afrikaaners', loss of political power should reduce their capacity to pose a perceived "real threat" to African interests and this should ameliorate African attitudes to them. However, this did not happen. Instead of group attitudes changing with the change in power relations, it was relative deprivation that changed. Why this effect? We propose the model shown in Figure 4.1 to explain this effect, and indeed most of the findings obtained in this study.

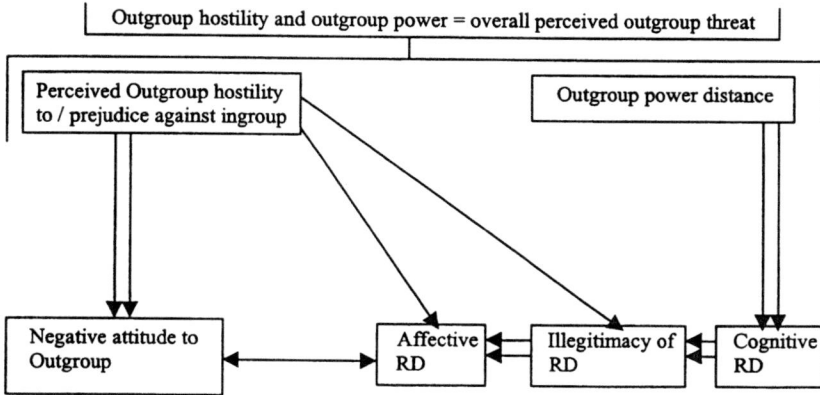

Figure 4.1. A simplified causal model of minority or disadvantaged ingroup attitudinal and relative deprivation response to majority or advantaged group power and threat with double arrows indicating strong relationships and single arrows weak relationships.

We suggest that perceived "real threat" from an advantaged or dominant outgroup may have two essential components that impact differently on relative deprivation and group attitudes: power – the capacity to harm – and hostility – the desire to harm. Both appear essential to "real threat." Power without hostility could elicit admiration and respect (as suggested by our findings for cognitive RD once illegitimacy and affective RD were controlled). Hostility without power might sometimes elicit just derision, rather than dislike. We suggest that the actual power differential between advantaged outgroup and ingroup is the most important direct determinant of RD to the outgroup, and particularly cognitive RD. Cognitive RD then together with perceived hostility or ill will from the outgroup affects illegitimacy of RD and affective RD. The power differential between outgroup and ingroup does not itself affect attitudes to that outgroup.

This explains why Africans perceived greater cognitive RD to English Whites, who possessed both economic and political power over Africans, but greater affective RD and illegitimacy of RD to Afrikaans Whites who were perceived as hostile to and prejudiced against Africans. It explains why Whites', and particularly Afrikaaners', loss of political power over Africans would therefore have reduced all indices of relative deprivation to both White groups. The decrease would be somewhat greater for Afrikaaners, since their power had been primarily political and secondarily economic, while the reverse had been the case for English speakers. At post-election, for example, illegitimacy of RD to Afrikaaners had decreased to the same level as that for English speakers, possibly reflecting the perception that Afrikaaners' almost exclusive control of political power and capacity to unfairly influence resource allocation had been lost and was now no different from that of English Whites.

The second component, perceived hostility from the outgroup, which Grant and Brown (1995) have termed social identity threat, is seen in this model as the most powerful direct determinant of attitudes to the advantaged outgroup. The perceived hostility of Afrikaaners to Blacks would then account for the extremely negative attitude of Africans to Afrikaaners in comparison to their much more favorable attitude to English Whites. Moreover, the perception of White Afrikaaners as racist and prejudiced against Blacks might well not have changed over the transition, accounting for the absence of attitude change to them.

In addition to its powerful direct effect on outgroup attitudes, perceived hostility or social identity threat from an advantaged outgroup is seen as having weaker impacts on illegitimacy of RD and affective RD building in a partly spurious zero-order correlation between these variables and outgroup attitudes, which would largely wash out when causality was directly assessed, exactly as in this study. In addition, the model also proposes weak bidirectional causal effects between affective RD and outgroup attitudes, which our results suggested seemed to be moderated by the degree of perceived intergroup competition. Because perceived outgroup hostility would reflect perceived intergroup competition, the model proposes that this variable has direct impacts on outgroup attitudes, indirect impacts mediated through illegitimacy and affective RD, and moderates the relationship between affective RD and outgroup attitudes.

The overall conclusion that seems suggested by the findings from this research therefore is that relative deprivation does not seem to play the major causal role in determining group and intergroup attitudes that theorists have traditionally assumed. As such, it may be better viewed as merely part of a more complex matrix of causalities in which the primary determining factors are other variables, such as perceived threat, in the sense of both outgroup power and threats to social identities, and in which relative deprivation may play a largely secondary role mediating the impact of more powerful factors.

REFERENCES

Abeles, R. (1976). Relative deprivation, rising expectations, and black militancy. *Journal of Social Issues, 32,* 119–137.
Appelgryn, A., & Bornman, E. (1996). Relative deprivation in contemporary South Africa. *Journal of Social Psychology, 136,* 381–397.

Appelgryn, A., & Nieuwoudt, J. (1988). Relative deprivation and the ethnic attitudes of blacks and Afrikaans speaking whites in South Africa. *Journal of Social Psychology, 128*, 311–324.

Brown, R. (1995). *Prejudice: Its social psychology*. Oxford: Blackwell.

Brown, R., Condor, S., Mathews, A., Wade, G., & Williams, J. (1986). Explaining intergroup differentiation in an industrial organization. *Journal of Occupational Psychology, 59*, 273–286.

Buthelezi, J. (1995). *Relative deprivation and intergroup attitudes in a survey of African students and some Township residents*. Unpublished Honours dissertation, University of the Witwatersrand, Johannesburg, South Africa.

Caplan, N. (1970). The new ghetto man: A review of recent empirical studies. *Journal of Social Issues, 26*, 59–73.

Caplan, N., & Paige, J. (1968). A study of ghetto rioters. *Scientific American, 219*, 15–22.

DeCarufel, A. (1981). The allocation and acquisition of resources in times of scarcity. In M. Lerner & S. Lerner (Eds), *The justice motive in social behavior: Adapting to times of scarcity and change* (pp. 317–341). New York: Plenum.

DeRidder, R., Schruijer, S., & Tripathi, R. (1992). Norm violation as a precipitating factor of negative intergroup relations. In R. DeRidder & R. Tripathi (Eds), *Norm violation and intergroup relations* (pp. 3–47). Oxford: Clarendon Press.

Dubé-Simard, L., & Guimond, S. (1986). Relative deprivation and social protest: The personal-group issue. In J. Olson, C. Herman, & M. Zanna (Eds), *Relative deprivation and social comparison: The Ontario symposium* (Vol. 4, pp. 201–216). Hillsdale, NJ: Lawrence Erlbaum.

Duckitt, J. (1994). *The social psychology of prejudice*. New York: Praeger.

Duckitt, J. (1995). *Standardized scales for the measurement of intergroup attitudes and evaluation*. Unpublished manuscript.

Finchilescu, G., & de la Rey, C. (1991). Understanding intra-group variations in prejudice – The role of perceived legitimacy and stability. *South African Journal of Psychology, 21*, 225–232.

Foster, D., & Nel, E. (1991). Attitudes and related concepts. In D. Foster & J. Louw-Potgieter (Eds), *Social psychology in South Africa* (pp. 121–170). Isando, South Africa: Lexicon.

Grant, P., & Brown, R. (1995). From ethnocentrism to collective protest: Responses to relative deprivation and threats to social identity. *Social Psychology Quarterly, 58*, 195–211.

Guelke, A. (1996). Dissecting the South African miracle. *Nationalism and Ethnic Politics, 2*, 141–154.

Guimond, S., & Dubé-Simard, L. (1983). Relative deprivation theory and the Quebec nationalist movement: The cognitive-emotion distinction and the person-group deprivation issue. *Journal of Personality and Social Psychology, 44*, 526–535.

Hanf, T., Weiland, H., & Vierdag, G. (1981). *South Africa: The prospects of peaceful change*. London: Rex Collings.

Kawakami, K., & Dion, K. (1995). Social identity and affect as determinants of collective action: Towards an integration of relative deprivation and social identity theory. *Theory and Psychology, 5*, 551–577.

LeVine, R., & Campbell, D. (1972). *Ethnocentrism, theories of conflict, ethnic attitudes, and group behavior*. New York: John Wiley.

Martin, J., Brickman, P., & Murray, A. (1984). Moral outrage and pragmatism: Explanations for collective action. *Journal of Experimental Social Psychology, 20,* 484–496.

McCrone, I. (1937). *Race attitudes in South Africa: Historical, experimental, and psychological studies*. London: Oxford University Press.

McPhail, C. (1980). Civil order participation: A critical examination of recent research. In M. Pugh (Ed.), *Collective behavior: A sourcebook* (pp. 157–174). St. Paul, MN: West.

Nieuwoudt, J., & Plug, C. (1983). South African ethnic attitudes: 1973–1978. *Journal of Social Psychology, 121,* 163–171.

Odén, B., Ohlson, T., Davidson, A., Strand, P., Lundahl, M., & Moritz, L. (1994). *The South African Tripod: Studies on economics, politics and conflict*. Uppsala: Scandanavian Institute of African Studies.

Plewis, I. (1985). *Analysing change: Measurement and explanation using longitudinal data*. Chichester, England: John Wiley.

Rogosa, D. (1979). Causal models in longitudinal research: Rationale, formulation and interpretation. In J. Nesselroade & P. Baltes (Eds), *Longitudinal research in the study of behavior and development* (pp. 263–302). New York: Academic.

Sparks, A. (1995). *Tomorrow is another country: The inside story of South Africa's negotiated revolution*. Sandton, South Africa: Struik Book Distributors.

Thompson, L. (1995). *A history of South Africa*. New Haven, CT: Yale University Press.

Van den Berghe, P. (1962). Race attitudes in Durban, South Africa. *Journal of Social Psychology, 57,* 55–72.

Vanneman, R., & Pettigrew, T. (1972). Race and relative deprivation in the urban United States. *Race, 13,* 461–486.

Walker, I., & Pettigrew, T. (1984). Relative deprivation theory: An overview and conceptual critique. *British Journal of Social Psychology, 23,* 301–310.

Wright, S., Taylor, D., & Moghaddam, F. (1990). Responding to membership in a disadvantaged group: From acceptance to collective protest. *Journal of Personality and Social Psychology, 58,* 994–1003.

FIVE

Is It Just Me?

The Different Consequences of Personal and Group Relative Deprivation

Heather J. Smith and Daniel J. Ortiz

Two professors discover that their salary is significantly lower than the salaries for faculty members at institutions with less stringent job requirements. One professor immediately joins the faculty union and actively participates in rallies and strike actions. The other professor redoubles her efforts to receive grants and merit pay. Why might these professors react so differently to the same disadvantage? According to relative deprivation theory, the same disadvantage framed in different ways will lead to different reactions. If the professor views herself as a representative faculty member deprived in comparison to faculty at other institutions (group relative deprivation), she should be motivated to support collective action. However, if the professor views herself as a unique individual deprived in comparison to other individual faculty (personal relative deprivation), she should be motivated to pursue individualistic opportunities.

Unfortunately, the initial promise of relative deprivation (RD) as an explanation for collective behavior has not been fulfilled. Some investigations strongly support RD models (e.g., Abrams, 1990; Pettigrew, 1978; Runciman, 1966; Vanneman & Pettigrew, 1972; Walker & Mann, 1987), but others do not (e.g., Gaskell & Smith, 1984; Thompson, 1989). In response to these inconsistencies, previous literature reviews have sought to clarify the theoretical antecedents and components of the concept (Crosby, 1976; Martin, 1986; Walker & Pettigrew, 1984), or to dismiss its value completely (e.g., Finkel & Rule, 1986; Gurney & Tierney, 1982). However, dismissing the usefulness of RD may be premature. For example, most negative reviews of the RD literature have neglected the theoretical distinction between group RD and personal RD (e.g., Finkel & Rule, 1986; McPhail, 1971). As originally introduced by Runciman (1966), people may compare themselves to other people and feel personally deprived, or they may compare themselves as members of an important reference group to another group and feel group deprived. It is feelings of group RD, not personal RD, that promote political protest and active attempts to change the social system (Pettigrew, 1964, 1967; Vanneman & Pettigrew, 1972; Walker & Mann, 1987). In contrast, personal RD is related to personal reactions to disadvantage such as quitting one's job, juvenile delinquency, or psychological depression (Kawakami & Dion, 1992; Mark & Folger, 1984).

However, many researchers use interpersonal comparisons to predict collectively oriented behavior (e.g., Long, 1975; Newton, Mann, & Geary, 1980; Useem, 1980). This tendency to confuse levels of analysis may explain why so many researchers have failed to find a relationship between feeling deprived and collective action. Feeling deprived can inspire participation in collective behavior, but only if the person feels deprived on behalf of a relevant reference group. The first part of this chapter reviews the preliminary results from a meta-analytic integration of RD research that includes measurements of both group and personal RD. The strongest relationship between RD and collective behavior and attitudes occurred when people feel deprived as members of an important reference group. In contrast, psychological stress, depression, and personal responses to disadvantage were more closely related to personal RD. A questionnaire designed to test the general meta-analytic conclusions confirms these patterns.

The second part of the chapter reviews recent research on authority relations that suggests why group RD and personal RD lead to such qualitatively different reactions. In this research, participants focus on the fairness of their treatment when the authority represents a valued reference group but they focus on the fairness of their outcomes when the authority represents an outgroup. The key difference is how self-relevant people view unfair treatment by the authority to be. When the authority represents an important reference group, unfair treatment is related to decreased feelings of respect and self-esteem, but when the authority represents an outgroup, the same relationship does not occur (Tyler, Degoey, & Smith, 1996). In other words, people place greater importance on treatment quality compared to outcomes when the authority represents an ingroup (because the way they are treated conveys self-relevant information: Huo, Smith, Tyler, & Lind, 1996). We suggest that people's reactions to poor treatment and outcomes from an ingroup authority are psychologically similar to people's reactions to disadvantaged interpersonal comparisons. People's reactions to poor treatment and outcomes from an outgroup authority are psychologically similar to people's reactions to disadvantaged intergroup comparisons. This research suggests that when a disadvantage is framed in intergroup terms, people are likely to place more importance on negative outcomes, and feel less personally threatened by poor treatment. Therefore, they will be more likely to endorse collective action and be less likely to feel physically stressed or psychologically depressed.

A META-ANALYSIS OF RELATIVE DEPRIVATION RESEARCH

The primary purpose of the meta-analytic review (Smith, Pettigrew, & Vega, 1994) was to include research that distinguished between personal and group RD. We expected measures of group RD to be more closely related to attitudes and participation in collective action whereas measures of personal RD should be more closely related to personal reactions to disadvantage.

The recognition of two patterns of RD raises a more subtle distinction between levels of analysis that also is easily confused empirically (Kawakami & Dion, 1992; Smith, Spears, & Oyen, 1994). Respondents are often asked to compare themselves to someone who is a member of another group. For example, suppose we ask a woman to compare her *personal* working situation with those of male employees. On the one hand, the comparison to *male* employees may mean that gender is the salient comparison dimension, thus suggesting an intergroup comparison. The employee sees herself as a representative female employee in comparison to male employees. On the other hand, the emphasis on her *personal* working situation may mean that unique personal characteristics are salient, thus suggesting an interpersonal comparison. The employee sees herself as an employee in comparison to another employee in the same company. In other words, we cannot distinguish between group and personal RD in this comparison because the same comparison could represent either an intergroup comparison, and measure feelings of group deprivation, or an interpersonal comparison, and measure feelings of personal deprivation.

The ambiguity illustrated by this example suggests that to engender feelings of group deprivation and collective behavior requires not only that the comparison target represent a particular group, but that the comparers view themselves as group representatives. Therefore, we distinguished between three types of social comparisons: (1) interpersonal comparisons between oneself and an ingroup member (e.g., a working woman compares her situation to another working woman), (2) comparisons between oneself and an outgroup member (e.g., a working woman compares her situation to a working man), and (3) intergroup comparisons between one's membership group and another group (a working woman compares the situation for working women with working men). We predict that collective behavior should be related to intergroup comparisons whereas individualistic reactions should be related to interpersonal comparisons between the respondent and an ingroup member. We expect comparisons between the respondent and an outgroup member to produce more ambiguous results because we do not know whether the respondent views the comparison as representing an intergroup situation (and therefore will be related to collective action) or as representing an interpersonal comparison (and therefore will be related to individual action).

Besides the distinction between personal and group relative deprivation, we believe there are two other reasons why researchers often fail to find strong relationships between feeling deprived and subsequent attitudes and behavior. First, RD is often defined as the difference between answers to two separate questions rather than the answer to a question that includes the comparison target. For example, respondents are often asked to place themselves, their peer group, and other ethnic or political groups on a ladder with the bottom rung labeled as the worst possible life and the top rung labeled as the best possible life (Cantril's self-anchoring striving scale, 1965). RD is defined by the difference between the placement of the respondent and various reference groups. However, using a difference score is problematic for two reasons. First, there is no guarantee that the respondent answered one question with the other question or questions in mind. Therefore, the investigators cannot assume the respondent made the comparison that they created with a difference score. Second, the reliability of difference scores is consistently lower than the questions that produce the score (Nunnally & Bernstein, 1994). Given these problems, we expect questions that include the comparison target to be more closely related to relevant dependent variables than measures constructed from difference scores.

The second reason the relationship between RD and behavior is often weak is the failure to measure how people *feel* about their disadvantage (Tyler & Smith, 1998). RD is defined as the belief that you (or your group) are worse off compared to another person or group coupled with feelings of anger and resentment. Therefore, we expect that RD measures that asked respondents about their feelings to be more closely related to dependent variables than questions that just asked whether respondents noticed a disadvantage.

To test our argument, we reviewed over 350 studies published or presented between 1967 and 1995 (located via personal letters, searches of computer databases, and reference searches through published articles and conference publications). Unlike traditional qualitative reviews, a meta-analytic integration of research results enables us to determine whether the effect sizes are as weak or nonexistent as some reviewers claim. More important, a meta-analysis can test if, as we predict, the results from studies that more closely measure the theoretical constructs originally intended do provide stronger evidence for the role of RD in motivating behavior.

To be included in the final study, the research investigation met five rules of inclusion. First, RD must be considered a *causal variable*. This requirement excludes most experimental investigations of RD designed to investigate the antecedent conditions of feeling deprived (e.g., Bernstein & Crosby, 1980; Folger & Martin, 1986; Olson, 1986). Second, individual respondents must be *asked directly about their experience*. This requirement excludes investigations in which feelings of deprivation were inferred via aggregate measures of income inequality (Gurr, 1968, 1970) or from demographic variables collected from individual respondents (e.g., Geschwender & Geschwender, 1973; Pinard, Kirk, & Von Eschen, 1972). Third, RD must be defined as a *comparative construct*. This requirement excludes measures in which people rated their feelings of injustice or resentment about their personal or group situation without reference to another person or group (Dube & Guimond, 1986, study #3; Van Kyk & Nieuwoudt, 1990). Fourth, RD must refer to discrepancies that *disadvantage the person or group*. This requirement excludes measures defined as RD on the behalf of others (see Tougas & Beaton, this volume). Finally, *the relation between the respondent and the comparison target must be clear*. For example, if the measure was a comparison between two outgroups, it was excluded. Similarly, if the measure was a comparison between a smaller and larger ingroup, it was excluded.

The effect size index that we will present is a weighted Cohens D that gives more weight to effect sizes that are reliably estimated (the effect size is weighted by the reciprocal of variance, Hedges & Olkin, 1985). For most meta-analyses, the empirical study is the preferred unit of analysis. However, many studies in this literature include several different measures of RD, each with different comparison targets. Each combination offers a different test of our hypotheses. RD studies also often include two different independent samples (e.g., African American and Caucasian-American respondents). This means that a single study can contribute a number of different tests to the meta-analysis (one test might represent the relationship between a disadvantaged interpersonal comparison and support for collective action, another test might represent the relationship between a disadvantaged intergroup comparison and support for collective action). Given our expectation that different comparison targets will yield stronger or weaker relationships, the analyses presented in the following sections focus on individual tests, even though a focus on individual tests can violate assumptions of independence (the number of tests per independent sample ranged from 1 to 36). Interestingly, our choice means that the results are more conservative: the more tests reported in a study, the lower the average effect size ($r(130) = -.24$, $p < .05$). However, when possible, key analyses are retested with the individual sample as the unit of analysis (the effect size represents an average of all the statistical tests reported for the sample).

Is Relative Deprivation Significantly Related to Collective Behavior?
The first question is whether RD is related to collective behavior. For example, social scientists trying to explain the widespread occurrence of urban riots and civil disorders in the United States during the late 1960s linked participation in riots to measures of both subjective and objective deprivation. In 1971, McPhail presented a first quantitative review of this research. Of the 39 tests he classified as tests of the relative deprivation hypothesis, 32% were nonsignificant, 61% indicated a low magnitude of association, 7% represented a moderate association, and less than 1% represented a high association between feeling deprived and participation in urban riots. Although a majority of tests were statistically significant, they certainly did not reveal a powerful effect. Subsequently, RD was dismissed as an explanation for collective behavior as researchers shifted toward resource mobilization models of collective behavior (Klandermans, 1989).

However, a closer look at the 39 tests represented in McPhail's review reveals a wide variety of measures. The RD measures include difference scores and nondifference scores, measures that asked and did not ask about feelings, comparisons between one's current personal situation and one's expectations, comparisons to other ingroup and outgroup members and experiences and opinions with police malpractice. In contrast, we argue that the best measure of the relationship between RD and collective behavior will include the comparison in the question, ask about feelings, and focus on group-to-group comparisons.

The data set used to test our argument included 35 studies (the majority were published journal articles). Most of the research represented populations in the United States. However, the research also included samples from Canada, the Netherlands, England, Australia, West Germany, Portugal, Chile, and Austria. The majority of the research focused on members of ethnic minorities. However, ethnic majorities, groups with shared occupational status, groups with shared political status, and random samples of the population were also studied. Outcome measures include self-reported rioting, militancy, using violence to achieve political goals, readiness to block a road, block bulldozers, or spike trees, approval of violent politics or civil disobedience, and pressuring employers to hire more ingroup members.

The overall effect size for the relationship between RD and collective behavior is relatively small; $d+ = .24$ for the 35 studies, $d+ = .21$ for the 48 samples, and $d+ = .20$ for the 223 tests. These small effect sizes appear to confirm the pessimistic conclusions of earlier reviews of the literature. However, the average effect size for the 130 tests that included the comparison target within the question was significantly greater ($d+ = .27$) than the average effect size for the 93 tests that used difference scores ($d+ = .14$, $Qb = 227.50$, $p < .05$). Clearly, difference scores are associated with a weaker relationship between RD and collective behavior. Next, we limited the analysis to those questions that included the comparison target and then we distinguished between those questions that asked about feelings and those that did not. The 53 tests that excluded feelings ($d+ = .18$) reveal a significantly weaker relationship than the 77 tests that included feelings ($d+ = .35$, $Qb = 173.12$, $p < .05$).

Finally, we can examine whether, for those RD measures that included the comparison target and feelings within the question, particular comparison targets yield stronger relationships (see Figure 5.1). As we expected, group-to-group comparisons ($d+(17) = .63$) were significantly more closely related to collective behavior and attitudes than comparisons between the respondent and an ingroup member ($d+(7) = .19$, $\chi^2 = 133.36$, $p < .05$) and comparisons to personal experience ($d+(36) = .34$, $\chi^2 = 68.87$, $p < .05$). However, as we might expect given the potential ambiguity of comparisons to specific outgroup members, the average effect size for these comparison measures was significantly smaller ($d+(7) = .39$) than group-to-group comparisons ($\chi^2 = 12.18$, $p < .05$), and these measures were not significantly different from comparisons to ingroup members ($\chi^2 = 6.50$, ns). Interestingly, measures that asked respondents to compare their current group situation to the group's situation in either the past or the future failed to show an effect size significantly greater than any of the other types of comparisons shown in Figure 5.1 ($d+(11) = .10$).

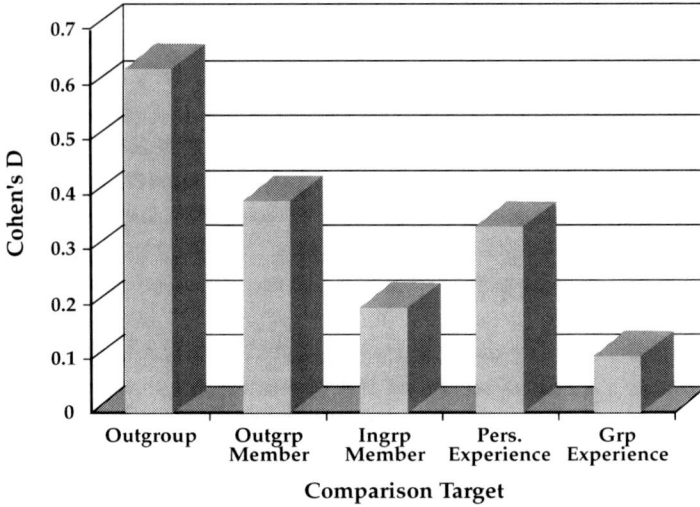

Figure 5.1. Mean effect sizes for tests of collective behavior.
Note. N=77. Comparison target and feelings are included in the measure of relative deprivation.

When individual samples are used as the unit of analysis, the pattern remains the same. Group-to-group comparisons $(d+(9) = .54)$ were significantly more closely related to collective behavior and attitudes than comparisons between the respondent and ingroup member $(d+(4) = .17, \chi^2 = 37.58, p < .05)$ and comparisons to personal experience $(d+(4) = .26, \chi^2 = 40.80, p < .05)$.[1] In this case, comparisons to outgroup members $(d+(4) = .36)$ yielded a smaller but not significantly different effect size than group-to-group comparisons $(\chi^2 = 4.16, ns)$. This effect size also was not significantly different from the average effect size for comparisons to ingroup members $(\chi^2 = 3.99, ns)$. Again, the study that asked respondents to compare their current group situation to either the past or the future failed to show an effect size significantly greater than the other types of comparisons $(d+(1) = .10)$.

These results show that if we consider RD measures that better capture the theoretical construct, there is a strong relationship between RD and collective behavior, particularly if we limit the analysis to single questions that include feelings and group-to-group comparisons. In fact, the mean effect size is as large as many other social psychological phenomena $(d+ = .63, r = .31,$ Cohen, 1977$)$. These results suggest that previous reviewers were too quick to dismiss RD as an explanation of collective behavior and attitudes. In particular, the superiority of group-to-group comparisons supports Runciman's original distinction and recent social identity interpretations of relative deprivation (Ellemers, this volume; Kawakami & Dion, 1992; Smith & Spears, 1996; Walker & Pettigrew, 1984). Before comparisons can motivate collective behavior, we must view the comparison in group terms – our ingroup versus an outgroup. This requirement suggests why group-to-group comparisons outperformed the more ambiguous comparisons between the single respondent and an outgroup member.

Is Relative Deprivation Significantly Related to Individual Behavior?
The second question is whether RD measures are related to measures of individual behavior. In contrast to measures of collective behavior, measures of personal RD, not group RD, should be more closely related to individual behavior. However, we still expect better measures of RD – questions that include the comparison target and ask about feelings – to be more closely related to individual reactions. Eleven studies are included in the final data set (the majority are journal articles). The majority of research occurred in United States (but Canada, the Netherlands, Poland, and Portugal are also represented). Most research focused on groups with a shared occupational status (e.g., university professors in Poland). Ethnicity was not investigated. Outcome measures included official records of delinquency, the propensity to date rape, work for church committees, absence from work, hypothetical reactions to poor grades, academic activities, looking for another job, physical exercise, and talking to one's work supervisor.

The overall effect size for the relationship between RD and individual behavior is very weak; $d+ = .10$ for the 11 studies, $d+ = .10$ for the 13 samples, and $d+ = .11$ for the 83 tests. However, as we argued above, these overall effect sizes are combined across better and worse measures of RD. If we distinguish between measures that include the comparison target and those that do not, the 29 tests that include the comparison yield a bigger effect size ($d+ = .11$) than the four tests that do not ($d+ = .02$), but the difference is not significant ($Qb = .40$, ns).

If we decompose the tests that include the comparison target as part of the question, the 26 tests that asked about feelings were significantly more closely related to individual reactions ($d+ = .22$) than the 53 tests that did not ask about feelings ($d+ = .10$, $Qb = 18.55$, $p < .05$). However, in this case, different comparison targets do not seem to be associated with different average effect sizes (see Figure 5.2). The average effect size for the 18 tests for the person to ingroup member comparisons was .22, for the four tests of person to outgroup member comparisons was .26, and for the four tests of group-to-group comparisons was .19. Focused contrasts yield no signif-

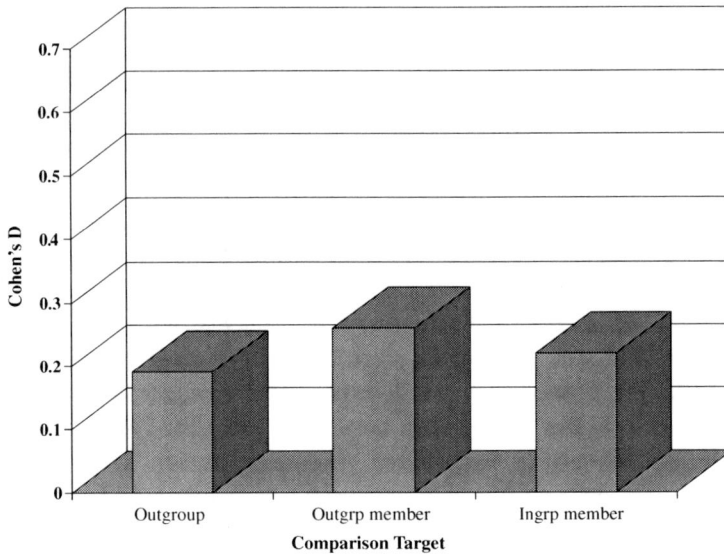

Figure 5.2. Mean effect sizes for tests of individual behavior.
Note. N=26. Comparison target and feelings are included in the measure of relative deprivation.

icant differences. Unfortunately, the analyses could not be repeated using single samples as the unit of analysis.

Based on this set of research results, the relationship between individual behavior and RD is small – even under what we would consider the best of circumstances – with the comparison target and feelings included in the question and limited to comparisons to other ingroup members ($d+$ = .22, r = .11). Before proposing possible explanations for this pattern, it is important to recognize how much smaller the number of tests included in this data set is compared to the number of tests of the collective behavior hypothesis. For example, the data includes no comparisons to personal experience, and it may be that it is these types of comparisons that elicit the strongest individual reactions (see Tougas & Beaton, this volume).

However, the small relationship may not be so surprising given the wide range of individual behaviors studied and the degree to which individual behavior is multiply determined. In fact, one might argue that the repertoire of individual reactions to a disadvantaged situation is greater than the repertoire of collective reactions. Certainly, the smaller data set for individual behavior includes a wider range of reactions than the data set for collective behavior. If this is true, finding a relationship between personal RD and reactions will be more difficult than finding a relationship between group RD and reactions. However, before we dismiss the value of personal RD to individual behavior and reactions, we should consider a third question.

Is Relative Deprivation Significantly Related to Changes in Internal States?

The third question is whether relative deprivation measures are related to measures of changes in internal states (e.g., self-esteem, physical stress, and psychological depression). Again, the best measure should include the comparison target within the question, ask about feelings, and focus on interpersonal comparisons. Twelve studies are included in the final data set (the majority are journal articles). Most of the research was conducted in the United States and focuses on women. However, the data set also includes research conducted in Canada, the Netherlands, England, and Australia, and contains investigations of minority group members, the unemployed, and high school teachers. Outcome measures include stress symptom checklists, blood pressure and medical history, powerlessness, depression and anxiety checklists, and social competence.

The overall effect size for the relationship between RD and internal states is small; $d+ = .34$ for the 12 studies, $d+ = .28$ for the 22 samples, and $d+ = .23$ for the 64 tests. However, as we previously argued, these overall effect sizes are combined across better and worse measures of RD. If we distinguish between measures that include the comparison target and those that do not, the 47 tests that include the comparison target are significantly more closely related to internal states ($d+ = .35$) than are the 17 tests that do not ($d+ = .19$, $Qb = 51.67$, $p < .05$). Within those measures that include the comparison target, the 45 tests that include feelings are more closely related to internal states ($d+ = .37$) than the two tests that do not include feelings ($d+ = .19$, $Qb = 8.39$, $p < .05$).

Finally, comparison target does make a difference (see Figure 5.3). Simple contrasts confirm that comparisons to ingroup members ($d+(22) = .40$) are significantly more closely related to internal states than are group-to-group comparisons ($d+(12) = .20$, $\chi^2 = 9.19$, $p < .05$). Similarly, personal experiences ($d+(6) = .67$) are more closely related to internal states than to group-to-group comparisons ($\chi^2 = 7.90$, $p < .05$). In this case, comparisons to outgroup members yield a strong effect size ($d+(5) = .46$) that is not significantly different from comparisons to ingroup members ($\chi^2 = 3.99$, *ns*) nor from group-to-group comparisons ($\chi^2 = 4.16$, *ns*).

If a single sample is used as the unit of analysis, the pattern of results is similar. Comparisons to an ingroup member yield the strongest relation-

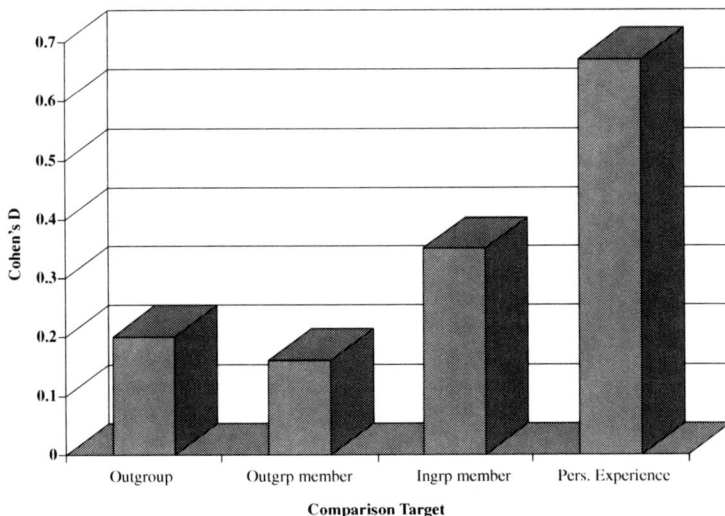

Figure 5.3. Mean effect sizes for tests of internal states.
Note. N=35. Comparison target and feelings are included in the measure of relative deprivation.

ship ($d+(3)$ = .76), comparisons to personal experience the next strongest relationship ($d+(3)$ = .69) and group-to-group comparisons the weakest ($d+(1)$ = .19). Group comparisons are significantly weaker than comparisons to ingroup members (χ^2 = 27.01, $p < .05$) and comparisons to personal experience (χ^2 = 16.90, $p < .05$).

Unlike measures of individual behavior, tests of internal states yield a more theoretically consistent relationship between RD and reactions. Comparisons to ingroup members (with the comparison target and feelings included in the question) reveal the strongest relationship to internal states whereas group comparisons reveal the weakest. Perhaps it is not surprising to find a stronger relationship between feeling personally deprived and other measures of internal states than between feeling personally deprived and particular behaviors. In fact, low self-esteem, depression or greater physiological stress might mediate the relationship between personal RD and particular actions. However, more striking is the absence of a strong relationship between measures of internal states and group RD. A lack of fit between the level of the comparison and the dependent variable might explain the lack of relationship between group comparisons and self-evaluations ($d+(9)$ = .20). For example, if collective self-esteem (Crocker & Luhtanen, 1990) rather than personal (or global) self-esteem, was measured, we might see a stronger relationship (see Tougas & Beaton, this volume). However, there is also a weak relationship between group-to-group comparisons and physiological stress measures $(d+(3) = .19)$, suggesting that this lack of relationship is not simply measurement error.

Experimental Evidence

Together, the meta-analytic results suggest that if relative deprivation is measured correctly; with the comparison target included in the question, asking about feelings, and at the right level of fit, it is related to important outcomes. The mean effect size for the best measures of RD and collective behavior $(d+ = .63, r = .31)$ and for the best measures of RD and internal states $(d+ = .67, r = .33)$ would be considered representative of large effect sizes (Cohen, 1977). The only weak relationship was between the best measures of RD and individual behavior $(d+ = .26, r = .13)$. Given the range of populations and the types of dependent variables studied, these results are impressive.

However, all the research included in the meta-analysis is correlational. This means that comparison information was measured rather than manipulated, limiting any causal conclusions. Therefore, in a recent study (Smith, Muller, & Shull, 1999), participants read one of three possible social comparisons and then indicated how they felt and whether they supported a collective reaction to the problem. By manipulating the comparison information presented, we can be more confident that disadvantageous group-to-group comparisons are more likely to promote collective action. An experimental design also allows us to keep all the comparison information the same except for how the comparison is framed (e.g., as either an intergroup or an interpersonal comparison). In contrast, we cannot know what information respondents in previous studies used when they were asked to compare the situation of working men to women, or their situation to other working women.

Not only did we manipulate comparison information, we also measured the extent to which people identified with their group. We argue that the reason group-to-group comparisons are most closely related to collective action is because the respondent is reacting as a group member and not as a unique individual. Of course, knowing that one is a group member, and truly caring about one's group membership are two different things (see Ellemers, this volume). Therefore, we would expect participants who identify more closely with their reference group to react more strongly to disadvantageous intergroup comparisons than participants who identify less closely with the reference group. Recent experimental research shows that initial levels of group identification are critical to how people deal with their disadvantaged group status (see Doosje, Ellemers, & Spears, 1999; Spears, Doosje, & Ellemers, 1999). For example, when group identity was threatened, those who identified closely with their group saw themselves as a more typical group member and the group as more homogeneous compared to low identifiers. People who did not identify with the group were less committed to the group and wanted to change group membership even if it did not seem possible (Ellemers, Barreto, & Spears, 1999). Most important, these differences between high and low identifiers are most evident when the intergroup context is made salient (Spears, Doosje, & Ellemers, 1999). Describing a disadvantaged intergroup comparison should make the intergroup context salient. Therefore, we expected students who identified more closely with their university to be more sensitive to a disadvantaged intergroup comparison than those who did not. A first questionnaire measured respondents' identification with Sonoma State University (SSU). Respondents completed a second questionnaire several weeks later in which the type of comparison information the participants read was manipulated. Participants either read about a disadvantageous intergroup comparison between SSU and Cal Poly students (a rival university), a disadvantageous interpersonal comparison between themselves and other SSU students, or a disadvantageous interpersonal comparison between themselves and other Cal Poly students. Following the comparison information, students were asked a series of questions about their reactions to the information.

The results from this questionnaire study confirm and refine the patterns revealed in the meta-analysis. For example, participants who read the disadvantaged intergroup comparison were more likely to endorse collective action (e.g., picketing a trustee meeting) and to view their groups as effective than did participants who read the interpersonal comparisons, but only if they identified closely with the group. Participants who did not identify with the group actually rated their group as significantly less effective after reading the disadvantaged intergroup comparison. Further, in contrast to the meta-analytic results, we do find a relationship between an internal states measure and the intergroup comparison. High identifiers were more upset by the disadvantaged group comparison and less bothered by the negative interpersonal comparisons than were low identifiers.

The questionnaire study also demonstrates the problem of comparisons to an outgroup member even for those respondents who identify closely with the reference group and who might be expected to interpret any comparison information in group terms. Mean ratings for collective action and group efficacy following the disadvantaged comparison to an outgroup member fell between the mean ratings following disadvantaged group-to-group comparison and the disadvantaged person to ingroup comparison.

The results from this study confirm the relative deprivation prediction that disadvantages framed in intergroup terms promote collective action. However, the results also suggest that framing a disadvantage in group terms will only increase sensitivity to the collective situation for those participants who are closely identified with the disadvantaged group. For participants who are not identified with the group, framing the disadvantage in group terms might make them more inclined to distance themselves from the collective problem.

DISADVANTAGED COMPARISONS AND THE PSYCHOLOGY OF AUTHORITY RELATIONS

How do we explain the qualitative difference between reactions to disadvantaged intergroup and interpersonal comparisons – particularly when people identify closely with the reference group? The key may be in how people conceptualize their relationship to the comparison target. When the comparison target represents an outgroup, people may be more concerned with outcome differences and less concerned with the implications for their personal self-image than when the comparison target represents an ingroup. Therefore, they may be more willing to challenge the inequity. To illustrate this argument, we can examine people's reactions to the treatment and outcomes given by an outcome authority compared to their reactions to the same treatment and outcomes given by an ingroup authority (Huo, Smith, Tyler, & Lind, 1996; Tyler, Degoey, & Smith, 1996).

In one recent study, we distinguished between employees in a multicultural organization who viewed a supervisor of a different ethnicity as a fellow member of the larger organization (an interpersonal relationship) and employees who viewed their supervisor as a representative of a different ethnic group (an intergroup relationship, Huo, Smith, Tyler, & Lind, 1996). Employees who identified more closely with the larger organization based their acceptance of the supervisor's resolution to the conflict on whether they felt respectfully treated. In contrast, employees who identified less closely with the larger organization based their acceptance on whether they got the outcome they wanted. In other words, people reacted less confrontationally to unfavorable outcomes when they perceived the source of these outcomes as part of their ingroup. Employees might be willing to tolerate huge discrepancies in paychecks if they view the management as one of their own, but if they view the management as repre-

senting an outgroup, the same discrepancy might prompt strong condemnation (Martin & Harder, 1994).[2]

Why should the group affiliation of the authority influence people's reactions to unfavorable outcomes? According to the group value model of procedural justice (Lind & Tyler, 1988) and the related relational model of
authority (Tyler & Lind, 1992), the answer lies in people's desire to seek self-
relevant information through evaluations of the quality of their interaction
with important reference group representatives. The group value model
incorporates the social identity premise (Hogg & Abrams, 1988; Tajfel &
Turner, 1986) that people use groups, and the authorities that represent those
groups, as sources of information about their self-worth (Tyler, Degoey, &
Smith, 1996). An important premise of the group-value model is that people's relationship to the group should moderate the importance they place on
how they are treated by group authorities. Because treatment quality conveys relationship information about people's value to a group, such information should be particularly important to people when they are dealing with
an authority who represents a valued ingroup. When dealing with an outgroup authority, the self-relevant implications of treatment quality are less
important. The group value model proposes that treatment quality matters
to people because it provides relational information about their position
within a valued ingroup, which in turn shapes their self-concept. In other
words, fair treatment by an ingroup authority communicates respect for the
individual. Feelings of respect, in turn, shape a person's sense of self-worth.
The assumption underlying this hypothesis is that treatment quality is taken
as an indicator of the group's general opinions. In particular, respectful treatment by a key group representative indicates whether other group members
respect the person.

We tested this argument in two recent experiments (Smith, Tyler, Huo,
Ortiz, & Lind, 1998) in which the group affiliation of an authority responsible for outcomes was manipulated. In one experiment, a graduate student responsible for grading a social skills test was presented to students
as either an ingroup member (from the student's university) or an outgroup member (from a rival university). Later, the graduate student
entered the room and treated the student fairly or unfairly by either carefully grading the student's work performance, or doing a superficial job.
Independently, the student received either a favorable outcome or an
unfavorable outcome. Regardless of the outcome, participants who were
treated unfairly by the testgrader from the participant's university
reported feeling significantly less respect from other people than participants treated unfairly by the testgrader from a rival university.

A second experiment confirmed this pattern of results. In this study, psychology students participated in a computer simulation of several typical business tasks (Lind, Kray, & Thompson, 1998). Participants were told that if they were successful, they would have the opportunity to participate in a $100 subject payment lottery. Following each task, participants could email messages to an unseen supervisor that explained any problems. The unseen supervisor responded to the participants' email messages with either three very polite and considerate messages or an initially polite message followed by two rude and insensitive messages. As in the first study, the supervisor was from either the participant's university or a rival university. As expected, fair treatment by an ingroup authority led to feelings of greater respect, particularly when the outcomes were negative.

A third study investigated the same relationships in a field setting. In a questionnaire, students described and evaluated a recent conflict with a university faculty or staff member. Because of the correlational nature of this study, we operationalized the construct of authority group affiliation in a slightly different manner than in the previous experiments. In the two previous experiments, we assumed that students value their membership in their university and manipulated the university affiliation of the authority to create ingroup and outgroup authority conditions. In contrast, in this study, we acknowledged that objective group membership is only a proxy of the extent to which people value their group memberships. Hence, we explicitly measured students' identification with their university. We assumed that students who identified highly with the university would be more likely to view faculty and staff as ingroup authorities. Similarly, students who identified less closely with the university would be more likely to view faculty and staff as representing an outgroup. Finally, unlike the two experiments, in which participants experienced a brief interaction with an authority figure, this study explores conflicts in which those involved have stronger, longer-term relationships with potentially greater consequences. As we predicted, the results show that when students identified more closely with the university, fair treatment was positively related to both feelings of respect and self-esteem, confirming in a field setting the pattern of results found in the two experiments. Clearly, an ingroup authority who treats people poorly communicates information about whether people in general respect the person.

However, this research also reveals an unexpected pattern of results. In all three studies, rude treatment by an outgroup authority was associated with feelings of *greater* respect. As shown in Figure 5.4, when outcomes were unfavorable and the authority represents an outgroup, poor treat-

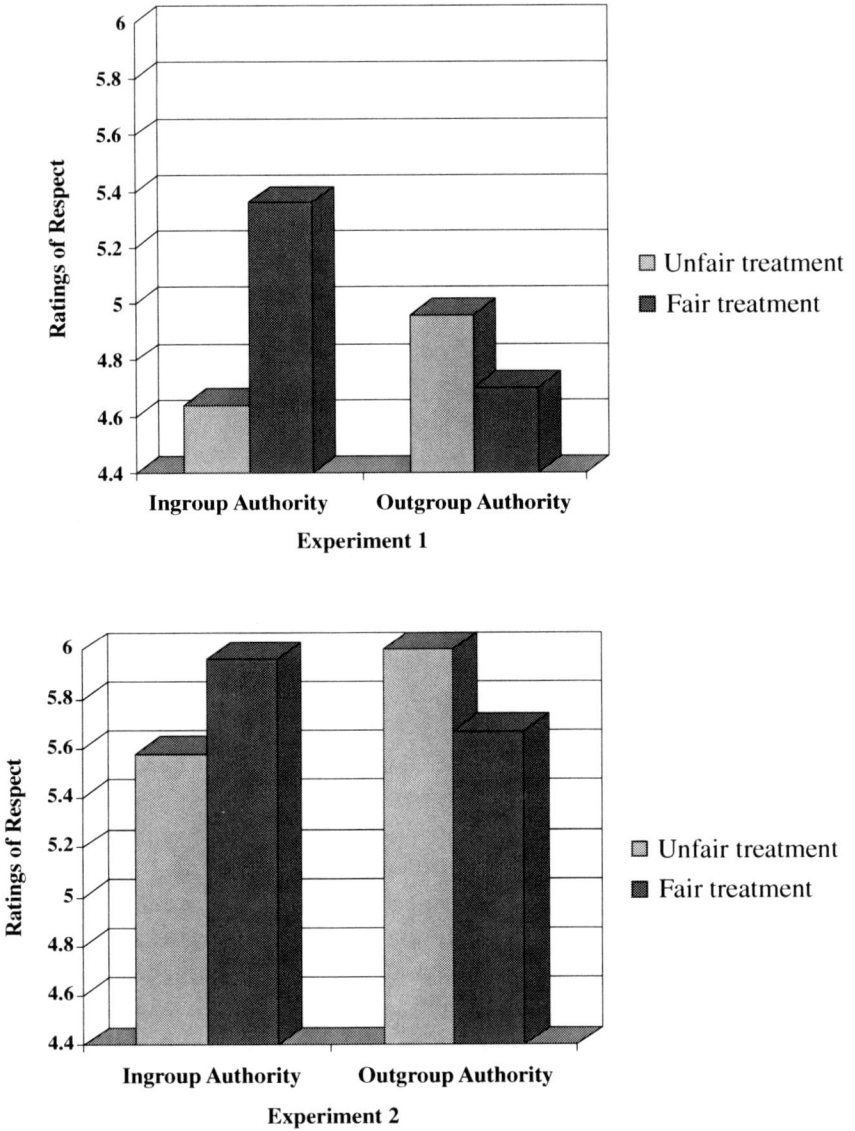

Figure 5.4. Mean respect ratings for two experiments.
Note. Ratings of respect could range from low (1) to high (7). Data from Smith, Tyler, Huo, Oritz & Lind (1998).

ment quality actually lead to greater feelings of respect than did good treatment quality. Why do participants report more respect rather than less when treated unfairly by an outgroup authority? One possible explanation may be that people are more likely to view negative behavior by an ingroup authority as legitimate but negative behavior by an outgroup authority as illegitimate. Therefore, it may have been easier to discount and even react against negative feedback from an outgroup authority (Ruggiero & Taylor, 1997). Recent research on psychological disengagement suggests that one reason the self-esteem of African American students is not as sensitive to intellectual performance feedback as is the self-esteem of European Americans is their perceptions that such tests are racially biased (Major, Spencer, Schmader, Wolfe, & Crocker, 1998). Similarly, research on minorities' reactions to discrimination suggests that attributing negative feedback to discrimination protects performance self-esteem (Ruggerio & Taylor, 1997). If true, we would expect respondents to rate a situation with an outgroup authority as more illegitimate than the same situation with an ingroup authority. However, in both experiments and the questionnaire study, group affiliation did not influence ratings of procedural and outcome fairness. In other words, people rated poor treatment and unfavorable outcomes from an ingroup authority as unfair as they rated poor treatment and unfavorable outcomes from an outgroup authority.

A second possibility is that group membership offers people an attributional resource for explaining negative reactions by the outgroup that does not threaten their personal self-worth (Crocker & Major, 1989). For example, when interacting with an outgroup authority, people might use stereotypes about the unfairness, selfishness, and unreasonableness of outgroup members toward *any* ingroup member to decide that how they were treated was not related to anything uniquely "personal" about them. In fact, people may be more likely to blame the system for inequitable outcomes when they define the situation in intergroup terms. In contrast, people may be more likely to take personal responsibility for inequitable outcomes when they define the situation in interpersonal terms. In a different set of experiments, we first replicated the typical tendency for people to rationalize poor personal outcomes, even when they are the product of a clearly unfair and arbitrary disadvantage (Smith & Spears, 1996). However, when we made a shared disadvantaged group membership salient, participants no longer viewed their poor outcomes as the product of their personal lack of effort or ability. Differences in attributions can explain why unfair treatment by outgroup authorities is less likely to be associated with negative self-evaluations and stress.

A third possibility is that interpreting the situation in intergroup terms may give people a greater sense of social support. This sense of social support can protect them against physiological stress and negative self-evaluations. Often, the first response to a possible unfair event is to try to verify the unfairness (Bies & Tripp, 1996; Koss, Goodman, Browne, Fitzgerald, Keita, & Russon, 1994). However, in intergroup contexts, people act as representative group members rather than as unique individuals (Turner, 1999). Therefore, in intergroup contexts, people may feel more confident that their experience is not unique or ambiguous. In a recent experimental study (Ruggiero, Taylor, & Lydon, 1997), women who learned that another woman had failed a test possibly evaluated by a sexist judge (defined as a manipulation of informational support) were significantly more likely to attribute their performance to discrimination compared to women who did not have this knowledge. Similarly, women who thought that they would have the opportunity to meet with someone after the test (defined as a measure of emotional support) were significantly more likely to attribute their performance to discrimination compared to women without this opportunity. In this experiment, social support is represented by interactions with other group members. In contrast, we are suggesting that simply framing the same disadvantage in intergroup terms reduces ambiguity (thereby providing informational support) and feelings of isolated uniqueness (thereby providing emotional support). In other words, viewing the situation as a representative group member provides people with consensus information that is not psychologically available when people think of themselves as unique individuals.

An important question is whether the increased respect we find in this data is linked to real behavior or not. If the increased respect reported by participants is simply defensive, we would not expect them to be more likely to participate in collective behavior (e.g., participate in a rally or sign a petition). Alternatively, framing a disadvantage in intergroup terms may give people the psychological resources to challenge an inequitable situation. In fact, these results might explain a classic paradox described in the relative deprivation literature. It is not necessarily the most deprived who are more likely to lead collective actions, but the moderately deprived (Caplan & Paige, 1968; Gurin & Epps, 1975). Previous authors have suggested that more advantaged members of disadvantaged groups have the material resources to pursue collective action. The more advantaged members of disadvantaged groups might also have more interactions with outgroup members and authorities. These interactions, if defined in intergroup terms, should increase feelings of respect. Greater respect from one's ingroup is associated with more behavior to help that group (Smith & Tyler 1997; Tyler, Degoey, & Smith, 1996). This research suggests that if people view the authority as an outgroup member, unfair treatment will lead to feeling greater respect, not less, and perhaps offer a psychological resource for pursuing collective action.

Research on authority relations suggests two reasons why disadvantaged intergroup comparisons are more likely to prompt an active collective response and less likely to influence internal states than are disadvantaged interpersonal comparisons. First, participants' reactions to conflicts are more closely related to outcome discrepancies when they view the source of those discrepancies as an outgroup member. When people define a disadvantage in intergroup terms, they will be less likely to tolerate unfavorable outcomes. Second, unfair treatment from an outgroup authority can lead to more rather than less respect and self-esteem. This finding coupled with other research that suggests that people are less likely to "rationalize" unfair personal outcomes when they interpret the situation in intergroup terms suggests that a salient group membership can empower people to actively respond to disadvantages.

CONCLUSIONS

The research reviewed in this chapter illustrates how important the distinction between group RD and personal RD is for understanding people's reactions to disadvantage. First, the pessimistic conclusions of previous reviewers of the RD literature appear to be premature. RD is a powerful concept if it is measured correctly (with the appropriate comparison target and feelings included in the question). Second, the distinction between group RD and personal RD illustrates how framing the same situation in either personal or group terms can lead to very different reactions. Research on authority relations suggests that when a disadvantage is defined in intergroup terms, people may be more concerned with outcome differences and less concerned with the implications for their personal self-image than when the same disadvantage is defined in interpersonal terms. Therefore, they may be more willing to challenge the inequity. Not only might people feel less devastated by a disadvantage they interpret in intergroup terms, they may actually feel more empowered to deal with it.

NOTES

1. One effect size was removed from the category of personal experience because, unlike the other studies, the RD measures in this study involved U.S. adults' answers to 15 questions about their frustration with their housing, income, medical care, and work. Each of the 15 answers was weighted by how much responsibility the respondent assigned to the state for their situation (Muller, 1980). Removal of this study sharply reduced the estimate of heterogeneity for this category. If this effect size is included, the average effect size increases to .58.

2. Of course, one important question yet to be explored is whether continuous large outcome discrepancies might lead people to reassess the situation and be more likely to view the authority as an outgroup member.

REFERENCES

Abrams, D. (1990). *Political identity: Relative deprivation, social identity and the case of Scottish nationalism.* Economic & Social Research Council 16–19 Initiative. Occasional Paper no. 24. Social Statistics Research Unit, City University London.

Bernstein, M., & Crosby, F. J. (1980). An empirical examination of relative deprivation theory. *Journal of Experimental Social Psychology, 16,* 442–456.

Bies, R. J., & Tripp, T. M. (1996). Beyond distrust: "getting even" and the need for revenge. In R. Kramer & T. R. Tyler, (Eds.), *Trust in organizations.* Beverly Hills, CA: Sage.

Cantril, H. (1965). *The pattern of human concerns.* New Brunswick, NJ: Rutgers University Press.

Caplan, N., & Paige, J. M. (1968). A study of ghetto rioters. *Scientific American, 219,* 15–21.

Cohen, J. (1977). *Statistical power analysis for the behavioral sciences.* New York: Academic Press.

Crocker, J., & Luhtanen, R. (1990). Collective self-esteem and ingroup bias. *Journal of Personality and Social Psychology, 58,* 60–67.

Crocker, J., & Major, B. (1989). Social stigma and self-esteem: The self-protective properties of stigma. *Psychological Review, 96,* 608–630.

Crosby, F. (1976). A model of egoistical deprivation. *Psychological Review, 83,* 85–113.

Doosje, B., Ellemers, N., & Spears, R. (1999). Commitment and intergroup behavior. In N. Ellemers, R. Spears, & B. Doosje, (Eds.), *Social identity: Context, commitment, content* (pp. 84–106). Oxford: Blackwell.

Dube, L., & Guimond, S. (1986). Relative deprivation and social protest: The personal-group issue. In J. M. Olson, C. P. Herman, and M. P. Zanna, (Eds.), *Relative deprivation and social comparison: The Ontario symposium* (Vol. 4, pp. 201–216). Hillsdale, NJ: Lawrence Erlbaum.

Ellemers, N., Barreto, M., & Spears, R. (1999). Commitment and strategic responses to social context. In N. Ellemers, R. Spears, & B. Doosje, (Eds.), *Social identity: Context, commitment, content* (pp. 127–146). Oxford: Blackwell.

Finkel, S., & Rule, J. (1987). Relative deprivation and related psychological theories of civil violence: A critical review. *Research in Social Movements: Conflicts and Change, 9,* 47–69.

Folger, R., & Martin, C. (1986). Relative deprivation and referent cognitions: Distributive and procedural justice effects. *Journal of Experimental Psychology, 22*, 531–546.

Gaskell, G., & Smith, P. (1984). Relative deprivation in Black and White youth: An empirical investigation. *British Journal of Social Psychology, 23*, 121–131.

Geschwender, B. A., & Geschwender, J. A. (1973). Relative deprivation and participation in the civil rights movement. *Social Science Quarterly, 54*, 405–411.

Gurin, P., & Epps, E. (1975). *Black consciousness, identity and achievement: A study of students in historically black colleges.* New York: John Wiley.

Gurney, J., & Tierney, K. (1982). Relative deprivation and social movements: A critical look at twenty years of theory and research. *Sociological Quarterly, 23*, 33–47.

Gurr, T. R. (1968). A causal model of civil strife: A comparative analysis using new indices. *American Political Science Review, 62*, 1104–1124.

Gurr, T. R. (1970). *Why men rebel.* Princeton: Princeton University Press.

Hedges, L. V., & Olin, I. (1985). *Statistical methods for meta-analysis.* New York: Academic Press.

Hogg, M. A., & Abrams, D. (1988). *Social identifications: A social psychology of intergroup relations and group processes.* London and New York: Routledge.

Huo, Y. J., Smith, H. J., Tyler, T. R., & Lind, E. A. (1996). Superordinate identification, subgroup identification, and justice concerns: Is separatism the problem; Is assimilation the answer? *Psychological Science, 7*, 40–45.

Kawakami, K., & Dion, K. (1992). The impact of salient self-identities on relative deprivation and action intentions. *European Journal of Social Psychology, 23*, 525–540.

Klandermans, B. (1989). Grievance interpretation and success expectancies: The social construction of protest. *Social Behavior, 4*, 113–125.

Koss, M. P., Goodman, L. A., Browne, A., Fitzgerald, L. F., Keita, G. P., & Russon, N. F. (1994). *No safe haven: Male violence against women at home, at work and in the community.* Washington, DC: American Psychological Association.

Lind, E. A., Kray, L., & Thompson, L. (1998). The social construction of injustice: Fairness judgments in response to own and others' unfair treatment by authorities. *Organizational Behavior and Human Decision Processes, 75*, 1–22.

Lind, E. A., & Tyler, T. R. (1988). *The social psychology of procedural justice.* New York: Plenum.

Long, S. J. (1975). Malevolent estrangement: Political alienation and political justification among Black and White adolescents. *Youth and Society, 7*, 99–129.

Major, B., Spencer, S., Schmader, T., Wolfe, C., & Crocker, J. (1998). Coping with negative stereotypes about intellectual performance: The role of psychological disengagement. *Personality and Social Psychology Bulletin, 24*, 34–50.

Mark, M., & Folger, R. (1984). Response to relative deprivation: A conceptual framework. *Review of Personality and Social Psychology, 5*, 192–218.

Martin, J. (1986). The tolerance of injustice. In J. Olson, C. P. Herman, & M. Zanna, (Eds.), *Relative deprivation and social comparison: The Ontario symposium* (Vol. 4, pp. 217–242). Hillsdale, NJ: Lawrence Erlbaum.

Martin, J., & Harder, J. W. (1994). Bread and roses: Justice and the distribution of financial and socio-emotional rewards in organizations. *Social Justice Research, 7*, 241–264.

McPhail, C. (1971). Civil disorder participation: A critical examination of recent research. *American Sociological Review, 36,* 1058–1073.

Muller, N. (1980). The psychology of political protest and violence. In T. R. Gurr (Ed.), *Handbook of political conflict* (pp. 69–100). New York: Free Press.

Newton, J. W., Mann, L., & Geary, D. (1980). Relative deprivation, dissatisfaction and militancy: A field study in a protest crowd. *Journal of Applied Social Psychology, 10,* 384–397.

Nunnally, J. C., & Bernstein, I. H. (1994). *Psychometric theory.* New York: McGraw-Hill.

Olson, J. M. (1986). Resentment about deprivation: entitlement and hopefulness as mediators of the effects of qualifications. In J. M. Olson, C. P. Herman, and M. Zanna, (Eds.), *Relative deprivation and social comparison: The Ontario symposium* (Vol. 4, pp. 57–77). Hillsdale, NJ: Lawrence Erlbaum.

Pettigrew, T. F. (1964). *A profile of the Negro American.* Princeton, NJ: Van Nostrand.

Pettigrew, T. F. (1967). Social evaluation theory. In D. Levine (Ed.), *Nebraska symposium on motivation* (Vol 15, pp. 241–315). Lincoln: University of Nebraska Press.

Pettigrew, T. F. (1978). Three issues in ethnicity: Boundaries, deprivations and perceptions. In J. M. Yinger & S. J. Cutler (Eds.), *Major social issues* (pp. 25–49). New York: Free Press.

Pinard, M., Kirk, J., & Von Eschen, D. (1969). Processes of recruitment in the sit-in movement. *Public Opinion Quarterly, 33,* 555–369.

Ruggiero, K., & Taylor, D. (1997). Why minority members perceive or do not perceive the discrimination that confronts them: The role of self-esteem and perceived control *Journal of Personality and Social Psychology, 72,* 373–389.

Ruggerio, K. M., Taylor, D. M., & Lydon, J. E. (1997). How disadvantaged group members cope with discrimination when they perceive that social support is available. *Journal of Applied Social Psychology, 27,* 1581–1600.

Runciman, W. G. (1966). *Relative deprivation and social justice: A study of attitudes to social inequality in twentieth-century England.* Berkeley: University of California Press.

Smith, H. J., Miller, A., & Shull, S. (1999). *Worse than whom?: Comparison target and feeling relatively deprived.* Unpublished manuscript, Sonoma State University.

Smith, H. J., Pettigrew, T. F., & Vega, L. (1994). *Measures of relative deprivation: A conceptual critique and meta-analysis.* Paper presented at the annual meeting of the American Psychological Association, Los Angeles, California.

Smith, H. J., Spears, R., & Oyen, M. (1994). The influence of personal deprivation and salience of group membership on justice evaluations. *Journal of Experimental Social Psychology, 30,* 277–299.

Smith, H. J., & Spears, R. (1996). Ability and outcome evaluations as a function of personal and collective (dis)advantage: A group escape from individual bias. *Personality and Social Psychology Bulletin, 22,* 690–704.

Smith, H. J., & Tyler, T. R. (1997). Choosing the right pond: How group membership shapes self-esteem and group-oriented behavior. *Journal of Experimental Social Psychology, 33,* 146–170.

Smith, H. J., Tyler, T. R., Huo, Y. J., Ortiz, D. J., & Lind, E. A. (1998). The self-relevant implications of the group-value model: Group membership, self-worth and treatment quality. *Journal of Experimental Social Psychology, 34,* 470–493.

Spears, R., Doosje, B., & Ellemers, N. (1999). Commitment and the context of social perception. In N. Ellemers, R. Spears, & B. Doosje (Eds.), *Social identity: Context, commitment, content* (pp. 59–83). Oxford: Blackwell.

Tajfel, H., & Turner, J. C. (1986). The social identity theory of intergroup behavior. In W. G. Austin & S. Worchel (Eds.), *Psychology of intergroup relations* (pp 7–24). Chicago: Nelson-Hall.

Thompson, J. L. (1989). Deprivation and political violence in Northern Ireland, 1922–1985. *Journal of Conflict Resolution, 33,* 676–699.

Turner, J. C. (1999). Some current issues in research on social identity and self-categorization theories. In N. Ellemers, R. Spears, & B. Doosje (Eds.), *Social identity: Context, commitment, content* (pp. 6–34). Oxford: Blackwells.

Tyler, T. R., Degoey, P., & Smith, H. J. (1996). Understanding why the justice of group procedures matters: A test of the psychological dynamics of the group-value model. *Journal of Personality and Social Psychology, 70,* 913–930.

Tyler, T. R., & Lind, E. A. (1992). A relational model of authority in groups. In M. Zanna (Ed.), *Advances in experimental social psychology,* (Vol. 25, pp. 115–191). New York: Academic Press.

Tyler, T. R., & Smith, H. J. (1998). Social justice and social movements. In D. Gilbert, S. T. Fiske, & G. Lindzey (Eds.), *Handbook of social psychology* (4th ed., Vol. 2, pp. 595–629). New York: McGraw Hill.

Useem, B. (1980). Solidarity model, breakdown model and the Boston anti-busing movement. *American Sociological Review, 45,* 357–369.

Van Kyk, A., & Nieuwoudt, J. (1990). The relationship between relative deprivation and the attitudes of rural Afrikaans-speaking women towards Blacks. *Journal of Psychology, 124,* 513–521.

Vanneman, R., & Pettigrew, T. F. (1972). Race and relative deprivation in the urban United States. *Race, 13,* 461–486.

Walker, I., & Mann, L. (1987). Unemployment, relative deprivation and social protest. *Personality and Social Psychology Bulletin, 13,* 275–283.

Walker, I., & Pettigrew, T. F. (1984). Relative deprivation theory: An overview and conceptual critique. *British Journal of Social Psychology, 23,* 310.

PART TWO

DEVELOPMENT

SIX

Personal and Group Relative Deprivation

Connecting the 'I' to the 'We'

Francine Tougas and Ann M. Beaton

When it was recognized that some groups (e.g., women and African Americans) were unfairly treated in the workforce, the Canadian and American governments, to name a few, took action via affirmative action programs to remedy the situation. These programs include strategies to eliminate systemic barriers and achieve fair representation of target group members at all levels and in every sector of the labor market. This entails profound social changes as members of designated groups access jobs they were previously denied on the basis of such characteristics as race or sex.

In this chapter, we focus on responses to programs designed to improve the conditions of women in the workforce. It will be shown that the attitudes of both those who might gain from the introduction of social change, the disadvantaged group (e.g., women), and those who might lose some long-standing privileges, the advantaged group (e.g., men), can be explained by referring to the concept of relative deprivation. By doing so, this chapter deals with questions raised by Pettigrew (1967) about the consequences of social evaluations. Indeed, relative deprivation refers to the affective reactions to disadvantageous personal and group comparisons. The comparisons identified by Walker and Pettigrew (1984), and believed to be important in the development of feelings of relative deprivation, are pivotal in the reactions of all parties concerned by the introduction of social change. It will also be suggested that our understanding of these attitudes would benefit from the inclusion of temporal comparisons in the evaluation of feelings of relative deprivation. Research in the area of relative deprivation has mainly focused on social comparisons, although temporal comparisons have been identified as a source of frustration (Crosby, 1976; Folger, 1977, 1986; Gurr, 1970; Pettigrew, 1967; Runciman, 1966; Walker & Pettigrew, 1984).

RELATIVE DEPRIVATION AMONG A DISADVANTAGED GROUP: THE CASE OF WOMEN

The Antecedents of Personal and Group Relative Deprivation

The investigation of the reactions of members of disadvantaged groups to strategies put in place to improve their conditions in the workforce focused on two types of relative deprivation, the personal and the group (Runciman, 1966). Personal relative deprivation referred to comparisons between one's conditions and those of members of the outgroup. The selection of self/outgroup comparisons is based on the belief that these are more pertinent in the case of group discrimination. For example, in the Beaton and Tougas (1997) study, which focused on discrimination on the basis of sex, female managers were asked to compare their own promotion and training opportunities to those of their male colleagues. In the case of group relative deprivation, female managers were asked to compare the situation of managers of both sexes within the organization (Beaton & Tougas, 1997; Tougas, Beaton, & Joly, 1990; Tougas, Beaton, & Veilleux, 1991; Tougas & Veilleux, 1988, 1989).

Relative deprivation not only implies social comparisons, but also the resulting emotional reactions. This concept has been defined as a feeling of discontent experienced as a result of invidious personal and group comparisons (Runciman, 1966). In the example presented previously, the affective component was measured by asking female managers to express their dissatisfaction with the outcome of the comparisons involving both sex groups.

Measuring both cognitive and affective components is important in the evaluation of attitudes toward social change: Perceiving unfair differences matters in the development of feelings of dissatisfaction, but it is only the latter that is significantly associated with favorable attitudes toward social change (Dubé & Guimond, 1986; Guimond & Dubé-Simard, 1983; Tougas, Dubé, & Veilleux, 1987; Veilleux, Tougas, & Rinfret, 1992). In the next section, it will be shown that feelings of resentment experienced as a result of perceived unfair disparities both at the personal and the group levels affect responses to affirmative action.

The Consequences of Personal and Group Relative Deprivation

The point of departure for our demonstration is the research establishing the link between personal and group relative deprivation. According to Runciman (1966, 1968), group relative deprivation is the product of a generalization of experiences of personal relative deprivation. In other words, individuals are believed to translate, at the group level, their personal disadvantageous experiences. Work on equity theory also supports the generalization hypothesis (Dion, 1986, Walster, Walster, & Berscheid, 1978).

This hypothesis was tested among female managers. As predicted, it was demonstrated that personal relative deprivation generalized to deprivation on behalf of one's group: Discontent based on invidious personal comparisons with male colleagues was linked to the recognition of intolerable inequalities between men and women in the workforce (Beaton & Tougas, 1997).

In distinguishing between personal and group relative deprivation, Runciman (1966) also discussed their role in the prediction of different types of behaviors. Specifically, he argues that group relative deprivation accounts for strategies aiming to improve the situation of the ingroup. Personal relative deprivation, however, is not believed to be linked to collective action. In fact, it was predicted to be associated with personal enhancement strategies (Runciman, 1966).

The precedence of group over personal relative deprivation in predicting promotion of social change was confirmed. For example, a study conducted by Guimond and Dubé-Simard (1983) among Francophone university students in Québec showed no significant link between personal relative deprivation, whether it implied self/ingroup or self/outgroup comparisons, and sociopolitical attitudes. In fact, only group relative deprivation was correlated with nationalist attitudes among Francophones of Québec. These results are consistent with those of other studies showing that group relative deprivation is especially predictive of willingness to engage in collective behaviors (Dubé & Guimond, 1986; Martin & Murray, 1984; Olson, Roese, Meen, & Robertson, 1995; Walker & Mann, 1987).

Having shown that group relative deprivation is a better predictor of collective actions than personal relative deprivation does not necessarily entail that personal relative deprivation has no impact on these behaviors. Research previously described, and confirming the generalization hypothesis, suggests that its impact is indirect: Personal experiences of discrimination are important in the development of feelings of group relative deprivation which in turn leads to the adoption of pro-group attitudes and behaviors. This suggests that both feelings of personal and group relative deprivation are important to understand why some people endorse and others oppose strategies designed to promote the situation of one's group.

The mediating role of group relative deprivation was confirmed among female managers (Beaton & Tougas, 1997). It was shown that while personal and group relative deprivation were associated, only the latter was linked to the promotion of social change. Indeed, only group relative deprivation mattered in the endorsement of support strategies for women in terms of networking and mentoring, and favorable reactions to affirmative action programs. The relevance of group relative deprivation in predicting

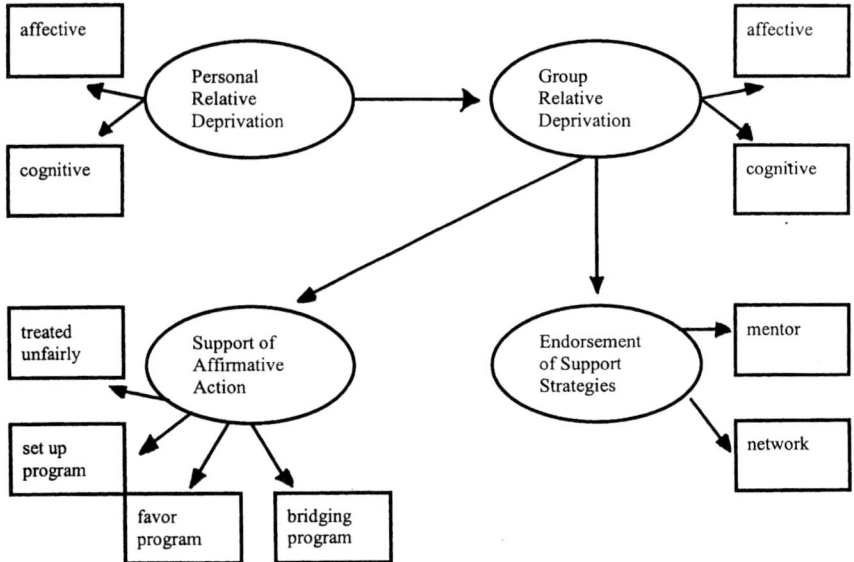

Figure 6.1. The consequences of personal and group relative deprivation among women managers.

support of affirmative action was further demonstrated in studies conducted with French Canadian female homemakers, office workers, and professionals (Tougas & Veilleux, 1988), and managers and professionals (Tougas, Beaton, & Joly, 1990; Tougas, Beaton, & Veilleux, 1991). These links are illustrated in Figure 6.1.

RELATIVE DEPRIVATION AMONG AN ADVANTAGED GROUP: THE CASE OF MEN

The Antecedents of Personal and Group Deprivation

We now turn to the study of the reactions of men. In this case, personal, and two types of relative deprivation involving the ingroup were investigated. We first look at the comparisons included in the evaluation of personal and group relative deprivation. For reasons outlined later, feelings of discontent of members of the advantaged group were assessed through temporal, often called intragroup, comparisons. According to Albert (1977), temporal comparisons are especially pertinent in situations of change and adjustments. In terms of the theory of temporal comparisons (Albert, 1977), maintaining a coherent sense of self-identity through one's different developmental stages is a natural drive. In fact, Albert argued that temporal comparisons are essential in the sense that individuals need to keep an enduring sense of self through periods of change (Albert, 1977). Because affirmative action was implemented to change deep-rooted values and norms of functioning that favored White males in organizations, it is believed that temporal comparisons are crucial in the study of the impact of relative deprivation on men's attitudes toward these programs.

Albert's theory refers to comparisons involving the self. Temporal comparisons involving a self-evaluative process have been the focus of much work conducted by Suls (Suls, 1986; Suls, Marco, & Tobin, 1991; Suls & Mullen, 1982; Suls & Sanders, 1982) who argues that temporal rather than social comparisons increase with age in the appraisal of one's life circumstances. Further research suggests that temporal comparisons may also be used to evaluate the situation of the ingroup.

According to Mummendey and her colleagues (Mummendey, Mielke, Wenzel, & Kanning, 1992), temporal comparisons are essential to both groups and individuals. In order to establish one's group position, it was suggested that individuals may compare its current to its past status, or use abstract standards without reference to other groups (Hinkle & Brown, 1990). The importance of temporal group comparisons was evaluated in a study conducted by Brown and Middendorf (1996). Results not only support the assumption that temporal comparisons matter in group status evaluations, but they also show, as suggested by Suls (1986), that preference for this type of comparison increases with age to the extent that participants of the age of 40 and over exhibited a marked preference for temporal over intergroup comparisons.

The investigation of feelings of relative deprivation focused on temporal comparisons of men averaging 40 years of age at the time of study. For example, present/past personal comparisons were used to assess personal relative deprivation: Male employees of a large Canadian firm were asked to evaluate whether the affirmative action program put in place had negatively affected their career opportunities (Tougas & Veilleux, 1991). In terms of group relative deprivation, measures included present/past group comparisons. In this case, the effects of the introduction of affirmative action on the ingroup's situation were evaluated among male managers (Veilleux & Tougas, 1989).

The Consequences of Personal and Group Relative Deprivation

The links between personal and group relative deprivation and responses to social change policy were also evaluated. As in the case of women, it was found that both types of relative deprivation were associated, and

that only group relative deprivation was a significant predictor of attitudes toward affirmative action. However, in the case of men, group relative deprivation was associated with opposition to affirmative action
policies (Tougas, Dubé, & Veilleux, 1987; Tougas & Veilleux, 1991; Veilleux
& Tougas, 1989). In other words, when men recognized that the policy had
a negative impact on their personal and group conditions, they were
firmly opposed to this type of strategies.

Relative Deprivation on Behalf of Others
The different forms of relative deprivation presented thus far account for the
opposition of men to affirmative action policies. We have yet to account for
some men's willingness to promote the situation of women. According to
Runciman (1968), altruistic behaviors on the part of members of an advantaged group can be explained in light of relative deprivation on behalf of
others. This concept refers to the feeling of discontent one experiences when
perceiving that members of another group are unfairly treated. This form of
relative deprivation has received little attention, with the exception of work
conducted in the area of the promotion of the situation of women. For
example, studies conducted among male students (Tougas et al., 1987) and
managers and professionals (Veilleux & Tougas, 1989) from various organizations reveal that discontent due to the inequitable treatment of women in
the workforce is associated with endorsement of prosocial measures for
women and affirmative action policies.

   The link between group relative deprivation and relative deprivation
on behalf of others was also investigated (Tougas & Veilleux, 1991). It was
predicted on the basis of equity theory (Walster et al., 1978) that feelings
of group deprivation had a negative impact on deprivation on behalf of
others. This is based on an egoistical view of human nature: Individuals
consider their own interests before those of others. Within the context of
affirmative action, the gains of one group might be seen as losses for
another. When a mutually beneficial solution is not believed to be feasible, individuals are bound to consider their own interests before those of
the outgroup.

   This hypothesis was integrated in a model also including personal relative deprivation and reactions to measures promoting the situation of
women. This model is illustrated in Figure 6.2. Hypotheses included in
this model were confirmed among a sample of male employees of a large
Canadian firm. As predicted, it was found that being personally dissatisfied with the perceived negative effects of affirmative action was linked to
group dissatisfaction (Tougas & Veilleux, 1991). Despite this association,

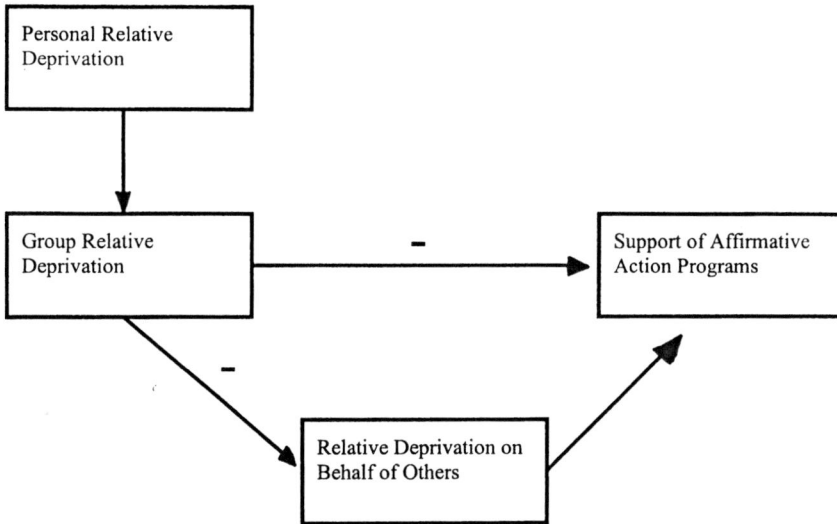

Figure 6.2. The influence of personal relative deprivation, group relative deprivation, and relative deprivation on behalf of others over support of affirmative action programs among men managers.

only group dissatisfaction led to opposition to affirmative action. Moreover, feeling deprived for one's group was found to be negatively related to relative deprivation on behalf of others, in this case women. Finally, the differing effects of group relative deprivation, and relative deprivation on behalf of others on attitudes toward prosocial measures were also confirmed: The former was associated with opposition to affirmative action, while the latter was linked to support of these strategies.

SUMMARY OF FINDINGS

In summary, studies previously reported clearly show that relative deprivation is significant in accounting for reactions of both women and men to policies implemented by governments and organizations to eliminate sex disparities. In fact, the importance of personal and group considerations in responses to affirmative action has consistently been demonstrated. Thus, the conclusion that the personal is political for both groups. This is in line with previous research showing that double deprivation is a significant predictor of group-oriented behaviors (Foster & Matheson, 1995).

The consequences of social evaluations were also investigated (Pettigrew, 1967). It was found that comparisons confirming a disadvantageous social position were part of experiences of resentment of women, and approval of social change. This is congruent with past studies relying on social comparisons to explain demands of social change by underprivileged groups (Foster & Matheson, 1995; Grant & Brown, 1995; Guimond & Dubé-Simard, 1983; Hafer & Olson, 1993; Olson et al., 1995; Walker & Mann, 1987).

Temporal and social comparisons were used to assess three types of deprivation among men: personal, group, and on behalf of another less fortunate group. According to predictions, studies conducted among men support the argument that temporal comparisons are crucial in situations of social change (Albert, 1977). Moreover, relative deprivation on behalf of others was found to be associated with altruistic attitudes: To a certain extent, endorsing policies designed to improve the situation of a disadvantaged group involves calling into question the legitimacy of one's privileged status.

The present chapter has examined only a few of the types of comparisons leading to relative deprivation. It is believed that reactions to social change measures stem from additional considerations of one's personal and group situation. In fact, studies suggest that individuals refer to a variety of different comparisons to interpret their relative personal (Wheeler & Miyake, 1992) or group (Taylor, Moghaddam, & Bellerose, 1989) standings. The next sections pertain to yet unexplored avenues of research that, in our opinion, would shed further light on the consequences of evaluations. These suggestions refer not only to determinants of reactions to other party initiatives of social change, but also individuals' implication in the process. In the following, we first look at comparisons involving the disadvantaged group.

FURTHER EXAMINATION OF EVALUATIONS
OF THE DISADVANTAGED GROUP

The role of temporal comparisons, often called intrapersonal comparisons (Guimond & Tougas, 1994), as determinants of feelings of personal dissatisfaction among underprivileged individuals was evaluated in the past (deCarufel, 1979; deCarufel & Schopler, 1979; Folger, 1977). According to Folger (1977, 1986), resentment is particularly high in situations in which inequities and unfair treatment have been socially recognized, but actions taken have failed to eliminate disparities in the distribution of resources. It is as if what was endured stoically cannot be tolerated once expectations are raised.

These results clearly suggest that including temporal comparisons would be most appropriate in the study of reactions of members of disadvantaged groups to measures of social support. In the case of affirmative action, it would be especially relevant. Indeed, affirmative action programs were introduced in part to reduce if not eliminate discrimination on the basis of sex in the workplace.

However, there is evidence that shows that expectations have not been met. For example, after over a decade since the adoption of the Canadian Employment Equity Act in Canada in 1986, women's disadvantaged status in the workforce has improved at a very modest pace, at best. According to the Annual Report on Employment Equity, in 1998, women earned 76.6% of men's average annual earning, an increase of 6% in the last 12 years. Furthermore, while 42.6% of women were hired by organizations covered under the Employment Equity Act in 1987, this rate has only slightly increased to 44.2% in 1998 (Human Resources Development, 1999). Finally, results continue to show that women remain concentrated in traditional areas of employment while underrepresented in nontraditional sectors (Human Resources Development, 1999).

A true test of the impact of temporal comparisons on feelings of personal deprivation among women within an affirmative action context would benefit from the following three considerations. First, the relevance of temporal and social comparisons in feelings of personal resentment should be evaluated. In doing so, efforts should be made to distinguish between different forms of temporal comparisons. It is believed that comparisons involving one's past and anticipated future situations (present/past; present/future) should be included. Social protest is not only due to deteriorating life conditions, but also to pessimistic views of the future (Gurr, 1970, 1971). Second, the impact of personal deprivation on feelings of collective resentment should be evaluated. As was shown earlier in this chapter, it is through group deprivation that personal resentment has an effect on promotion of social change. To be congruent, measures of group relative deprivation should also include temporal comparisons. A recent study showed that intragroup comparisons proved to be important in accounting for feelings of resentment of Black South Africans (Appelgryn & Bornman, 1996). Third, temporal comparisons should be included not only to predict attitudes toward social change, but also actions taken to improve the efficiency of social policies. In the past, it was shown that women demanded stronger affirmative action measures as it became obvious those in place did not produce the expected outcomes (Tougas & Beaton, 1992). Perhaps the impact of temporal comparisons would be more important than that of social evaluations when the inefficiency of social policies has been recognized. Remaining rather than being in a disadvantageous situation might better account for reactions to one's conditions especially when expectations were raised, but not met.

FURTHER EXAMINATION OF EVALUATION
OF THE ADVANTAGED GROUP

Temporal comparisons were used in the analysis of men's feelings as a result of the introduction of affirmative action for women. Indeed, feelings of resentment both at the personal and the collective levels were found to be triggered by intrapersonal comparisons involving the present and the past. This is only part of the picture. It seems that more could be learned by asking individuals to compare their present and anticipated situations. We could then be in a position to determine which of the following is more conducive to the development of feelings of deprivation: deteriorating conditions or grim predictions about the future. Answering this question is important in the sense that personal and group feelings of resentment have an impact, the former an indirect and the latter a direct one, on relative deprivation on behalf of others.

Relative deprivation on behalf of others is felt by those who are concerned about social inequities. It translates, as was suggested and shown, into altruistic attitudes and behaviors. Members of advantaged groups' commitment to the implementation of social programs is essential. Without the input and clear support of members of groups in power, the success of programs such as affirmative action is greatly compromised (Astin & Snyder, 1982; Hitt & Keats, 1984; Hitt, Keats, & Purdum, 1983; Larwood, Gutek, & Gattiker, 1984; Leach, Snider, & Iyer, this volume; Leck & Saunders, 1992). According to Blanchard (1989), support of affirmative action policies from authorities is a key element in producing an effective program. Those in a leadership position are more likely to control and manage resources that are directly related to the elaboration of affirmative action policies.

THE ROLE OF SOCIAL IDENTIFICATION IN THE
DEVELOPMENT OF RELATIVE DEPRIVATION

It is believed that a better understanding of the reasons why individuals experience relative deprivation would benefit not only from the study of different comparisons, whether temporal or social, but also from further exploration of the role of identity. The association between relative deprivation and identity has been approached from two different perspectives. In the first, it was argued that identity has an impact on feelings of relative deprivation (Guimond & Dubé-Simard, 1983; Tajfel, 1978; Tougas & Veilleux, 1988, 1989, 1990; Veilleux, Tougas, & Rinfret, 1992). More precisely, it was posited that identity is important in the development of feelings of relative deprivation. According to this argument, as group identity intensifies, people become more sensitive to invidious social comparisons (Guimond & Dubé-Simard, 1983; Smith, Spears, & Oyen, 1994; Tougas & Veilleux, 1988).

Results of studies evaluating the proposed link by way of a global measure of identity (i.e., cognitive, evaluative, and affective components) were ambiguous. Some supported the hypothesized relationship (Abrams, 1990; Tropp & Wright, 1999), while many did not (Tougas & Veilleux, 1988, 1989, 1990; Veilleux, Tougas, & Rinfret, 1992).

Instead of considering identity as an antecedent of relative deprivation, Walker and his colleague (Petta & Walker, 1992; Walker, 1999) viewed relative deprivation as a determinant of identity. According to these authors, comparisons resulting in negative outcomes have the potential to produce negative views of the self and the group. Both correlational and experimental data confirmed the proposed sequence both at the personal and group levels. Although personal relative deprivation had a negative impact on self-esteem, feelings of discontent on account of unfavorable comparisons involving the ingroup resulted in lowered collective self-esteem.

To summarize, studies evaluating the impact of identity and relative deprivation have produced unclear results. These inconsistent findings suggest that a refinement of hypotheses is in order. In contrast, it was shown that relative deprivation has an impact on identity as measured by personal and collective esteem. In the following, an integration of both perspectives is proposed. This is facilitated by the fact that both perspectives are based on social identity theory (Ellemers, this volume; Tajfel, 1978, 1982; Tajfel & Turner, 1979). According to this theory, the self-concept is a two-faceted entity. One is called personal identity, and it includes personal attributes and characteristics. The other, social identity, refers to the descriptors of the ingroups.

Crocker and her colleagues (Crocker, Blaine, & Luhtanen, 1993; Luhtanen & Crocker, 1992) argue that evaluations of self and group descriptors are also part of personal and group identities. According to these authors, "personal self-esteem is the self-evaluative (rather than self-descriptive) component of personal identity, and collective self-esteem is the self-evaluative component of social (or collective) identity" (Crocker et al., 1993).

The distinction between the descriptive and evaluative components of personal and social identities proposed by Crocker and her colleagues (Crocker et al., 1993; Luhtanen & Crocker, 1992) is pivotal in the proposal of an integrative approach to the link between identity and relative deprivation. It is first argued that the descriptive component of identity has an impact on personal and group relative deprivation. According to this argument, as beliefs about the characteristics of the ingroup become stronger, negative reactions to intergroup differences intensify. This argument also applies at the personal level: The probability of feelings of relative deprivation to emerge is higher as beliefs about one's descriptors become stronger. People who have strong beliefs about their personal or group identity want more for themselves, and as a result they become more sensitive to invidious social comparisons.

Predictions included in the second perspective constitute the second part of this integration. As such, it is posited that the evaluative component of personal and group identities is affected by invidious comparisons at the personal and group levels. According to the second perspective, feelings of personal and group relative deprivation have a negative impact on personal and collective self-esteem. Lower self-esteem is the consequence of invidious comparisons at the personal level. When comparisons producing negative outcomes refer to the ingroup, the impact is felt on collective self-esteem.

A predictive model including part of this integrative approach to the link between identity and relative deprivation was tested, and confirmed via structural equation modeling (Tougas, Lagacé, de la Sablonnière, & Kocum, 2000). It was found that as personal beliefs about one's characteristics (self-descriptive component of personal identity) became stronger, feelings of personal deprivation intensified. Moreover, it was shown that feelings of personal relative deprivation are negatively associated with self-esteem: Self-regard becomes more negative as feelings of personal relative deprivation increased. No attempt has yet been made to evaluate the relationship between identity and relative deprivation at the group level.

CONCLUSION

In conclusion, this chapter has dealt with the antecedents and consequences of relative deprivation. The focus was on three types of relative deprivation: The personal, the group, and the one on behalf of others. Studies conducted and presented in the first sections of this chapter have confirmed the significant role of temporal and social comparisons in the development of these three types of relative deprivation, and attitudes toward social change. Moreover, suggestions were offered to improve our understanding of the impact of comparisons in social action. Special attention was paid to the concept of relative deprivation on behalf of others in the context of affirmative action. The study of relative deprivation on behalf of others as a precursor to other types of altruistic behaviors is timely. Understanding what leads to altruistic behaviors is crucial as many Western societies rely more and more on volunteer efforts to counter inequities. It was argued and shown that this can be accomplished via the concept of relative deprivation on behalf of others.

Finally, in the last section an integrative approach to the relationship between identity and relative deprivation has been proposed. Further understanding of the role of identity in the emergence of feelings of relative deprivation might provide some answers to the question as to why some people experience resentment and discontent with their conditions, and others in the same situation don't. Further investigation of the effects of relative deprivation on self and collective esteem is also important in the sense that both are believed to have an impact on attitudes and behaviors related to the promotion of the self and the group (Petta & Walker, 1992; Walker, 1999): Self-esteem acts as a mediating variable between relative deprivation and action. At what point lowered self-esteem will trigger or prevent action, and what is the role of self-esteem in the adoption of different types of actions are crucial questions to determine why relative deprivation is sometimes weakly associated with attitudes and behaviors.

REFERENCES

Abrams, D. (1990). *Political identity: Relative deprivation, social identity and the case of Scottish nationalism.* Economic and Social Research Council 16–19 Initiative, Occasional Paper no. 24. Social Statistics Research Unit, City University, London.

Albert, S. (1977). Temporal comparison theory. *Psychological Review. 84,* 485–503.

Appelgryn, A. E. M., & Bornman, E. (1996). Relative deprivation in contemporary South Africa. *Journal of Social Psychology, 136,* 381–397.

Astin, H. S., & Snyder, M. B. (July/August, 1982). Affirmative action 1972–1982: A decade of response. *Change,* 26–31, 59.

Beaton, A. M., & Tougas, F. (1997). The representation of women in management: The more, the merrier? *Personality and Social Psychology Bulletin, 23,* 773–782.

Blanchard, F. A. (1989). Effective affirmative action programs. In F. A. Blanchard & F. J. Crosby (Eds.), *Affirmative action in perspective* (pp. 193–208). New York: Springer-Verlag.

Brown, R., & Middendorf, J. (1996). The underestimated role of temporal comparison: A test of the life-span model. *Journal of Social Psychology, 136,* 325–331.

Crocker, J., Blaine, B., & Luhtanen, R. (1993). Prejudice, intergroup behaviour and self-esteem: Enhancement and protection motives. In M. A. Hogg & D. Abrams (Eds.), *Group motivation: Social psychological perspective* (pp. 52–67). New York: Harvester-Wheatsheaf.

Crosby, F. (1976). A model of egoistical relative deprivation. *Psychological Review, 83*, 85–113.

deCarufel, A. (1979). Factors affecting the evaluation of improvement: The role of normative standards and allocator resources. *Journal of Personality and Social Psychology, 37*, 847–857.

deCarufel, A., & Schopler, J. (1979). Evaluation of outcome improvements resulting from threats and appeals. *Journal of Personality and Social Psychology, 37*, 662–673.

Dion, K. L. (1986). Responses to perceived discrimination and relative deprivation. In J. M. Olson, C. P. Herman, & M. P. Zanna (Eds.), *Relative deprivation and social comparison: The Ontario symposium* (Vol. 4, pp. 159–179), Hillsdale, NJ: Lawrence Erlbaum.

Dubé, L., & Guimond, S. (1986). Relative deprivation and social protest: The personal–group issue. In J. M. Olson, C. P. Herman, and M. P. Zanna (Eds.), *Relative deprivation and social comparison: The Ontario symposium* (Vol. 4, pp. 201–216). Hillsdale, NJ: Lawrence Erlbaum.

Folger, R. (1977). Distributive and procedural justice: Combined impact of 'voice' and improvement on experienced inequity. *Journal of Personality and Social Psychology, 35*, 108–119.

Folger, R. (1986). A referent cognitions theory of relative deprivation. In J. M. Olson, C. P. Herman, & M. P. Zanna (Eds.), *Relative deprivation and social comparison: The Ontario symposium* (Vol. 4, pp. 201–216). Hillsdale, NJ: Lawrence Erlbaum.

Foster, M. D., & Matheson, K. (1995). Double relative deprivation: Combining the personal and political. *Personality and Social Psychology Bulletin, 21*, 1167–1177.

Grant, P. R., & Brown, R. (1995). From ethnocentrism to collective protest: Responses to relative deprivation and threats to social identity. *Social Psychology Quarterly, 58*, 195–211.

Guimond, S., & Dubé-Simard, L. (1983). Relative deprivation theory and the Quebec nationalist movement: The cognition-emotion distinction and the personal-group deprivation issue. *Journal of Personality and Social Psychology, 44*, 526–535.

Guimond, S., & Tougas, F. (1994). Sentiments d'injustice et actions collectives: la privation relative. In R. Y. Bourhis & J.-Ph. Leyens (Eds.), *Stéréotypes, discrimination et relations intergroupes* (pp. 201–231). Liège: Mardaga.

Gurr, T. R. (1970). *Why men rebel*. Princeton, NJ: Princeton University Press.

Gurr, T. R. (1971). A causal model of civil strife: A comparative analysis using new indices. In J. C. Davies (Ed.), *When men revolt and why* (pp. 293–313). New York: The Free Press.

Hafer, C. L., & Olson, J. M. (1993). Beliefs in a just world, discontent, and assertive actions by working women. *Personality and Social Psychology Bulletin, 19*, 30–38.

Hinkle, S., & Brown, R. J. (1990). Intergroup comparisons and social identity: Some links and lacunae. In D. Abrams & M. A. Hogg (Eds.), *Social identity theory: Constructive and critical advances* (pp. 48–70). New York: Springer-Verlag.

Hitt, M. A., & Keats, B. W. (1984). Empirical identification of the criteria for effective affirmative action programs. *Journal of Applied Behavioral Science, 20,* 203–222.

Hitt, M. A., Keats, B. W., & Purdum, S. (1983). Affirmative action effectiveness criteria in institutions of higher education. *Research in Higher Education, 18,* 391–407.

Human Resources Development, Canada. (1999). *Annual Report: Employment equity Act.* Ottawa: Department of Supply and Services, Canada.

Larwood, L., Gutek, B., & Gattiker, U. E. (1984). Perspectives on institutional discrimination and resistance to change. *Group & Organization Studies, 9,* 333–352.

Leck, J. D., & Saunders, D. M. (1992). Canada's Employment Equity Act: Effects on employee selection. *Population Research and Policy Review, 11,* 21–49.

Luhtanen, R., & Crocker J. (1992). A collective self-esteem scale: Self-evaluation of one's own social identity. *Personality and Social Psychology Bulletin, 18,* 302–318.

Martin, J., & Murray, A. (1984). Catalysts for collective violence: The importance of a psychological approach. In R. Folger (Ed.), *The sense of injustice: Social psychological perspectives* (pp. 95–139). New York: Plenum.

Mummendey, A., Mielke, R., Wenzel, M., & Kanning, U. (1992). *Die Roller sozialer Vergleiche bei der Bewertung der eigenen Lebenssituation in Ostdeutschland.* [The role of social comparisons in evaluating own living conditions in Eastern Germany]. Unpublished manuscript, Universität Münster, Germany.

Olson, J. M., Roese, N. J., Meen, J., & Robertson, D. J. (1995). The preconditions and consequences of relative deprivation: Two field studies. *Journal of Applied Social Psychology, 25,* 944–964.

Petta, G., & Walker, I. (1992). Relative deprivation and ethnic identity. *British Journal of Social Psychology, 31,* 285–293.

Pettigrew, T. F. (1967). Social evaluation theory: Convergences and applications. In D. Levine (Ed.), *Nebraska symposium on motivation* (Vol. 15, pp. 241–315). Lincoln: University of Nebraska Press.

Runciman, W. G. (1966). *Relative deprivation and social justice: A study of attitudes to social inequality in twentieth-century England.* Berkeley: University of California Press.

Runciman, W. G. (1968). Problems of research on relative deprivation. In H. H. Hyman & E. Singer (Eds.), *Readings in reference group theory and research* (pp. 69–76). New York: Free Press.

Smith, H. J., Spears, R., & Oyen, M. (1994). People like us: The influence of personal deprivation and group membership salience on justice evaluations. *Journal of Experimental Social Psychology, 30,* 277–299.

Suls, J. (1986). Notes on the occasion of social comparison theory's thirtieth birthday. *Personality and Social Psychology Bulletin, 12,* 289–296.

Suls, J., Marco, C. A., & Tobin, S. (1991). The role of temporal comparison, social comparison, and direct appraisal in the elderly's self-evaluations of health. *Journal of Applied Social Psychology, 21,* 1125–1144.

Suls, J., & Mullen, B. (1982). From the cradle to the grave: Comparison and self-evaluation across the life-span. In J. Suls (Ed.), *Psychological perspectives on the self* (Vol. 1, pp. 97–125). Hillsdale, NJ: Lawrence Erlbaum.

Suls, J., & Sanders, G. S. (1982). Self-evaluation through social comparison: A developmental analysis. In L. Wheeler (Ed.), *Review of personality and social psychology* (Vol. 3, pp. 171–198). Beverly Hills, CA: Sage.

Tajfel, H. (1978). *Differentiation between social groups: Studies in the social psychology of intergroup relations.* London: Academic Press.

Tajfel, H. (1982). Social psychology of intergroup relations. *Annual Review of Psychology, 33*, pp. 1–40.

Tajfel, H., & Turner, J. C. (1979). An integrative theory of intergroup conflict. In W. G. Austin & S. Worchel (Eds.), *The social psychology of intergroup relations* (pp. 33–47). Monterey, CA.: Brooks/Cole.

Taylor, D. M., Moghaddam, F., & Bellerose, J. (1989). Social comparison in an intergroup context. *Journal of Social Psychology, 129*, 499–515.

Tougas, F., & Beaton, A. M. (1992). Women's views on affirmative action: A new look at preferential treatment. *Social Justice Research, 5*, 239–248.

Tougas, F., Beaton, A. M., & Joly, S. (1990). L'appui des femmes à l'action positive: Une question d'image ou de colère? *Science et Comportement, 20,* 211–222.

Tougas, F., Beaton, A. M., & Veilleux, F. (1991). Why women approve of affirmative action: The study of a predictive model. *International Journal of Psychology, 26,* 761–776.

Tougas, F., Dubé, L. & Veilleux, F. (1987). Privation relative et programmes d'action positive. *Revue canadienne des sciences du comportement, 19,* 167–177.

Tougas, F., Lagacé, M., de la Sablonnière, R., & Kocum, L. (2001). *Some consequences of integrating descriptors associated with experienced workers into self characterisations: The case of young retirees.*

Tougas, F., & Veilleux, F. (1988). The influence of identification, collective relative deprivation, and procedure of implementation on women's response to affirmative action: A causal modeling approach. *Canadian Journal of Behavioural Science, 20,* 16–29.

Tougas, F., & Veilleux, F. (1989). Who likes affirmative action?: Attitudinal processes among men and women. In F. A. Blanchard & F. J. Crosby (Eds.), *Affirmative action in perspective* (pp. 111–124). New York: Springer-Verlag.

Tougas, F., & Veilleux, F. (1990). The response of men to affirmative action strategies for women: The study of a predictive model. *Canadian Journal of Behavioural Sciences, 22,* 424–432.

Tougas, F., & Veilleux, F. (1991). Les réactions des hommes à l'action positive: une question d'intérêt personnel ou d'insatisfaction face aux iniquités de sexe? *Revue canadienne des sciences administratives, 8,* 37–42.

Tropp, L. R., & Wright, S. C. (1999). Ingroup identification and relative deprivation. An examination across multiple groups social comparisons. *European Journal of Social Psychology, 29,* 707–724.

Veilleux, F., & Tougas, F. (1989). Male acceptance of affirmative action programs for women: The result of altruistic or egoistical motives? *International Journal of Psychology, 24,* 485–496.

Veilleux, F., Tougas, F., & Rinfret, N. (1992). Des citoyens en colère: une question de privation relative et/ou d'identité sociale? *Revue canadienne des sciences du comportement, 24,* 59–70.

Walker, I. (1999). The effects of personal and group relative deprivation on personal and collective self-esteem. *Group Processes and Intergroup Relations, 2,* 365–380.

Walker, I., & Mann, L. (1987). Unemployment, relative deprivation, and social protest. *Personality and Social Psychology Bulletin, 13,* 275–283.

Walker, I., & Pettigrew, T. F. (1984). Relative deprivation theory: An overview and conceptual critique. *British Journal of Social Psychology, 23,* 301–310.

Walster, E., Walster, G. W., & Berscheid, E. (1978). *Equity, theory and research.* Boston: Allyn and Bacon.

Wheeler, L., & Miyake, K. (1992). Social comparison in everyday life. *Journal of Personality and Social Psychology, 62,* 760–773.

SEVEN

"Poisoning the Consciences of the Fortunate"

The Experience of Relative Advantage and Support for Social Equality

Colin Wayne Leach, Nastia Snider, and Aarti Iyer

Men of *ressentiment,* physiologically unfortunate and worm-eaten, a whole tremulous realm of subterranean revenge, inexhaustible and insatiable in outbursts against the fortunate and happy and in masquerades of revenge and pretexts for revenge: when would they achieve the ultimate, subtlest, sublimest triumph of revenge? Undoubtedly if they succeeded in *poisoning the consciences* of the fortunate with their own misery, with all misery, so that one day the fortunate began to be ashamed of their good fortune and perhaps said one to another: "it is disgraceful to be fortunate: there is so much misery!"
(Friedrich Nietzsche, 1887/1967, *On the Genealogy of Morals,* p. 124)

Most challenges to inequality are based in a profound sense of relative deprivation (see Wright & Tropp, this volume). This has led many to examine the resentment of the disadvantaged as the sine qua non of social change. In most cases, however, relative deprivation leads the disadvantaged into direct conflict with those either responsible for, or benefiting from, their deprivation. Unfortunately, we know little about how the advantaged experience *others'* deprivation relative to them. In this chapter we develop a phenomenology of relative advantage. We specify the various ways in which advantage can be experienced and discuss how each is related to support for social equality. As we shall see, however, there is a great deal working to prevent the recognition and disavowal of privilege. Even the most deprived may have a difficult time achieving the "poisoning of the consciences of the fortunate" that would constitute "the ultimate, subtlest, sublimest, triumph of revenge" against them. Understanding the ways in which advantage is experienced could go a long way in specifying the political potential (and limits) of relative deprivation-based challenges to inequality.

Relative advantage can be experienced in many different ways. This, and the absence of a sustained treatment in the extant literature, require an ecumenical use of sources. Where possible, we utilize empirical research, ranging in method from ethnography and qualitative interviews to quantitative surveys and experiments, in order to evaluate conceptualizations and claims. Few studies, however, have examined the *experience* of advantage directly, and we have, of necessity, extrapolated from studies that were not originally designed to fit within our approach.

Our discussion of the phenomenology of advantage is organized into three parts. First, we discuss how advantage can be taken for granted. Second, we look at the minimization of advantage. Third, we discuss situations in which advantage is recognized. As this last possibility is the one most likely to promote social equality, we focus on this condition and offer a detailed typology of the ways the advantaged can recognize their position.

TAKING ADVANTAGE FOR GRANTED

Advantaged groups secure in their position, due to their greater size or control over resources, can take their advantage for granted. This can result from three related processes: (1) the advantaged tend not to identify with their group, (2) advantaged groups are often "unmarked," and (3) the advantaged tend not to compare themselves to the disadvantaged.

First, when highly secure, advantage is not a salient form of group categorization, and the advantaged do not see themselves as members of a (privileged) group (McIntosh, 1992). In fact, secure majority groups tend to identify less strongly with their group than do minorities (Mullen, 1991). Weak group identification leads the advantaged to see themselves as individuals rather than as members of a group, rendering their group status invisible to them (DeMott, 1990).

The concept of markedness, taken from structural linguistics, offers a second explanation of the invisibility of privilege. Markedness explains how asymmetrical and hierarchical relations between two categories can *appear* to be relations between equal opposites (Waugh, 1982). The superior category often conveys more general information and is thus taken as the norm. The normativity of the superior category renders its privileged position invisible, while simultaneously marking the "difference" of the inferior category. The power of markedness in racial relations is particularly obvious in the following example (Williams, 1989, p. 430):

1. Americans are still prejudiced against Blacks.
2. Americans still earn less money than do Whites.

There is no difficulty understanding the first sentence, in which "American" is synonymous with "White." However, the second sentence, when "American" stands for "Black," seems confusing or ridiculous. Because whiteness is normative and unmarked in the United States (Frankenburg, 1993; McIntosh, 1992), "Whites" can stand for "Americans," even though not all Americans are White. The markedness of "blackness," however, makes the second sentence fail, as African Americans cannot stand for the culture as a whole.

Third, privilege may be rendered invisible as a result of myopic comparisons. This process can operate at both the intergroup and interpersonal levels. At the group level, RD researchers argue that the disadvantaged fail to experience RD because they compare their lots only to those similarly situated (see Runciman, 1966). Such "selective exposure" to others at a similar level of disadvantage prevents the comparisons to the advantaged necessary to the recognition of inequality. Although typically not applied in this way, this explanation of limited perceived inequality applies equally well to the fortunate. For example, Major and colleagues (see Major, 1994, for a review) have shown that members of advantaged groups tend to compare their lots to similarly situated others. In a typical experiment, men given greater pay than women for equal work tend not to notice the gender inequality because they attend to the similar pay received by other men, rather than the lesser pay given women.

Research on the interpersonal comparisons of individuals in advantaged positions also shows that the fortunate tend not to compare themselves with the disadvantaged. Here, advantage is typically operationalized as higher levels of self-esteem, possession of a valued attribute, or success at a task. In an experimental study of the comparison choices of those higher and lower in self-esteem after they received success or failure feedback, Wood, Giordano-Beech, Taylor, Michela, and Gauss (1994) found those higher in self-esteem to be relatively uninterested in comparisons with worse-off others after success. In line with Festinger's (1954) idea of a "unidirectional drive upward" in interpersonal comparison, the literature suggests that when people with secure advantages do compare, they tend to compare themselves with similar or slightly better-off others (see Collins, 1996, for a review).

Thus, at least three processes work to limit the recognition of secure advantage. Consequently, taking advantage for granted requires little active avoidance of the disparities between the well-off and the unfortunate. When taken for granted, relative advantage is "a reality enjoyed, but not acknowledged, a privilege lived in, but unknown" (Frankenberg, 1993, p. 9). Obviously, those with little consciousness of their advantage have little reason to respond to others' claims of relative deprivation. In fact, advantaged groups often respond strategically to criticisms of their advantage by minimizing inequalities of prestige or resources.

MINIMIZING ADVANTAGE

Those with privilege may be motivated to reduce the perceived discrepancy between themselves and others in hopes of avoiding accusations of injustice (Heider, 1958; see Exline & Lobel, 1999, for a review). If supported, such accusations could lead to challenges to the existing hierarchy – certainly not a desired outcome for the fortunate. Claims of injustice can also damage the self-image of the favored, if fairness is an important value for them (Hoffman, 1976). In one line of work, Mikula and colleagues (see Mikula, 1993, for a review) have studied victims' and perpetrators' perceptions of unfair incidents in close personal relationships. In response to an injustice reported by the victim, perpetrators minimized the degree of injustice. In addition, perpetrators minimized their role in the perceived injustice by stating that they had limited control and responsibility, and little intention to act as they did. Perpetrators also claimed that the victim deserved mistreatment, and that the mistreatment was justified. Relatedly, Montada and Schneider (1989) found those who endorsed the equity principle – that rewards should be distributed according to specific contribution, rather than need – tended to minimize their advantages over unfortunate others. Thus, the minimization of advantage appears rooted in general beliefs regarding the fairness of inequality.

Other researchers approach the minimization of advantage from an intergroup relations perspective. Most notably, van Knippenberg (1978, 1984) shows that both advantaged and disadvantaged groups engage in strategic representations of the differences between them; advantaged groups want to minimize the differences most in dispute, while disadvantaged groups want to maximize them. In one study, van Knippenberg (1978) studied students at two engineering schools of differing prestige. When judging the status of their own school alone, students at the higher prestige school affirmed their superiority. When evaluating the status of both schools together, however, those higher in prestige lowered their evaluation of their own status, thereby minimizing their relative advantage (see also Spears & Manstead, 1989; van Knippenberg & van Oers, 1984). By questioning the very existence of inequality, such strategic modesty can both limit self-critical guilt and undermine others' justice-based challenges.

RECOGNITION OF ADVANTAGE AND DOWNWARD COMPARISONS

Thus far, we have discussed the two main ways in which the relatively advantaged can avoid recognizing their privilege. There are, however, circumstances under which relative advantage is acknowledged. Recognition of advantage is typically based in a downward comparison with the unfortunate, in just the way that relative deprivation is based in an upward comparison with the privileged. Such downward comparisons can be experienced in many ways, ranging from sympathy to indignation to gloating. It is important to differentiate these ways of experiencing relative advantage, because they are not equally likely to result in support for equality. Thus, we offer a typology that orders the phenomenology of relative advantage along four conceptual dimensions: self–other focus, perceived legitimacy, perceived stability, and perceived control.

First, the degree to which the advantaged focus on themselves or on the disadvantaged is important to how privilege is experienced. Self–other focus determines which side of the inequality between the advantaged and the disadvantaged is most salient and in need of explanation. When self-focused, the advantaged can be moved to pride or guilt in response to their privilege, depending on its perceived legitimacy. In contrast, focusing on others can promote sympathy, moral outrage, or disdain toward the disadvantaged.

The perceived security of advantage also plays an important role in how it is experienced. Social identity theorists have identified two dimensions of perceived security: legitimacy and stability (see Tajfel & Turner, 1979; Turner & Brown, 1978). *Perceived legitimacy* is the second conceptual dimension in our typology of relative advantage. Advantages perceived as illegitimate require defense against outright challenge by others or guilt imposed by the self. Advantages perceived as legitimate, on the other hand, can promote pride in one's position (Ortony, Clore, & Collins, 1988). The third conceptual dimension, *perceived stability*, assesses the degree to which the advantaged see their position as likely to change. When advantage is unstable, the privileged may need to compete directly with the dis-advantaged to secure their position (Turner & Brown, 1978). Under other circumstances, instability may encourage the disavowal of or rebellion against advantage.

The fourth dimension important to the experience of relative advantage is *perceived control*. When self-focused, the advantaged evaluate their own control of the means by which they have gained their position. If the advantaged perceive a high degree of control, they should attribute their position to superior ability or effort, as outlined in attribution theory (see Weiner, 1995). Major, Testa, and Bylsma (1991) argue that the fortunate must perceive themselves as having control over their lot if they are to contrast themselves successfully to the less fortunate. If the fortunate believe they have little control over their circumstances, comparison to those worse off is insecure and can promote a fear of falling (Ybema & Buunk, 1995). When the advantaged have an other-oriented focus, they are evaluating the degree to which the less fortunate have control over their own circumstances. Perceiving the disadvantaged as responsible for their position is related to less sympathetic responses, while perceiving their misfortune as beyond their control encourages greater sympathy and helping on their behalf (see Weiner, 1995, for a review).

Self–other focus, and the perceived legitimacy, stability, and control of advantage are combined in a typology shown in Figure 7.1. Theoretically, there are eight possible self-focused and eight possible other-focused ways

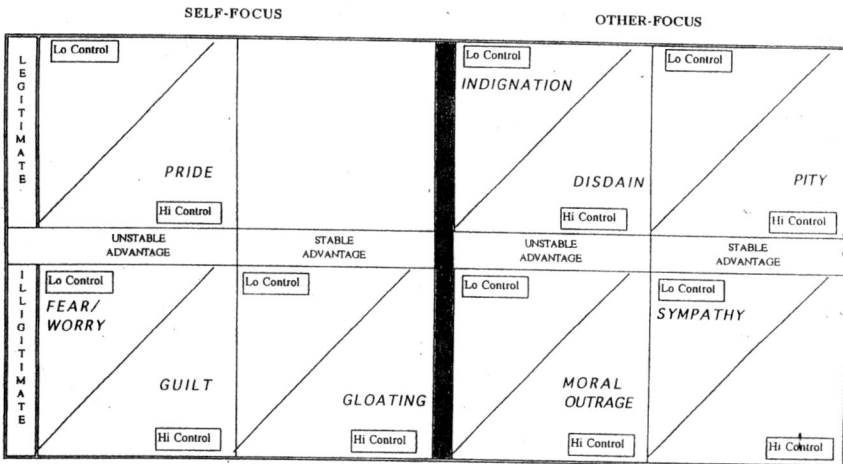

Figure 7.1. A typology of downward comparisons from relative advantage.

that relative advantage can be experienced. We do not, however, believe the phenomenology of advantage to be symmetrical. For example, we have no description of a self-focused experience of advantage that is perceived as legitimate and stable. This highly secure type of advantage is precisely what we expect to be most taken for granted. If such a secure advantage is taken for granted, there will be little self-focus and little conscious awareness of privilege. In the following sections, we describe each of the particular ways in which relative advantage can be experienced according to our typology.

Self-Focused
Gloating

> To see others suffer does one good, to make others suffer even more: this is a hard saying but an ancient, mighty, human, all-too-human principle to which even the apes might subscribe … Without cruelty there is no festival.
>
> (Nietzsche, 1887/1967, p. 67)

Gloating is the feeling of pleasure in response to another's disadvantage (Ortony et al., 1988). It is a direct, self-focused, affirmation of the superiors' advantage over others with little fear of reprisal. The stability of the advantage and the high degree of perceived control makes the kind of direct downward comparison necessary to gloating "safe" for the fortunate (see Gibbons & McCoy, 1991; Wood et al., 1994). Although made safe by a stable advantage, the absence of a strong legitimation for privilege necessitates the assertions of relative superiority characteristic of gloating (see Turner & Brown, 1978). Establishing superiority through gloating serves as explanation and justification of gross advantage (Montada & Schneider, 1989).

Considerable empirical work shows that advantaged groups directly assert their superiority over others when their advantage appears stable but illegitimate. For example, in a recent study of students at two competing universities, Smith and Spears (1996) provided one group with an unfair advantage by giving them an easier task. The collectively advantaged saw their group as superior in ability and did not see their advantage as unfair, despite the fact that their status was clearly produced by a biased experimenter. In fact, many experimental studies of ingroup favoritism show that groups accorded high status by means of success at a task distinguish themselves from less successful others by accentuating their positive attributes (see Bourhis, 1994; Mullen, Brown, & Smith, 1992, for reviews). Thus, fortunate groups exaggerate (or gloat over) advantages that both the fortunate and the unfortunate accept as true (e.g., Brown, 1978; Sachdev & Bourhis, 1985; Spears & Manstead, 1989; see also Mummendey & Schreiber, 1983; Mummendey & Simon, 1989). That both the advantaged and disadvantaged agree on the superiority of the advantaged assures the stability of their position and makes gloating safe.[2]

Because gloating is a direct, rather mean-spirited, affirmation of a highly secure and controllable advantage, it is unlikely to promote efforts at social equality; the advantaged who gloat are enjoying their position and have little interest in change. Interestingly, however, gloating by the privileged could promote resentment among the disadvantaged if they see the attempt at legitimation as excessive. Strong claims of superiority and displays of malicious glee by the advantaged in a situation where their position is stable can be seen as immodest, and can fuel claims of immorality by the disadvantaged (Raiffa, 1982). In fact, in their boys' camp studies, the Sherifs (1969) found that some of the losing groups that had endured gloating by the winners took the moral high ground and disparaged the other group as poor winners. Excessive gloating by the advantaged allowed the disadvantaged to exalt themselves as gracious losers.

Pride. Ortony et al. (1988, p. 136) describe pride as "approving of one's own praiseworthy action." It is widely believed that to promote pride in the context of unstable status, advantages must be gained through competition with others and attributed to the legitimate superiority of the fortunate.[3] There is, in fact, a long-standing notion that superiors depend on competitive comparisons with inferiors to secure their identity as advantaged (e.g., Adler, 1927/1957; Hegel, 1841/1961).

Although gloating over an advantage can serve to legitimate it, prideful responses to advantage are focused on a different type of insecurity. Here, the advantaged must compete with the disadvantaged for superiority because their position is not stable (see Mummendey & Simon, 1989). For example, Turner and Brown (1978) found that an experimentally created high status group that enjoyed a legitimate but unstable advantage showed a moderate level of ingroup favoritism, judging their own group to be somewhat superior to a lower status group. The level of ingroup favoritism was, however, lower than that shown by the high status group that gloated over an illegitimate, but stable advantage. Similarly, in one of their many experimental studies of ingroup favoritism under differing social structural conditions, Sachdev and Bourhis (1985) manipulated the stability of group status by providing one group with 70% control over outcomes and another 100% control. It was reasoned that the group with 70% control had a less stable position, as the outgroup with 30% control had some ability to determine their outcomes and future status. As expected, the group with 70% control showed much greater ingroup favoritism, as the group with complete control showed something similar to pity or noblesse oblige toward the disadvantaged group (see also Sachdev & Bourhis, 1991).

In the interpersonal comparison literature, Wills (1981) describes downward comparisons in response to unstable superiority as "active" attempts at self-esteem maintenance. This view of downward comparison in the service of identity maintenance is shared by Social Identity Theory (Tajfel & Turner, 1979). Various studies, with both everyday and laboratory groups, show ingroup favoritism increases group identification and pride (see Crocker, Blaine, & Luhtanen, 1993; Hinkle & Brown, 1991; Rubin & Hewstone, 1998, for reviews). In one study, Branscombe and Wann (1994) threatened participants' identity as "American," and then provided them with an opportunity to derogate a rival nationality. Those whose group esteem (national identity) dropped after a threat were more likely to subsequently derogate the rival nationality. This derogation was, in turn, related to an increase in participants' esteem as American. The threat to positive national identification was thus managed by derogating a national rival, which restored positive identity (or pride).

Clearly, prideful advantaged groups whose status is threatened by instability will be unsupportive of efforts to promote equality. Their dependence on competition with those lower in status to secure their position should promote strong hostility toward and little sympathy for the disadvantaged. Moreover, the pride they take in securing their advantage is based in a belief that their privilege is a legitimate reflection of their ability or effort; controllable and deserved advantages, gained through "honest" competition, are difficult to characterize as unfair or immoral (see Brown, 1978).

Guilt. Guilt is typically defined as a "dysphoric feeling associated with the recognition that one has violated a personally relevant moral or social standard" (Kugler & Jones, 1991, p. 318). Guilt in response to relative advantage results from a concentrated focus on the self and the belief that the advantage is illegitimate (Roseman, Spindel, & Jose, 1990). This direct type of guilt is based in the recognition of an immoral expropriative relationship, where the gains of the fortunate are based on the losses of the unfortunate. Those experiencing such guilt believe that their high degree of control has allowed them to secure an advantage, despite the illegitimacy and instability of their position. Such direct, self-blaming guilt seems, however, to be an unlikely response to relative advantage. As the earlier discussion of the minimization and invisibility of advantage suggests, the fortunate have little reason to accept such direct responsibility for the misfortune of others. As a result, the advantaged are more likely to feel guilt for unearned privilege where their advantage violates the moral standard of legitimacy indirectly, as in existential guilt or guilt by association.

Hoffman (1976) defines *existential guilt* as feeling guilty simply because one has unearned advantages over others. This is different from actual guilt, where the advantaged feel directly responsible for inequality. Existential guilt has been documented by Hassebrauk (1987), who asked study participants to imagine themselves in a situation of either advantage or disadvantage relative to another. Although it was clear that neither of the parties was responsible for the illegitimate inequality, those with the (imagined) advantage felt more guilty than did those with the (imagined) disadvantage. Even though these participants did not perceive themselves to be responsible for their advantage, they experienced feelings of guilt in response to the inequity. People experiencing existential guilt feel culpable even though they have done no direct harm to the unfortunate other, because they perceive their advantage as illegitimate (Montada & Schneider, 1989). Consistent with this reasoning, Chen and Tyler (1998) found that the experience of (existential) guilt in response to privilege was predicted by opposition to ideologies that legitimate inequality. When participants rejected explanations of advantage rooted in Social Darwinism (survival of the fittest), social domination (superiority of certain groups), or system legitimacy (belief that the status quo is good), they were more likely to experience guilt over their advantage.

The self-focused nature of existential guilt suggests that those who experience it will be too wrapped up in their own misery to help the disadvantaged (Hoffman, 1976). Research on the importance of self–other focus in prosocial emotion, motivation, and behavior is consistent with this view (e.g., Batson, Dyck, Brandt, & Batson, 1985). Montada and Schneider (1989), however, show that existential guilt may lead to indirect, relatively apolitical forms of help, such as giving money to charity. Ostrander's (1984) study of upper-class White women in the United States (as discussed in Hurtado & Stewart, 1997) also supports this view. The women whom Ostrander interviewed recognized their privilege, but they claimed that it was based on an "accident of birth," rather than their own intentional actions. These upper-class women did not want to take any responsibility for their privileged position. They did, however, perform some work for charities, in a rather individualized effort to help the less fortunate.

People who are advantaged by *guilt by association* may feel that those they are associated with are somehow responsible for the illegitimate disadvantage of the unfortunate (Hoffman, 1976). Fellow group members may have created the system that leaves some at a disadvantage, or they may have directly caused the misfortunes of others. The advantaged can thus feel partly responsible for the actions of their associates, even though they had little or no personal involvement. In two recent studies, Doosje, Branscombe, Spears, and Manstead (1998) demonstrate guilt by association. In one study Doosje et al. created two groups in a laboratory experiment designed to elicit feelings of group guilt. In another study, they examined Dutch guilt over the country's colonial treatment of Indonesians. In both studies, participants felt guilty when their group was *unambiguously* shown to have done harm to others in the past. However, when the group's harm to others was ambiguous, those highly identified with their group felt less guilt by association and appeared to disassociate themselves from the harm done by their fellow group members. As with direct guilt, people appear highly motivated to avoid the responsibility for disadvantage implied by guilt by association.

Despite the fact that people try to avoid guilt, it can serve a positive social function. When experienced at moderate levels, guilt can promote efforts for restitution and forgiveness (O'Connor, Berry, Weiss, Bush, & Sampson, 1997). For example, the Dutch in Doosje et al.'s (1998) study who experienced guilt over their country's colonial past were likely to advocate compensation for the victims. Thus, the indirect responsibility characteristic of guilt by association may prevent the paralyzing self-criticism of guilt proper and thereby encourage the advantaged to support equalizing efforts. Unfortunately, existential guilt is probably too self-focused to lead to real efforts for social change; at best, it may encourage rather individualized, indirect forms of help.

Worry

> Now my dad gave me his old Jaguar, I mean this is like a $50,000 car that I'm driving around [...] But have I earned it? Have I deserved this? I am very aware of the fact that I deserve none of the shit that I have. I am very grateful. I am very aware of the fact that [my father] could fall over and die and then I am on my own and nobody is going to step in there and pick up. That's it, it's over.

(Ortner, 1998, p. 427)

In recent work on social class and culture in the United States, anthropologist Sherry Ortner (1998) details worry about losing privilege (see also Newman, 1988). Ortner's respondents believe their advantage is both unstable and illegitimate, and perceive themselves as having little control over their position.

Thus, it is not surprising that they are deeply afraid of losing their privilege and ending up like those below them in the economic hierarchy.

The debilitating effects of downward comparison to those worse-off have also been shown in the interpersonal comparison literature. Theorists argue that those who worry about downward mobility must see themselves as similar to a worse-off other, who comes to represent a feared possible future (Wills, 1991). As in Ortner's (1998) research, such fearful individuals typically perceive little control over their future. This reasoning was supported in a recent study by Ybema and Buunk (1995) who exposed disabled people to information about another disabled person who was coping better or worse than themselves. Those who believed they had little control over their situation identified more strongly with the worse-off other than those perceiving greater control (see also Buunk, Collins, Taylor, VanYperen, & Dakof, 1990). In a study of breast cancer patients, Taylor and Lobel (1989) found such identification with badly off others to be associated with fear of meeting a similar fate (see also Montada & Schneider, 1989).

Despite the fact that worry occurs under the conditions most conducive to challenges by the disadvantaged (see Ellemers, 1993) and leads the relatively advantaged to identify closely with the disadvantaged, worry is not likely to be associated with support for social equality. Although advantage is perceived as illegitimate and unstable, and is thus ripe for protest from below, worry over losing privilege is based in a belief that the advantaged have little control over their status. Feelings of low personal efficacy are unlikely to promote any effort to improve their lot or that of the disadvantaged (Schroeder, Penner, Dovidio, & Piliavin, 1995). In addition, fear of losing privilege is highly self-focused, and should inhibit a sympathetic, other-focused, concern for the disadvantaged. As with guilt, the excessive self-focus typical of this negative emotional experience should lead to reduced motivation and effort to help others. In our view, there is only one possible way in which concern over a highly insecure advantage can promote social change efforts. It is possible that extreme worry about downward mobility can lead to such a strong identification with the disadvantaged that the advantaged recategorize themselves as belonging to the disadvantaged group. In essence, the advantaged would have to cease experiencing themselves as advantaged for worry to lead to support for social equality. The classic example here is the case in which laborers in the ethnic, regional, or gender majority respond to the fear of falling downward to the level of ethnic minority, immigrant, or gender minority workers by identifying with those worse-off and recategorizing them-

selves as workers facing a common external threat. Such downward identification may promote group solidarity and collective efforts to change
the system seen as unfairly disadvantaging all workers.

Other-Focused

Disdain. We argued that an advantage seen as legitimate and unstable
would lead to pride when the fortunate focused on their own fortunes, as
the instability of the advantage encourages competitive downward comparisons that favor the fortunate. When focused on the disadvantaged,
however, such competitive comparisons downward should result in disdain. If advantage is legitimized, the disadvantaged are believed responsible for their inferior position and are seen as undeserving of better. The
fact that the status arrangement is unstable suggests, however, that the
disadvantaged may gain an undeserved improvement in their position,
and this results in disdain.

As with the legitimate, unstable hierarchy in pride, attributions are
extremely important to disdain. When self-focused, self-serving intergroup
attribution for the successes of the advantaged leads to exaggerated pride,
as previously discussed. When other-focused, biased intergroup attributions evaluate misfortune harshly; this is the other-focused side of the "ultimate attribution error" (Pettigrew, 1979). In a review of studies, Hewstone
(1990) has shown that advantaged and other ingroups hold outgroups more
responsible for negative acts than for positive acts. This was also the case in
Islam and Hewstone's (1993) study of intergroup attribution in Bangladesh.
Here, the Muslim majority believed the Hindu minority to be highly responsible for negative actions, but saw the Hindus' positive acts as the result of
external pressure or luck. There was also some, albeit weak, evidence that
holding the outgroup responsible for negative acts was related to greater
anger in response to these actions. The previously mentioned study of
Montada and Schneider (1989) provides stronger support for the link
between blame and anger directed at the disadvantaged. Their respondents
were most angry at disadvantaged groups, such as immigrants and the
unemployed, when they believed the groups' disadvantage to be controllable and thereby avoidable (see also Weiner, 1995).

Feelings of disdain on the part of the privileged are highly unlikely to
lead to support for social change that will improve the circumstances of
those less fortunate. Rather, disdain can be a powerful weapon against
efforts to reduce inequality. Those with unstable advantage are able to use
disdain to better secure their position, by arguing that the disadvantaged
are, in fact, to blame for their own misfortune. This sort of other-focus in
the context of an unstable but legitimate advantage not only solidifies

opposition to social change, it also facilitates a kind of pitiless contempt for those seen as responsible for their own misfortune. Disdain can, therefore, lead to disregard for the well-being of the disadvantaged or, in extreme cases, active hostility and mistreatment.

(Moral) Indignation

> [L]et's abolish Indian Affairs. That's our tax dollars – not yours. Let's see you work for a living and to build and buy your own homes and pay for your own education ... As to speaking out for the Indians. Why should we? Nobody speaks out for us! If we have a problem we can't even go to the 'White Man's Affairs' for help – there is none.
>
> (Jacobson, as cited in Dunk, 1991, pp. 116–117)

In an ethnography of White male working-class culture in northwestern Ontario, Thomas Dunk (1991) provides a variety of examples of moral indignation directed toward Native Canadians. "The Boys" believed that "Indians" were inferior, and therefore incapable of advancing on their own, but they were also extremely envious of native people. Although the Native Canadians were the least powerful segment of society, in the minds of "the Boys" they represented local White powerlessness (p. 103). The men with whom Dunk talked felt alienated from the state and its power base in southern Ontario. They believed that the government did not care about them, even though they were "hard-working taxpayers." In contrast, they believed that Native Canadians benefited unfairly from government largesse. As shown in the opening quote, "the Boys'" perception of unfair gains by the low status group led them to make rather hostile statements regarding "Indians" and led to strong opposition to government policies targeted to benefit the group. As illustrated in this example, the experience of insecure advantage as moral indignation is based on the perception that advantage is unstable, as the disadvantaged are (unfairly) improving their position. Like Dunk's (1991) working-class informants, the indignant perceive little control over the means by which their advantage is secured. This makes the perceived gains made by the disadvantaged all the more threatening. As is also apparent in the Dunk example, indignation is directed as much at the authority seen as unfairly aiding the disadvantaged (in this case the government) as it is directed at the disadvantaged themselves.

In some cases, like that described by Dunk, members of advantaged groups experience indignation because they believe that they do not enjoy the benefits of their membership in a high status group, while lower status groups are believed to have unfair advantages (see Bobo, 1988). In fact, a group advantage can serve to highlight a personal disadvantage, making it appear more extreme in comparison to the position of fellow group members (see Smith & Spears, 1996). A number of perspectives expect lower status members of higher status groups to experience the greatest indignation toward disadvantaged groups believed to be unfairly gaining. Such assumptions can be found in analyses of "poor White racism" (Cox, 1948/1970) and authoritarian aggression (Adorno, Frenkel-Brunswik, Levinson, & Sanford, 1950). In a classic study, Pettigrew and Riley (1971) applied this reasoning in their analysis of support for the avid segregationist George Wallace, who ran in the U.S. presidential election of 1968. Wallace supporters in the urban North tended to be men strongly identified with the working class who had lower, but not the lowest, levels of education and income. These men experienced a great deal of alienation and disenfranchisement and felt forgotten by authorities they believed were unfairly favoring African Americans, who were perceived as making unfair gains on their position (see also Vanneman & Pettigrew, 1972). It was these mens' feelings of relative deprivation as deserving members of the industrious and forgotten working class that led them to express support for the segregationist populism of Wallace.

Although moral indignation involves downward comparison to those less fortunate, this comparison does not lead the privileged to recognize their structural advantage. In many ways, their (sometimes modest) privilege remains invisible despite this comparison. In fact, as previously discussed, the comparison can even make the privileged believe that it is they who are being unfairly disadvantaged. Thus, moral indignation is more likely to result in negative sentiment, and potentially punitive actions, against the disadvantaged than it is to result in support for efforts to reduce real inequities.

Pity/Noblesse Oblige

> One should not overlook the almost benevolent nuances that the Greek nobility, for example, bestows on all the words it employs to distinguish the lower orders from itself; how they are continuously mingled and sweetened with a kind of pity, consideration, and forbearance.
>
> (Nietzsche, 1887/1967, p 37)

We argued that when an advantage is extremely secure, it is often taken for granted. In cases when others' disadvantages are attended to, the fortunate may feel pity, rather than the disdain or indignation that accompanies a less secure advantage. The security of the fortunates' advantage allows a somewhat "benevolent" reaction to the disadvantaged in the form of pity. Although seemingly positive, pity relies on a view of the disadvantaged as inferior. A number of sociologists have discussed the ways in which advantaged groups secure in their dominance can show paternalistic benevolence toward subordinates (e.g., van den Berghe, 1967). Jackman (1994) describes paternalism as a "velvet glove" that covers the "iron fist" of domination, as the appearance of benevolence obscures gross inequality. In her view, paternalism is a highly efficient way to manage relative advantage, as a benevolent appearance discourages resentment on the part of the disadvantaged. Paternalism therefore makes superiority more palatable for both dominants and subordinates by representing it as a natural, caring relationship rather than one of injustice, exploitation, or conflict.

There is a great deal of empirical support for the notion that advantaged groups with highly secure (i.e., legitimate and stable) status do not gloat over their advantages. For example, in a large-scale cross-cultural study of ethnic groups in East Africa, Brewer and Campbell (1976) found groups with higher socioeconomic status to show less ethnocentrism. Presumably, such groups had a secure enough status that ethnocentric ingroup favoritism was less necessary than it was for those with lower status. In a meta-analytic integration of studies of ingroup favoritism among naturally existing groups, Mullen et al. (1992) also showed that higher status groups exhibited somewhat less ingroup favoritism than groups of moderate or low status. Larger groups, which presumably should have more secure status, were also found to express less ingroup favoritism than groups smaller in size (see also Sachdev & Bourhis, 1991). In another line of research, Mummendey and colleagues (Mummendey & Schreiber, 1983; Mummendey & Simon, 1989) have found ingroups to evaluate outgroups as superior on dimensions valued by the outgroup, but seen as unimportant to the ingroup's sense of identity (see also Spears & Manstead, 1989; van Knippenberg & van Oers, 1984). Turner and Brown (1978) provide more definitive support for the experience of pity by advantaged groups with highly secure status. In their study, the only high status group that did not show any ingroup favoritism was the one accorded a legitimate and stable advantage. Given their unchangeable and unchallengeable superiority, there was no need for the advantaged to judge themselves superior to the other group; hence, they were able to express noblesse oblige (see also Sachdev & Bourhis, 1985).

Thus, in situations in which advantage is experienced as legitimate and stable, the privileged are in a position to pity those less fortunate. As described in discussions of paternalism, pity on the part of the fortunate is typically associated with positive feelings toward the disadvantaged, although such feelings fit well within a clear and direct assertion of relative superiority. Pity can even lead the privileged to express some desire for improving the situation of the disadvantaged. That said, pity is not likely to lead to any real change or reduction in systematic inequity, because the structures of advantage are so stable that they appear natural and immutable. It is because there is no real danger of change that the advantaged are in a position to view the less fortunate with apparent benevolence. At the first hint of potential instability in their advantage, however, the fortunate are likely to view the disadvantaged in a more hostile, disdainful way (Fiske & Glick, 1995).

Sympathy. Understanding the antecedents and consequences of sympathetic responses to the disadvantaged is a central goal of those who study helping behavior. From this perspective, sympathy is based in identification with the other and their misfortune, rather than focusing on the sadness or personal distress the potential helper feels in response to the other's plight. For example, Batson and Coke (1981, p. 4), define a sympathetic response as "elicited by and congruent with the perceived welfare of someone else." It is argued that sympathy leads to helping, even when costs to the helper are great, because the focus on the other makes the other's need more salient than the potential cost of helping (see Batson et al., 1985; Dovidio, Allen, & Schroeder, 1991; Thompson, Cowan, & Rosenhan, 1980).

Sympathy for the disadvantaged is most likely when their misfortune is perceived to be illegitimate (Montada & Schneider, 1989) and beyond their control (Betancourt, 1990). Research on attribution theory shows that explaining poverty or other disadvantages as the result of illegitimate or uncontrollable circumstances is related to more sympathy, greater willingness to help, and stronger support for ameliorative social programs (see Weiner, 1995, for a review; see also Kluegel & Bobo, 1993).

Although the role of self–other focus, legitimacy, and control in sympathy is clear, the role of stability is much less obvious. It is argued in the literature on prosocial behavior that perceiving another's misfortune as stable encourages helping, because intervention is the only means by which the position of the disadvantaged can be improved. A stable misfortune clarifies the need for help, thus promoting greater helping by the advantaged (Batson & Coke, 1981). This view of stability presumes, however, that the misfortune is perceived as modifiable and that the advantaged perceive themselves as able to improve the situations of others. Research on prosocial behavior has, in fact, shown perceived efficacy to help to be an important predictor of intervention (Schroeder et al., 1995). Given a highly stable, unchangeable disadvantage, the fortunate may not perceive themselves as able to change the position of the less fortunate, and they would therefore be unlikely to help. Thus, sympathy in the context of a stable disadvantage may not lead to intervention on the part of the more fortunate. It seems clear, however, that sympathy would predispose the advantaged to aiding the less fortunate, if they mounted their own attempt at change, thereby making their disadvantage appear unstable.

Moral Outrage. There are numerous examples of members of advantaged groups working against a system of privilege that unfairly benefits them and damages others. White abolitionists, male supporters of the suffrage and feminist movements, and Las Casas' opposition to the colonial Spanish treatment of native peoples are some of the more obvious examples. Moral outrage is considered both a powerful statement against illegitimate advantage and a direct call to action in support of the disadvantaged. The call to action is based in the belief that existing status arrangements are controllable and changeable through principled opposition. Although similar in many ways, moral outrage is differentiated from feelings of guilt by its explicit focus on the position of the other. Calls to action made by advantaged group members often warn against becoming mired in guilt and work to limit it by identifying unfair systems as the target of resistance. For example, in their answer to the question, "Are We Men the Enemy?," Blood, Tuttle, and Lakey (1992, p. 138) say,

Some people say that men are the enemy when it comes to fighting sexism. We do not agree; blame and guilt don't help in understanding why people function as they do or in getting them to change.
    Does this mean we are not responsible for what is happening? Not at all! As men, we are all involved in the oppression women experience, and we benefit from it each day. Yet this is no reason to fix blame on ourselves as "the oppressor" [...] Over many years society has forced men and women into these roles of domination and submission.

In their attempt to mobilize opposition to inequality, the authors strike a delicate balance between encouraging personal responsibility for and outrage against an illegitimate system. They seem well aware of the possibility that men confronting their own gender advantages will have much reason to disavow them or, if they are acknowledged, to become immobilized by guilt. Although men are not considered ultimately responsible for the advent of sexism, which is attributed to society, they are deemed responsible for mounting a moral opposition.

According to Montada and Schneider (1989), those with advantages who experience moral outrage avoid the potentially damaging self-criticism associated with guilt by holding an external agent responsible for the inequitable system. In their study, moral outrage was related to holding powerful others responsible for support of the needy, while guilt was not related to the belief that powerful others were responsible. Because the self is not implicated in the judgment of illegitimacy, the advantaged who feel moral outrage have little to lose in bringing about social equality and should therefore engage in prosocial behavior. Consistent with this reasoning, Montada and Schneider (1989) show moral outrage to be more strongly related to willingness to engage in political activity on behalf of the disadvantaged than feelings of guilt, sympathy, or fear. In fact, the more moral outrage respondents felt in response to the disadvantaged, the more respondents were willing to sign a petition and participate in a demonstration against the disadvantage.

Those with relative advantage should experience moral outrage when their position is illegitimate, unstable, and controllable, and they focus on the disadvantage of others. Interestingly, illegitimate, unstable, and controllable advantages have also been found to promote feelings of relative deprivation and challenges by the disadvantaged (Ellemers, 1993; this volume). These circumstances appear to most strongly support dramatic opposition to systems of inequality by *both* the advantaged and the disadvantaged.

THEORETICAL IMPLICATIONS

We believe our typology provides a useful integration of a wide range of ideas and research. It offers a testable model for studying the experience of relative advantage and support for social equality. There are, however, many issues that require further attention, three of which we will address. First, we utilized theory and research across the social structural, intergroup, interpersonal, and individual levels, with little attention to the possibility that phenomena operate differently at these levels of analysis. It may not be the case, for example, that emotions such as guilt or pride operate in the same way when experienced by individuals as opposed to large collectivities. Although it is important to apply ideas across levels of analysis, we must know whether the ideas work in a similar way at each level. This is an important question for future research. It is also unclear whether the various methodologies employed to study relative advantage all access the same level of the phenomenon. It is possible that experimental studies with small, ad hoc groups may not capture the same aspects of advantage assessed in more naturalistic studies of preexisting collectivities (see Mullen et al., 1992). To fully understand the dynamics of relative advantage we must understand how various methodologies access different aspects of the phenomenon. It is extremely important to know, for example, that in experimental studies in which group status is determined by success at a task given by the experimenter, advantage is experienced as stable (Bourhis, 1994). With awareness of the particularities of method and level of analysis, an integrative, cross-disciplinary approach seems possible.

Second, in our attempt to address both the social structural and phenomenological aspects of unfair advantage we have invited the age-old "base-superstructure" problem in the social sciences (see Hall, 1977). The problem is that it is difficult to endorse the view that the social structure, or "base," has the ability to determine psychological experience without slipping into a "vulgar materialism" that sees psychology as only an epiphenomenal, "superstructural" by-product. Attempts to avoid vulgar materialism can all too easily fall into an equally problematic idealism, in which psychological experience is altogether removed from its social structural context. Our typology of relative advantage attempts to balance base and superstructure by viewing both as mutually determinate (Hall, 1977). From a materialist perspective, we assume that relative advantage is based in the reality of social structures that benefit certain people. Although we expect the actual legitimacy, stability, and control of advantage to be related to the perception of these structural conditions, it is the perception that is expected to determine the psychological experience of advantage as pride, indignation, or outrage.

The difficulty of examining both structural position and the experience of it is evidenced in our discussion of moral indignation on the part of the relatively advantaged. We argued that indignation is most likely when those who experience (a perhaps limited) advantage in one domain also feel threatened by the perceived advancement of those they believe to be inferior. In the case of "poor White racism," for example, working-class Whites, who benefit from skin color privilege, may also experience economic deprivation relative to higher status Whites and ethnic minorities seen as benefiting unfairly from government largesse. In this case, the advantaged are not a singular, homogenous group that share an equal degree of privilege. Thus, it is difficult to know whether some working-class Whites' indignation is based in an active denial of (an albeit limited) advantage, or whether it is based in a realistic conflict with close competitors whom they see as advancing by unfair means (Pettigrew & Riley, 1971). Although, for the purposes of this chapter, we assume relative advantage to be quite obvious, sometimes it is not. Establishing true material position is an exceedingly difficult task, but a necessary one if we are to examine the ways in which people experience and shape reality.

The third implication of our approach is that the experience of relative advantage is dynamic, moving from one type to another, as people's environments, and their perceptions of it, change. In some cases, the degree to which advantage is acknowledged can change. For example, the well-off who take their advantage for granted can be made aware of their position if others' disadvantage is made salient. In other situations, one downward comparison based experience of advantage can lead to another. For example, gloating over a stable, but illegitimate advantage can over time establish an advantage as legitimate. A newly legitimized and stable advantage can then be experienced as pity, if other-focused. It is also possible that the advantaged can have conflicting feelings about their position. Memmi (1957, pp. 56–57) described the colonialist as caught between what we call gloating and guilt: "the repeated, even earnest, affirmation of the excellence of one's ways and institutions, one's cultural and technical superiority do not erase the fundamental condemnation which every colonialist carries in his heart. ... Deep within himself, the colonialist pleads guilty."

CONCLUSIONS

In this chapter, we have considered three different ways in which relative advantage can be experienced. First, the advantaged can take their good fortune for granted when it is highly secure. This sort of invisible privilege is typically not associated with support for social equality, as the fortunate are blissfully unaware of their membership in an advantaged group. In such situations, when the disadvantaged depend on support from the advantaged, the disadvantaged must first make privilege visible. To promote social equality, the disadvantaged must encourage the fortunate to acknowledge their position and encourage them to make the kind of sympathetic downward comparisons that promote efforts at justice.

Second, the privileged can minimize their advantage to limit others' claims of injustice or to limit their own guilt. Strategic modesty by the advantaged works against potential threats to their position by putting the presence of a relative advantage into question. In response, the disadvantaged seeking more equality will have to establish first that a discrepancy exists.

Third, relative advantage can be acknowledged. We offered a typology of the various ways that explicit advantage can be experienced. We also argued that such acknowledgment relies on downward comparisons to the less fortunate. Four conceptual dimensions – self–other focus, perceived legitimacy, perceived stability, and perceived control – were used to differentiate the various comparisons and describe their phenomenology. These dimensions also help an understanding of how each experience of relative advantage is related to support of social equality.

Our typology suggests that support for equality on the part of the advantaged will be greatest when their position is experienced as highly insecure. To experience the moral outrage most associated with efforts at systemic change, relative advantage must be seen as both unstable (changeable) and illegitimate (challengeable). The advantaged must also focus on the (unstable and illegitimate) position of the disadvantaged and believe themselves to have control over the means by which status is attained, if they are to feel the kind of moral impetus necessary to structural change. Interestingly, these conditions are precisely the ones shown to lead to moral outrage and system challenges by the disadvantaged. Thus, in the case of moral outrage, the advantaged and the disadvantaged experience their positions in complementary ways that promote similar sorts of action. Obviously, this is not always the case.

The advantaged and disadvantaged seem often to perceive their positions differently, and to have different ideas about whether existing societal arrangements are in need of alteration. The likelihood of social change is therefore determined jointly by the experience and behavior of the advantaged and the disadvantaged. One of the central points of this chapter is that examinations of relative deprivation, moral outrage, and change efforts among the disadvantaged are important to an understanding of social justice, but they are not sufficient. Focusing solely on the disadvantaged can lead to "victim blame" by raising questions about why the disadvantaged fail to take action, without understanding the structural constraints on their efforts for change (Vanneman & Cannon, 1987). As we noted earlier, when the disadvantaged do mobilize to challenge inequities, this can lead them into direct conflict with the advantaged. Given this fact, the way in which advantage is experienced must also be examined if we are to know the true potential for social equality. Our typology can, if combined with existing work on the experience of relative disadvantage, provide a truly dialectical perspective by examining movement toward equality as a function of *both* groups' experience and action.

Unfortunately, our survey of the experience of relative advantage does not lead to positive projections regarding their support of equality. There is, in fact, a great deal working to prevent those with advantage from recognizing their privilege. Even when the advantaged do recognize their position through comparison with the less fortunate, this will not necessarily lead to support for efforts at equality. Out of the nine possible ways of experiencing advantage outlined in the typology, in only three conditions did the advantaged seem likely to support equality. Thus, we must conclude that even the most egregious and unfair advantage will not necessarily lead to the "poisoning of the consciences of the fortunate" that would lead them to willingly abandon their position. It is important to note, however, that while the advantaged can play an important role in facilitating *or* impeding equality, such efforts are not fully dependent on them. In some cases, as in South Africa recently, the disadvantaged pursue and attain social change despite resistance. In other cases, attempts at change from below can transform the way the advantaged experience their position, as in Gandhi's and M. L. King Jr.'s moral "politics of conversion." Although the phenomenology of relative advantage tends to work in opposition to social equality, it need not.

NOTES

1. This chapter was recognized with an Honorable Mention in the 1999 Gordon Allport Intergroup Relations Prize awarded by the Society for the Psychological Study of Social Issues. Our thinking about the issues presented in this chapter has benefited from discussions with Philip Kubzansky, Tamsin Lorraine, Julie Seager Volckens, and Russell Spears. We also owe a great deal to Tom Pettigrew's interdisciplinary work applying social comparison theory to the study of intergroup relations. We thank the following for their comments on a previous draft: Nyla Branscombe, Heather Smith, Richard H. Smith, Lara Z. Tiedens, and Iain Walker.
2. The experimental setting can, in many ways, reinforce the stable and consensual nature of advantage by providing groups with seemingly objective feedback that is unlikely to change in the course of the experimental situation. In this way experimental studies can powerfully mimic stable and illegitimate group relations maintained by the arbitrary decisions of those with unassailable power (i.e., the experimenter; see Reicher, 1997; Spears, 1994, for discussions).
3. Often, relatively advantaged groups take pride in their accomplishments by accentuating the importance of their own attributes as an explanation of their success. In an extension of Allport's pioneering ideas, Pettigrew (1979) has described this phenomenon as part of an "ultimate attribution error" in intergroup relations (see Islam & Hewstone, 1993; see also Hewstone, 1990, for a review).

REFERENCES

Adler, A. (1927/1957). *Understanding human nature*. New York: Premier Books.

Adorno, T. W., Frenkel-Brunswik, E., Levinson, D. J., & Sanford, R. N. (1950). *The authoritarian personality*. New York: Harper and Row.

Batson, C. D., & Coke, J. S. (1981). Empathy: A source of altruistic motivation for helping? In J. P. Rushton & R. M. Sorrentino (Eds.), *Altruism and helping behavior*. Hillsdale, NJ: Lawrence Erlbaum.

Batson, C. D., Dyck, J. L., Brandt, J. R., & Batson, J. G. (1985). Five studies testing two new egoistic alternatives to the empathy-altruism hypothesis. *Journal of Personality and Social Psychology, 55*, 52–77.

Betancourt, H. (1990). An attribution-empathy model of helping behavior: Behavioral intentions and judgements of help-giving. *Personality and Social Psychology Bulletin, 16*, 573–591.

Blood, P., Tuttle, A., & Lakey, G. (1992). Understanding and fighting sexism: A call to men. In M. L. Andersen & P. Hill Collins (Eds.), *Race, class, and gender: An anthology* (pp. 134–146). Belmont, CA: Wadsworth.

Bobo, L. (1988). Group conflict, prejudice, and the paradox of contemporary racial attitudes. In P. Katz & D. Taylor (Eds.), *Eliminating racism: Profiles in controversy* (pp. 85–114). New York: Plenum Press.

Bourhis, R. Y. (1994). Power, gender, and intergroup discrimination: Some minimal group experiments. In M. P. Zanna & J. M. Olson (Eds.), *The psychology of prejudice: The Ontario symposium* (Vol. 7, pp. 171–208). Hillsdale, NJ: Lawrence Erlbaum.

Branscombe, N. R., & Wann, D. L. (1994). Collective self-esteem consequences of outgroup derogation when a valued social identity is on trial. *European Journal of Social Psychology, 24*, 641–657.

Brewer, M. B., & Campbell, D. T. (1976). *Ethnocentrism and intergroup attitudes: East African attitudes*. New York: John Wiley.

Brown, R. (1978). Divided we fall: An analysis of relations between sections of a factory workforce. In H. Tajfel (Ed.), *Differentiation between social groups* (pp. 395–429). London: Academic Press.

Buunk, B. P., Collins, R. L., Taylor, S. E., VanYperen, N. W., & Dakof, G. A. (1990). The affective consequences of social comparison: Either direction has its ups and downs. *Journal of Personality and Social Psychology, 59*, 1238–1249.

Chen, E., & Tyler, T. R. (1998, August). *Advantage without guilt: World views and attitudes toward the disadvantaged*. Paper presented at the annual convention of the American Psychological Association, San Francisco, CA.

Collins, R. L. (1996). For better or worse: The impact of upward comparison on self-evaluations. *Psychological Bulletin, 119*, 51–69.

Cox, O. C. (1948/1970). *Caste, class, & race*. New York: Modern Reader.

Crocker, J., Blaine, B., and Luhtanen, R. (1993). Prejudice, intergroup behavior and self-esteem: Enhancement and protection motives. In M. Hogg & D. Abrams (Eds.), *Group motivation: Social psychological perspectives* (pp. 52–67). New York: Harvester Wheatsheaf.

DeMott, B. (1990). *The imperial middle. Why Americans can't think straight about class*. New York: William Morrow.

Doosje, B., Branscombe, N. R., Spears, R., & Manstead, A. S. R. (1998). Guilt by association: When one's group has a negative history. *Journal of Personality and Social Psychology, 75,* 872–886.

Dovidio, J. F., Allen, J. L., & Schroeder, D. A. (1990). Specificity of empathy-induced helping: Evidence for altruistic motivation. *Journal of Personality and Social Psychology, 59,* 249–260.

Dunk, T. W. (1991). *It's a working man's town: Male working-class culture in Northwestern Ontario.* Montreal and Kingston: McGill-Queen's University Press.

Ellemers, N. (1993). The influence of socio-structural variables on identity management strategies. In W. Stroebe & M. Hewstone (Eds.), *European Review of Social Psychology, 4,* 27–57.

Exline, J. J., & Lobel, M. (1999). The perils of outperformance: Sensitivity about being the target of a threatening upward comparison. *Psychological Bulletin, 125,* 307–333.

Festinger, L (1954). A theory of social comparison processes. *Human Relations, 7,* 117–140.

Fiske, S. T., & Glick, P. (1995). Ambivalence and stereotypes cause sexual harassment: A theory with implications for organizational change. *Journal of Social Issues, 51,* 97–115.

Frankenberg, R. (1993). *White women, race matters: The social construction of whiteness.* Minneapolis: University of Minnesota Press.

Gibbons, F. X., & Boney McCoy, S. (1991). Self-esteem, similarity, and reactions to active versus passive downward comparison. *Journal of Personality and Social Psychology, 60,* 414–424.

Hall, S. (1977). Rethinking the "base and superstructure" metaphor. In J. Bloomfield (Ed.), *Class, hegemony, and party* (pp. 43–72). London, England: Lawrence & Wishart.

Hassebrauk, M. (1987). Ratings of distress as a function of degree and kind of inequity. *Journal of Social Psychology, 126,* 269–270.

Hegel, G. W. F (1841/1961). *The phenomenology of mind* (translated by J. B. Baille). London: Allan & Unwin.

Heider, F. (1958). *The psychology of interpersonal relations.* New York: John Wiley.

Hewstone, M. (1990). The "Ultimate Attribution Error"?: A review of the literature on intergroup causal attribution. *European Journal of Social Psychology, 20,* 311–335.

Hinkle, S., & Brown, R. (1991) Intergroup comparisons and social identity: Some links and lacunae. In D. Abrams & M. A. Hogg (Eds.), *Social identity theory: Constructive and critical advances* (pp. 48–70). London: Harvester Wheatsheaf.

Hoffman, M. L. (1976). Empathy, role-taking, guilt, and development of altruistic motives. In T. Lickone (Ed.), *Moral development and behavior: Theory, research, and social issues* (pp. 281–313). New York: Academic Press.

Hurtado, A., & Stewart A. J. (1997). Through the looking glass: Implications of studying whiteness for feminist methods. In M. Fine, L. Weis, L. C. Powell, & L. Mun Wong (Eds.), *Off white: Readings on race, power, and society* (pp. 297–311). New York: Routledge.

Islam, M. R., & Hewstone, M. (1993). Intergroup attributions and affective consequences in majority and minority groups. *Journal of Personality and Social Psychology, 64,* 936–950.

Jackman, M. R. (1994). *The velvet glove: Paternalism and conflict in gender, class, and race relations.* Berkeley: University of California Press.

Kluegel, J. R., & Bobo, L. (1993). Dimensions of white's beliefs about the black–white socioeconomic gap. In P. M. Sniderman, P. E. Tetlock, & E. G. Carmines (Eds.), *Prejudice, politics, and the American dilemma* (pp. 127–147). Stanford: Stanford University Press.

Kugler, K., & Jones, W. H. (1992). On conceptualizing and assessing guilt. *Journal of Personality and Social Psychology, 62,* 318–327.

Major, B. (1994). From social inequality to personal entitlement: The role of social comparisons, legitimacy appraisals, and group membership. In M. P. Zanna (Ed.), *Advances in experimental social psychology* (Vol. 26, pp. 293–355). San Diego: Academic Press.

Major, B., Testa, M., & Bylsma, W. H. (1991). Responses to upward and downward social comparisons: The impact of esteem-relevance and perceived control. In J. Suls & T. A. Wills (Eds.), *Social comparison: Contemporary theory and research* (pp. 237–260). Hillsdale, NJ: Lawrence Erlbaum.

McIntosh, P. (1992). White privilege and male privilege: A personal account of coming to see correspondences through work in Women's Studies. In M. L. Andersen & P. Hill Collins (Eds.), *Race, class, and gender: An anthology* (pp. 70–81). Belmont: Wadsworth.

Memmi, A. (1957). *The colonizer and the colonized.* Boston: Beacon Press.

Mikula, G.(1993). On the experience of injustice. In W. Stroebe & M. Hewstone (Eds.), *European Review of Social Psychology, 4,* 223–244.

Montada, L., & Schneider, A. (1989). Justice and emotional reactions to the disadvantaged. *Social Justice Research, 3,* 313–344.

Mullen, B. (1991). Group composition, salience, and cognitive representations: The phenomenology of being in a group. *Journal of Experimental Social Psychology, 27,* 1–27.

Mullen, B., Brown, R., & Smith, C. (1992). Ingroup bias as a function of salience, relevance, and status: An integration. *European Journal of Social Psychology, 22,* 103–122.

Mummendey, A., & Schrieber, H. (1983). Better or just different? Positive social identity by discrimination against or by differentiation from outgroups. *European Journal of Social Psychology, 13,* 389–397.

Mummendey, A., & Simon, B. (1989). Better or just different? III: The impact of importance of comparison dimension and relative ingroup size upon intergroup discrimination. *British Journal of Social Psychology, 28,* 1-16.

Newman, K. S. (1988). *Falling from grace: The experience of downward mobility in the American middle class.* New York: Free Press.

Nietzsche, F. (1967). *On the genealogy of morals* (W. Kaufmann & R. J. Hollingdale, Trans.). New York: Random House. (Original work published. 1887)

O'Connor, L. E., Berry, J. W., Weiss, J., Bush, M., & Sampson, H. (1997). Interpersonal guilt: The development of a new measure. *Journal of Clinical Psychology, 53,* 73–89.

Ortner, S. B. (1998). Generation X: Anthropology in a media-saturated world. *Cultural Anthropology, 13,* 414–440.

Ortony, A., Clore, G. L., & Collins, A. (1988). *The cognitive structure of emotions.* New York: Cambridge University Press.

Pettigrew, T. F. (1979). The ultimate attribution error: Extending Allport's cognitive analysis of prejudice. *Personality and Social Psychology Bulletin, 5,* 461–476.

Pettigrew, T. F., & Riley, R. T. (1971). The social psychology of the Wallace phenomenon. In T. F. Pettigrew (Ed.), *Racially separate or together?* (pp. 231–256). New York: McGraw-Hill.

Raiffa, H. (1982). *The art and science of negotiation.* Cambridge: Belknap/Harvard University Press.

Reicher, S. (1997). Laying the ground for a common critical psychology. In T. Ibanez & L. Iniguez (Eds.), *Critical social psychology* (pp. 83–94). London: Sage.

Roseman, I. J., Spindel, M. S., & Jose, P. E. (1990). Appraisals of emotion-eliciting events: Testing a theory of discrete emotions. *Journal of Personality and Social Psychology, 59,* 899–915.

Rubin, M., & Hewstone, M. (1998). Social identity theory's self-esteem hypothesis: A review and suggestions for clarification. *Personality and Social Psychology Review, 2,* 40–62.

Runciman, W. G. (1966). *Relative deprivation and social justice: A Study of attitudes to social inequality in twentieth-century England.* Berkeley: University of California Press.

Sachdev, I., & Bourhis, R. Y. (1985). Social categorization and power differentials in group relations. *European Journal of Social Psychology, 15,* 415–434.

Sachdev, I., & Bourhis, R. Y. (1991). Power and status differentials in minority and majority group relations. *European Journal of Social Psychology, 21,* 1–24.

Schroeder, D. A., Penner, L. A., Dovidio, J. F., & Piliavin, J. A. (1995). *The psychology of helping and altruism: Problems and puzzles.* New York: McGraw-Hill.

Sherif, M., & Sherif, C. W. (1969). *Social psychology.* New York: Harper Row.

Smith, H. J., & Spears, R. (1996). Ability and outcome evaluations as a function of personal and collective (dis)advantage: A group escape from individual bias. *Personality and Social Psychology Bulletin, 22,* 690–704.

Spears, R. (1994). Why depopulation should not (necessarily) be taken personally: A reply to "Repopulating the depopulated pages of social psychology" by Michael Billig. *Theory and Psychology, 4,* 337–344.

Spears, R., & Manstead, A. S. R. (1989). The social context of stereotyping and differentiation. *European Journal of Social Psychology, 19,* 101–121.

Tajfel, H., & Turner, J. C. (1979). An integrative theory of intergroup conflict. In W. G. Austin & S. Worchel (Eds.), *The social psychology of intergroup relations* (pp. 33–47). Monterey: Brooks/Cole.

Taylor, S. E., & Lobel, M. (1989). Social comparison activity under threat: Downward evaluation and upward contacts. *Psychological Review, 96,* 569–575.

Thompson, W. C., Cowan, C. L., & Rosenhan, D. L. (1980). Focus of attention mediates the impact of negative affect on altruism. *Journal of Personality and Social Psychology, 38,* 291–300.

Turner, J. C., & Brown, R. (1978). Social status, cognitive alternatives and inter-group relations. In H. Tajfel (Ed.), *Differentiation between social groups* (pp. 201–234). London: Academic Press.

van den Berghe, P. L. (1967). *Race and racism*. New York: John Wiley.

van Knippenberg, A. (1978). Status differences, comparative relevance and inter-group differentiation. In H. Tajfel (Ed.), *Differentiation between social groups* (pp. 171–200). London: Academic Press.

van Knippenberg, A. (1984). Intergroup differences in group perceptions. In H. Tajfel (Ed.), *The social dimension: European developments in social psychology* (Vol. 2, pp. 560–578). Cambridge: Cambridge University Press.

van Knippenberg, A., & van Oers, H. (1984). Social identity and equity concerns in intergroup perceptions. *British Journal of Social Psychology, 23,* 351–361.

Vanneman, R., & Cannon, L. W. (1987). *The American perception of class.* Philadelphia: Temple University Press.

Vanneman, R. D., & Pettigrew, T. F. (1972). Race and relative deprivation in the urban United States. *Race, 13,* 461–486.

Waugh, L. R. (1982). Marked and unmarked: A choice between unequals in semi-otic structure. *Semiotica, 38,* 299–318.

Weiner, B. (1995). Inferences of responsibility and social motivation. In M. P. Zanna (Ed.), *Advances in experimental social psychology* (Vol. 27, pp. 1–47). San Diego: Academic Press.

Williams, B. F. (1989). A class act: Anthropology and the race to nation across eth-nic terrain. *Annual Review of Anthropology, 18,* 401–444.

Wills, T. A. (1981). Downward comparison principles in social psychology. *Psychological Bulletin, 90,* 245–271.

Wills, T. A. (1991). Similarity and self-esteem in downward comparison. In J. Suls & T. A. Wills (Eds.), *Social comparison: Contemporary theory and research* (pp. 51–78). Hillsdale, NJ: Lawrence Erlbaum.

Wood, J. V., Giordano-Beech, M., Taylor, K. L., Michela, J. L., & Gaus, V. (1994). Strategies of social comparison among people with low self-esteem: Self-pro-tection and self-enhancement. *Journal of Personality and Social Psychology, 67,* 713–731.

Ybema, J. R., & Buunk, B. P. (1995). Affective responses to social comparison: A study among disabled individuals. *British Journal of Social Psychology, 34,* 279–292.

EIGHT

The Embeddedness of Social Comparison

C. David Gartrell

Think about the last time you made an unscheduled visit to a physician, medical clinic, or hospital for some symptom or injury. Did you talk to anyone prior to going for medical consultation? With whom did you talk? Why? If you're like me when my foot mysteriously swelled up one morning last month, you probably talked with a relative and perhaps a friend or two. I wanted to know what they thought might be causing the swelling, whether they'd ever experienced anything like this, whether they would worry if it happened to them, and what I might do next.[1] I learned a lot by comparing my mysterious symptoms with these social contacts: they suggested a sprain or an insect bite; that the swelling looked unusual; that, yes, they would worry if it was their foot; and that checking with the doctor at the clinic was probably a good idea. Not just any acquaintance or stranger would do for these consultations; I compared my symptoms with people I knew and trusted (though acquaintances or strangers would have done in a pinch). My comparisons were *embedded* in my personal social network of relatives and friends.

The answer to the question "Who compares with whom?" – a basic issue in research on social comparison – appears to have a great deal to do with "who is in contact with whom." Psychologists have only recently begun to recognize the importance of personal contacts in comparison choices; their explanations have focused, not suprisingly, on the individual, her goals and motives, to learn about, improve, protect, or enhance herself. Their preferred method – laboratory experimentation – uproots people from the moorings of ongoing social relationships. Psychologists' recent calls for greater attention to the "social context" of comparing have come just as field studies have begun to reveal how comparing is shaped by patterns of social ties among people – that is, by *social networks*. But psychologists are not sociologists. They lack the tools to study directly the "social context" of comparing.

In this chapter I use a powerful sociological tool – social network analysis – to answer the question "Who compares with whom?" I offer a new conceptualization of social comparisons as a *type of tie* linking any two people; the collection of such ties can be thought of as a *network of comparisons*, and we can study it in relation to networks of social relationships, such as friendship. Networks are typically clumped and clustered, with subgroupings (cliques) and other structural features that focus comparisons and create the conditions for distinctive ideas and standards as people interact and influence one another. Asking "Who compares with whom?" prompts two types of questions about these networks. First, does the comparison network *match or correlate* with networks of social relationships? To put this another way, if person A is a friend of B, does A tend to compare with B? I examine this question empirically by studying comparisons of grades among a class of university students. Second, what effect do *patterns* in the networks of social relationships have on comparisons? In the discussion that concludes this chapter, I argue that by providing a representation of network patterns that make up the social context of comparison, social network analysis opens exciting new doors to understanding how the social environment affects social evaluation processes.

THEORY

Social comparison, the way that people learn about their abilities, opinions, and outcomes by comparing with others, is a basic human activity. It is basic in the sense that it is at least as old as written human history (see Matthew 16:1–20) and it lies at the heart of the social evaluation theories that Pettigrew reviewed in his 1967 *Nebraska Symposium* chapter (hereafter, *NSM*) – theories of comparison level, reference groups, relative deprivation, and equity and distributive justice. Pettigrew identified the question "who compares with whom?" as being fundamental to all of social evaluation theory both in NSM (1967, p. 243) and in subsequent work (1978, p. 29; Walker & Pettigrew, 1984, p. 308). This question continues to be the "Achilles heel" of social evaluation theory (Pettigrew, 1978, p. 36), in part because of the way the comparison process has been construed in psychology.

Inspired initially by Festinger's (1954) theory, social psychologists have sought to explain "who compares with whom" by portraying people as active choosers of comparison others, directed in their choices by an array of individual motives and goals, such as self-enhancement, self-improvement, and self-evaluation (for a review, see Wood, 1989). In this portrait of social life, the individual appears as an active causal agent who stands out against a rather nonproblematic environment (Guiot, 1978). In the volitional, individualistic language of the social comparison literature, people "seek" social information, "search for," "screen," and "select" others who are their comparison "targets" (Wood, 1996, p. 521). Ultimately, the comparer's "epistemic motivations" are based on "the perceived benefits and costs of attaining an answer (or a specific answer) to a comparative question ... [which] ... vary across situations, cultures, or personality types" (Kruglanski & Mayseless, 1990, p. 197).

Important as individuals' motives are in comparison choices, it is apparent that comparisons arrive as the sometimes unbidden by-products of social relations with other people: "the neighbor who takes frequent, exotic vacations, or ... the colleague who is awarded three large grants in one year" (Wood, 1989, p. 244). Many such comparisons will not be relevant or "diagnostic" (Gilbert, Giesler, & Morris, 1995) in the sense that they are not useful for self-evaluation (Wills & Suls, 1991; Wood & Taylor, 1991). I may envy my neighbor's frequent, exotic vacations until I recall that she won the lottery and that her financial situation and mine are now worlds apart. In an ingenious series of experiments, Gilbert and his colleagues have shown that people make such nondiagnostic comparisons, and even experience transitory emotional reactions in response to them, but then "mentally undo" the comparisons by discounting their relevance (Gilbert et al., 1995). Discounting is likely to happen if the comparer does not identify with the referent, considers the referent to be invalid, or has poor information about the referent (Markovsky, 1985). Thus, social comparison may be as much about our *reactions* to information that we unavoidably encounter in everyday social life as about *choices* we make among comparison "targets."

The idea that social comparison is sometimes thrust on us is compatable with the notion that comparisons are *embedded* in social networks of acquaintances, friends, relatives, and other social contacts (Gartrell, 1987; Granovetter, 1985). People become aware of others' outcomes, abilities, and opinions through such contacts (Gartrell, 1982). As social comparison research shifted from laboratories, where experimental subjects often do not know one another or expect to interact (Erickson, 1988; Wood, 1996), to field settings where people are socially interconnected, evidence of the embeddedness of social comparing has steadily emerged. Pettigrew anticipated this trend in NSM. Noting that social comparison research had not considered "the larger social context in which the social comparison process operates," he cites evidence from two field studies (Hyman, 1942; Katz & Lazarsfeld, 1955) of the significance of circles of friends and co-workers in social comparison (1967, pp. 248–249). Later in the same work, Pettigrew discusses the Coleman Report's finding that having close friends of the opposite race is a vital mediating link between the racial composition of the classroom and its racial consequences. Specifically, in "more than half" White classrooms, Black students with close White friends tended to have both higher achievement scores and higher college aspirations. Friendship operated in a similar fashion for White students (1967, p. 292). Although comparisons were not measured directly, presumably these opposite race close friends provided comparative reference points that were critical to students' self-evaluations.

Field studies in organizations have consistently shown that people learn about others' wages, salaries, benefits, and working conditions through personal contacts (Gartrell, 1987). For instance, in 1977–78, I spent a year working with, observing, and interviewing 98 blue-collar workers at the Cambridge, Massachussets, Department of Public Works (DPW). Among other questions, I asked these workers how their pay compared with the pay for jobs outside of the DPW. Half of the comparisons that they spontaneously cited involved jobs they had heard about through friends (41%) or relatives (9%). Relatives were more important as sources of information about the salaries of doctors (13%) and lawyers (22%). As Wooten (1955) has observed, norms of secrecy often shroud professional and managerial salaries, where pay is assumed to reflect personal qualities and capabilities. Closer social bonds with relatives were used to probe pay differences across the social barrier of occupational status.

Within the DPW, the organization of work affected opportunities for social contact among workers and, consequently, their comparisons of pay and job content. For instance, I found that laborers on rubbish trucks were keenly aware of the job demands of laborers on street construction crews. "There they are, leaning against their shovels. It takes ten of them to dig a hole!" was a common refrain. The rubbish workers often passed by these street construction crews in the course of the workday. As the most mobile, visible workers at the DPW, rubbish laborers also attracted the most comparisons from other laborers. Studies of wage and salary comparisons among workers have likened their comparisons to a kind of "glue" that creates interdependence in pay structures – whether within a firm, or between firms, among wage-setting units – such that changes in one area create pressures for changes throughout the system. (Doeringer & Piore, 1979, pp. 88–89).

The tale of my swollen foot was inspired by field studies of the effects that comparing with friends has on health-related attitudes and behaviors (see, e.g., Klein & Weinstein, 1997, on unrealistic optimism; Misovich, Fisher, & Fisher, 1997, on AIDS-related attitudes and behavior). In a rare example in this stream of literature of the explicit use of network imagery and terminology, Suls et al. (1997) show how illness-related social comparisons develop within "lay networks" of friends, family, and other social contacts. Comparison depends on the type of illness process. In "symptom-induced social comparison," people seek out others in order to understand ambiguous bodily symptoms. For example, Suls and his colleagues found that most of the college students whom they interviewed reported having spoken with friends and relatives prior to a medical consultation about a recent illness. Middle-aged and older adults were less likely to seek out such information, "perhaps because the elderly have more experience and knowledge about interpreting the meaning of symptoms" (1997, p. 208), although a substantial majority still seek out comparison information from their lay network. "Context-induced" social comparison occurs most frequently when a member of the social network is verifiably ill with some contagious disorder, or when parties share exposure situations, such as food poisoning or environmental toxins (1997, p. 210). The individual observes his or her physical condition and attempts to match the signs and symptoms experienced with those presented by the contagious other. Finally, in cases of "mass psychogenic illness," ambiguous symptoms that are not really indicative of actual physical disease spread among people who know one another or work together closely. Kerchoff and Back's (1968) "June bug" study is a well-known example. In this type of contagion, people monitor their own symptoms and compare with others' reports of illness.

Undergraduate subjects in social comparison experiments often seem like isolated social atoms, yet field studies reveal the embeddedness of their social comparisons outside the laboratory. Wheeler and Miyake (1992) had undergraduate students keep comparison diaries over a period of weeks, using the "Rochester Social Comparison Record." Comparisons, particularly similar comparisons, were more likely with close friends than with those who were less close. People avoid dissimilar comparisons with close friends in order to avert threats to self-esteem – both their own and their friends' (1992, p. 761). The tendency to make similar comparisons with close friends was stronger when the comparisons involved were on a more controllable, "lifestyle" dimension, which Wheeler and Miyake take as further evidence that these students were concerned with protecting their self-esteem as well as their close friendships.

Wheeler and Miyake's findings are consistent with the central tenets of Tesser's (1986) "self-evaluation maintenance" (SEM) model. The "closeness" of our social relationships with referent others is a key variable in the SEM process. "Closeness" refers to anything that tends to put two people into a unit relationship. Comparing with close others who outperform us can threaten our own positive self-evaluation if we wish to do well on the dimension being compared (Tesser refers to this as the "comparison" process). If the comparison dimension is not relevant to our self-definition, then we may bask in the reflected glory of a close other's achievement (the "reflection" process). An impressive array of experimental and field research supports the SEM model's predictions that people will maintain their self-evaluations by adjusting one of the three variables central to the SEM process: closeness (e.g., "I don't really like doing things with him anyways"), performance (e.g., "His form was bad; he just got lucky") or relevance (e.g., "Bowling isn't important to me anyway").

Pelham and Wachsmuth (1995) have extended the SEM model by arguing that its "comparison" and "reflection" processes are akin to two general perceptual tendencies, "contrast" and "assimilation." Contrast effects occur when we encounter highly talented others and come to feel less talented by comparison; assimilation involves a "birds of a feather" heuristic in which evidence of the flaws or talents of others is taken as a stand-in for evidence about ourselves (1995, p. 835). A "minimum level of psychological closeness" is necessary for both types of effects to occur. Pelham and Wachsmuth's studies reveal that assimilation with close others is most likely when people are certain of their beliefs or abilities.

Although social comparison theory has only recently discovered social relations, the idea that networks of social contacts provide the conduits through which comparing occurs can be traced back through a half-century of research on reference groups, relative deprivation, subjective social class, equity, and justice, as well as through applications of this research in such areas as social support, diffusion of innovations, and race relations (for an extended review, see Gartrell, 1987). Taken together with the field studies spawned by social comparison theory, this research constitutes broad evidence of the importance of interpersonal bonds as a basis of comparing. Yet as an answer to the question "who compares with whom?," this evidence is incomplete in an important way.

When respondents are asked to record or otherwise report their comparisons, we learn much about the characteristics of their comparative referents and about the nature of their relationships to these referents, yet we learn nothing about their relationships to those with whom they do *not* compare. In order to estimate properly the effects of social relations on comparing, one must be able to assess both comparing and noncomparing.[2] One way to do this is to present respondents with an array of potential referent others, observe with whom they compare and whom they ignore, and what types of social relationships undergird both types of responses. If every member of the array evaluates every other member, the joint product of their evaluations is a social network: "a finite set or sets of actors and the relation or relations defined on them" (Wasserman & Faust, 1994, p. 20). Such a network can be represented by a matrix in which the (i,j)th entry is actor i's evaluation of referent j, or by a graph in which social ties are represented by lines connecting actor i with referent j. For instance, Figures 8.1 and 8.2 present graphs of networks of comparing and of friendship among a group of 23 university students (these data are discussed at length in the next section).[3] Defining the boundary of a network can be difficult, yet natural boundaries often demarcate finite groups such as classrooms or firms.

Two types of hypotheses can be derived about social comparison within such a network. The first, which constitutes the empirical focus of this chapter, involves *dyadic* relationships: how is actor i's tendency to compare with partner j related to i's other social ties with j? As we shall see in the next section, the statistical model that I use to assess these relationships assumes multiple actors evaluating and being evaluated by multiple partners (Kenny & Lavoie, 1984). The second type of hypothesis, to which I return at the other end of this chapter, addresses how *patterns* of relations within the network shape social comparisons among network members. Both draw on Erickson's (1988) pathbreaking discussion of the relational basis of attitudes.

Erickson argues that, at the dyadic level, social comparison of attitudes is influenced by four properties of social relations: frequency of interaction; multiplexity; strength of ties; and asymmetry. Since in my study the relevent social relations are overwhelmingly symmetric (the (i,j)th tie is the same as the (j,i)th tie), my analysis focuses on the first three of these dyadic properties:

> Hypothesis 1: *The more frequently actor i interacts with partner j, the more likely i is to compare with j.*

Erickson notes that comparing with a little-known other is less likely to boost confidence in one's opinion than is comparing with nonstrangers. A similar argument can be made for comparisons of grades. The more i interacts with *j*, the more opportunity *i* has to learn about *j*'s performance-related abilities.

Hypothesis 2: The more multiplex actor i's relationship is with partner j, the more likely i is to compare with j.

The experimental literature on comparing emphasizes similarity, either on performance or on performance-based attributes, as the basis of comparison (Kruglanski & Mayseless, 1990; Suls & Wills, 1991; Wood, 1989). Erickson points out that sharing relationships may itself be a type of similarity. An actor who interacts with a partner across a variety of different types of relationships is thus more likely to compare with this partner.

Hypothesis 3: The stronger actor i's tie with partner j, the more likely i is to compare with j.

Strong ties "may be a form of widely salient similarity that leads to frequent comparison" (Erickson, 1988, p. 103). Moreover, if comparisons are reciprocal, a feeling of closeness may be necessary for actor and partner to feel comfortable revealing information about their respective performances. Closeness is also important when actors evaluate certain kinds of attitudes and opinions with partners (Erickson, 1988, p. 102).

Finally, I include a central proposition from Festinger's (1954) classic statement of social comparison theory:

Hypothesis 4: The more similar actor i is to partner j, the more likely i is to compare with j.

Festinger proposed that people choose similar others as reference points because they provide subjectively more precise, stable information. I interpret "similarity" to refer to both similarity on the dimension under evaluation (e.g., exam grades) as well as dimensions surrounding the dimension under evaluation (e.g., general academic ability) (Goethals & Darley, 1977; Suls et al., 1978; Wood, 1989; Zanna, Goethals, & Hill, 1975).

METHOD

Respondents
The respondents were 23 of 25 students enrolled in a third-year course in social networks at the University of Victoria. The students participated on a voluntary basis, and I tried to encourage a spirit of co-investigation. To this end we talked about various parts of the project and examined portions of the data during lab sessions held as part of the course.

Data and Measurement

The data were collected late in November 1992 during one class session. A computerized questionnaire presented the students with a list of 23 names (Gartrell & Gartrell, 1989). They were subsequently asked 22 questions about those whom they recognized from this list. The questions concerned a range of social relations, such as friendship, as well as questions about comparing grades on course assignments and exams. In the end, the data consisted of one 23 × 23 matrix for each of the 22 questions.

The dependent variable in this study is social comparison. The matrix COMPARE represents the volume of i's comparison with j as the sum of three (0,1) matrices: whether student i compared with j on the last lab assignment handed back; comparing on the midterm exam; and comparing on any other assignments. Cell elements in COMPARE thus range from 0 (no comparison) to 3 (compared on assignments and midterm).

Hypotheses 1–3 reflect the relationship between various properties of ties at the dyadic level and social comparison. On the assumption that interaction relevant to grade comparisons is primarily verbal, I measured FREQUENCY as the extent to which student i talks with j (0 = never, 2 = often). Following the lead of Marsden and Campbell (1984), I operationalized strength in terms of a sense of closeness with other. The matrix STRENGTH reflects how close i considers herself to be to j (1 = not at all close, 7 = very close). Finally, MULTIPLEXITY is measured as the sum of 10 binarized relations, including proximity (sit next to in class or in lab), shared foci (in other courses with now or before), sharing course work (discussing readings or assignments, studying with, exchanging notes), friendship and social contact outside class.

I included two measures of similarity to reflect two interpretations of the impact of similarity on comparing in social comparison theory. Under the first interpretation, people are thought to compare with others who are similar on the dimension under evaluation. Accordingly, my first measure reflects i's similarity with j on those items that make up the dependent variable, COMPARE (i.e., the last assignment, any other previous assignments, and the midterm exam). Specifically, SIMILARITY (Course) is the average over these three items of the absolute value of the difference between the standardized (z) scores of students i and j on each item. Smaller scores represent greater similarity.

Under the second interpretation of similarity, people are thought to compare with others who are similar on dimensions related to the dimension under evaluation (Goethals & Darley, 1977). My second measure is based on grade-point averages (GPA), and reflects i's similarity to j in general academic ability. The variable SIMILARITY (GPA) was formed as the absolute value of the difference between the standardized *(z)* GPAs of students *i* and *j*. Again, smaller values represent greater similarity between *i* and *j*.

Analysis

Models for estimating the conformity of two sociomatrices have been devised by Wasserman (1987), for dichotomous data, and by Kenny (1994; Kenny & Lavoie, 1984) for valued data. Kenny's "social relations model" discerns three types of effects from the data in a sociomatrix (Kenny, 1994). An "actor" effect represents person *i*'s average level of a given behavior in relation to a variety of partners (e.g., a tendency to like others); a "partner" effect represents the average level of the behavior that an actor elicits from a variety of partners (e.g., a tendency to be liked by others); and a "relationship" effect represents actor *i*'s behavior in relation to a particular partner, *j*, above and beyond their actor and partner effects (e.g., *i*'s particular liking of *j*, above and beyond *i*'s tendency to like others, and *j*'s own likeability). Relationship effects are asymmetric or directional; *i*'s response to *j* may be different from *j*'s response to *i*.

The data were analyzed with Kenny's (1994) SOREMO program. Table 8.1 presents univariate results for each of the variables in the analysis. The variance partitioning suggests that with the exception of similarity in course marks, the data are overwhelmingly dyadic.[4] That is, there is relatively little variation associated with actors' tendencies to evaluate partners, or with partners tendencies to receive evaluations. Instead, the variation consists primarily of the way particular actors respond to particular partners. To take an example, the lack of actor and partner variation in STRENGTH suggests that, on the one hand, students cannot be differentiated in terms of their tendency to feel close, nor on the other hand are there "stars" – students who are particularly the object of others' feelings of being close. Feelings of being close vary according to particular actor–partner relationships.

Because relationship effects are asymmetric, it is possible to correlate *(i,j)* effects with *(j,i)* effects. These "reciprocity" correlations are both large and substantively interesting (Table 8.1). In particular, if student *i* compares with *j,j* tends also to have compared with *i* (*r* = .79). This result reflects the fact that comparing grades is *dyadic* – it takes place in social interactions between students. To my knowledge, this is the first time such an effect has been systematically demonstrated in the comparison literature.

The relationship effect of person *i* interacting with *j* in one matrix (e.g., *i*'s tendency to feel close to *j*) can be correlated with the relationship effect of *i* with *j* in a second matrix (e.g., *i*'s tendency to compare with *j*). This

Table 8.1. *Univariate Results*

		Variance Partitioning			
	Mean	Actor	Partner	Relationship	Reciprocity
Compare	.19	.01	.00	.99	.79*
Frequency	.24	.02	.03	.95	.72*
Strength	.62	.03	.04	.93	.86*
Multiplexity	.87	.01	.02	.97	.87*
Similarity (GPA)	1.20	.08	.08	.84	1.00*
Similarity (Course)	1.11	.26	.26	.48	1.00*

*$p < .01$

"intrapersonal" correlation assesses, in this example, the extent to which i's feeling strongly tied to j is associated with i's comparing with j.[5] Intrapersonal correlations in the left-most column of Table 8.2 represent empirically the relationships conjectured in Hypotheses 1–4.

My first three hypotheses are strongly supported. Student i is more likely to compare with j to the extent that i interacts more frequently with j ($r = .77$); the closer i feels to j ($r = .79$); and the more multiplex i's relationship is with j ($r = .83$). These effects are both substantial and statistically significant. By contrast, there is little support for Hypothesis 4. Both SIMILARITY correlations are in the predicted direction, greater (i,j) difference (and less similarity) tending to be associated with less (i,j) comparison (–.09 and –.11). Yet both effects are very small and neither is statistically significant.

Table 8.2. *Bivariate Results*

	Com-pare	Fre-quency	Strength	Multi-plexity	Simi-larity (GPA)	Simi-larity (Course)
Compare	—	.64**[a]	.79**	.76**	–.09	–.11
Frequency	.77**[b]	—	.75***	.78***	–.09	–.08
Strength	.79**	.80***	—	.84**	–.07	–.09
Multiplexity	.83***	.91***	.86**	—	–.09	–.10
Similarity (GPA)	–.09	–.09	–.07	–.09	—	.25
Similarity (Course)	–.11	–.08	–.09	–.10	.25	—

[a] Interpersonal correlations are above the diagonal (e.g., if i talks more frequently with j, then j tends to compare more often with i).
[b] Intrapersonal correlations are below the diagonal (e.g., if i talks more frequently with j, then i tends to compare more often with j).
** $p < .01$ *** $p < .001$

Table 8.3. *Multivariate Results*

	Model[a]	
	A	**B**
Similarity (GPA)	$-.07^b$	$-.01$
Similarity (Course)	$-.09$	$-.02$
Frequency		$.06$
Multiplexity		$.53$
Strength		$.29$
R^2	$.02$	$.71$

[a] The dependent variable is Compare.
[b] Beta.

The first row of Table 8.2 contains "interpersonal" correlations of the relationship effects for student i with student j on each independent variable with the relationship effect of j with i. For instance, we see that the more frequently i interacts with j, the more likely j is to compare with i ($r = .64$). The interpersonal correlations for frequency, strength, and multiplexity are, like their intrapersonal counterparts, strong and statistically significant. These results reinforce the notion that comparing ties that occur along with other social relations tend to be reciprocal.[6]

The relative impacts of similarity and interpersonal bonds can be estimated in a hierarchical regression analysis (Table 8.3). Entered first on the grounds of temporal priority, the similarity variables have a very small impact ($R^2 = .02$). Mirroring their significance in the univariate results, the set of interpersonal bonds variables has a substantial impact (R^2 change = .69). The betas suggest that multiplexity has the largest net impact on comparison; the range of i's relationships with j is particularly important in determining i's tendency to compare with j.

DISCUSSION

The answer to the question "who compares with whom" has much to do with "who is tied to whom." Comparisons hinge on social relations; the greater the strength, frequency, and especially, the multiplexity of i's relationship with j, the more likely i is to compare with j. These are substantial effects (Cohen, 1977). Similarity – either in performance or in general academic ability – has much less to do with comparing. Moreover, the grade comparisons we have observed here are dyadic; if i compares with j, j tends to compare with i.

These findings have three powerful implications for social comparison theory and research. First, treating social comparisons as *(i,j)* ties in a social network allows us to estimate, for the first time, the magnitude of the effect of social relations on social comparing. Field studies of social comparison have repeatedly shown that people's comparisons are rich in social bonds, yet this evidence is incomplete in that it does not address how people are related to those with whom they do not compare.

Second, the network approach encourages us to view comparing as a product of social interaction, rather than as a one-sided evaluation by an actor uprooted from any social moorings. My finding that comparisons are dyadic is consistent with a growing body of evidence that comparisons are often by-products of social relations (Gartrell, 1982, 1987). When I ask my students how their comparisons happen, they usually describe grade comparing as a routine part of everyday conversation. Blue-collar workers learn about the wages and job characteristics of other workers through a similar sort of "talk" (Gartrell, 1982, p. 129). To find that comparing is a sometime feature of conversations in ongoing social relationships could not be more banal. Yet the fact that this point needs to be made at all reveals the degree to which social relations have been excluded from the traditional "comparison context" (Wood, 1996, p. 533).

Finally, while most studies of social comparison involve only a single comparison at a single point in time, "in everyday life, people probably make comparisons on more than one dimension simultaneously, with multiple comparison targets, not just once but repeatedly" (Wood, 1996, p. 533). A network is defined in terms of "multiple targets" (a set of actors) who "repeatedly" compare (each is tied to the others by multiple comparison ties) on more than one dimension (more than one type of comparison relation is possible). It is precisely this complexity to which a network approach to comparing is well suited.

Every study has its limitations, and mine is no exception. Hypothesis 4 was tested with two measures of similarity, both pertaining to academic achievement, and the hypothesis was not supported. Given the centrality of similarity and dissimilarity in the comparison literature, it could be argued that my construal of similarity should be broadened to include nonacademic attributes with known relationships to social comparison (see, e.g., Wood, 1989, pp. 235–238; Suls & Wills, 1991). Unfortunately, the literature offers few theoretically coherent suggestions as to which attributes should be considered (Wood, 1989), or of the conditions under which similarity or dissimilarity is preferred (Kruglanski & Mayseless, 1990).

A broader construal of similarity could be important in a different sense. My research demonstrates that social relationships have substantial effects on social comparing. It is well known in the literature on interpersonal attraction that friendships are often based on similarity of attitudes, self-concepts, and demographic characteristics (Byrne, 1971; Carli, Ganley, & Pierce-Otay, 1991; Deutsch, Sullivan, Sage, & Basile, 1991; Kandel, 1978; Newcomb, 1961). If interpersonal relationships reflect broad similarities of outlook and background, and if comparisons are embedded in networks of such relationships, then similarity may well influence comparing through its effect on the development of social bonds. This possibility is congruent with the suggestion that people may avoid comparisons that are nondiagnostic (Gilbert et al., 1995) or threatening (Tesser, 1986) by limiting social contacts with other people. At the same time, it is important to recognize that friendship choice is not entirely free. Rather, relationships are constrained by opportunities to interact that often have little to do with personal choice (Feld, 1981; Wellman, Carrington, & Hall, 1988), such as those that occur when students are assigned to university classes (Erickson, 1988, p. 105).

Because I did not measure the relevance of grades to my students, my results do not directly address the SEM model developed by Tesser. However, if we assume that students are concerned about grades and consider academic performance to be relevant to their self-concepts, then my data can speak to the SEM model. The model predicts that "when relevance is high, the better another's performance the lower the closeness" (Tesser, 1991, p. 121). The similarity variables in this study do not differentiate between i's superiority over j and j's superiority over i; they simply measures departures from equivalence. To measure differences in performance I created two additional variables, SUPERIORITY (Course) and SUPERIORITY (GPA), by undoing the absolute value transformation from SIMILARITY (Course) and SIMILARITY (GPA). SUPERIORITY represents i's superiority over j in course assignments. The SEM model predicts that as j is more superior to i (as SUPERIORITY becomes more negative), i should be less close to j (STRENGTH, FREQUENCY, and MULTIPLEXITY should be positively correlated with SUPERIORITY). The intrapersonal correlations for these variables appear in Table 8.4.

The correlations are in the predicted direction, but are very small and statistically insignificant. A second superiority variable representing the degree to which i's GPA exceeded j's produced similar results (Table 8.4). Both superiority variables were only very weakly correlated with comparing. To what might we attribute this lack of support for the SEM model?

I recently asked three of the students who had been in the class to tell me about their grade comparisons:

Table 8.4. *Intrapersonal Comparisons*

	Superiority (GPA)[a]	Superiority (Course)
Compare	.01	−.01
Frequency	.03	.02
Strength	.00	.00
Multiplexity	.01	.00

[a] The correlation between Superiority (GPA) and Superiority (Course) is .07.

(Respondent #2): We'd go over the assignments over coffee sometimes, talk about what we'd got in the different sections of the assignment – "oh, you got this here," sort of thing. ... There's a norm operating such that one shouldn't be critical of a friend when he gets a mark worse than ones' own. The norm is to be supportive and listen to bitching. Support the other and help to deflect other's upset towards the prof, who assigned the grade. When one is doing less well, one may perceive that the other deserved the better grade through their efforts. I've never thought of this as a competetive process with friends, never been threatened by their performance.

(Respondent #23): Fairness was very important. We were very concerned with the accuracy of the grading, with evaluating what the prof had done in relation to what we expected to get. We'd ask "why is there a one-mark difference between you and me?" We helped each other to do better. We were supportive of one another. We tried to explain to each other what the differences in grades were. There was no threat; if you did better, you'd be quieter, in order not to hurt the others' feeling.

Both stress the supportive nature of the comparing; it was done to ensure that the instructor [myself!] had treated the students fairly. Listening to others and deflecting resentments of grade differences toward the instructor are also important supportive mechanisms. By contrast, the world of SEM is steeped in competition, where comparisons are laden with threatening implications that are sometimes resolved in rather unfriendly ways:

Suppose that Albert's good friend Bob makes a 90 on a biology test on which Albert made an 80. Suppose, further, that it is important to Albert's self-definition to do well in biology. ... Albert can do a variety of things: He can alter the closeness of his relationship with Bob ... he can mislabel or hide Bob's slides for the next test ... he can spend less time studying biology ... reducing the importance of biology to his self-definition. (Tesser, 1986, p. 440)

Students in the dog-eat-dog world of SEM are out for themselves in a way that conjures up the social atoms of traditional social comparison research whom we encountered at the outset of this chapter. Of course, the sociology students in my class may have been every bit as upset as Albert the biology student when their close friends did better than they did. But the few students whose comments appear here approach these comparative discrepancies in a way that protects their social relationships. In contrast, comparison research has emphasized various comparative goals whose implications are primarily individual, such as self-evaluation, self-esteem, and self-improvement (Suls & Wills, 1991; Wood, 1989; Wood & Taylor, 1991) – all terms prefaced by the word "self." My students' remarks are a reminder that nurturing social relationships with others is also an important goal.

In their recent work, Tesser and his colleagues have recognized that the original SEM model failed to consider people's investments in their social relationships. An "extended" version of the model holds that as romantically involved couples become more interdependent and communal in orientation, they appear to become more motivated or more adept at extending empathy and sympathy toward their partners when they outperform or are outperformed themselves on self-relevant activities (Beach et al., 1998). My results suggest that such empathic, communally oriented responses are not restricted to romantic couples; they also occur among groups of students. My students' concerns about whether their friends are treated fairly arise as they create and recreate their social lives together. They do this precisely because they are *not* social atoms.

Neither is their social landscape merely dyadic. It consists of small subgroups, or cliques, whose members are more densely tied to one another than to the surrounding network (Wasserman & Faust, 1994). Reference group processes such as communication, comparison, influence, and conformity take place within the web of interrelationships that define cliques. In her pathbreaking analysis, Erickson suggests how properties of these subgroups, such as their density (ratio of actual to potential ties), are translated into attitude similarity. Students #2 and #23 were part of one such clique, along with two other students (Figures 8.1 and 8.2). Their comments suggest that the meaning of comparisons develops within their group. For instance, both students stressed that their comparisons were supportive, made in part to ensure fair treatment, rather than being assessments of their position vis-à-vis competitors. Of course, theirs is but one of several subgroups which we might find in an analysis of cliques in this network, as even a glance at Figures

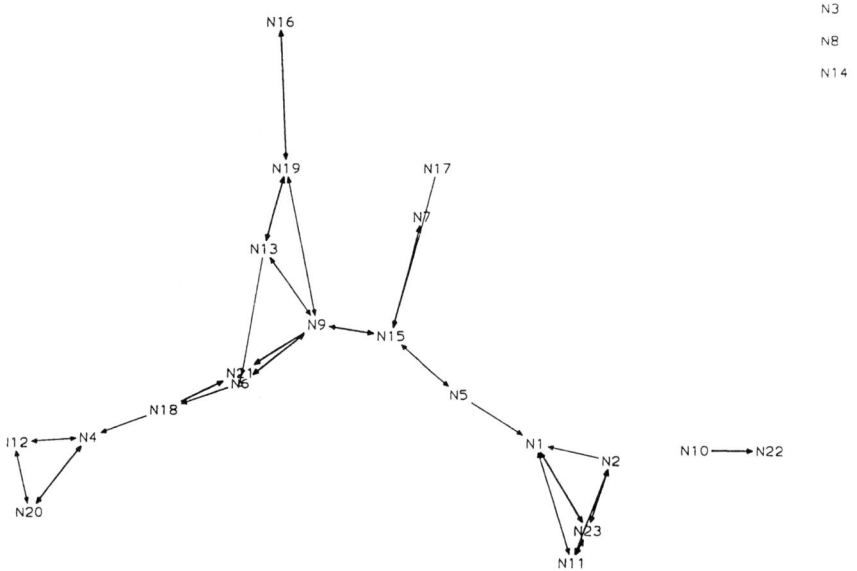

Figure 8.1. Grade comparisons among 23 students.

8.1 and 8.2 suggests. The members of another subgroup might well hold quite distinctive views about the nature of social comparison. Consider the comments of a third member of the same clique:

(Respondent #1):   We didn't feel threatened by comparing in our group, because we'd been friends outside of the class before it got started. Our friendship was very durable – whether one of us wasn't doing as well as the others wasn't important to continuing the friendships. I think this would be true of friendships formed on the basis of any attributes other than performance. Where friendships are less durable, I think you might find that another person's good performance could be threatening, especially if you keep "coming in second" all the time.

These remarks affirm that SEM processes exist, but they also suggest that SEM may have a particular social structural locus outside of long-standing cliques.

The key point here is that patterns of social relations within the overall network affect both the pattern and meaning of comparisons. Social network analysis defines social structure in terms of such patterned social relations (Wasserman & Faust, 1994, p. 3). In future work, I plan to extend my analysis of grade comparisons from dyads to examine aspects of relational structures, such as cliques, and their implications for social comparisons.[7] The intent of this line of analysis is to explore the social structural features of social com-

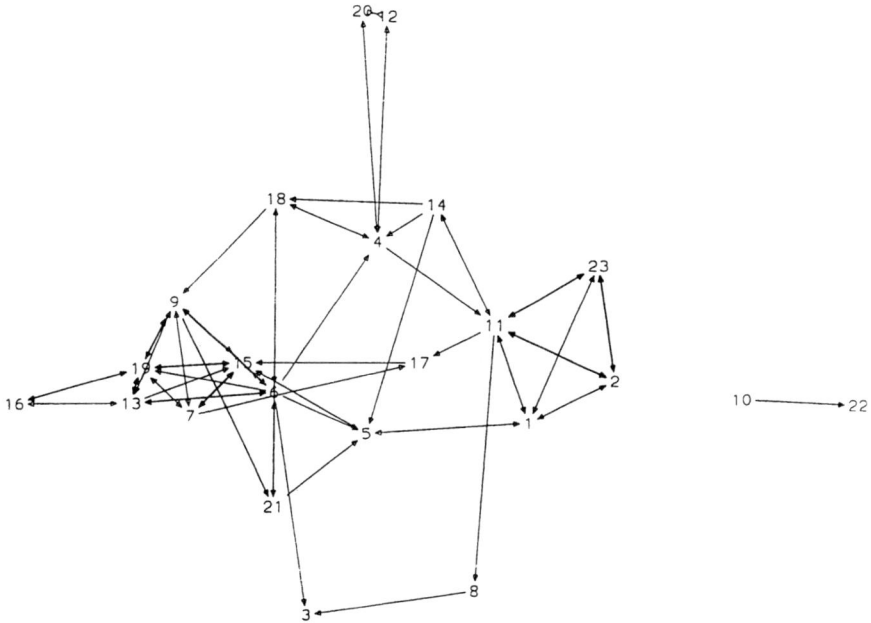

Figure 8.2. Friendship among 23 students.

parison "environments" that social comparison research has long sought to represent (Pettigrew, 1967; Wood, 1989, 1996), as well as the meanings of comparison processes within these structures. I hope these efforts will continue what I have begun here: opening an intellectual door through which a predominantly psychological research tradition may begin to explore the sociological terrain in which comparisons are embedded.

ACKNOWLEDGMENTS

A draft of this chapter was presented at the International Social Networks Conference in London, on July 5, 1995. I am grateful to the students of Sociology 326 (Social Networks) who provided me with the data and to all the students who have made terrific comments on this work over the years. Dave Kenny patiently answered my questions about the SOREMO program, the Social Relations Model, and Beatles' trivia (be sure to visit his website!). The following is an incomplete list of others who have made helpful comments on my work: Tanis Abuda, Morgan Baker, Gordon Behie, Jim Ennis, Bonnie Erickson, Mark Granovetter, Penny Hocking, Terry Nosanchuk, and Marni Wilkinson. Although their identities have not been changed, they are innocent of any errors that remain in this chapter. Special thanks to Iain

Walker and Heather Smith for their editorial comments and encouragement,
and to Tom Pettigrew for his inspiration and guidance over the years.

NOTES

1. This example draws on the work of Suls, Martin, and Leventhal (1997).
2. An early discussion of this issue may be found in Merton and Kitt (1950, p. 69), who suggest offering subjects ordered arrays of comparative contexts that exhaust their potential reference points.
3. Line thickness reflects the number of comparisons, in Figure 8.1, and the strength of friendship, in Figure 8.2. Both graphs were produced by KrackPlot (Krackhardt, Lundberg, & O'Rourke, 1993) based on a two-dimensional multidimensional scaling of geodesic path distances among all pairs of students.
4. Observation *(i,j)* is missing if *i* reported not recognizing or not talking with *j*. I assumed missing data were O's, reflecting contact or no comparison. Analysis is currently under way with a modified version of SOREMO that can handle missing observations.
5. Kenny terms this an "intrapersonal" correlation because the same person is the actor in each variable (Kenny, 1994, p. 18).
6. The intra- and interpersonal correlations are equal due to the symmetry of the similarity variables.
7. Social comparison implications of other social structural features of networks, such as structural equivalence, have been explored by Erickson (1988) and Burt (1982).

REFERENCES

Beach, S. R., Tesser, A., Fincham, F., Jones, D., Johnson, D., & Whitaker, D. (1998). Pleasure and pain in doing well, together: An investigation of performance-related affect in close relationships. *Journal of Personality and Social Psychology, 74*, 923–938.
Burt, R. S. (1982). *Toward a structural theory of action.* New York: Academic Press.
Byrne, D. (1971). *The attraction paradigm.* New York: Academic Press.
Carli, L. L., Ganley, R., & Pierce-Otay, A. (1991). Similarity and satisfaction in roommate relationships. *Personality and Social Psychology Bulletin, 17*, 419–426.
Cohen, J. (1977). *Power analysis for the behavioral sciences.* New York: Academic Press.
Deutsch, F. M., Sullivan, L., Sage, C., & Basile, N. (1991). The relation among talking, liking and similarity between friends. *Personality and Social Psychology Bulletin, 17*, 406–411.
Doeringer, P., & Piore, M. J. (1971). *Internal labor markets and manpower analysis.* Lexington: Heath.
Erickson, B. H. (1988). The relational basis of attitudes. In B. Wellman & S. Berkowitz (Eds.), *Social structures: A network approach.* Cambridge: Cambridge University Press.
Feld, S. (1981). The focused organization of social ties. *American Journal of Sociology, 86*, 1015–1035.

Festinger, L. (1954). A theory of social comparison processes. *Human Relations, 7,* 117–140.

Gartrell, C. D. (1982). On the visibility of wage referents. *Canadian Journal of Sociology, 7,* 17–43.

Gartrell, C. D. (1987). Network approaches to social evaluation. *Annual Review of Sociology, 13,* 49–66.

Gartrell, C. D., & Gartrell, M. J. (1989). *NETQUEST: A computer-based questionnaire for relational data.* Department of Sociology, University of Victoria.

Gilbert, D. T., Giesler, R. B., Morris, K. A. (1995). When comparisons arise. *Journal of Personality and Social Psychology, 69,* 227–236.

Goethals, G. R., & Darley, J. M. (1977). Social comparison theory: An attributional approach. In J. Suls & R. L. Miller (Eds.), *Social comparison processes: Theoretical and empirical perspectives.* Washington: Hemisphere.

Granovetter, M. S. (1985). Economic action, social structure, and embeddedness. *American Journal of Sociology, 91,* 481–510.

Guiot, J. M. (1978). Some comments on social comparison processes. *Journal for the Theory of Social Behaviour, 8,* 29–43.

Hyman, H. H. (1942). The psychology of status. *Archives of Psychology, 38*(269).

Kandel, D. (1978). Similarity in real-life adolescent friendship pairs. *Journal of Personality and Social Psychology, 36,* 306–312.

Katz, E., & Lazarsfeld, P. F. (1955). *Personal influence.* Glencoe: Free Press.

Kenny, D. A. (1994). *SOREMO Version v. 1.* Unpublished manuscript, University of Connecticut.

Kenny, D. A., & La Voie, L. (1984). The social relations model. In L. Berkowitz (Ed.), *Advances in experimental social psychology* (Vol. 18, pp. 141–182). New York: Academic Press.

Kerchoff, A., & Back, K. (1968). *The June bug: A study of hysterical contagion.* New York: Appleton-Century-Crofts.

Klein, W. M., & Weinstein, N. D. (1997). Social comparison and unrealistic optimism about personal risk. In B. P. Buunk & F. X. Gibbons (Eds.), *Health, coping, and well-being: Perspectives from social comparison theory.* Mahwah, NJ: Lawrence Erlbaum.

Krackhardt, D., Lundberg, M., & O'Rourke, L. (1993). KrackPlot: Pictures worth a thousand words. *Connections, 16,* 37–47.

Kruglanski, A. W., & Mayseless, O. (1990). Classic and current social comparison research: Expanding the perspective. *Psychological Bulletin, 108,* 195–208.

Markovsky, B. (1985). Toward a multilevel distributive justice theory. *American Sociological Review, 50,* 822–839.

Marsden, P. V., & Campbell, K. E. (1984). Measuring tie strength. *Social Forces, 63,* 482–501.

Merton, R. K., & Kitt, A. (1950). Contributions to the theory of reference group behavior. In R. K. Merton & P. Lazarsfeld (Eds.), *Continuities in social research: Studies in the scope and method of "The American Soldier."* Glencoe: Free Press.

Misovich, S. J., Fisher, J. D., & Fisher, W. A. (1997). Social comparison processes and AIDS risk and AIDS preventive behavior. In B. P. Buunk & F. X. Gibbons (Eds.), *Health, coping, and well-being: Perspectives from social comparison theory.* Mahwah, NJ: Lawrence Erlbaum.

Newcomb, T. (1961). *The acquaintance process.* New York: Holt, Rinehart and Winston.

Pelham, B. W., & Wachsmuth, J. O. (1995). The waxing and waning of the social self: Assimilation and contrast in social comparison. *Journal of Personality and Social Psychology, 69,* 825–838.

Pettigrew, T. F. (1967). Social evaluation theory. In D. Levine (Ed.), *Nebraska symposium on motivation* (Vol. 15, pp. 241–311). Lincoln: University of Nebraska Press.

Pettigrew, T. F. (1978). Three issues in ethnicity: Boundaries, deprivations, and perceptions. In J. M., Yinger & S. J. Cutler (Eds.), *Major social issues.* New York: Free Press.

Suls, J. M., Gastorf, J., & Lawhon, J. (1978). Social comparison choices for evaluating a sex- and age-related ability. *Personality and Social Psychology Bulletin, 4,* 102–105.

Suls, J. M., Martin, R., & Leventhal, H. (1997). Social comparison, lay referral, and the decision to seek medical care. In B. P. Buunk & F. X. Gibbons (Eds.), *Health, coping, and well-being: Perspectives from social comparison theory.* Mahwah, NJ: Lawrence Erlbaum.

Suls, J., & Wills, T. A. (Eds.), (1991). *Social comparison: Contemporary theory and research.* Hillsdale, NJ: Lawrence Erlbaum.

Tesser, A. (1986). Some effects of self-evaluation maintenance on cognition and action. In R. M. Sorrentino & E. T. Higgins (Eds.), *Handbook of motivation and cognition: Foundations of social behavior.* New York: Guilford.

Tesser, A. (1991). Emotion in social comparison and reflection processes. In J. Suls & T. A. Wills (Eds.), *Social comparison: Contemporary theory and research.* Hillsdale, NJ: Lawrence Erlbaum.

Walker, I., & Pettigrew, T. F. (1984). Relative deprivation theory: An overview and conceptual critique. *British Journal of Social Psychology, 23,* 301–310.

Wasserman, S. (1987). Conformity of two sociometric relations. *Psychometrika, 52,* 3–18.

Wasserman, S., & Faust, K. (1994). *Social network analysis.* Cambridge: Cambridge University Press.

Wellman, B., Carrington, P., & Hall, A. (1988). Networks as personal communities. In B. Wellman & S. Berkowitz (Eds.), *Social structures: A network approach* (pp. 130–184). Cambridge: Cambridge University Press.

Wheeler, L., & Miyake, K. (1992). Social comparison in everyday life. *Journal of Personality and Social Psychology, 62,* 760–773.

Wills, T. A., & Suls, J. (1991). Commentary: Neo-social comparison theory and beyond. J. Suls & T. A. Wills (Eds.), *Social comparison: Contemporary theory and research.* Hillsdale, NJ: Lawrence Erlbaum.

Wood, J. V. (1989). Theory and research concerning social comparisons of personal attributes. *Psychological Bulletin, 106,* 231–248.

Wood, J. V. (1996). What is social comparison and how should we study it? *Personality and Social Psychology Bulletin, 22,* 520–537.

Wood, J. V., & Taylor, K. L. (1991). Serving self-relevant goals through social comparison. In J. Suls & T. A. Wills (Eds.), *Social comparison: Contemporary theory and research.* Hillsdale, NJ: Lawrence Erlbaum.

Wooten, B. (1955). *The social foundations of wage policy.* New York: Norton.

Zanna, M. P., Goethals, G. R., & Hill, J. F. (1975). Evaluating a sex-related ability: Social comparison with similar others and standard setters. *Journal of Experimental Social Psychology, 11,* 86–93.

NINE

Japanese and American Reactions to Gender Discrimination

Matthew Crosby, Kazuho Ozawa, and Faye Crosby

You need not have majored in sociology or anthropology to know that there is no society on earth in which either opportunities or burdens are distributed evenly among its members. And, as any elementary text records, all societies develop distributional norms, some of which may be codified as law. On the basis of either ascribed statuses, like family, clan, or caste, or achieved statuses, like education and training, certain roles are reserved for some people while other roles are open to other people. Almost any society relies on both ascribed and achieved statuses to distribute goods and burdens, although different societies do so in different degrees.

The effect of established distributional norms is to keep people content even when they bear a large share of the burdens or receive a small share of the rewards. As long as the burdens and rewards appear not to be disproportionate according to some internalized set of criteria, people express little sense of grievance. That deprivations are felt relative to some standard, and not due to absolute situations, is, of course, the central tenet of relative deprivation theory (Crosby, 1976; Pettigrew, 1967; Runciman, 1966).

Societies are always changing their norms. Every extant culture is a "culture in transition." Because of interactions with other societies and because of ever-changing realities in the physical world, each society is constantly renegotiating what it sees as "normal" by way of how opportunities and burdens are divided among its population.

Japan's distributional rules are of great interest to contemporary Western observers. Ever since Detroit began to lose its market to Asian competitors, Americans have shown a curiosity bordering on obsession with Japan's economic affairs (Fingleton, 1995; LeFeber, 1996; Schaller, 1996). In Japan, meanwhile, a growing cadre of policy makers, commentators, and scholars have become interested in explaining their country to the West, exemplified in the body of work known as "Nihonjinron" (Johnson, 1995; Yoshino, 1992). Japan's economic recession has only heightened, not dampened, the cross-national fascination.

One aspect of Japan's norms that excites special interest among feminists and others is the role of gender in the distribution of economic opportunities, rewards, and burdens (Brinton, 1989, 1993; Condon, 1985; Iwao, 1993; National Women's Education Center, 1990). Traditionally, women have not had the chance to excel in high status positions and, until quite recently, women filled only very constrained roles in Japanese businesses (White, 1992; WuDunn, 1995a). Although some changes have occurred during the last decade or two, Japan is exhibiting some difficulty sustaining its movement toward gender equity during the current times of economic recession (Japan, 1995; Kristof, 1995; WuDunn, 1995b).

The primary aim of this chapter is to consider issues of gender equity in Japan in light of the concept of relative deprivation. First we review statistics on the current position of women in the Japanese paid labor force. Then we turn to a small study in which matched samples of American and Japanese college students reacted to an instance of sex discrimination. The choice of college students is intentional for they are the future professionals and managers in the United States and especially in Japan. We also explore some of the earlier research on relative deprivation as well as directions for the future. As expected, we find that both Japanese women and men are more forgiving of the discrimination than are American women and men. We conclude where we begin: with the concept of relative deprivation.

SEX DISCRIMINATION IN THE WORKPLACE IN JAPAN

Women workers in Japan enjoy both constitutional and statutory safeguards (Upham, 1987), but the safeguards are weak. The Japanese constitution states that "there shall be no discrimination in political, economic or social relations because of race, creed, sex, social status or family origin," and both Article 4 of the Labor Standards Act (1947) and the Equal Employment Opportunity Act (1985) also prohibit sex discrimination, but the language is precatory for there is no system of penalties.

Perhaps that is why women's wages lag behind men's. In 1992, the national averages for starting salaries for workers without college degrees were 186,900 yen per month for males and 180,100 for females. For graduates of four-year colleges, the gap was wider; males earned 370,400 yen per month, while females earned 251,100 (Science of Labour Research Institute, 1992). A survey conducted in 44 prefectures in March 1993 found that one in five employers admitted to discriminating in salary between women and men with the same qualifications. Asked about specific aspects, 21.5% replied that they discriminated in starting salary; 26.9% that they discriminated in family allowance payments; and 10.7% that they discriminated in terms of retirement money (Rodosho, 1993).

Even greater than wage discrimination is discrimination in terms of hiring, promotion, and retention. In 1992, 78% of men were in the paid labor force while only 50% of women were. Women managers and executives are rare in Japan, in part because the woman's place is still seen to be in the home. The 1993 Survey on Women revealed that 23.1% of those sampled excluded women from regular office work, and 20% from executive positions (Rodosho, 1993). In another survey, nearly half the employers felt that women lacked "the necessary knowledge, experience, and judgments" for management positions (Rodosho fujin kyoku, 1993). It is typical in Japan for women to be invited to enter a company with the expectation that they will leave at the time of their marriage. Later they may work as part-time employees with lower wages and no benefits (Rodosho fujin kyoku, 1993). That is why most women are denied job training given to men or are required to take special entrance tests from which men are exempt (Nihon fujin dantai rengokai, 1993). Sexism can also be seen in the phenomenon known as "hidden unemployment," which occurs when women want to work, but because of the difficulty of finding a job or discrimination in the workplace are forced to give up and get married. With so many women being counted as off the rolls of those who are actively seeking employment, there is a great discrepancy between the unemployment rate for women and the percentage rate for nonworking women. For 1992, the former was 2.2%, while the latter was 50.7%. In contrast, the unemployment rate for men was 2.1%, although 77.9% of men were employed.

The large numbers of female part-time workers in Japan is also evidence of how women are treated as an expendable labor commodity, as opposed to men who generally receive full-time employment for life. The predominately female part-time workforce in Japan has been called the "safety valve" of the Japanese economy. Part-time workers are paid less, are not entitled to benefits, and have contracts that can be terminated on very short notice. So, when there is a need for cheap labor, more part-time workers are hired, but when there is a downturn in economic climate, they are usually the first to be laid off (Science of Labor, 1992).

Antifemale discrimination may not exclusively be the result of the current economic climate, but may also reflect deep-rooted attitudes in Japanese society. For example, a 1982 survey shows that although that 73% of Japanese mothers aspire to university education for their sons, only 27.7% of that same sample aspired to university education for their daughters (Brinton, 1993). This lack of expectation may translate into a lack of ambition on the part of young women to enter a four-year university and pursue a high-level career. In the end, all these obstacles act as deterrents for the Japanese woman to gain an equal place in the workforce. It is a vicious cycle that discourages women from competition in the workforce. Although attitudes are slowly changing, there is clearly still a lot to be done to equalize the roles of men and women in the workplace.

REACTIONS TO INJUSTICE

Past research has shown that individuals often do not link their own personal situation with abstract categories. In the case of sex discrimination, although an individual may realize that sex discrimination does exist in the abstract, she may be reluctant to apply this information to her own case. In fact, in earlier studies, relative deprivation theory has accounted for a situation in which working women expressed low feelings of personal grievance even though they may be more or less outraged about the position of working women in general (Crosby, 1982). The separation of the group and the individual may also be seen in legislation, in which categorical measures or "quotas" are rejected due to a perceived lack of attention to individual circumstances.

The data presented here have been obtained in a cross-cultural study of reactions to affirmative action. The goal of the larger study was to determine whether the Japanese, being more collectivistic, would be more supportive than Americans of categorical remedies to documented instances of sex discrimination. Categorical remedies are those that slot people into different categories rather than considering each individual as a unique case. Before measuring the students' responses to proposed remedies, we also measured their responses to the problem itself that was an instance of sex discrimination. Those reactions form the focus of this chapter.

Methods

The experiment is described in detail elsewhere (Ozawa, Crosby, & Crosby, 1996). Suffice it here to note that our participants attended

Amherst College in Amherst, Massachusetts, and Doshisha University in Kyoto, Japan, and that the data were collected in the spring and fall of 1994. At both locations, students were approached by an older female student of their own nationality and asked if they would participate in a study. Thirty-five women students and 30 men students were approached at Doshisha, and all agreed to participate in the study. At Amherst 34 women students and 27 men students were approached, and all but six of the women and two of the men agreed to participate. We eliminated from the study students who had spent time in the other country, reducing the number of Japanese participants to 33 women and 25 men. The average ages of the Americans and of the Japanese were 19.0 years and 19.4 years, respectively.

The materials were presented to the students in their native language. The materials started by noting "we are interested in looking at how American and Japanese university students think about certain business practices that may occur in either country." Soon after came a description of an instance of sex discrimination. It read:

In normal years the Toba Company hires 500 new graduates from America's [Japan's] major universities to fill entry level management jobs. The economic recession has, however, caused serious problems for Toba. In 1992, they hired only 55 new graduates – just about one-tenth the normal amount. Fifty of those hired were men and 5 were women. Because the number of applicants for the available jobs was so great, the company was extremely selective in its hiring choices. A recent study of Toba's Division of Institutional Research (a division of the Human Relations department) revealed that 20 of the men who were hired had qualifications that were less impressive than those of women applicants who were not offered positions.

Respondents then rated their reactions using Likert scales for each of three questions. They indicated how they felt about what the Toba Company had done (Feelings); whether they felt the company had acted properly or improperly (Judgments); and whether they saw the company as unfair (Fairness). Feelings, Judgments, and Fairness were all measured on five-point scales, with a higher number indicating more upset or disapproval.

Next, students were asked to elaborate on their reactions. The verbatim answers from the Japanese participants were translated into English. All answers were then coded along two dimensions: Disapproval and Justice. To code for Disapproval, we rated the verbatim answers for the degree to which participants disapproved of what the Toba Company had done, with a 3 meaning total disapproval, and a 1 meaning total approval.

Equivocal answers earned a score of 2. We also rated the extent to which the answer was framed in terms of justice. A score of 3 meant that the answer was framed entirely or almost entirely in terms of what the students saw as just or fair or what they thought people deserved, and a score of 1 meant that the answer never touched on issues of justice, fairness, or deservingness. An answer that was partially framed in terms of justice, fairness, or deservingness was given a score of 2.

Twelve verbatim answers were coded by two independent raters and they agreed on both ratings 11 of 12 times.

Results

The Japanese and American participants did not differ from each other in the extent to which justice concerns predominated in how they framed their open-ended answers. The Japanese students did not, on average, frame their responses wholly in terms of justice concerns. Nor did they wholly ignore justice. On the three-point scale, their scores fell nearly at the midpoint. The average score of the Americans was virtually identical to that of the Japanese. The lack of national differences in the degree of preoccupation with justice issues in this data set is collaborated by other analyses of the same data set, reported elsewhere (Ozawa et al., 1996).

Nor did the women and men in either country differ from each other. Women were as likely as, but no more likely than, men to frame their open-ended responses to the case of sex discrimination in terms of justice. The lack of gender differences is consistent with other investigations of gender and morality (Crosby, 1991, ch. 5).

Although the devotion to justice did not differ according to gender or nationality, both nationality and gender were very important determinants of the degree to which participants saw as improper what the Toba Company had done. Women in both countries were more likely than their male counterparts to feel upset about the company's actions, to judge them improper, to classify them as unfair, and to disapprove of them. Gender differences emerged on all three variables measured by a rating scale (Feeling, Judgment, and Fairness) and on the Disapproval rating scored from the open-ended narratives. Tables 9.1, 9.2, 9.3, and 9.4, display the statistically reliable gender effects.

As noticeable as gender differences were national differences. American participants were significantly more likely than Japanese participants to feel that the Toba Company had acted poorly, to judge the actions improper, and to disapprove of them. Only the Fairness variable produced no reliable national differences.

Table 9.1. *Mean Feeling Scores by Gender and Nationality*

	Nationality	
Gender	Japanese	American
Women	4.0 (33)	4.6 (28)
Men	3.7 (25)	3.9 (25)

Notes: Scores are means, and can potentially range from 1 (no bad feeling about what the Toba Company did) to 5 (much bad feeling about what the Toba Company did). Numbers in parentheses show the number of participants per condition. There are main effects for Gender ($F = 10.87$; df = 1, 107; $p < .001$) and for Nationality ($F = 7.52$; df = 1, 107; $p < .007$). The interaction was not significant.

Looking at the tables, one can detect an interesting pattern: Japanese women and American men tend to be similar in their reactions. American women are the most upset about the gender discrimination; and Japanese men are the least upset. This presents a paradox of sorts: although statistically speaking, Japanese women appear to be worse-off in terms of equity income and other factors than women in America, Japanese women appear to express less of a sense of grievance about this fact.

Table 9.2. *Mean Judgment Scores by Gender and Nationality*

	Nationality	
Gender	Japanese	American
Women	3.8 (33)	4.4 (28)
Men	3.2 (25)	3.8 (25)

Notes: Scores are means, and can potentially range from 1 (the Toba Company did not act improperly) to 5 (the Toba Company did act properly). Numbers in parentheses show the number of participants per condition. There are main effects for Gender ($F = 10.25$; df = 1, 107; $p < .002$) and for Nationality ($F = 11.11$; df = 1, 107; $p < .001$). The interaction was not significant.

Table 9.3. *Mean Fairness Scores by Gender and Nationality*

Gender	Nationality	
	Japanese	American
Women	4.3 (33)	4.4 (28)
Men	4.1 (25)	3.9 (25)

Notes: Scores are means, and can potentially range from 1 (the Toba Company was fair) to 5 (the Toba Company was unfair). Numbers in parentheses show the number of participants per condition. There is a main effect for Gender ($F = 5.83$; df = 1, 107; $p < .02$), but not for Nationality. The interaction was not significant.

There are a number of ways in which this apparent anomaly can be explained. For example, the gap between statistics and attitude can be explained using past and present models of relative deprivation. In Crosby's 1976 model of relative deprivation, five necessary preconditions of relative deprivation are outlined. According to the model, for a person to experience relative deprivation, one must want X; feel entitled to X; see that someone else currently has X; think it feasible to obtain X; and have no sense of personal responsibility for not possessing X at present (Crosby, 1976). Later, an additional sixth factor of high past and low future expecta-

Table 9.4. *Mean Disapproval Scores by Gender and Nationality*

Gender	Nationality	
	Japanese	American
Women	2.3 (33)	2.7 (28)
Men	2.0 (25)	2.3 (25)

Notes: Scores were derived from verbatim transcripts, and can potentially range from 1 (no disapproval), through 2 (equivocation), to 3 (disapproval expressed). Numbers in parentheses show the number of participants per condition. There are main effects for Gender ($F = 8.78$; df = 1, 103; $p < .004$) and for Nationality ($F = 9.22$ df = 1, 107; $p < .003$). The interaction was not significant.

tions was added. If one examines the Japanese case in terms of preconditions for relative deprivation, the low level of outrage of Japanese women
compared to American women can be explained in terms of the absence of
feelings of feasibility and entitlement to equality in the workplace. As
Crosby noted, "to the extent that society tells Person that because of both
general and particular factors she can attain X, Person will believe that it is
feasible to attain X and will blame herself if she fails to do so" (Crosby,
1976, p. 91). In the Japanese case, until recently it would be fair to say that
the conditions for deprivation have not all been fulfilled.

After empirical testing, Crosby revised her model of relative deprivation and reduced the number of preconditions from five or six to two. The
new model predicts only wanting and deserving as the essential preconditions of relative deprivation. In this model, "to feel aggrieved about a situation, people must feel that there is a discrepancy between what they have
and what they want and a discrepancy between what they have and what
they deserve" (Crosby, 1982, p. 160). Although Crosby herself notes that
this is not a complete model, it does have one distinct advantage over previous, more complicated constructs – namely, a focus on wanting as the
most important precondition for deprivation. The advantage of placing
wanting at the center of relative deprivation theory is that it allows for the
influence of social and cultural factors on individual behavior, rather than
postulating universal cognitive structures.

Regarding equality in the workplace, Japanese women's attitudes may
be at least partly explained through an examination of the general societal
expectations for working women in Japan. A large-scale longitudinal
study conducted by NHK of approximately 5,000 Japanese participants
conducted at five-year intervals between 1973 and 1988 found that
although women's attitudes about work and home life have changed dras-
tically in the last 20 years, there are still large numbers of women and men
who believe that the woman's place is in the home (NHK yoron chosa bu,
1991). The NHK study asks respondents whether they believe that after
marriage the wife should concentrate on domestic duties, work until children are born, or continue to work even after children have been born. In
1973, only about 24% of women wished to continue work after the birth of
their children, but by 1988 the number had risen to 38%. Likewise, the percentage of men who gave the same response rose from 16% in 1973 to 28%
by 1988. However, although the percentage of Japanese favorably inclined
to working mothers is growing, these numbers still reveal that the majority of Japanese believe that the woman should continue to work only until
marriage or the birth of her children. It should come as no surprise that

attitudes such as these have a big impact on women's perception of what is fair and attainable in the workplace setting.

Through a similar examination of Japanese society, one could also argue that outrage against injustice in Japanese society has been muted by the increasing rise in the standard of living in the post war period that masks gender inequality. In 1988, over 85% of Japanese men and women felt themselves either "satisfied" or "somewhat satisfied" with their current standard of living. It is possible that the overall increase in income may have obscured any dissatisfaction.

These historical factors can be said to be some of the characteristics of postwar Japanese society. Although Japanese society is no more or less "unique" than any other, cross-cultural research highlights the importance of considerations of societal and cultural factors in addition to theoretical models. Models can tell us to what extent Japanese and Americans conceive of sex discrimination in terms of fairness and feeling. These models cannot, however, elucidate what determines these factors in the first place – how do Japanese conceive of "justice" and is this different from American respondents' ideas of justice? An even more fundamental question is how the Japanese and Americans perceive their own societies. Persistent myths of homogeneity may be more likely to prevent the simple division of Japanese society into "haves" and "have-nots" by Japanese respondents, while the ideal of individualism may lie behind some American feelings of resentment against obstacles to personal success. An understanding of these details cannot help enhancing existing models of relative deprivation.

THE IMPLICATIONS OF CROSS-CULTURAL RESEARCH

Cross-cultural research of the kind employed in this study has the potential for wide application that reaches beyond the field of psychology and relative deprivation research. As a method of prediction, relative deprivation may have limited use, but as Crosby, Muehrer, and Loewenstein (1986, p. 29) note, "if we think of relative deprivation as a concept, and not as a model, we may stop asking how well it predicts and start asking how well it explains."

Some of the uses of relative deprivation as a concept in political science, for example, were hinted at in Pettigrew's 1967 article, "Social Evaluation Theory: Convergences and Applications." In this article, Pettigrew cites Davies' model of revolution in which factors such as rising expectations and differences in living standards contribute to a general feeling of relative deprivation. Building on Pettigrew's observations, studies in a similar vein have continued to enrich the research on relative deprivation in a number of different ways. First, the introduction of interdisciplinary methods drawing from two or more disciplines has the potential for cross-fertilization and the opening of new fields of study. Second, within the theory of relative deprivation itself, Pettigrew signaled a shift from personal to group deprivation – a distinction that became increasingly important to explain large-scale protest (see chapters in this volume by Ellemers, Smith & Ortiz, Tougas & Beaton, and Wright & Tropp).

The latter point is especially pertinent to the field of political science and international relations, which is largely concerned with relations on an interstate or transnational level. The division between personal relative deprivation (dissatisfaction in relation to others within one's own group) and group relative deprivation (dissatisfaction with one's group in society) was originally used to explain different feelings of deprivation within a given society. Dubé and Guimond (1986) use "perception of intergroup equality" and "measure of group discontent" to explain Quebec nationalism, suggesting that identification with the group and its prospects are the most important factors in social protest. Given that the nation forms one significant nexus of group identification, it should be possible to apply relative deprivation theory not only to nationalist movements within societies, but also to nations and nationalism within the larger sphere of "international society." In the emerging discourse of globalism, relative deprivation may help to explain some of the problems that continue to plague world politics, such as the North/South divide, development, and trade friction.

WHAT IS AND WHAT OUGHT TO BE

Returning to the Japanese case, clearly the findings of our small study are consistent with the impression conveyed by our review of the position of women in the Japanese economy. Our data provide a good illustration of the relative insensitivity to gender issues in Japan as contrasted with the United States. From the numbers, it would seem that outrage or upset is a less probable response to sex discrimination in Japan than in the United States.

This impression is further strengthened if one looks at the actual paragraphs written by the Japanese and American participants after they learned of the Toba Company's hiring practices. Consider these statements articulated by the American participants:

If the statistics about the qualifications of the hired and unhired applicants are correct, the company's actions were unjustifiable and wrong. If under-qualified men were hired over qualified women, apparently on the basis of gender, this is blatant prejudice and an unfair hiring practice. (male)

or

It is stupid to hire men that are less qualified than women. There is nothing else to say. (female)

or

Employment positions should be offered to the person who is the most qualified, regardless of race, color, or gender. Anything less is an obvious example of discrimination. (female)

Such statements indicate an uncompromising stance in which sex discrimination is not to be tolerated.

Not all Americans were as categorical as the three just quoted. Said one American female, for example, at the end of her answer: "I would like to know the reasons behind their hiring procedures." Another participant pleaded that he needed "more info. to criticize or support their actions!" But rarely did an American provide an answer such as this one from a White male participant: "I support the sort of things the Toba Company did. Men are naturally more qualified to deal with the pressure of management positions."

In contrast to the generally unyielding responses of the American participants were the generally conciliatory responses of the Japanese respondents. Typical of the Japanese reactions are these:

It is not fair that it is not the most qualified people who were hired as a result of a supposedly very strict selection. However, in reality, it seems like people for management positions are not yet hired purely for their abilities, and so it might have been necessary for the company to take this kind of action in order to carry things on smoothly as a company. So although I can not say it was completely bad, it was definitely not good. (female).

and

The fact that the hiring standard was lower for men means that the abilities of women were not recognized, and that is bad and unfair. However, considering the above, the company's and society's demands must be included. And so Toba's actions can't be labeled good or bad. I would like to know why Toba doesn't want to employ women. (male).

The question arises: How well do responses on a paper and pencil questionnaire predict actual behavior? Should we expect, on the basis of the present study, that American women will prove least tolerant – in their actions – of sex discrimination while Japanese men will prove most tolerant? Is there not a vast literature that speaks to the lack of correspondence between attitudes, measured as we have done, and behaviors – especially when the attitudes concern prejudice (Crosby, Bromley, & Saxe, 1980)?

Although it would be foolhardy to attempt to predict the actions of any one individual in our study from her or his responses to our story of the Toba Company, it does make sense to expect that the four groups will, by and large, differ in their behaviors, on average, in a manner consistent with our results. In the United States, women have taken more of a lead than men in the battle against sex discrimination. It will be interesting to see whether the same will prove true in Japan.

If Japanese gender politics follow the same course as American gender politics, furthermore, we should expect to see Japanese women expressing the most distress over sex discrimination in the labor place at the very moment when their situation begins to improve (Crosby, 1982). Deprivations are not absolute, but rather are felt relative to some standard. As the standard changes, so do the feelings; and expectations have a way of rising faster than reality changes. Now that Japan is suffering economic anxiety, the women's movement is likely to lose ground. Not having gained sufficient momentum to sustain its forward thrust, the fledging movement for women's rights in Japan is likely to stall completely until the economy improves.

In the best of all possible academic worlds, we would revisit Amherst College and Doshisha University at five-year intervals. It would be instructive to chart the changing reactions to the kind of behavior performed by the Toba Company and described in our materials. More instructive still would be a plan to map the changes in the attitudes we measure on campus onto changes that occur in the wider societies. Every society is constantly in transition; and in a perfect world we could extend our small study into the future as a peephole through which to watch the changes.

ACKNOWLEDGMENTS

We would like to express our appreciation to Shinobu Kitayama, Rebecca Polasio, and especially Theodore Singelis for help with materials; to Elizabeth Aries, Meredith Howard, and Russell Weigel for help in data collection; to Julie Kmeic for her superb help in data management; and to Kristen Heydenberk for her general assistance. We are grateful to the Committee for Faculty Development at Smith College.

REFERENCES

Brinton, M. (1989). Gender stratification in contemporary urban Japan. *American Sociological Review, 54,* 549–564.

Brinton, M. (1993). *Women and the economic miracle: Gender and work in postwar Japan.* Berkeley: University of California Press.

Condon, J. (1985). *A half step behind.* New York: Dodd, Mead, and Co.

Crosby, F. J. (1976). A model of egoistical relative deprivation. *Psychological Review, 83,* 85–113.

Crosby, F. J. (1982). *Relative deprivation and working women.* New York: Oxford University Press.

Crosby, F. J. (1991). *Juggling: The unexpected advantages of combining work and home to women and their families.* New York: Free Press.

Crosby, F. J., Bromley, S., & Saxe, L. (1980). Recent unobtrusive studies of black and white discrimination and prejudice: A literature review. *Psychological Bulletin, 87,* 546–563.

Crosby, F. J., Muehrer, P., & Loewenstein, G. (1986). Relative deprivation and explanation: Models and concepts. In J. M. Olson, C. P. Herman, & M. P. Zanna (Eds.), *Relative deprivation and social comparison: The Ontario symposium* (Vol. 4, pp 17–32) Hillsdale, NJ: Lawrence Erlbaum.

Dubé, L., & Guimond, S. (1986). Relative deprivation and social protest: The personal-group issue. In J. M. Olson, C. P. Herman, & M. P. Zanna (Eds.), *Relative deprivation and social comparison: The Ontario symposium* (Vol. 4, pp 201–216). Hillsdale, NJ: Lawrence Erlbaum.

Fingleton, E. (1995). *Why Japan is still on track to overtake the U.S. by the year 2000.* Boston: Houghton Mifflin.

Iwao, S. (1993). *The Japanese woman.* New York: Free Press.

Japan. *Ms. Magazine.* January/February, 1995. p. 16.

Johnson, C. (1995). *Japan: Who governs?* New York: W.W. Norton.

Kristof, N. D. (1995, December 13). Japan's feminine falsetto falls right out of favor. *New York Times,* December 13.

LeFeber, W. (1996). *The clash: A history of U.S.-Japan relations.* New York: W.W. Norton.

National Women's Education Center. (1990). *Women in a changing society: The Japanese scene.* N.P.: UNESCO Women's Series.

NHK yoron chosa bu. (1991). *Gendai Nihonjin no ishiki kozo.* NHK Bukkusu.

Nihon fujin dantai rengokai. (Ed.), (1993). *Fujin hakusho 1993.* Tokyo: Harupu shuppan.

Ozawa, K., Crosby, M. M., & Crosby, F. J. (1996). Individualism and resistance to affirmative action: A comparison of Japanese and American samples. *Journal of Applied Social Psychology, 26,* 1138–1152.

Pettigrew, T. F. (1967). Social evaluation theory. In D. Levine (Ed.), *Nebraska symposium on motivation* (Vol. 15, pp. 241–311). Lincoln: University of Nebraska Press.

Rodo no kagaku 47(2). (1992). Kawasaki: Rodo kagaku kenkyujo.

Rodosho. (Ed.), (1993). *Rodo hakusho.* Tokyo: Okurasho.

Rodosho fujin kyoku. (Ed.), (1993). *Hataraku josei no jitsujo.* Tokyo: Okurasho.

Runciman, W. G. (1966). *Relative deprivation and social justice: A study of attitudes to social inequality in twentieth-century England.* Berkeley: University of California Press.

Schaller, M. (1996). *Altered states: The United States and Japan.* New York: Oxford University Press.

Upham, F. (1987). *Law and social change in postwar Japan.* Cambridge, MA: Harvard University Press.

White, M. (1992). Home truths: Women and social change in Japan. *Daedalus, 121*, 61–82.

WuDunn, S. (1995a). Many Japanese women are resisting servility. *New York Times.* July 9.

WuDunn, S. (1995b). In Japan, still getting tea and no sympathy. *New York Times.* August 27.

Yoshino, Kosaku. (1992). *Cultural nationalism in contemporary Japan: A sociological enquiry.* New York: Routledge.

TEN

Collective Action in Response to Disadvantage

Intergroup Perceptions, Social Identification, and Social Change

Stephen C. Wright and Linda R. Tropp

Between May and August 1981, ten Irish Republicans imprisoned in the H-Block of the Long Kesh prison in Northern Ireland starved to death in a hunger strike. Their demands were quite simple. They wanted to be recognized not as criminals, but rather as political prisoners. They wanted their cause to be recognized as a political cause and their actions – which the British government described only as criminal – to be recognized as political acts designed to achieve changes that they believed would improve the status and treatment of their group. Their protest rallied the support of much of the Catholic community in Northern Ireland and drew international attention and sympathy for the prisoners and their cause. However, Margaret Thatcher and the British government remained unmoved in their opposition to the prisoners' demands and each of the ten young men suffered a slow and painful death. Although the British government never admitted to having conceded to the demands of the hunger-strikers, many of the privileges normally granted only to political prisoners were subsequently given to other Irish Republicans in prisons in Northern Ireland. But more important perhaps, the Hunger Strike of 1981 remains a pivotal moment in conflict in Northern Ireland (see Feehan, 1983; Sands, 1981).

How can we explain the actions of Bobby Sands and his fellow prisoners? Although a complete answer to this question is certain to be complex and multifaceted, in this chapter we will consider some of what social psychology can contribute to that answer. We propose that one place to begin would be to consider the broader class of behavior to which this most dramatic of examples belongs: *collective action*. That is, we might consider the broader question of why a person might forgo his or her personal interests and choose instead to take actions designed to benefit the ingroup as a whole?

BRIEF BACKGROUND TO SOCIAL PSYCHOLOGICAL RESEARCH ON COLLECTIVE ACTION

Although collective action has been widely discussed in the literature, most of the social psychological research on intergroup relations has not studied collective action directly. Several of the models that dominated the social psychological study of intergroup relations in the 1960s, 1970s, and 1980s, such as Equity theory (Adams, 1965; Walster, Walster, & Berscheid, 1978), Distributive Justice theory (Homans, 1961) and Relative Deprivation theory (Crosby, 1976; Folger, 1986; Runciman, 1966; Stouffer, Suchman, DeVinney, Starr, & Williams, 1949; Walker & Pettigrew, 1984) did describe behavioral outcomes. Still, most of the research inspired by these theories failed to measure behaviors per se, but rather measured emotional and cognitive outcomes such as anger and resentment, feelings of satisfaction, and/or perceptions of justice (e.g., Austin & Walster, 1974; Bernstein & Crosby, 1980; Crosby 1982; deCarufel & Schopler, 1979; Dion, 1986; Folger & Martin, 1986; Folger, Rosenfield, & Robinson, 1983; Olson & Ross, 1984; Tripathi & Srivastava, 1981).

There are a number of potential explanations for this lack of attention to behavior. One culprit may be social psychology's predilection for laboratory research (see Kelly & Breinlinger, 1995; Reicher, 1996) and the difficulties in designing studies that can elicit and measure meaningful action in this research context. Another explanation may be the common assumption that frustration, anger, and moral outrage are the essential determinants of action (e.g., Brickman, Folger, Goode, & Schul, 1981; Crosby, 1976; Mark & Folger, 1984). The strength of this assumption is perhaps most clearly demonstrated in Kramnick's (1972) claim that research on perceived injustice was "obvious and trite, for surely only angry men turn to revolution" (p. 56). The underlying assumption of a rather simple linear relationship between strong emotional reactions and collective action may have reduced efforts to focus directly on the more difficult task of measuring action.

Whatever the causes of social psychology's lack of attention to action, the result has been that, until recently, the study of collective action had been left primarily to sociology. And, unfortunately for social psychology, the dominant sociological perspectives during the 1970s and 1980s all but dismissed psychological variables as irrelevant for understanding collective action participation. The resource mobilization approach (e.g., McCarthy &

Zald, 1977) held that structural and organizational variables determine the likelihood of collective action, and that incorporating psychological variables would not add to the explanatory power of models predicting disadvantaged group behavior. Although sociological perspectives have since expanded to include more psychological concepts (see Gamson, 1992; McAdam, McGarthy, & Zald, 1996; Snow & Benford, 1992), the mainstream of social psychology has made few contributions to this discussion.

Fortunately, we now find ourselves in the midst of a revitalization of the social psychology of collective action. Tajfel and his colleagues' (Tajfel, 1978a; Tajfel & Turner, 1979) Social Identity Theory (SIT) has formed the basis for a new perspective on groups and intergroup relations. This perspective has dominated European and Australian social psychology for the last two decades, and in the late 1990s has arguably achieved a similar position in North American psychology of groups and intergroup relations. The general concept of "social identity" and the fresh perspective on the self that SIT implied has spawned a number of broader models of identity, the most influential of which has been Self-Categorization Theory (Turner, Hogg, Oakes, Reicher, & Wetherell, 1987). However, it is only recently that significant research efforts have concentrated on the specific behavioral outcomes associated with disadvantaged group membership that were so central to the initial model. In addition, Tajfel and Turner's (1979) initial model is being strengthened by emerging perspectives in sociology and more traditional theories of intergroup relations, such as relative deprivation theory and equity theory (see Ellemers, 1993; Hinkle, Fox-Cardamone, Haseleu, Brown, & Irwin, 1996; Kawakami & Dion, 1995; Kelly & Breinlinger, 1996; Klandermans, 1997; Simon, 1998). Creative laboratory investigations and recent field research have tested, and in some cases integrated, aspects of these theoretical perspectives (e.g., Foster & Matheson, 1999; Kawakami & Dion, 1993; Petta & Walker, 1992; Simon et al., 1998; Smith, Spears, & Oyen, 1994), igniting a new interest in the social psychological underpinnings of collective action. In this chapter, we follow in the tradition of these new approaches by considering the social psychological determinants of collective action, with special attention to members of societally disadvantaged groups.

DEFINING COLLECTIVE ACTION

The term "collective action" has been used in a variety of ways and, of course, the definition that one chooses has important implications for any analysis of its determinants. We take a decidedly psychological perspective, defining collective action in terms of the intentions and perceptions of the actors. *A group member engages in collective action any time that she or he is acting as a representative of the group and where the action is directed at improving the conditions of the group as a whole* (Wright, Taylor, & Moghaddam, 1990a). This definition follows directly from Tajfel's (1978a) distinction between interpersonal and intergroup behavior; where interpersonal behavior occurs in interactions between individuals acting on the basis of their unique personal identities and intergroup behavior occurs when the individual's behavior is guided by his or her social identities. Thus, collective action is intergroup behavior because it involves the individual's response as guided by his or her self-representation as a member of a particular group. However, it is a specific case of intergroup behavior, because it is also strategic in that it is intended to improve the status or treatment of the relevant ingroup.

This definition is perhaps best understood by contrasting collective action with alternative responses. Rather than acting to promote the ingroup's interests, group members could choose behaviors designed to improve their personal situation; in other words, they could take *individual action*. In this case, the actor focuses on his or her personal situation and takes actions that distance him or her from the ingroup's disadvantaged position, while improving his or her chances of acquiring a more advantaged position. This distinction between individual action and collective action is consistent with the distinction made in SIT between an "individual mobility" and a "social change" orientation. Tajfel and Turner (1979) proposed that members of low status groups could either attempt to leave their group in favor of a higher status outgroup (individual mobility), or they could attempt to raise the relative status of their disadvantaged ingroup (social change). Thus, in terms of action, the individual–collective distinction depends on whether the intended beneficiary of the desired change in status or treatment is the individual or the ingroup as a whole (see also Branscombe & Ellemers, 1998; Ellemers, 1993; Hogg & Abrams, 1988).

Collective action can be taken by members of any group. Members of relatively advantaged groups can and do engage in actions designed to maintain and enhance the status of their group. They construct discriminatory barriers to protect the privileged position of their ingroup (e.g., Gardner, 1972), and build social institutions that legitimate oppression and even violence against disadvantaged groups (Jackman, 1998). In some cases, individual acts of discrimination can represent efforts to substantiate and maintain the ingroup's higher status position (Sachdev & Bourhis, 1991). However, most of the theorizing and research on collective action has focused on members of societally disadvantaged groups. In this case, there is a third interesting alternative to individual or collective action – *inaction*. Disadvantaged group members can take no action to improve either their individual or collective position. It is important to recognize that inaction can be associated with a wide range of cognitive and affective experiences. In addition to willing acceptance of one's group's position, inaction can also accompany feelings of resentment, dissatisfaction, anger, frustration, and outrage, as well as stress symptoms, depression, and resignation (see Crosby, 1976; Mark & Folger, 1984; Olson, Herman, & Zanna, 1986; Walker & Pettigrew, 1984). Equity theory (Adams, 1965; Tyler, Boeckmann, Smith, & Huo, 1997), for example, recognizes that feelings of inequity can be restored either by direct action or by altering one's perceptions of the situation in the absence of action. Similarly, SIT outlines a set of psychological strategies designed to enhance the *perceived* status of the ingroup while not directly affecting the group's actual status. These were labeled "social creativity" (Tajfel & Turner, 1979) and included strategies such as seeking new dimensions for intergroup comparisons, focusing on social comparisons with an even more disadvantaged outgroup, and enhancing the salience of an alternative group categorization (see also Lemaine, 1974; Mummendey & Simon, 1989). In short, inaction can be associated with a variety of cognitive and affective reactions, ranging from passive acceptance of the ingroup's low status position, to efforts to revise one's understanding of the ingroup's status, to hopeful patience that the ingroup's situation will soon improve, to angry resignation. Nonetheless, in and of themselves, these responses do not involve actual, overt behaviors and thus the outcome is very likely to be little change in the relative position of the individual and the ingroup.

THE ROAD TO COLLECTIVE ACTION

The present chapter outlines a set of psychological processes that can enhance or diminish the likelihood that group members will engage in collective action. These include: (a) the individual's self-representations as group members and his or her level of ingroup identification, (b) social comparisons with other groups in the social structure, (c) assessments of the permeability of intergroup boundaries, and (d) perceptions of the legitimacy and stability of the intergroup context.

Self-Representation: Recognizing Oneself as a Member of a Social Category

It is obvious that in order to engage in collective action the individual must recognize his or her membership in the relevant group. Thus, a psychological analysis of collective action might logically begin by considering what will lead people to think of themselves as members of a social category, and when that category membership will serve as the foundation for thought and action. Basic to this question is the distinction, alluded to earlier, between one's personal identity and one's social identity; where one's personal identity includes those attributes that make one unique and distinct from others, and one's social identity involves those aspects of the self that connect one to others through group memberships. The distinction between personal and social aspects of the self is a cornerstone of SIT (Tajfel & Turner, 1979), Self-Categorization Theory (Turner et al., 1987), and other theoretical accounts on the self (Brewer, 1991; Brewer & Gardner, 1996; Sedikides & Brewer, in press; Taylor & Dube, 1986). When personal identities are salient within a given social context, people will be more likely to think and act as unique individuals. In contrast, when social identities are salient, a process of *depersonalization* occurs, wherein individuals perceive themselves less as individuals and more as representatives of the relevant social category (Turner et al., 1987). The first roots of collective action are found in these salient social identities, in that individuals who recognize their membership in a social group and act as representatives of that group are more likely to engage in action intended to benefit the group.

Each of us belongs to a large number of groups and, thus, there are many different social identities that can attract our self-representation at a given time. As such, it is necessary to consider how specific group memberships become the salient aspects of individuals' self-conceptions. Broadly speaking, Tajfel's (1978a) conceptualization of social identity stated that the salience of a given group membership rests upon two factors: (1) immediate situational and contextual cues that focus the individual's attention on the group membership, and (2) the psychological salience of that group membership for the individual. Self-categorization theorists expanded on Tajfel's ideas by proposing an "accessibility × fit" formulation of self-categorization processes (see Oakes, Haslam, & Turner, 1994, for a review). According to this perspective, self-categorization occurs as a result of the interaction between the perceived relevance or appropriateness of a categorization within a given situation ("fit") and the individual's preparedness to refer to oneself in terms of the social category ("accessibility").

Fit: Situational Salience of Group Identity. Many factors can enhance the situational salience of a particular group categorization for the individual. The power of local contextual cues to evoke collective self-representations has been reviewed extensively by self-categorization theorists (see Oakes et al., 1994; Turner et al., 1987). For example, if a group membership is distinctive, such as when the group is underrepresented and/or physically different from others in a given context, the relevant category distinction will become more salient (e.g., Lord & Saenz, 1985; Taylor, Fiske, Etcoff, & Ruderman, 1978).

Accessibility: Psychological Salience of Group Identity. At the same time, when entering a given social context, a given group categorization may be more *psychologically* salient for some individuals than for others. Group categorizations will be more readily accessible as a dominant self-representation to the extent that they have proven useful or relevant across past social experiences and interactions. Increased accessibility of a category can result from frequent or repeated use of that category (Bargh, Lombardi, & Higgins, 1988; Macrae, Bodenhausen, & Milne, 1995) over a history of accumulated social experiences. Thus, representation of one's group in the broader society can impact the salience of a category, such that the group membership is more salient for members of minority groups who have grown accustomed to being perceived as different (Brewer, 1991; Mullen, 1991), oftentimes regardless of their actual numerical representation in the given context.

The notion of accessibility may be particularly useful for understanding self-categorizations associated with membership in a disadvantaged group. For members of disadvantaged groups, group membership is likely to play a prominent role in many social interactions with others (see Goffman, 1963). Disadvantaged group members are readily aware of biases against their group, and may feel that they are being evaluated on the basis of their group membership (Crocker & Major, 1989; Frable, 1993; Jones et al., 1984). In turn, members of disadvantaged groups may approach social situations with a preconceived awareness of their group membership, along with anticipation of how they will be treated due to that membership (see Crocker, Major, & Steele, 1998).

A research example can demonstrate the dual importance of accessibility and situational salience for individuals' self-conceptions. McGuire, McGuire, Child, and Fujioka (1978) assessed "spontaneous" self-concepts (i.e., self-generated identity attributes) among White, Black, and Hispanic students. The authors found that 17% of the Black and 14% of the Hispanic students mentioned ethnicity as part of their self-descriptions, as compared with only 1% of the White population of students. These results suggest that, due to a history of experiences across a variety of contexts, "ethnicity" had become a more accessible category for self-definition among ethnic minority students. At the same time, McGuire et al. (1978) also discovered that White students from more ethnically diverse class-rooms were more likely to include ethnicity in their spontaneous self-descriptions than White students in more homogeneous, predominantly White classrooms. This additional finding reveals that, even among members of the majority group, contextual influences can make ethnicity a rel-atively more accessible construct for self-definition.

Ingroup Identification. Much of the theorizing on accessibility has fol-lowed a largely cognitive approach, emphasizing the frequency with which particular group memberships are recognized and salient in social situations. At the same time, however, social identities are valued by indi-viduals – and are therefore significant for individuals' self-conceptions – beyond their repeated salience in social situations. Indeed, Tajfel (1981) stated that social identity derives from *both* people's "knowledge of their membership in a social group (or groups) together with the value and emotional significance of that membership" (p. 255). The strength of these feelings toward one's group has been discussed in terms of *ingroup identi-fication.* Group identification has generally been regarded as the personal importance that a particular group membership holds for the individual (see Ellemers, this volume; Ellemers, Spears, & Doosje, 1997; Tajfel, 1981), or the psychological attachment that individuals feel toward their groups (Lau, 1989). We define group identification as the individual's psychologi-cal connection with a group, based on the significance that the group membership holds for one's sense of self – that is, the extent to which the ingroup is "included" as part of the self (see Tropp & Wright, in press).

It appears increasingly clear that identification with the ingroup is an important factor in the prediction of collective action. Research from a social identity perspective has shown that, even among members of disad-vantaged groups, individuals with high levels of ingroup identification are more committed to the ingroup (Ellemers et al., 1997) and desire more for their ingroup (Tropp & Wright, 1999; Wann & Branscombe, 1995) than individuals with lower levels of ingroup identification. Further, evidence for the association between ingroup identification and collective action has been found in research on pro and anti-abortion lobbies (Hinkle et al., 1996), union participation (Kelly & Kelly, 1994), participation in the women's movement (Kelly & Breinlinger, 1995), participation in the gay movement in the United States. (Simon et al., 1998, Study 2), and in research on laboratory-created groups (see Branscombe & Ellemers, 1998;

Ellemers et al., 1997). In the words of Doosje and Ellemers (1997), "'die-hard' members (i.e., those people who identify strongly with their group) are more predisposed to act in terms of the group, and make sacrifices for it, than are 'fair-weather' members" (p. 358).

Determining the Position of the Ingroup Within an Intergroup Context: Social Comparisons

An individual's self-representation as a group member and feelings of identification with that group constitute only the foundation for collective action. Individuals' thoughts and feelings about their groups do not occur in a vacuum; rather, they occur within a context in which other groups exist, and where the social position and attributes of one's group can be compared to those of others. Indeed, status (whether one's own or that of one's group) is interpreted and evaluated through the process of social comparison (Major, 1994; Pettigrew, 1967) and the perceived status of the ingroup in the broader social structure plays a pivotal role on the road to collective action. Therefore, we will turn our attention to the role of social comparison in creating perceptions of disadvantage and the recognition that the disadvantage is collective in nature.

Perception of Disadvantage. Clearly, one factor associated with interest in action should be whether a social comparison results in a sense of disadvantage relative to the comparison target. Research inspired by Relative Deprivation Theory has focused extensively on this topic (see Olson et al., 1986; Tyler et al., 1997). Relative deprivation has been defined as one's sense of deprivation in comparisons with other individuals or social groups (Runciman, 1966). In particular, relative deprivation research has focused on feelings of deprivation among members of disadvantaged groups, which result from comparisons with relatively advantaged individuals or groups (Vanneman & Pettigrew, 1972; Walker & Pettigrew, 1984). Rather than necessarily reflecting objective circumstances, these feelings of deprivation stem from individuals' subjective assessments of their own situation, in relation to the perceived situation of the target of their social comparisons (Taylor & Moghaddam, 1994).

Recognition of Disadvantage on a Collective Level. Runciman (1966) established an important theoretical distinction between personal (egois-tic) deprivation, which develops from comparisons between oneself and more advantaged individuals, and group (fraternal) deprivation, which results from comparisons between one's ingroup and more advantaged outgroups. Recent attempts to link ideas from Social Identity Theory and Relative Deprivation Theory have considered the connections between the level of self-representation (personal or social identities) and the types of social comparisons that will be made and, thus, the type of relative deprivation that will result (e.g., Ellemers, this volume; Smith & Ortiz, this volume; Smith et al., 1994). Social identity and self-categorization theories propose that when group membership is salient, attention is focused on collective outcomes and the status of the group, rather than on one's own personal outcomes or status (see Hogg & Abrams, 1988; Tajfel, 1981). Salient group identities would, therefore, lead individuals to engage in intergroup comparisons, which can result in greater feelings of group deprivation (see Kawakami & Dion, 1993, for an extended discussion).

Research has also suggested that people who are highly identified with the ingroup report greater levels of group deprivation than people who are less strongly identified with the group (Abrams, 1990; Petta & Walker, 1992; Tropp & Wright, 1999). For example, in a study of Italian immigrants in Australia, Petta and Walker (1992) found that identification with the ethnic ingroup was most strongly associated with perceptions of group deprivation, while only weakly associated with personal deprivation. It appears that recognition that the ingroup holds a relatively disadvantaged position leads to stronger feelings of deprivation for individuals for whom that group membership is more central to their self.

Ingroup Identification, Relative Deprivation, and Multiple Targets of Social Comparison

Our own research (Tropp & Wright, 1999) confirms this association between strength of ingroup identification and reports of relative deprivation among disadvantaged groups members. However, we have also considered another thorny question in the relevant social comparison literature: how to deal with the issue of multiple targets of social comparison. Not only can the disadvantaged group member make either personal or group-level comparisons, but within most social contexts there is more than one available outgroup that can serve as a target of comparison (see Taylor & Moghaddam, 1994). Clearly, which of these outgroups becomes the active target of social comparison will have a major impact on the strength of one's feelings of deprivation (either personal or group). More specifically, the relative status of the target may be particularly relevant (Walker & Pettigrew, 1984). One is likely to perceive more deprivation as a result of comparisons with a more advantaged target, and less when comparing to a target that is similar to the ingroup (Crosby, 1982). As a first effort to link the concepts of ingroup identification, group versus personal relative deprivation, and multiple targets of social comparison, we selected a sample of high and low identifiers from two traditionally disadvantaged groups in the United States (Latinos and African Americans).

Based on their scores on a measure of ethnic identification, participants were initially classified as either high-identifiers (top 40% of respondents) or low-identifiers (bottom 40% of respondents). Latino(a) and African-American respondents answered a series of relative deprivation items that directed them to make five separate social comparisons: two group-level comparisons and three personal-level comparisons. They were asked to consider the position of their ethnic group: (a) compared to other disadvantaged groups ("other minorities"), and (b) compared to a clearly advantaged outgroup ("Whites"). They were also asked to consider their own personal situation: (a) compared to other members of their own ethnic group, (b) compared to members of other disadvantaged groups minority groups ("other minorities"), and (c) compared to members of a clearly advantaged outgroup ("Whites").

Separate analyses were conducted for responses regarding group-level deprivation and personal deprivation. In terms of group-level relative deprivation, compared to low-identifiers, high-identifiers reported significantly greater personal and group deprivation. However, reports of deprivation varied depending on the target of social comparison, such that respondents reported significantly more deprivation in comparisons with Whites than in comparisons with other minorities. Further, these two main effects were qualified by a significant Ingroup Identification × Comparison Target interaction. Specifically, while high-identifiers reported more deprivation than low-identifiers in comparisons with other minorities; this difference between high- and low-identifiers was even greater in comparisons with Whites (see Figure 10.1).

A similar pattern was found for the personal-level comparisons. The difference between high-identifiers and low-identifiers was small for comparisons with other ingroup members; both high and low identifiers were satisfied with their personal situation relative to ingroup members. However, high-identifiers were significantly less satisfied than low-identifiers with their personal position relative to members of other minority groups. When the comparison target was Whites, the difference between high-identifiers and low-identifiers became even larger, with high-identifiers indicating clear feelings of personal deprivation (see Figure 10.2).

These findings provide support for the importance of both ingroup identification and the target of social comparison in determining the psy-

deprivation

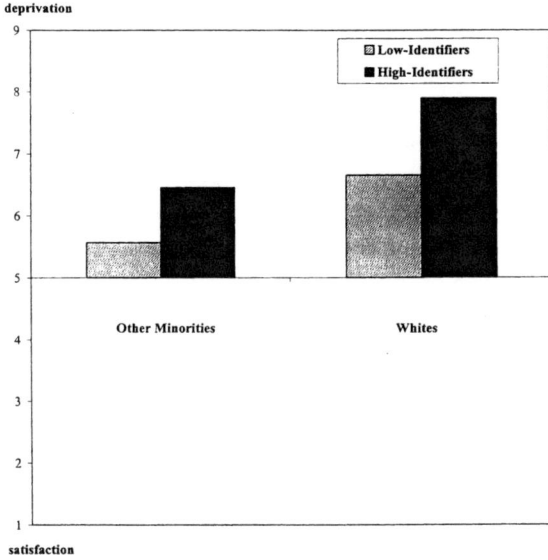

Figure 10.1. Assessments of collective (group-level) relative deprivation among high- and low-identifiers, in comparisons with other minorities, and Whites.

deprivation

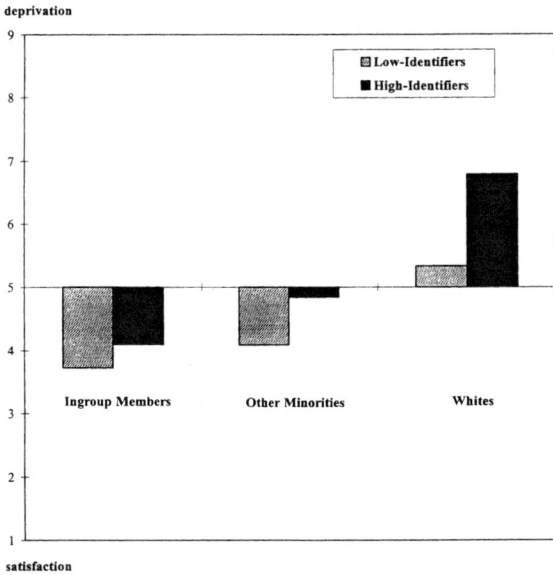

Figure 10.2. Assessments of personal (individual-level) relative deprivation among high- and low-identifiers, in comparisons with ingroup members, other minorities, and Whites.

chological outcomes of membership in a disadvantaged group. More
specifically, high identification with the ingroup and comparison to a
clearly advantaged outgroup (in this case, Whites) combined to produce
the strongest feelings of group-level and personal-level relative deprivation. These findings become important for our discussion of collective
action when we consider that other research has shown that feelings of
collective deprivation can serve as an initial impetus for action directed at
changing the status and outcomes of the ingroup. Feelings of group deprivation have been connected to perceptions of social injustice (Martin, 1986;
Vanneman & Pettigrew, 1972), as well as support for separatist and nationalistic attitudes (Abrams, 1990; Guimond & Dube-Simard, 1983), social
protest (Birt & Dion, 1987; Walker & Mann, 1987), and programs that can
enhance the welfare of one's group (Tougas & Beaton, this volume; Tougas
& Veilleux, 1988). For example, in a longitudinal study, Abrams (1990)
examined causal relationships between ingroup identification, relative
deprivation, and support for nationalism among Scottish youth. His findings showed that ingroup identification was a significant predictor of
group deprivation and, in turn, these two factors predicted nationalistic
attitudes. Similarly, Tougas and Veilleux (1988), in a study involving a
diverse sample of women, found that support for affirmative action (a
program designed to enhance the opportunities of women) was associated
both with higher identification with the ingroup (women) and feelings of
relative deprivation associated with a comparison between men and
women. In summary, we would predict that it will be those individuals
who identify strongly with their ingroup and who make group-level social
comparisons with more advantaged outgroups that will feel the most relatively deprived and will be most likely to support collective strategies for
social change.

*Extending the Prediction of Collective Action: Emphasizing the
Intergroup Relationship.* Although high levels of ingroup identification
and strong feelings of group-level relative deprivation may provide the
foundation, our approach proposes that we consider other psychological
processes on the road to collective action. It may be more than the relative
advantage or disadvantage of the comparison target that propels individuals to support collective strategies for social change. Additionally, it may
be the particular *intergroup relationship* that surrounds the status difference between the groups (see Wright, 1997; in press-a). Our research on
Latinos and African Americans (Tropp & Wright, 1999) provides an illustrative example. For both groups of respondents, group-level compar-

isons to Whites lead to clear feelings of collective relative deprivation. Comparisons to other minorities also led to significant, albeit lower, feelings of collective deprivation. However, these two social comparisons may differ in more than just the magnitude of the relative advantage of the comparison outgroup. Social comparisons with Whites may represent a comparison with the *dominant* group in the status hierarchy; the group that is seen to be responsible for the subordinate status of the ingroup; the group that maintains and supports the status quo; the group that is perceived to have a greater degree of control over and access to resources and higher status positions (see Sidanius & Pratto, 1993). Thus, it may be that in order for collective action to be undertaken, in addition to perceiving one's group as relatively disadvantaged (relatively deprived), the target of comparison must be understood to have had some agency in creating or maintaining the group status hierarchy. As such, support for collective action should be related specifically to feelings of deprivation relative to a *dominant* outgroup. This view is consistent with those who have argued that collective action requires the isolation of a particular villain (i.e., the "they" that is set in contrast to the "we") to whom blame for the ingroup's disadvantaged position can be attributed (see Gamson, 1992; Klandermans, 1997; Snow & Benford, 1992).

This position would lead to the prediction that reports of deprivation in comparisons with a dominant group would predict interest in collective action, while deprivation resulting from comparisons with members of other nondominant outgroups would not. To test this hypothesis, we used regression analyses to determine how well ingroup identification and feelings of relative deprivation associated with group-level and personal-level social comparisons with the dominant outgroup (Whites) and other non-dominant outgroups (other minorities) could predict Latino and African American respondents' support for collective action (Tropp & Wright, in press).

We also considered the distinction between cognitive and affective components of relative deprivation: where the cognitive component represents an individual's *perceptions* of deprivation, and the affective component reflects the individual's *emotional responses* to the deprivation they perceive (see Walker & Pettigrew, 1984). There is some evidence that it may be the affective component rather than the cognitive component that best predicts attitudes and behaviors associated with collective action (e.g., Guimond & Dube-Simard, 1983; Smith & Pettigrew, 2001; Tougas & Veilleux, 1988). In other words, the perception of inequality alone may not be sufficient to encourage collective action. Rather, it is the anger, resentment, or dissatisfaction that can result from that perception that serves as a driving force behind collective action. Thus, we predicted that the affective component of group-level relative deprivation associated with comparisons with the dominant outgroup (Whites) and ingroup identification should be the two primary (perhaps only) predictors of support for collective action.

Predicting Collective Action: Ingroup Identification, Target of Comparison, Affective and Cognitive Relative Deprivation. Ingroup identification was assessed using a standardized, composite measure, which combined items from several different identity scales (e.g., Cheek, Tropp, Chen, & Underwood, 1994; Luhtanen & Crocker, 1992; Tropp & Wright, in press). Possible scores ranged between 1 and 7, with greater values indicating higher levels of ingroup identification.

Relative deprivation (RD) was assessed using four social comparisons. Two group-level measures asked respondents to make social comparisons: (a) between their ethnic ingroup and other disadvantaged groups (other minorities), and (b) between their ethnic ingroup and the dominant outgroup (Whites). Two personal-level items asked respondents to make social comparisons: (a) between their personal situation and that of members of other disadvantaged groups (other minorities); and (c) between their personal situation and that of members of the dominant outgroup (Whites).

For each of the five comparison targets, two items were included. The first assessed the cognitive component (perception) of RD ("Would you say that you are [your ethnic group is] better off or worse off than ..."), and the second assessed the affective component (emotional responses) of RD ("How angry or satisfied are you about your [ethnic group's] situation relative to..."). For each item, possible scores ranged between 1 and 9, with higher values corresponding to greater reports of deprivation.

Support for collective action was measured with a single item ("Members of our ethnic group must stick together and work as a group to change the position of all the members of the group"). Respondents were asked the extent to which they endorsed the item on a 9-point scale, where higher scores corresponded to stronger support for collective action.

Correlations were conducted between support for collective action and each of the ingroup identification and RD measures (Ns ranging from 295 to 301). Results from these analyses indicated that ingroup identification and most of the RD measures were significantly correlated with support for collective action (see Table 10.1). Overall, greater support for collective action was associated with higher levels of ingroup identification, and greater per-

Table 10.1. *Correlations between Support for Collective Action and Measures of Ingroup Identification and Relative Deprivation*

	Support for Collective Action
Ingroup identification	.32***
Other minorities	
Personal RD – cognitive	.10^
Personal RD – affective	.16**
Group RD – cognitive	.28***
Group RD – affective	.28***
Whites	
Personal RD – cognitive	.29***
Personal RD – affective	.23***
Group RD – cognitive	.40***
Group RD – affective	.48***

$^p < .10$ $*p < .05$ $**p < .01$ $***p < .001$

sonal and group deprivation in comparisons with both other minorities and Whites. As shown in Table 10.1, support for collective action was most strongly related to group deprivation in comparisons with Whites and least related to personal deprivation in comparisons with other minorities.

A standard regression analysis (N = 279) was conducted using the ingroup identification and the eight RD measures as predictors of support for collective action (see Table 10.2). The overall model was significant, R^2 = .28, $F(9,269)$ = 11.48, $p < .001$. As can be seen in Table 10.2, only two measures uniquely accounted for a significant portion of the variance in support for collective action: Ingroup Identification and Affective Group RD in comparison with Whites.

Additionally, a hierarchical regression analysis was conducted to examine whether Ingroup Identification and Affective Group RD in comparisons with Whites would account for a significant portion of the variance after the other predictor variables were entered into the model. At the first stage, the seven remaining predictor variables were entered into the model. The model was significant at this stage, $F(7,271)$ = 8.38, $p < .001$, accounting for 18% of the variance in support for collective action. At this stage, only the Cognitive Group RD item regarding comparisons with Whites accounted for a significant portion of variance in support for collective action (Beta = .27, sr = .20, t = 3.58, $p < .001$). At the second

Table 10.2. *Summary of Standard Regression Analysis Using Ingroup Identification and Relative Deprivation Measures as Predictors of Support for Collective Action*

	B	Beta	r	sr	t
Ingroup identification	.33	.20	.34	.18	3.54***
Other minorities					
Personal RD – cognitive	−.01	−.01	.10	−.01	−.15
Personal RD – affective	.01	.01	.15	.01	.23
Group RD – cognitive	.10	.09	.27	.07	1.31
Group RD – affective	−.07	−.06	.29	−.04	−.79
Whites					
Personal RD – cognitive	.06	.07	.29	.04	.84
Personal RD – affective	−.04	−.05	.23	−.04	−.73
Group RD – cognitive	.03	.03	.39	.02	.30
Group RD – affective	.44	.38	.48	.23	4.35***

* $p < .05$ ** $p < .01$ *** $p < .001$

stage, Ingroup Identification and the Affective Group RD in comparison with Whites were added to the model. The full model accounted for 28% of the variance in support for collective action, demonstrating a significant increase in the amount of variance accounted for beyond that predicted by the seven other predictor variables (R^2 change = .10, F change = 18.53, $p < .001$).

Conclusions and Summary. Generally, these results indicate that ingroup identification and relative deprivation both contribute substantially to the prediction of support for collective action. However, beyond this, three more specific conclusions can be drawn regarding the relationships between relative deprivation and support for collective action. First, group deprivation, and not personal deprivation, predicts support for collective action. These findings are consistent with previous findings (e.g., Abrams, 1990; Birt & Dion, 1987; Walker & Mann, 1987). In addition, although cognitive and affective components of collective RD are both correlated with support for collective action, the cognitive component accounts for virtually no unique variance beyond that accounted for by the affective component. The prominence of affective over cognitive RD in predicting collective action is also consistent with previous research (e.g., Guimond & Dube-Simard, 1983; Smith & Pettigrew, 2001; Tougas & Veilleux, 1988).

Finally, and perhaps most interestingly, group deprivation that results from comparisons with a dominant outgroup (in this case, Whites) is a strong predictor of support for collective action, while group deprivation resulting from comparisons with other disadvantaged outgroups (other minorities) adds virtually no predictive power. This may result, in part, because people generally feel more deprived in comparisons to the dominant target. However, it is also consistent with the prediction that comparison with the dominant group is the most appropriate comparison for determining the need for social change. It may be that only when relative deprivation involves comparisons with the agent of the intergroup inequality – the group responsible for the present status hierarchy – that collective action will be perceived as the appropriate response.

Individual Mobility or Social Change: Assessing Boundary Permeability

For the most part, we have been considering psychological processes that have focused on the individual and his or her relationship with the relevant ingroup and how these contribute to interest in collective change – processes such as self-representations and identification with the ingroup, perceptions of collective disadvantage, and feelings of deprivation. However, in describing the importance of social comparisons with a *dominant* outgroup (as opposed to other outgroups that might hold a more advantaged position), we have also alluded to the importance of the individual's understanding and interpretation of the existing social structure as a crucial determinant of participation in collective action. How the individual evaluates the structural relationship between the relevant groups will play a pivotal role in his or her subsequent behavior. Social Identity theory (Tajfel & Turner, 1979; see also Hogg & Abrams, 1988) has pointed to three important assessments: (a) the permeability of the intergroup boundaries (i.e., can the individual move from the lower to higher status group?); (b) the stability of the intergroup status hierarchy (i.e., is the low status position of the ingroup open to change?); and (c) the legitimacy of the intergroup status hierarchy (i.e., is the low status position of the ingroup appropriate/deserved?). Our earlier discussion of relative deprivation foreshadowed the importance of legitimacy assessments. Clearly, feelings of anger and dissatisfaction about the status of one's group require not only the recognition that the ingroup is disadvantaged, but also feelings of entitlement that imply perceptions of illegitimacy (see Major, 1994). We will consider the assessment of legitimacy and stability shortly. However, in other writings

(Wright, 1997, in press-b) we have argued, in a manner consistent with Tajfel (1978a) and others (see Ellemers, in press), that the assessment of boundary permeability may be the primary of these three assessments in determining disadvantaged group behavior.

Once an individual recognizes that the ingroup holds a relatively disadvantaged position, he or she will then evaluate the ease with which individuals can move from one group to another – that is, he or she will assess the degree to which individual upward mobility is possible (Hogg & Abrams, 1988; Tajfel & Turner, 1979; Taylor & McKirnan, 1984). If individual upward mobility seems possible, the individual adopts an "individual mobility orientation" (Tajfel, 1981). This orientation is marked by dissociation from the disadvantaged ingroup, a focus on improving one's own position, and a preference for individual actions. Thus, the belief that the intergroup boundaries are permeable will serve to reduce or prevent interest in collective action. However, if the intergroup boundaries are perceived to be closed, the individual will adopt a "social change orientation" (Tajfel, 1981). This orientation is marked by increased identification with the ingroup, an enhanced motivation to improve the position of the ingroup, and an interest in collective action (see Ellemers, 1993; Wright & Taylor, 1998; Wright et al., 1990a).

The apparent simplicity of this basic model is very appealing. However, there are a number of complexities that not only strengthen the model but also broaden the importance of this initial assessment of permeability as a determinant of collective action. So in addition to providing a more complete discussion of the importance of perceptions of legitimacy and stability, we will consider two important extensions to the discussion of boundary permeability: (a) the distinction between internal (psychological) and external (structural) barriers to boundary permeability; (b) the importance of considering the permeability as a continuum, rather than a dichotomy and the significance of a context we label "tokenism."

Internal and External Barriers to Boundary Permeability. Broadly speaking, an assessment of boundary permeability considers two types of barriers to leaving the disadvantaged ingroup: *external* barriers and *internal* barriers. External barriers include physical and structural factors that reduce individual's chances of moving from the disadvantaged group into a more advantaged social group. Some of these external barriers include ascribed characteristics that cannot be changed (e.g., race, gender), social norms and practices that prevent members of the disadvantaged group from leaving their own group or joining the outgroup (e.g., prejudice and discrimination, both direct and institutional, by the advantaged group), or geographical distances that separate the groups.

Most of the existing work on boundary permeability has focused on these types of physical and structural factors, and this narrow focus has prompted some controversy. For example, Taylor and McKirnan's (1984) "Five-Stage Model" of intergroup relations proposes that individual action will always precede collective action, and it is the failed attempts at individual mobility that lead to the recognition that group boundaries are closed, which in turn leads to collective action. Others, however, have criticized this sequential model, pointing to the presence of personal and psychological factors that can also influence group members' assessments of boundary permeability, and their preferences for individual or collective strategies (e.g., Branscombe & Ellemers, 1998; Ellemers et al., 1997; Wright, Taylor, & Moghaddam, 1990b). These personal and psychological factors can be described as *internal* barriers to perceiving boundary permeability. For example, strong ingroup identification serves to tie the individual psychologically to the ingroup, and this psychological attachment to the ingroup is likely to lead the individual to believe that he or she simply could not leave the group. Thus, even if the actual (external) barriers to moving into a more advantaged group are minimal, strong identification serves as a psychological barrier to perceived boundary permeability (see also Ellemers et al., 1997; Spears, Doosje, & Ellemers, 1997).

Thus, one interpretation of the previously described research on importance of ingroup identification as a predictor of interest in collective action is that ingroup identification steers interest away from individual action and toward collective action, by reducing the individual's perception that he or she could leave the disadvantaged ingroup and move into the more advantaged outgroup. Thus, ingroup identification increases interest in collective action by reducing the perceived permeability of group boundaries.

In summary, assessment of boundary permeability involves an analysis of both external and internal barriers. The individual considers both the structural barriers and those imposed by his or her own relationship with or position within the ingroup. When either or both of these assessments result in perceptions that boundaries between the groups are open, individual mobility will be seen as appropriate and desirable. However, when a disadvantaged group member cannot (or will not) abandon his or her membership in the disadvantaged group to become part of the dominant group, individual action is no longer perceived as an option, and he or she must choose between collective action and inaction.

Cognitive Alternatives: Assessing Legitimacy and Stability

The decision to take collective action over inaction rests on the disadvantaged group member's ability to imagine a situation in which the relative positions of the two groups are different. In SIT terms, he or she must recognize "cognitive alternatives" to the present status relationship. Tajfel and Turner (1979) propose that the recognition of cognitive alternatives depends on two assessments: *legitimacy*, an evaluation of the justice or fairness of the present status relationship; and *stability*, an evaluation of the likelihood that the present status relationship can be changed.

Legitimacy. The concepts of "legitimacy" and "justice" are basic to many theoretical perspectives in intergroup relations (see, e.g., Jost & Major, in press; Major, 1994; Olson, Herman, & Zanna, 1986; Runciman, 1966; Tajfel, 1981; Tyler et al., 1997; Walker & Pettigrew, 1984), and to a number of theories of social movements (e.g., Gamson, 1992; Klandermans, 1997). As described earlier in our discussion of relative deprivation, in addition to recognizing that one's group is disadvantaged relative to another group, members must also feel dissatisfaction, even anger, about the position of their group. These feelings of dissatisfaction and anger are closely linked to perceptions of the legitimacy of the social structure. Feeling dissatisfied with one's position indicates a sense of *entitlement* (see Major, 1994), the feeling that one deserves more. If a disadvantaged group member believes that his or her ingroup deserves more, this directly implies that the present state of affairs is unfair or illegitimate (Major, 1994). The feeling of illegitimacy that results from the assessment that one's group deserves higher status or better treatment is an essential step on the road to collective action, because this feeling provides the motivation and the justification for actions that may be socially disruptive and potentially costly or even dangerous (Tajfel, 1981; see also Hogg & Abrams, 1988).

Stability, Agency and Collective Control. In addition to perceiving illegitimacy, SIT proposes that disadvantaged group members must also see instability in the present social order. When disadvantaged group members believe that the relative positions of the groups are part of a fixed social hierarchy, an immutable reality, they will be disinclined to engage in collective action. In contrast, when they believe that the relative positions of the groups can change, they become interested in collective action (Tajfel, 1981; see also Kelly & Breinlinger, 1996; Martin, Brickman, & Murray, 1984). A number of others have presented conceptually similar constructs. For example, Gamson (1992) and Klandermans (1997) have used the term *agency frame* to refer to the extent that group members feel capable of producing collective action that can successfully reduce or remove the injustice they face. Bandura (1997) defines *collective efficacy* as "the group's shared belief in its conjoint capability to organize and execute the courses of action required to produce given levels of attainment" (p. 477).

Although these concepts of agency frame and collective efficacy are very similar to Tajfel and Turner's concept of stability, they are not identical. The distinction between the SIT's stability and these two other concepts can be most easily understood by referring to theories of *perceived control* (e.g., Abramson, Seligman, & Teasdale, 1978). According to this perspective, in order to feel that one has control of one's outcomes one must make two simultaneous judgments. First, the individual must believe that that the situation can be changed if certain actions are taken (that outcomes are contingent on behavior). At the group level, this judgment corresponds with SIT's concept of *stability*. Second, the individual must also believe that the relevant agent (oneself or the group) is able to execute the behaviors necessary to produce the desired change. This second judgment corresponds to the concept of *agency* or *collective efficacy*. Thus, from this perspective, a lack of *collective control* can result from either a belief that the status relationship between the groups cannot be changed no matter what actions are taken, or from a belief that the relevant ingroup lacks the necessary resources or abilities to produce the desired change.

Assessing Legitimacy and Collective Control When Group Boundaries Are Closed. It is clear that the assessments of legitimacy and collective control are most accurately considered as continuous; that is, situations will be seen as "more or less just" and "more or less stable." However, action and inaction represent discrete categories (one either takes action or one does not) and there would need to be a relatively discrete point at which the situation is seen as "unstable enough" and/or "illegitimate enough" to warrant action. In this sense, while assessments of stability and legitimacy are made on a continuum, for each individual in a given situation there is a relatively discrete point at which these assessments initiate a qualitative switch in the individual's behavioral strategy.

With that introduction, the combination of the assessments of legitimacy and collective control leads to four alternatives (see Figure 10.3). At one extreme, the relative position of the groups is believed to be both legitimate and uncontrollable; that is, the status differences are based on principles or norms that are accepted by both the advantaged and disadvantaged groups, and neither group questions their place in the

	Legitimate	Illegitimate
Uncontrollable	Inaction With Acceptance	Inaction With Anger/Frustration
Controllable	Collective Normative Action	Collective Non-normative Action

Figure 10.3. Assessing legitimacy and collective control when group boundaries are closed.

social structure. In SIT terms, cognitive alternatives to the present situation are not recognized and collective action not considered. The result is inaction. At the other extreme, the inequalities between the groups are seen as illegitimate and controllable. Neither the principles that support the status hierarchy nor the inevitability of the hierarchy is accepted. Disadvantaged group members see unfairness, believe the situation can change, and believe that the ingroup has the necessary resources and capabilities to achieve that change. The result is collective action.

It is likely that controllability and illegitimacy will be correlated in ways that will make one of these two extreme alternatives likely. That is, conditions that undermine the stability of the status hierarchy are also likely to raise doubts about its legitimacy. Similarly, conditions that undermine the legitimacy of the present social structure should motivate disadvantaged group members to consider and perhaps even seek out evidence of its controllability (Tajfel, 1978b). Alternatively, the pressure could be in the other direction. That is, clear evidence that the situation is uncontrollable should lead individuals to alter their perceptions so that the situation appears increasingly legitimate (see Pettigrew, 1961, for a discussion of the "psychology of the inevitable"). Also, strong beliefs in the legitimacy of the existing group hierarchy should reduce both the search for evidence that the situation can be changed and efforts to build the resources necessary to produce change.

Despite the pressures that move perceptions toward either the illegitimate/controllable or the legitimate/uncontrollable extremes, it is worth considering the two mixed situations that fall in between the two extremes. It is possible that the status hierarchy might be considered illegitimate but uncontrollable, or legitimate but controllable. Not only are these two situations possible, there are contexts where they can be relatively enduring. Take, for example, a nation ruled by a strong military dictatorship. Much of the population may see the status differences between rich and poor as unfair, but may also see little chance that the distribution will ever be more equitable. The principles or beliefs that sustain intergroup inequalities are challenged, yet the relative status of the two groups appears unchangeable. Under these circumstances, collective action is unlikely. Of course, the resulting inaction does not indicate "acceptance" of the social situation, but rather an angry or begrudging admission that things cannot be changed.

It should be noted, however, that when this anger and resentment are not expressed in actions, observers from both the advantaged and the disadvantaged groups may interpret this inaction as de facto acceptance. The advantaged group may believe that disadvantaged group members share their understanding of the principles and myths that legitimize the status hierarchy. At the same time, this misinterpretation can also have important implications for the actions of other ingroup members. Research on a process labeled "pluralistic ignorance" (Miller & McFarland, 1987) shows that even when most group members do not agree with the direction taken by their group, when others fail to act on their misgivings, each individual member can mistakenly assume that he or she alone disagrees. The resulting normative pressures lead the individual to conform to the group's chosen direction despite the fact that most of them privately do not support this course of action. In this way, pluralistic ignorance provides a partial explanation for why inaction would persist even when, if suggested, collective actions might be supported by many disadvantaged group members.

In the other "mixed" case, the situation is perceived to be legitimate and controllable. This situation is consistent with a two-party democratic political system such as in the United States. Members of the party that does not hold power (i.e., the disadvantaged group) generally accept their present low status position as legitimate. As long as they believe that the rules of democracy were followed, they recognize that they failed to get the necessary votes and, thus, must settle for a lower status position. However, they also believe that this situation is controllable; that they may well be able to garner the necessary votes to change the status hierarchy in the next election. Thus, the perceptions of controllability and legitimacy coexist because the means by which group status is determined (democratic elections) and the inherent instability of their present positions are accepted by both groups. In this case, perceived control will inspire interest in collective action, but only collective actions that conform to the rules of the social system.

This raises an important additional distinction relevant to our discussion of collective action. Resembling Martin's (1986) distinction between "positive" and "negative" behavior, and Simpson and Yinger's (1985) distinction between "aggression" and "reformism," Wright and his colleagues (Wright et al., 1990a) propose a distinction between normative and nonnormative collective actions. Normative actions conform to the shared rules of the existing social system, while nonnormative actions violate the existing social rules. Like the distinction made at the beginning of this chapter between collective and individual action, the distinction between normative and nonnormative action is also expressly psychological. If the actor believes that his or her action is consistent with the relevant societal expectations, then the action would be designated normative. However, if the actor is aware that his or her behavior is inconsistent with the expectations of the broader social system, the action is nonnormative. Notice, however, that this does not involve the actors' perception of the appropriateness, legitimacy, or morality of their actions. She or he simply needs to be aware that the action, no matter how justified, violates some societal expectation or convention. In addition, this distinction is not synonymous with the violent/nonviolent distinction (Martin, Scully, & Levitt, 1990). Many forms of civil disobedience are nonviolent but are also understood to be inconsistent with normative practices. On the other hand, in some intergroup contexts (e.g., in a football game) acts of violence are an accepted part of the intergroup interaction.

The important point here is that perceptions that the low status position of the ingroup can be changed (i.e., perceiving collective control) will open the doors for collective action. However, when the present low status position of the ingroup is also perceived as just and appropriate (i.e., perceived legitimacy), collective action will be limited to normative forms. From the perspective of the disadvantaged group, limiting themselves to actions that are consistent with the rules and practices of the social system is not

	Legitimate	Illegitimate
Uncontrollable	Individual Normative Action	Individual Non-normative Action
Controllable	Individual Normative Action	Collective Action

Figure 10.4. Assessing legitimacy and collective control when group boundaries are highly restricted (tokenism).

problematic as long as their perceptions of collective control are accurate (i.e., as long as the normative channels for social change are actually effective). In our example of two-party democratic process, limiting party members' actions to those prescribed by the rules of the electoral process is reasonable as long as the electoral process is indeed fair. When the normative avenues for change are ineffective (e.g., if the election is fixed), limiting actions to those allowed by the present process may result in little real social change. Thus, while perceived controllability appears to play a pivotal role in the initiation of collective action, perceived illegitimacy is critical for nonnormative (i.e., socially disruptive) forms of collective action to be considered.

In summary, when intergroup boundaries are closed, the assessment of legitimacy and collective control will lead to inaction whenever the intergroup context is perceived to be uncontrollable. When this stable intergroup context is seen as illegitimate, this inaction will likely be associated with anger and/or frustration. However, when the intergroup context is perceived to be controllable, normative forms of collective action will result if the context is also seen to be legitimate. Nonnormative collective

action designed to change the social structure will occur only when the
intergroup context is perceived to be both controllable and illegitimate.

Restricted Group Boundaries: Responding to Tokenism

Although theories like SIT have represented boundary permeability as a
continuous variable, most of the relevant research has operationalized
boundary permeability as a dichotomous distinction between "open" and
"closed" contexts. Elsewhere (see Wright, in press-b for a review) we have
argued that in contemporary North American society, and many other
intergroup contexts, individual mobility is neither completely impossible
(closed) nor is it entirely meritocratic (open). Instead, group boundaries
are often restricted (Farley, 1985; Martin, 1986; Pettigrew & Martin, 1987),
such that a small number of disadvantaged group members are accepted
into advantaged positions, while access is systematically blocked for most
qualified members of the disadvantaged group. Extreme restrictions on
boundary permeability result in a form of intergroup discrimination
referred to as "tokenism" (Moreland, 1965). In a number of studies
(Wright, 1997; Wright & Taylor, 1998; Wright et al., 1990a), we have shown
that disadvantaged group members faced with an entirely closed context
prefer disruptive forms of collective action. However, when as few as 2%
of the qualified ingroup members are allowed access to advantaged positions, individual actions become the response of choice. Thus, it appears
that even the slightest hint of boundary permeability may undermine
interest in collective action.

Our research suggests that this tokenism effect is multiply determined.
In part, tokenism leads to a preference for individual action by focusing
attention on personal identities and encouraging interpersonal social comparisons with the few successful tokens who now hold high status positions (Wright, 1997). By comparison, a completely closed intergroup
context leads to intergroup social comparisons with the advantaged outgroup. Thus, tokenism undermines interest in collective action by refocus-
ing attention away from the intergroup social comparisons that form the
basis for interest in collective action. However, there is also evidence that
tokenism may undermine collective action by obfuscation of the two
assessments of the intergroup context, the perceived legitimacy and stability of the intergroup status hierarchy (Wright, 1997).

*Assessing Legitimacy and Control When Group Boundaries Are
Restricted.* Inherent in tokenism is a paradox. On the one hand, tokenism
is like a closed context in that group membership is used as a criterion to

prevent individual mobility. Therefore, tokenism might be seen as discriminatory and thus lead to feelings of illegitimacy. On the other hand, tokenism is like an open context in that merit remains a partial criterion for success. For a few disadvantaged group members, individual merit results in success. This mingling of merit and discrimination can lead to uncertainty about the legitimacy of the social order (Wright, in press-b). Consistent with this interpretation, Wright and Taylor (1998) found that participants in a laboratory experiment who were faced with a tokenism context consistently perceived less collective injustice than those faced with completely closed intergroup boundaries.

If tokenism leads to uncertainty about the illegitimacy of the ingroup's low status, it should also lead to uncertainty about how other ingroup members will respond. Perceived instability hinges on the belief that collective action can be effective (Kelly, 1993), and confidence that ingroup members will mobilize can be a prominent factor in assessing the efficacy of collective action (Klandermans, 1997). Thus, uncertainty about illegitimacy may coincidentally raise uncertainty about ingroup support for collective action, and hence uncertainty about the instability of the ingroup's status.

Thus, all three assessments of the intergroup context necessary for collective action are compromised in the tokenism context. As some degree of permeability persists, tokenism can lead to a focus on one's personal position and therefore to a preference for individual action. Additionally, tokenism can undermine assessments of both the illegitimacy and controllability of status inequalities, thereby making collective action seem less appropriate and/or less likely to succeed. As a result there is a strong tendency for disadvantaged group members who are faced with a context of tokenism to prefer individual action. Indeed, only when group members receive clear information that strongly emphasizes the collective injustice of tokenism and points out the potential instability of the intergroup context will collective action occur in response to tokenism (Wright, 1997).

SUMMARY AND CONCLUSIONS

Inequality in the distribution of resources and status, and the resulting stratification of groups into relatively advantaged and disadvantaged positions, is a basic feature of most social contexts (Sidanius, 1993; Taylor & McKirnan, 1984). Groups occupying a dominant position are motivated to maintain their collective privilege (Apfelbaum, 1979; Ng, 1982; Tajfel, 1982) and, in the words of Martin Luther King Jr., "Privileged groups rarely give up their privileges without strong resistance." Thus, changes in the status hierarchy depend primarily on the actions of the disadvantaged group. Further, as suggested by the slogan "United we stand – Divided we fall," change in the social order is most dependent on the propensity of the disadvantaged group members to engage in *collective action* (see Gamson, 1990; Tarrow, 1994).

Yet it is clear that the road to collective action is fraught with obstacles and often individual social mobility becomes the action of choice for members of disadvantaged groups. However, collective action does occur. As was the case in 1981 in Long Kesh prison in Northern Ireland, collective acts can have dramatic and tragic consequences. In this chapter, we have considered some of the variables relevant to predicting collective action. Our analysis has been expressly psychological, in that it focuses on the emotions, perceptions, and assessments of individuals. It is our conclusion that the roots of disruptive collective action, the kind of collective action most likely to change the existing social structure, can be found in: (a) the individual's psychological connection with the ingroup (ingroup identification); (b) the propensity to make group-level social comparisons with a dominant outgroup that lead to strong feelings of collective relative deprivation; (c) the individual's assessment of, and subsequent rejection of, the possibility for individual upward mobility; and (d) the assessment of the ingroup's low status position as illegitimate and controllable.

Thus, it is not surprising that Bobby Sands and his fellow Irish Republicans were highly identified with the Irish Republican movement. In fact, the very essence of their demands – recognition as members of a the Irish Republican political movement and, thus, as political prisoners – makes their ingroup identification abundantly apparent. Second, we see in Bobby Sands' own writing constant references to the poor treatment of the Irish Catholics at the hands of the British and Loyalists (the Protestants). Third, the hunger strikers' strong ingroup identification created psychological barriers to leaving the ingroup, and the history of conflict and discriminatory practices on both sides of the conflict prevented movement between social groups in Northern Ireland. Also, they were prisoners with bars and walls to serve as clear barriers to changing their group identity. Fourth, the perceived illegitimacy of the British "occupation" of Northern Ireland is amply apparent in the writings of the Irish Republicans. Finally, in 1981, there was real confidence among the prisoners that the British would capitulate to their demands. In fact, as the national and international attention to the hunger strikes grew and as the first strikers died, the British government's unwillingness to concede became increasingly astonishing to the prisoners and their followers.

For what seems like a long time, social psychology has moved away from the study of action in favor of cognition, away from broader societal phenomena – what Tom Pettigrew (1991; 1996) has called "macro-level" phenomena – in favor of intrapersonal phenomena – what Tom has called "micro-level" phenomena. However, it is our perception that this is changing, and that social psychology now finds itself in the midst of a resurgence of what some have called truly 'social' social psychology (see Pettigrew, 1988; 1991; Taylor & Brown, 1979). One outcome of this "resurgence" has been a growing interest and an increasing diversity of research approaches focusing on the social psychology of collective action. This chapter reflects and, we hope, assists this revitalized interest by focusing attention on a number of interrelated processes that contribute to disadvantaged group members understanding their social position in a way that will promote action directed at social change.

REFERENCES

Abrams, D. (1990). *Political identity: Relative deprivation, social identity, and the case of Scottish nationalism.* Economic and Social Research Council 16–19 Initiative, Occasional Paper no. 24. Social Statistics Research Unit, City University, London.

Abramson, L., Seligman, M., & Teasdale, J. (1978). Learned helplessness in humans: Critique and reformulation. *Journal of Abnormal Psychology, 87,* 49–74.

Adams, J. S. (1965). Inequity in social exchange. In L. Berkowitz (Ed.), *Advances in experimental social psychology* (Vol. 2, pp. 267–299). New York: Academic Press.

Apfelbaum, E. (1979). Relations of domination and movements for liberation: An analysis of power between groups. In W. G. Austin & S. Worchel (Eds.), *The social psychology of intergroup relations* (pp. 188–204). Monterey, CA: Brooks/Cole.

Austin, W., & Walster, E. (1974). Reactions to confirmation and disconfirmation of expectations of equity and inequity. *Journal of Personality and Social Psychology, 30,* 208–216.

Bandura, A. (1997). *Self-efficacy: The experience of control.* New York: Freeman.

Bargh, J. A., Lombardi W. J., & Higgins, E. T. (1988). Automaticity of chronically accessible constructs in person X situation effects on person perception: It's just a matter of time. *Journal of Personality and Social Psychology, 55,* 599–605.

Bernstein, M., & Crosby, F. J. (1980). An empirical examination of relative deprivation theory. *Journal of Experimental Social Psychology, 16,* 172–184.

Birt, C. M., & Dion, K. L. (1987). Relative deprivation theory and responses to discrimination in a gay male and lesbian sample. *British Journal of Social Psychology, 26,* 139–145.

Branscombe, N. R., & Ellemers, N. (1998). Coping with group-based discrimination: Individualistic versus group-level strategies. In J. K. Swim & C. Stangor

(Eds.), *Prejudice: The target's perspective* (pp. 243–266). San Diego, CA: Academic Press.

Brewer, M. B. (1991). The social self: On being the same and different at the same time. *Personality and Social Psychology Bulletin, 17*, 475–482.

Brewer, M. B., & Gardner, W. (1996). Who is this "we"? Levels of collective identity and self representations. *Journal of Personality and Social Psychology, 71*, 83–93.

Brickman, P., Folger, R., Goode, R., & Schul, Y. (1981). Microjustice and macrojustice. In M. J. Lerner & S. C. Lerner (Eds.), *The justice motive in social behavior.* New York: Plenum.

Cheek, J. M., Tropp, L. R., Chen, L. C., & Underwood, M. K. (1994, August). *Identity orientations: Personal, social, and collective aspects of identity.* Paper presented at the annual meeting of the American Psychological Association, Los Angeles, CA.

Crocker, J., & Major, B. (1989). Social stigma and self-esteem: The self-protective properties of stigma. *Psychological Review, 96*, 608–630.

Crocker, J., & Major, B., & Steele, C. (1998). Social stigma. In D. T. Gilbert, S. T. Fiske, & G. Lindsey (Eds.), *The handbook of social psychology* (4th ed., Vol. 2, pp. 504–553). New York: McGraw-Hill.

Crosby, F. J. (1976). A model of egoistical relative deprivation. *Psychological Review. 83*, 85–113.

Crosby, F. J. (1982). *Relative deprivation and working women.* New York: Oxford University Press.

deCarufel, A., & Schopler, J. (1979). Evaluation of outcome improvement resulting from threats and appeals. *Journal of Personality and Social Psychology, 37*, 662–673.

Dion, K. L. (1986). Responses to perceived discrimination and relative deprivation. In J. M. Olson, C. P. Herman, & M. P. Zanna (Eds.), *Relative deprivation and social comparison: The Ontario symposium* (Vol. 4, pp. 159–179). Hillsdale, NJ: Lawrence Erlbaum.

Doosje, B., & Ellemers, N. (1997). Stereotyping under threat: The role of group identification. In R. Spears & P. J. Oakes, (Eds.), *The social psychology of stereotyping and group life* (pp. 257–272). Oxford: Blackwell.

Ellemers, N. (1993). The influence of socio-structural variables on identity management strategies. In W. Stroebe & M. Hewstone (Eds.), *European review of social psychology* (Vol. 4, pp. 27–57). Chichester: John Wiley.

Ellemers, N. (in press). Individual upward mobility and the perceived legitimacy of intergroup relations. In J. Jost & B. Major (Eds.), *The psychology of legitimacy: Emerging perspectives on ideology, justice, and intergroup relations.*

Ellemers, N., Spears, R., & Doosje, B. (1997). Sticking together or falling apart: Ingroup identification as a psychological determinant of group commitment versus individual mobility. *Journal of Personality and Social Psychology, 72*, 617–626.

Farley, R. (1985). Three steps forward and two back? *Ethnic and Racial Studies, 8*, 4–28.

Feehan, J. (1983). *Bobby Sands and the tragedy of Northern Ireland.* Dublin: Mercier Press.

Folger, R. (1986). A referent cognitions theory of relative deprivation. In J. M. Olson, C. P. Herman, & M. P. Zanna (Eds.), *Relative deprivation and social comparison: The Ontario symposium* (Vol. 4, pp. 217–242). Hillsdale, NJ: Lawrence Erlbaum.

Folger, R., & Martin, C. (1986). Relative deprivation and referent cognitions: Distributive and procedural justice effects. *Journal of Experimental Social Psychology, 22,* 531–546.

Folger, R., Rosenfield, D., & Robinson, T. (1983). Relative deprivation and procedural injustice. *Journal of Personality and Social Psychology, 45,* 268–273.

Foster, M. D., & Matheson, K. (1999). Perceiving and responding to the personal/group discrimination discrepancy. *Personality and Social Psychology Bulletin, 25,* 1319–1329.

Frable, D.E.S. (1993). Dimensions of marginality: Distinctions among those who are different. *Personality and Social Psychology Bulletin, 19,* 370–380.

Gamson. W. A. (1990). *The strategy of social protest.* Belmont, CA: Wadsworth.

Gamson, W. A. (1992). The social psychology of collective action. In A. D. Morris & C. McClurg Mueller (Eds.), *Frontiers in social movement theory* (pp. 53–76). New Haven, CT: Yale University Press.

Gardner, J. W. (1972). *In common cause.* New York: W. W. Norton.

Goffman, E. (1963). *Stigma: Notes on the management of spoiled identity.* Englewood Cliffs, NJ: Prentice-Hall.

Guimond, S., & Dube-Simard, L. (1983). Relative deprivation theory and the Quebec Nationalist Movement: The cognition-emotion distinction and the personal-group deprivation issue. *Journal of Personality and Social Psychology, 44,* 526–535.

Hinkle, S., Fox-Cardamone, L., Haseleu, J. A., Brown, R., & Irwin, L. M. (1996). Grassroots political action as an intergroup phenomenon. *Journal of Social Issues, 52,* 39–51.

Hogg, M. A., & Abrams, D. (1988). *Social identification: A social psychology of intergroup relations and group processes.* London: Routledge.

Homans, G. C. (1961). *Social behavior: Its elementary forms.* New York: Harcourt Brace.

Jackman, M. R. (1998, August). *Violence and legitimacy in expropriative intergroup relations.* Paper presented at The Psychology of Legitimacy: Emerging Perspectives on Ideology, Justice, and Intergroup Relations, Stanford, CA.

Jones, E. E., Farina, A., Hastorf, A. H., Markus, H., Miller, D. T., & Scott, R. A. (1984). *Social stigma: The psychology of marked relationships.* New York: Freeman.

Jost J., & Major, B. (Eds.) (in press). *The psychology of legitimacy: Emerging perspectives on ideology, justice, and intergroup relations.*

Kawakami, K., & Dion, K., L. (1993). The impact of salient self-identities on relative deprivation and action intentions. *European Journal of Social Psychology, 23,* 525–540.

Kawakami, K., & Dion, K. L. (1995). Social identity and affect as determinants of collective action: Toward an integration of relative deprivation and social identity theories. *Theory and Psychology, 5,* 551–577.

Kelly, C. (1993). Group identification, intergroup perceptions and collective action. In W. Stroebe & M. Hewstone (Eds.), *European review of social psychology,* (Vol. 4, pp. 59–83). Chichester: John Wiley.

Kelly, C., & Breinlinger, S. (1995). Identity and injustice: Exploring women's participation in collective action. *Journal of Community and Applied Social Psychology, 5,* 41–57.

Kelly, C., & Breinlinger, S. (1996). *The social psychology of collective action: Identity, injustice and gender.* Washington, DC: Taylor & Francis.

Kelly, C., & Kelly, J. (1994). Who gets involved in collective action?: Social psychological determinants in individual participation in trade unions. *Human Relations, 47,* 63–88.

Klandermans, B. (1997). *The social psychology of protest.* Oxford: Blackwell.

Kramnick, I. (1972). Reflections of revolution: Definition and explanation in recent scholarship. *History and Theory, 11,* 26–63.

Lau, R. R. (1989). Individual and contextual influences on group identification. *Social Psychology Quarterly, 52,* 220–231.

Lemaine, G. (1974). Social differentiation and social originality. *European Journal of Social Psychology, 4,* 17–52.

Lord, C. G., & Saenz, D. S. (1985). Memory deficits and memory surfeits: Differential cognitive consequences of tokenism for tokens and observers. *Journal of Personality and Social Psychology, 49,* 918–926.

Luhtanen, R., & Crocker, J. (1992). A collective self-esteem scale: Self-evaluation of one's social identity. *Personality and Social Psychology Bulletin, 18,* 302–318.

Macrae, C. N., Bodenhausen, G. V., & Milne, A. B. (1995). The dissection of selection in person perception: Inhibitory processes in social stereotyping. *Journal of Personality and Social Psychology, 69,* 397–407.

Major, B. (1994). From social inequality to personal entitlement: The role of social comparisons, legitimacy appraisals, and group membership. In M. P. Zanna (Ed.), *Advances in experimental social psychology* (Vol. 26, pp. 293–355). San Diego, CA: Academic Press.

Mark, M. M., & Folger, R. (1984). Responses to relative deprivation: A conceptual framework, *Review of Personality and Social Psychology, 5,* 192–218.

Martin, J. (1986). The tolerance of injustice. In J. M. Olson, C. P. Herman, & M. P. Zanna (Eds.), *Relative deprivation and social comparison: The Ontario symposium* (Vol. 4, pp. 217–242). Hillsdale, NJ: Lawrence Erlbaum.

Martin, J., Brickman, P., & Murray, A. (1984). Moral outrage and pragmatism: Explanations for collective action. *Journal of Experimental Social Psychology, 20,* 484–496.

Martin, J., Scully, M., & Levitt, B. (1990). Injustice and the legitimation of revolution: Damning the past, excusing the present, and neglecting the future. *Journal of Personality and Social Psychology, 59,* 281–290.

McAdam, D., McGarthy J. D., & Zald, M. N. (Eds.), (1996). *Comparative perspectives on social movements: Political opportunities, mobilizing structures, and cultural framings.* New York: Cambridge University Press.

McCarthy, J. D., & Zald, M. N. (1977). Resource mobilization and social movements: A partial theory. *American Journal of Sociology, 82,* 1212–1241.

McGuire, W. J., McGuire, C. V., Child, P., & Fujioka, T. (1978). Salience of ethnicity in the spontaneous self-concept as a function of one's ethnic distinctiveness in the social environment. *Journal of Personality and Social Psychology, 36,* 511–520.

Miller, D. T., & McFarland, C. (1987). Pluralistic ignorance: When similarity is inter-preted as dissimilarity. *Journal of Personality and Social Psychology, 53,* 298–305.

Moreland, J. K. (1965). Token desegregation and beyond. In A. M. Rose & C. B. Rose (Eds.), *Minority problems* (pp. 229–238). New York: Harper & Row.

Mullen, B. (1991). Group composition, salience, and cognitive representations: The phenomenology of being in a group. *Journal of Experimental Social Psychology, 27,* 297–323.

Mummendey, A., & Simon, B. (1989). Better or different? III. The impact of importance of comparison dimension and relative in-group size upon inter-group discrimination. *British Journal of Social Psychology, 28,* 1–16.

Ng, S. H. (1982). Power and intergroup discrimination. In H. Tajfel (Ed.), *Social identity and intergroup relations* (pp. 179–206). London: Cardiff University Press.

Oakes, P. J., Haslam, S. A., & Turner, J. C. (1994). *Stereotyping and social reality.* Oxford: Blackwell.

Olson, J. M. Herman, C. P., & Zanna, M. P. (Eds.). (1986). *Relative deprivation and social comparison: The Ontario symposium* (Vol 4). Hillsdale NJ: Erlbaum.

Olson, J. M., & Ross, M. (1984). Perceived qualification, resource abundance and resentment about deprivation. *Journal of Experimental Social Psychology, 20,* 425–444.

Petta, G., & Walker, I. (1992). Relative deprivation and ethnic identity. *British Journal of Social Psychology, 31,* 285–293.

Pettigrew, T. F. (1961). Social psychology and desegregation research. *American Psychologist, 16,* 1045–1112.

Pettigrew, T. F. (1967). Social evaluation theory: Convergences and applications. In D. Levine (Ed.), *Nebraska symposium on motivation* (Vol. 15, pp. 241–311). Lincoln: University of Nebraska Press.

Pettigrew, T. F. (1988) Influencing policy with social psychology, *Journal of Social Issues, 44,* 205–219.

Pettigrew, T. F. (1991). Towards unity and bold theory: Popperian suggestions for two persistent problems in social psychology. In C. W. Stephan, W. G. Stephan, & T. F. Pettigrew (Eds.), *The future of social psychology: Defining the relationship between sociology and psychology* (pp. 13–27). New York: Springer-Verlag.

Pettigrew, T. F. (1996). *How to think like a social psychologist.* New York: HarperCollins.

Pettigrew, T. F., & Martin, J. (1987). Shaping the organizational context for black American inclusion. *Journal of Social Issues, 43,* 41–78.

Reicher, S. (1996). Social identity and social change. In W. P. Robinson (Ed.), *Social groups and identities: Developing the legacy of Henri Tajfel* (pp. 317–336). Oxford: Butterworth and Heinemann.

Runciman, W. G. (1966). *Relative deprivation and social justice: A study of attitudes to social inequity in twentieth-century England.* Berkley: University of California Press.

Sachdev, I., & Bourhis, R. Y. (1991). Power and status differentials in minority and majority group relations. *European Journal of Social Psychology, 21,* 1–24.

Sands, B. (1991). *Skylark sing your lonely song: An anthology of the writings of Bobby Sands.* Cork, Ireland: Mercier Press.

Sedikides, C., & Brewer, M. B. (Eds.). (in press). *Individual self, relational self, and collective self: Partners, opponents, or strangers?* Philadelphia: Psychology Press.

Sidanius, J. (1993). The psychology of group conflict and the dynamics of oppression: A social dominance perspective. In S. Iyengar & W. J. McGuire (Eds.), *Explorations in political psychology* (pp. 183–219). Durham, NC: Duke University Press.

Sidanius, J., & Pratto, F. (1993). The inevitability of oppression and the dynamics of social dominance. In P. M. Sniderman, P. E. Tetlock, & E. G. Carmines (Eds.), *Prejudice, politics, and the American dilemma* (pp. 173–211). Stanford, CA: Stanford University Press.

Simon, B. (1992). Intragroup differentiation in terms of ingroup and outgroup attributes. *European Journal of Social Psychology, 22*, 407–413.

Simon, B. (1998). Individuals, groups, and social change: On the relationship between individual and collective self-interpretations and collective action. In C. Sedikides & J. Schopler (Eds.), *Intergroup cognition and intergroup behavior* (pp. 257–282). Mahwah, NJ: Lawrence Erlbaum.

Simon, B., Loewy, M., Stuermer, S., Weber, U., Freytag, P., Habig, C., Kampmeier, C., & Spahlinger, P. (1998). Collective identification and social movement participation. *Journal of Personality and Social Psychology, 74*, 646–658.

Simpson, G. E., & Yinger, J. M. (1984). *Racial and cultural minorities: An analysis of prejudice and discrimination* (5th ed.). New York: Plenum.

Smith, H. & Pettigrew, T. F. (2001). *Relative deprivation: A conceptual critique and meta-analysis.* Unpublished paper. Department of Psychology, University of California at Santa Cruz.

Smith, H., Spears, R., & Oyen, M. (1994). "People like us": The influence of personal deprivation and group membership salience on justice evaluations. *Journal of Experimental Social Psychology, 30*, 277–299.

Snow, D. E., & Benford, R. (1992). Master frames and cycle of protest. In A. D. Morris & C. McClurg Mueller (Eds.), *Frontiers in social movement theory* (pp. 133–155). New Haven, CT: Yale University Press.

Spears, R., Doosje, B., & Ellemers, N. (1997). Self-stereotyping in the face of threats to group status and distinctiveness: The role of group identification. *Personality and Social Psychology Bulletin, 23*, 538–553.

Stouffer, S. A., Suchman, E. A., DeVinney, L. C., Starr, S. A., & Williams, R. M. (1949). *The American soldier: Adjustment to army life* (Vol. 1). Princeton, NJ: Princeton University Press.

Tajfel, H. (1978a). Interindividual behavior and intergroup behavior. In H. Tajfel (Ed.), *Differentiation between social groups: Studies in the social psychology of intergroup relations.* London: Academic Press.

Tajfel, H. (1978b). *The social psychology of minorities* (Report No. 38). London: Minority Rights Group.

Tajfel, H. (1981). *Human groups and social categories: Studies in social psychology.* Cambridge: Cambridge University Press.

Tajfel, H. (1982). *Social identity and intergroup relations.* Cambridge: Cambridge University Press.

Tajfel, H., & Turner, J. C. (1979). An integrative theory of intergroup conflict. In W. G. Austin & S. Worchel (Eds.), *The social psychology of intergroup relations* (pp. 33–48). Monterey, CA: Brooks/Cole.

Tarrow, S. G. (1994). *Power in movement: Social movements, collective action and politics.* New York: Cambridge University Press.

Taylor, D. M., & Brown, R. J. (1979). Towards a more social social psychology? *British Journal of Social and Clinical Psychology, 18,* 173–180.

Taylor, D. M., & Dube, L. (1986). Two faces of identity: The "I" and the "We". *Journal of Social Issues, 42,* 81–98.

Taylor, D. M., & McKirnan, D. J. (1984). A five stage model of intergroup relations, *British Journal of Social Psychology, 23,* 291–300.

Taylor, D. M., & Moghaddam, F. M. (1994). *Theories of intergroup relations: International and social psychological perspectives* (2nd ed.). Westport, CT: Praeger.

Taylor, S. E., Fiske, S. T., Etcoff, N. L., & Ruderman, A. J. (1978). Categorical and contextual bases of person memory and stereotyping. *Journal of Personality and Social Psychology, 36,* 778–793.

Tougas, F., & Veilleux, F. (1988). The influence of identification, collective relative deprivation, and procedure of implementation on women's response to affirmative action: A causal modeling approach. *Canadian Journal of Behavioural Sciences, 20,* 15–28.

Tripathi, R. C., & Srivastava, R. (1981). Relative deprivation and intergroup attitudes. *European Journal of Social Psychology, 11,* 313–318.

Tropp, L. R., & Wright, S. C. (1999). Ingroup identification and relative deprivation: An examination across multiple social comparison. *European Journal of Social Psychology, 29,* 707–724.

Tropp, L. R., & Wright, S. C. (in press). Inclusion of ingroup in the self: Conceptualization and measurement. *Personality and Social Psychology Bulletin.*

Turner, J. C., Hogg, M. A., Oakes, P. J., Reicher, S. D., & Wetherell, M. S. (1987). *Rediscovering the social group: A self-categorization theory.* New York: Blackwell.

Tyler, T. R., Boeckmann, R., Smith, H., & Huo, Y. (1997). *Social justice in a diverse society.* Boulder, CO: Westview Press.

Vanneman, R. D., & Pettigrew, T. F. (1972). Race and relative deprivation in the urban United States. *Race, 8,* 461–486.

Walker, I., & Mann, L. (1987). Unemployment, relative deprivation, and social protest. *Personality and Social Psychology Bulletin, 13,* 275–283.

Walker, I. & Pettigrew, T. F. (1984). Relative deprivation theory: An overview and conceptual critique, *British Journal of Social Psychology, 23,* 301–310.

Walster, E., Walster, G. W., & Berscheid, E. (1978). *Equity: Theory and research.* Boston: Allyn & Bacon.

Wann, D. L., & Branscombe, N. R. (1995). Influence of level of identification with a group and physiological arousal on perceived intergroup complexity. *British Journal of Social Psychology, 34,* 223–235.

Wright, S. C. (1997). Ambiguity, shared consensus and collective action: Generating collective protest in response to tokenism. *Personality and Social Psychology Bulletin, 23,* 1277–1290.

Wright, S. C. (in press-a). Strategic collective action: Social psychology and social change. In R. Brown & S. Gaertner (Eds.), *Intergroup processes: Blackwell handbook of social psychology* (Vol. 4). Oxford: Blackwell.

Wright, S. C. (in press-b). Restricted intergroup boundaries: Tokenism, ambiguity and the tolerance of injustice. In J. Jost & B. Major (Eds.), *The psychology of legitimacy: Emerging perspectives on ideology, justice, and intergroup relations*. New York: Cambridge University Press.

Wright, S. C., & Taylor, D. M. (1998). Responding to Tokenism: Individual action in the face of collective injustice. *European Journal of Social Psychology, 28,* 647–667.

Wright, S. C., Taylor, D. M., & Moghaddam, F. M. (1990a). Responding to membership in a disadvantaged group: From acceptance to collective action. *Journal of Personality and Social Psychology, 58,* 994–1003.

Wright, S. C., Taylor, D. M., & Moghaddam, F. M. (1990b). The relationship of perceptions and emotions to behavior in the face of collective inequality. *Social Justice Research, 4,* 229–250.

PART THREE

INTEGRATION

ELEVEN

Social Identity and Relative Deprivation

Naomi Ellemers

PROGRESS IN SOCIAL PSYCHOLOGY: KNOWLEDGE EXTENSION OR ACCUMULATION OF THEORIES?

In his seminal paper of 1967, Pettigrew identified converging insights from different theoretical approaches, to integrate these in his social evaluation theory. What seemed most impressive from the outset was his attempt to "clean house" in social psychological theory, and to combine knowledge from different perspectives to get a handle on important social phenomena. Thirty years later, we are in the position to judge how this has affected further theoretical development in this area: Have research efforts indeed been directed at integrating and combining similar theoretical perspectives, leading to broader insights, as Pettigrew provisioned? Unfortunately, we cannot confirm that this has unequivocally been the case. Even though there is a large body of theoretical and empirical work in social psychology addressing social evaluation processes, the past three decades have witnessed a proliferation of divergent arguments, concepts, and approaches. Accordingly, from time to time, the concern is expressed that contemporary work focuses too much on "single hypothesis" theories, which can only explain narrowly defined phenomena and may therefore undermine development of a common body of knowledge. Nevertheless, partly due to the complexity of the phenomena at hand, researchers have continued to work in this perhaps too fragmented way, and this research policy is reinforced by scientific output ratings in which the productivity of researchers is commonly judged by the number of research papers published in peer-reviewed journals, while the writing of an integrative monograph is sometimes not even acknowledged. As a result, to paraphrase Newton:

Instead of seeing further because we are standing on the shoulders of giants (although it has been suggested that this statement originates from an earlier source, see Merton, 1965), it sometimes feels like we are reinventing the same wheel, but calling it by a different name. This raises the important question of whether these combined efforts have actually yielded theoretical progress or mainly resulted in the accumulation of different theories.

One important consequence of the ongoing specialization of psychological researchers is that over the years the gap between experimental research on psychological processes on the one hand, and investigations of social phenomena on the other, seems to have widened instead of narrowed. The need for experimental control when trying to gain insight into the cognitive processes underlying social perception and social behavior has resulted in the use of standardized stimuli and measures that are far removed from the social phenomena they should be relevant to. At the same time, the greater methodological sophistication in the field has made it less accepted to draw general theoretical conclusions from real-life observations. Additionally, even within each of these research traditions, it is common practice to emphasize distinct insights instead of aiming at converging or overarching theoretical models (see Taylor & Moghaddam, 1987).

Work on social identity theory and relative deprivation theory constitutes a case in point (see also Ellemers, 1993a; Kawakami & Dion, 1995) with the relative deprivation perspective focusing on the explanation of social behavior, while social identity research has mainly addressed the psychological processes involved in the perception of self and others in terms of group memberships. But there are more closely related theoretical perspectives that try to understand people's responses to social injustice, by specifying the likely consequences for the perception of self and others as well as for the resulting motives and social behaviors. For instance, theories on social justice (Lind & Tyler, 1988; Tyler & Lind, 1992), referent cognitions (Folger, 1987) and counterfactual thinking (Roese & Olson, 1995) focus on the cognitive processes that determine the way people evaluate their own situation, theories on social comparison (Major, Testa, & Bylsma, 1991) and self-esteem maintenance (Tesser, 1988) specify the motivational consequences, while theories on system justification (Jost & Banaji, 1994) and social dominance (Sidanius & Pratto, 1993) address the societal consequences of social injustice (as is evident from other chapters in this volume).

Despite the fact that at an operational level there seems to be considerable overlap, theoretical specifications and empirical studies mainly point to the distinctive contribution of each perspective, rather than trying to achieve a more integrative theoretical analysis in which these perspectives are explicitly related to each other. To the extent that this implies that each perspective addressed a different specific issue, this need not be problematic. However, when researchers working within a particular tradition expand their theorizing and move into adjacent areas, they sometimes end up developing an argument that has already been specified and sometimes even tested in another theoretical context (e.g., Deaux & Ethier, 1998; Rothgerber & Worchel, 1997). Again, to some extent this is an inevitable way in which science develops. At the same time, however, it is important to realize that real scientific progress is often made when ideas from different theoretical perspectives are *connected* with each other (see also Mackie & Smith, 1998). From this point of view, relatively little effort seems to be devoted to finding common ground in central theoretical constructs, to identifying common or complementary predictions, or to building an overarching theoretical framework. Obviously, this would be a daunting enterprise, and I would not pretend to be able to accomplish such an integration. Nevertheless, with the present contribution I will try to take a first step in this direction, as an attempt to demonstrate the promise and fruitfulness of thinking about possible connections between these separate literatures.

Relative Deprivation Theory and Social Identity Theory: Similarities and Differences

The aim of this chapter is to join insights from social identity theory and relative deprivation theory, by considering how they can complement and extend each other and reviewing research that may help to specify the role of group identification as a central bridging construct. Although relative deprivation theory and research has mainly focused on the behavioral consequences of (perceived) outcome inequality and social injustice – for instance, in employment situations (e.g., Major, 1994; Martin, 1981) – work on social identity theory has typically been used to derive hypotheses about intergroup perceptions in a broad range of experimental and applied settings, including randomly created laboratory groups as well as sports teams (e.g., Wann & Branscombe, 1990) and more recently also work teams in organizations (e.g., Hogg, 1996). Nevertheless, it may well be that these differences mainly concern a difference in emphasis rather than principle, and indeed from both perspectives similar issues and processes have been considered.

To some extent, these perspectives have developed separately because social identity theory is mostly a psychological theory, while relative deprivation theory originates from a sociological/political science tradition and has mainly been used in work on collective action. Accordingly, social identity theory and research has mostly focused on cognitive and motivational determinants of personal versus social identification, while relative deprivation theory and research has mainly addressed behavioral consequences of individual versus group deprivation to be able to predict who is likely to participate in collective action. Furthermore, whereas social identity theory has been developed on the basis of laboratory experimentation, relative deprivation theory was constructed to account for behavioral observations in natural settings (see also Kawakami & Dion, 1995; Tyler, Boeckmann, Smith, & Huo, 1997).

In both theories there is an interesting and complementary mismatch between the processes they describe and the actual observations made in empirical research. Although relative deprivation theory specifies the conditions under which feelings of deprivation are likely to result, empirical observations mainly assess the behavior that supposedly emanates from them, instead of trying to capture more directly the psychological processes involved in the development of deprivation feelings (see Tyler et al., 1997). Conversely, social identity theory distinguishes between possible behavioral strategies that may be used under different circumstances to address an unsatisfactory identity, while research in this area has mainly looked at how people make intergroup comparisons. In a way, this seems to provide a natural connection between the two, as empirical findings obtained within the framework of relative deprivation theory are relevant to predictions derived from social identity theory and vice versa. Obviously, the overlap between these two theoretical perspectives has been noted before – for instance, by Kawakami and Dion (1995), who focus on the distinction between individual and group level deprivation as possible precursors of collective action. Others have tried to develop more general theoretical models incorporating different aspects of social comparison and social inequality as well as possible responses to this (e.g., Martin, 1981; Taylor & McKirnan, 1984).

At first sight it therefore seems that these two perspectives mainly differ in their emphasis, as is evident from the centrality of particular processes, or their focus on specific issues. However, a somewhat more detailed comparison is necessary in order to assess to what extent the two perspectives would indeed yield complementary or converging predictors. Therefore, I will now consider three key issues in turn that may help to integrate insights from relative deprivation theory and social identity theory, namely: (1) what comparisons are people likely to make in order to evaluate their current standing, (2) what is the resulting behavioral preference, and (3) to what extent do improvement versus protection motives result in similar or different cognitive and behavioral responses.

Evaluation of the Status Quo. Relative deprivation theory emphasizes that the evaluation of one's current situation is in principle independent of one's objective outcomes. Instead, it depends on how they relate to so-called referent outcomes (see Folger, 1987). These referent outcomes may stem from a variety of sources, such as comparisons with other individuals or groups, with one's own future perspectives, or with past expectations (see Levine & Moreland, 1987). Thus, the evaluation of a particular situation supposedly depends on the choice of comparison or referent outcome.

Social comparison research has addressed the question under what circumstances a particular comparison is likely to occur. This has revealed that people may either compare with someone who is better-off than they are (upward comparison), or with someone who is worse-off (downward comparison), depending on the specific goal of the comparison – namely, self-improvement or self-enhancement (see Major, Testa, & Bylsma, 1991). Furthermore, it has been suggested that people are more likely to engage in interpersonal rather than intergroup comparisons, as the latter comparison target is likely to be more dissimilar to the self (Martin, 1981; see also Festinger, 1954). However, this seems somewhat incompatible with results of relative deprivation research (e.g., Major, 1994), showing that people are more inclined to acknowledge group deprivation than individual deprivation.

Likewise, little systematic attention has been devoted to the question of whether people prefer social comparisons rather than temporal comparisons: in most studies, research participants could only choose from different social comparison targets. However, a recent study in which participants could *either* use temporal or social comparison information revealed that, when they have this choice, people may primarily evaluate their current situation in view of previous expectations and future possibilities, rather than by comparing with others (see Ouwerkerk, Ellemers, Smith, & Van Knippenberg, 2000). Although feasibility of alternative outcomes has been listed as one of the preconditions for relative deprivation to occur (see Cook, Crosby, & Hennigan, 1977), the effects of different temporal perspectives on comparison preferences have not been investigated systematically.[1]

Social identity theory also acknowledges the possibility that different comparisons can be made, depending on the salient social context (Oakes, 1987), and that comparisons between one's own situation and that of other individuals or groups determine the favorability of the resulting personal or social identity (see Tajfel, 1975; 1978; Tajfel & Turner, 1979). However, an important difference with relative deprivation or social comparison theory is that social identity theory also allows a specification of what comparison is likely to be made under which circumstances.

Similar to the idea that the feasibility of alternative outcomes is important, in his original theoretical formulations Tajfel (1975; 1978) assigns a central role to the idea of so-called "cognitive alternatives" to the status quo. According to the theory, the availability of cognitive alternatives depends on the extent to which current outcomes seem subject to change. In this context, Tajfel refers to different kinds of belief systems regarding the social structure: to the extent that intergroup boundaries seem permeable, alternative outcomes should be available to individuals, while the conviction that group statuses are unstable implies that group outcomes might be different. Thus, the feasibility of alternative outcomes or the availability of cognitive alternatives may either apply to individuals or to groups. It is further argued that this may lead people to primarily think of themselves and others either in individualistic or in group terms (see also Turner, 1987). In other words, according to a social identity perspective, people's comparison preferences depend on what are considered relevant entities in a particular social context. Viewed from this perspective, the crucial difference between interpersonal and intergroup comparisons is the level of abstraction at which individuals define themselves and others, rather than the level of (dis)similarity between the self and the comparison target.

Thus, the question of which comparisons people are likely to make is central to both relative deprivation theory and social identity theory. However, although no specific predictions about comparison preference can be derived from relative deprivation theory, social identity theory suggests that the availability of cognitive alternatives to the present situation determines whether people are likely to engage in interpersonal or intergroup comparisons. Thus, the distinction that is made in social identity theory between the feasibility of different individual outcomes (permeability of group boundaries) on the one hand, and the likelihood that collective outcomes might change (stability of group status) on the other hand, enables us to specify that while people may be equally dissatisfied about the status quo, their resentment may either focus on the fact that they belong to this particular group, or on the position of the group as a whole (see Ellemers, Van Knippenberg, & Wilke, 1990).

Behavioral Responses. When we aim to predict the likely consequences to the experience of disadvantage, the perceived injustice of current outcomes emerges as an important factor in relative deprivation theory ("entitlement") as well as social identity theory ("legitimacy"). In fact, although they restrict their discussion to personal deprivation, Cook et al. (1977) argue that "relative deprivation *is* a sense of violated entitlement" (p. 312, italics in original). This emphasis on perceived illegitimacy of current outcomes is maintained in more recent theoretical formulations that also speak to the collective experience of relative deprivation. Specifically, it has been proposed that dissatisfaction with current outcomes only turns into resentment and thus constitutes grounds for collective action when the discrepancy between what is and what ought to be seems unjustifiable (e.g., Folger, 1987; see also Major, 1994).

Again, the approach in social identity theory is slightly different, as legitimacy is considered a "sociostructural" variable, just like permeability of group boundaries or stability of group status. Thus, rather than constituting the main factor that motivates people to take action, it has been argued that the legitimacy of current outcomes should be considered as a factor that determines the *nature* of this action, because it may either pull together (in the case of collective injustice) or drive apart (when they have suffered unjust treatment individually) group members. Accordingly, it has been established that collective injustice resulting in low group status enhances ingroup identification and elicits intergroup competition, while those who end up members of a lower status group because of individual unjust treatment resist identification with this group, and display competitiveness toward their fellow group members (see Ellemers, Wilke, & Van Knippenberg, 1993). Converging findings were obtained in a recent series of experiments by Wright (1997), who found that group members are more inclined to engage in collective protest as they consider their group's plight more unjust.

Thus, relative deprivation theory proposes that perceived injustice of current outcomes is an important motivator of behavioral action, aimed at redressing this injustice. Additionally, social identity theory allows us to predict the likely nature of the ensuing behavior, by proposing that the way people are treated can also affect people's self-definition. Consequently, legitimacy considerations may determine whether people are more likely to engage in interpersonal or in intergroup comparisons, and as a result they may point the way as to which forms of action (as an individual or as a group member) seem most appropriate.

Improvement versus Protection. A final issue concerns the fact that social identity theory mainly focuses on the consequences of lower social status, while relative deprivation theory maintains that deprivation feelings may occur regardless of one's objective social standing. Consequently, from a relative deprivation perspective it would seem that high status group members may experience identity threat just as well as low status group members – for instance, because their superior standing is challenged by others. This raises the interesting question of which cognitive and behavioral strategies high status group members are likely to use in order to protect their current position in the social hierarchy. For instance, in a laboratory experiment, participants were confronted with the possibility that they might lose membership in a highly attractive (high status minority) group, by emphasizing that group boundaries were permeable. In response to this, group members displayed increased ingroup identification, which can be seen as an indication that they tried to hold on to their group membership (Ellemers, Doosje, Van Knippenberg, & Wilke, 1992).

To some extent, this seems to suggest that those with higher status in principle display similar strategic responses as lower status group members. Nevertheless, it can be argued that systematic differences will occur. For instance, among lower status group members, the use of individualistic strategies (such as the pursuit of individual upward mobility) constitutes the primary option, except when this is objectively or subjectively unfeasible (i.e., when group boundaries are impermeable, see Ellemers, Van Knippenberg, De Vries, & Wilke, 1988, or when individuals are highly committed to their group, see Ellemers, Spears, & Doosje, 1997). For those who belong to a higher status group, however, initial preferences for individual versus group-level strategies may well be reversed. That is, when the superior status of one's group is threatened, it is likely that group members first try to preserve their group's position, and only engage in individual level strategies (i.e., seek acceptance in the other group) when their group's loss of status is inevitable (see Ellemers & Bos, 1998).

In other words, contrary to the pattern observed in lower status groups, it seems plausible that for high status group members the pursuit of group-level strategies prevails over the use of individual level strategies. Again, this illustrates how the combination of insights from social identity theory and relative deprivation theory may offer new directions for theoretical progress and empirical research.

Social Identification as a Central Construct
Although there are various differences between the two perspectives, there also appears to be considerable correspondence as to the main variables that are considered of interest in social identity theory and relative

deprivation theory. This confirms that they may be seen as complementary perspectives in which, depending on the specific issue at hand, one may be seen as an elaboration or specification of the other. More important, however, it seems that a combination of insights from these two theoretical frameworks raises novel research questions that may yield important additional insights. Three central issues that were discussed previously considered predictions from both perspectives about the kind of comparison that is likely to be made, the behavioral response this should elicit, and the question of whether protection and improvement motives elicit similar or different strategic preferences. In the remainder of this chapter, I will argue that social identification is a central construct linking relative deprivation to social identity predictions, and review some relevant empirical work that may illustrate this.

As we have briefly indicated, in relative deprivation theory an important distinction is made between individual-level (egoistic) deprivation and group-level (fraternal) deprivation (see Runciman, 1966). Although some have opted to focus on one form of deprivation only (e.g., Cook et al., 1977), others have explicitly addressed the differences between the two as well as their behavioral implications. Research into this issue has consistently revealed that the two forms of deprivation yield fundamentally different responses, in the sense that personal deprivation is likely to elicit experience of stress, while group-level deprivation seems an important precursor for collective action (Dion, 1986; Dubé & Guimond, 1986; Guimond & Dubé-Simard, 1983; Tripathi & Shrivastava, 1981; Vanneman & Pettigrew, 1972; Walker & Mann, 1987). Consequently, in order to predict the consequences of deprivation feelings, it is crucial to know whether people are likely to make interpersonal comparisons, which possibly result in the experience of personal deprivation, or intergroup comparisons that may give rise to group deprivation. In this context it should be emphasized that the level of comparison that is used does not necessarily depend on the properties of the social situation, nor can it be predicted from instrumental considerations such as the extent to which people's individual fates are bound to the group to which they belong. In fact, it turns out that there is no logical or self-evident connection between the two forms of deprivation. This can be illustrated by the literature on the so-called personal/group discrepancy, which reveals that people may be perfectly happy about their personal situation, even though they indicate that their group as a whole is disadvantaged (e.g., Major, 1994; Martin, 1981). In other words, people can respond differently to the same situation, and to understand their behavior it is important to predict who will be most likely to perceive the situation in interpersonal or rather in inter-group terms.

Although, as indicated previously, social identity theory mainly focuses on the consequences of lower social status, relatively much effort has been devoted to the different strategies group members may choose to cope with identity threat, as well as the conditions under which people are likely to opt for each of these strategies. In this context it has been proposed that strategy choice should be related to the extent to which people identify with their group, and this has been corroborated in empirical research (see Branscombe & Ellemers, 1998, for an overview). The cognitive underpinnings of this rela-tionship have been specified in self-categorization theory (Turner, 1987), where it is explicitly indicated that people may define themselves on differ-ent levels of abstraction (e.g., as individuals or as group members). Furthermore, the level of self-categorization determines what are relevant entities in the social environment. Most relevant to the present discussion is the assumption that when people define themselves as separate individuals they are likely to engage in interpersonal comparisons, while intergroup comparisons are expected to ensue when people primarily consider them-selves in terms of their group membership.

Thus, it seems that the construct of group identification may enable us to connect social identity predictions with insights from relative depriva-tion theory. However, to be able to make this connection successfully, we have to be more explicit about what this concept of group identification entails, and specifically whether the term group identification only indi-cates the cognitive organization of individuals into a social category, or whether it is essential that it incorporates the emotional consequences of social categorization. In the relative deprivation literature some discussion has been devoted to the question of whether relative deprivation mainly refers to the cognitive acknowledgment of a discrepancy between current outcomes and referent outcomes, or whether the resulting feelings of unjust disadvantage are crucial for behavioral responses to occur (see Guimond & Dubé-Simard, 1983; Martin, Brickman, & Murray, 1984). Similar questions have been raised by those who have attempted to apply insights from social identity theory to predict work-related behavior in an organizational context (see Ouwerkerk, Ellemers, & De Gilder, 1999, for an overview). The more interesting theoretical proposition, which is sup-ported by empirical data, emphasizes that group identification is more than the cognitive awareness of some common group membership. Specifically, it has been demonstrated that individual effort on behalf of the group cannot be explained from purely instrumental motives, and that people may even favor their group when it is obvious that they themselves cannot benefit from this (e.g., Diehl, 1990).

In a recent attempt to distinguish between different components of social identity, Ellemers, Kortekaas, and Ouwerkerk (1999) obtained support for the assumption that cognitive self-categorization can be separated from emotional involvement with the group. This not only emerged in the different subscales of their identity measure, but also in the finding that self-categorization and emotional involvement are affected by different group characteristics, such as relative group size and relative group status, respectively. Furthermore, and most relevant to our present discussion, it turned out that only emotional group involvement predicted group members' behavioral responses – that is, their displays of ingroup favoritism in group ratings and outcome allocations.

Where Do Differences in Identification Come From? Theory and research examining variations in group identification have mainly focused on the effects of group status (e.g., see Hinkle & Brown, 1990; Messick & Mackie, 1989, or Mullen, Brown & Smith, 1992, for overviews). Empirical support for the overall assumption that low group status generally elicits less ingroup identification than high group status has been obtained in various studies (e.g., Ellemers, 1993a). Nevertheless, the more interesting question is whether it is possible to establish factors that are likely to result in differential levels of ingroup identification, *given identical group status*. In other words, when considering the possible responses of those who belong to disadvantaged social groups, it is important to specify the circumstances under which these group members are likely to distance themselves from the rest of the group or display solidarity with their fellow ingroup members.

Arguably, there is some intercultural variation in this, in the sense that the overall inclination to identify as a group member is less strong in individualistic cultures while people in collectivistic cultures are more inclined to make intergroup comparisons (Triandis, 1990). Regardless of this differential base rate of identification, however, in line with self-categorization theory (Turner, 1987) the distinction between high and low identifiers is not intended as an individual difference variable. Rather, the level of identification supposedly reflects the extent to which people are willing to perceive themselves in terms of a particular group membership in a specific context.

A first issue that has to be considered is the *basis* for group membership. In this context it is important to distinguish between group memberships that are self-selected or externally assigned. Although this distinction has been mentioned in the literature (Luhtanen & Crocker, 1991) it has not systematically been addressed as a variable of interest. Nevertheless, it does covary with other group characteristics, and may therefore explain seemingly inconsistent findings in the literature. For instance when comparing field observations with results from laboratory studies (see Mullen et al., 1992), it is relevant to acknowledge that the former studies usually relied on natural group memberships (such as study major) that were self-selected, while individuals are usually assigned to groups that are created experimentally. Initial evidence suggests that such issues may moderate the extent to which individuals feel committed to a lower status group (Turner, Hogg, Turner, & Smith, 1984). When the possible effects of this difference were more explicitly assessed in a recent experiment (Ellemers et al., 1999), the empirical evidence confirmed that people identified more strongly with self-selected than with externally assigned group memberships.

A second factor that may help explain variations in identification with a lower status group refers to the way in which present outcomes have come about, or more specifically to the perceived legitimacy of the current situation. As previously noted, in this context legitimacy can be considered as a possible cause of group identification, instead of as a factor that merely influences the intensity of emotional responses to disadvantage. Thus, in addition to the question whether current positions result from fair or unfair treatment, we have to assess whether this treatment is directed at separate individuals or at the group as an entity in order to predict the likelihood that people will primarily think of themselves in individual or in group terms. As a result, to the extent that people consider their current inferior standing the result of collective unjust treatment, they are more likely to identify with their group. Conversely, when they are accorded low group status because of individual injustice, people resist identification with a lower status group (see Ellemers, Wilke, & Van Knippenberg, 1993). In other words, when illegitimate treatment evokes the impression of having a common enemy, this is likely to increase group cohesion (see also Rabbie & Bekkers, 1978).

In addition to these 'historical' aspects of the present situation, we have indicated the importance of future perspectives for improvement as determinants of ingroup identification. In line with early formulations of social identity theory (Tajfel, 1974; 1975; 1978; Tajfel & Turner, 1979), initial efforts in this direction focused on the effects of specific characteristics of the social structure (sociostructural variables). The general argument is that levels of group identification do not merely reflect the current standing of one's group, but also incorporate the ways in which the situation is likely to change. Specifically, to the extent that group boundaries are permeable, individuals may try to avoid the association with this particular group, as a way toward individual status improvement (individual mobility). Conversely, when the relative positions of groups vis-à-vis each other are subject to change, people may be more inclined to think of themselves in terms of their group membership. In other words, the level at which these so-called cognitive alternatives to the present situation are available determines the nature of movable agents in the social structure. Furthermore, the extent to which individuals or groups are perceived as salient entities is likely to affect people's inclination to engage in interpersonal or intergroup comparisons, and this should be evident from the extent to which they identify as group members. Empirical support for this general argument was obtained in a series of laboratory experiments with minimal groups, in which the perceived permeability of group boundaries and the stability of group statuses was experimentally manipulated (see Ellemers, 1993a, for an overview). The results of these studies indicate that members of lower status groups are relatively willing to identify with this group when the group's status is unstable. Conversely, the awareness that individuals may change groups (permeable group boundaries) results in a decrease of identification with lower status groups.

These sociostructural characteristics essentially indicate how the different groups are related to each other, but there are reasons to assume that *within-group* relations may just as well affect levels of ingroup identification. Specifically, in different experiments it turned out that people are less likely to identify with a lower status group, the higher their individual ability compared to other group members (see Ellemers, 1991). In principle, this finding attests to the fact that instrumental considerations may affect the extent to which people are inclined to identify with social groups. However, recent data demonstrated that intragroup relations may also affect levels of ingroup identification in ways that are less easy to explain from a purely instrumental point of view. Specifically, members of a group that was rated negatively by others were more inclined to show ingroup identification as they received more personal respect from their fellow ingroup members (see Branscombe et al., 1999).

Finally, in addition to the extent to which the individual's value is acknowledged *within* the group, it is important to consider the extent to which the individual can obtain a distinct identity *through* the group (see also Branscombe et al., 1999). In line with arguments proposed by Simon (1997; Simon & Hamilton, 1994) and Brewer (1991), it would seem that relatively small groups offer their members more of a distinct social identity than majority groups. Accordingly, independent of the relative status position of the group, its relative size is likely to determine the extent to which people think of themselves as group members. Indeed, there is by now converging empirical support for the assumption that minority group members generally show higher levels of ingroup identification than those who belong to the majority (e.g., Ellemers & Van Rijswijk, 1997; Simon, Pantaleo, & Mummendey, 1995; see also Branscombe et al., 1999).

What Are the Consequences of Differential Identification? A recurrent point of critique concerning relative deprivation theory is that, although it is acknowledged that various kinds of comparisons can be made (see Levine & Moreland, 1987), the theory does not allow prediction of which specific comparison is likely to be preferred under what circumstances (e.g., Taylor & Moghaddam, 1987; Tyler et al., 1997). As a consequence, the comparison that has been made can only be inferred post hoc. As we have seen, social identity and self-categorization theory and research, however, more explicitly maintain that situational factors affect the cognitive salience of various alternative outcomes (see also Haslam & Turner, 1992; Oakes, 1987), which in turn determines what kind of comparison is likely to be seen as most informative to the situation at hand. Thus, we propose that Tajfel's original assumption (1975), that people may either think of themselves and act as individuals or as group members, can be applied to predict whether interpersonal or intergroup comparisons are likely to be made. Specifically, the level of ingroup identification that may vary as a function of the factors discussed in the previous section should lead people to conceive of themselves and others primarily in individualistic or in group terms.

To corroborate and specify this argument, I will now review a recent program of research that systematically examined the cognitive and motivational consequences of high versus low group identification. A first indication that those who identify strongly with their group are more inclined to perceive the world in terms of social groups was obtained in a study by Doosje, Ellemers, and Spears (1995). They obtained converging results when investigating consequences of naturally occurring variations in group identification among members of real-life groups, and when examining the effects of experimentally manipulated differences in identification with artificially created groups. When the ingroup compared negatively to a relevant outgroup, high identifiers perceived the ingroup as well as the outgroup as homogeneous entities, which testifies to their inclination to define the social environment in group terms. By contrast, low identifiers emphasized intragroup differences, presumably to indicate that they preferred to consider themselves and others as separate individuals, instead of in terms of their group memberships.

Further support for this account was obtained in a study by Spears, Doosje, and Ellemers (1997), who investigated the extent to which group members were likely to self-stereotype when faced with a group threat. Converging results were obtained across four experiments, where the threat concerned the relative status of the ingroup or the group's distinctiveness, while this threat was either self-perceived or allegedly derived from other people's perceptions. Consequently, a meta-analysis across the four experiments showed that in response to group threat high-identifiers emphasized their prototypicality as group members, while low-identifiers were less inclined to perceive themselves in stereotypical group terms.

In addition to these implications of group identification at the cognitive level, in further empirical work we examined the behavioral consequences of high versus low group identification. These studies consistently revealed that those who identify strongly are more likely to stand by their group and are more willing to expend individual effort intended to improve their group's position. In a study with artificially created laboratory groups, Ellemers and Van Rijswijk (1997) led participants to believe that there were specific differences between these groups, in order to investigate whether this information would restrict claims of ingroup superiority. As expected, they generally observed a "social creativity" strategy (see Lemaine, 1974), in the sense that participants acknowledged the "established" differences between the groups, but displayed ingroup favoritism on more ambiguous comparative dimensions. Relevant to the present investigation is that this tendency to depict the ingroup in a positive way was more pronounced as participants identified more strongly with their group.

Although Ellemers and Van Rijswijk (1997) classified participants into high- versus low-identifiers on the basis of spontaneously occurring differences in identification, in a further study, Ellemers, Spears and Doosje (1997) experimentally induced different levels of identification. In their first experiment the ingroup held lower status than the comparison group, while in the second experiment the relative statuses of the groups were unknown. In both cases it turned out that high-identifiers were inclined to stick together with the rest of their group, while low-identifiers expressed the desire to leave the ingroup, and continue as a member of the other group. Converging results were obtained in different experimental paradigms.

In a series of laboratory experiments, we examined the combined effects of ingroup identification and intergroup performance comparisons on group performance motivation and individual effort on behalf of the group (see Ouwerkerk et al., 1999). These studies consistently revealed that, when the ingroup compared negatively to the relevant outgroup, this elicited negative affective responses in group members. As a result, some group participants also disidentified with the group. Consequently, when presented with an (unexpected) opportunity to improve their group's performance with an additional task, only those who still identified strongly with their group were motivated to do so. One experiment that allegedly compared the performances of natural groups (students with different majors) accordingly revealed that high-identifiers actually worked harder than low-identifiers to improve the group's performance after an unfavorable intergroup comparison.

Further converging evidence that the level of group identification may affect group members' willingness to exert themselves on behalf of the group was obtained in a laboratory study that examined dyadic collaboration in an asymmetrical power relation. Specifically, the goal of this study was to assess whether subordinates' willingness to display cooperative behavior depends on the extent to which they identify with their superior. For this purpose, participants always held the subordinate position in the team, and were either assigned to an ingroup (same study major) or outgroup (other study major) superior. The results confirmed that people generally engaged in more cooperative behavior as they feel more committed to their partner (Ellemers, Van Rijswijk, Bruins, & De Gilder, 1998).

Finally, we examined to what extent social pressure or social desirability might affect displays of group-favoring behavior. Although we did establish that high-identifiers are more likely than low-identifiers to comply to group norms (see Ellemers, Barreto, & Spears, 1999), it also turned out that high-identifiers are intrinsically motivated to work for the group. That is, while low-identifiers only show group-serving behavior when they can be held personally accountable for their behavior, high identifiers invest in the group regardless of whether their behavioral choices are made in public or in private (Barreto & Ellemers, 1998).

To summarize, a variety of laboratory experiments and studies among members of natural groups attests to the importance of group identification as a crucial moderator of people's cognitive and behavioral responses to their group membership. Specifically, the level of identification determines: (1) which elements in the social structure are seen as homogeneous entities that can be compared to each other, (2) to what extent people are likely to perceive themselves in terms of a particular group membership, and (3) whether they are willing to exert themselves on behalf of the group. Again, these findings underline the importance of social identification as a theoretical construct that may help us understand and predict how social actors are likely to respond to experienced threat or disadvantage.

Does Experimental Work on Social Identity Help Us to Understand Social Behavior?

Although, as we have indicated, converging results have been obtained from investigations of artificially created and naturally occurring groups, obviously the nature of the dependent measures that are most commonly used in this kind of research (such as point allocations, or cooperative behavior in an experimental group task) are far removed from the social behavior we would like to predict. Arguably, actual social behavior is usually more visible, more effortful, and more costly than the behavioral intentions or behavioral displays that can be tapped in a laboratory investigation. Hence, there is still a considerable gap between this experimental work and the social problems this should be applied to. To conclude this chapter, I will therefore consider some recent work suggesting that the processes observed in the laboratory may actually constitute a valid analogy of the psychological mechanisms that operate in real life.

One applied domain that has attracted attention from relative deprivation as well as social identity researchers is that of political action. Although relative deprivation researchers have argued that intergroup comparisons and the ensuing experience of collective disadvantage are likely precursors of participation in collective action, those who work from a social identity tradition set out to demonstrate that strength of group identification predicts whether or not people are likely to participate in collective action.

Considerable discussion in the literature on political action has been devoted to the question of whether participation in collective action primarily ensues from (personal) instrumental considerations (Klandermans, 1997) or can be attributed to psychological group involvement (Reicher, 1987; see also Kelly & Breinlinger, 1996). Obviously, for those who realize that others are likely to experience problems similar to theirs, joining forces may seem to increase the chances that political change might actually be achieved. Nevertheless, relative deprivation theory emphasises that the subjective experience of deprivation as well as the associated behavioral responses may occur relatively independently of the actual situation people find themselves in. Indeed, as we have seen, the relationship between the experience of personal deprivation and the perception of group deprivation is far from clear-cut (Major, 1994; Martin, 1981).

Accordingly, recent work in this area has established that in addition to instrumental considerations, more psychological factors also predict the likelihood that individuals will engage in collective action on behalf of their group. Specifically, in a study among Dutch and Spanish farmers, it turned out that although the intention to participate in collective action was partly determined by the estimated chances of success, significant proportions of additional variance were explained by the emotions individual participants experienced in reaction to the fate of other farmers, as well as the extent to which they identified with their professional group. In a similar vein, Simon et al. (1998) concluded from two field studies that participation in a political movement on behalf of the elderly in Germany as well as participation in a Gay rights movement in the United States was jointly determined by a rational cost/benefit analysis *and* identification with the group in question.

Additional evidence that psychological construal of the social situation and level of identification are essential to the experience of relative deprivation and the ensuing responses, was obtained in a field investigation among native entrepreneurs in Amsterdam (Ellemers & Bos, 1998). Although indicators such as the degree of professionalism, the level of education, the "survival rate," and profit level point out that the native shopkeepers are objectively better-off than their immigrant colleagues, the native entrepreneurs feel threatened. The native shopkeepers, who still constitute the overwhelming majority (with 87% of the businesses), greatly overestimated the proportion of immigrant enterprises in the area (at 40%), and felt strongly deprived as a group. Indeed, the more they identified with native entrepreneurs as a group, the more they thought native shopkeepers are disadvantaged.

The experience of group deprivation could not be predicted from the success of their own business or from personal deprivation feelings. In fact, additional results supported the notion that interpersonal instead of intergroup comparisons underlie the experience of personal deprivation. Specifically, those who felt more deprived as individuals were equally likely to hold negative perceptions of other shopkeepers, regardless of whether they were natives or immigrants. As a result, it was the *combination* of *strong group* deprivation and *lack of personal* deprivation that resulted in the least positive perception of the immigrant entrepreneurs.

A final goal of this study was to assess whether the experience of deprivation among those with higher social standing would elicit similar coping responses as are commonly observed among truly disadvantaged groups. Parallel to the pattern that is usually observed in lower status groups, the experience of group deprivation led participants to discredit the other group. However, contrary to the preference for individual mobility in lower status groups, among this sample the experience of personal deprivation led people to be *less* inclined to integrate with the other group. This confirms the previously expressed notion that, although members of higher and lower status social groups may experience similar levels of deprivation regardless of their objective standing, their cognitive and behavioral responses are likely to differ, given that these are aimed at status improvement in the one case, and status protection in the other.

In contrast to the large amount of effort that has been expended to understand collective action in real-life situations, relatively little attention has been devoted to investigating the precursors or consequences of individualistic responses to the experience of disadvantage. A series of studies on upwardly mobile women in male-dominated organizations may help to shed some light on this. As we have seen from the experimental work reviewed in this chapter, the combination of low ingroup status and the opportunity to gain access to a higher status group should result in decreased ingroup identification, accentuation of intragroup heterogeneity, self-presentation as a nonprototypical group member, and perhaps even discrimination toward former ingroup members.

A first investigation (Ellemers, 1993b) among female professors in the Netherlands (who constitute 4% of all full professors) revealed that they claim to have more masculine traits than their male colleagues do. Converging evidence was obtained in another study in a male-dominated government organization (Ellemers, in press). Although in lower ranks women report less masculine and more femine traits, the women in higher ranks indicate that they are equally masculine and less feminine than their male colleagues. These results confirm the notion that an individualistic response to social disadvantage, in this case, being successful as a woman in a male-dominated organization, entails self-presentation as a nonprototypical group member.

Accentuating the difference between oneself and other ingroup members, however, may also result in a stronger perception of the rest of the group in stereotypical terms. Indeed, this mechanism might account for the intriguing finding that female university faculty in the Netherlands held more gender-stereotypical perceptions of the work commitment of male and female PhD students than did male faculty (Ellemers, in press). In fact, the greater gender differentiation of PhDs by female faculty does not stem from a more accurate insight into women's work motives, as it is not reflected in the self-descriptions of the PhDs in question. In fact, similar results were obtained in another male-dominated government organization (Ellemers, in press). Although there was no difference in self-reported work commitment or ambition among male and female employees, especially the women in this organization perceived their female colleagues as less ambitious and less committed to their careers than their male colleagues.

Thus, these observations among women in organizations converge with the general pattern that emerged from relevant experimental work. To the extent that members of disadvantaged groups perceive social differences at an individual level, they disidentify with their group, and present themselves as nonprototypical group members to overcome the burden of discrimination. However, the sad result of this lack of identification is that they may then be most inclined to discriminate against other ingroup members, so that the focus on interpersonal differences may legitimize and ultimately even stabilize the group's inferior standing.

Closing Comments

My aim in this chapter was to connect insights from relative deprivation theory with work on social identity theory, by focusing on the central role of ingroup identification. In doing this, first I argued that social identification affects the comparison preferences that determine how people evaluate the status quo. Second, I proposed that perceived legitimacy not only motivates people to undertake action to redress social disadvantage, but that it may also determine the likely nature and focus of such action. Third, I considered the likely consequences of the assumption that socially advantaged may just as well experience deprivation that may elicit strategic behavior aimed at protecting their current standing. In order to illustrate the workings of these psychological mechanisms I have tried to subsume a large number of studies in different research settings by focusing on social identification as an important variable underlying a variety of other cognitive and behavioral responses. In so doing, I have not only considered the likely antecedents and consequences of social identification, but also tried to illustrate possible consequences of these mechanisms for actual behavior in real social settings.

NOTES

1. In his Referent Cognitions Theory, Folger (1987) proposes the concept "likelihood of amelioration" to specify the psychological antecedents of relative

deprivation. Whereas the perceived feasibility of alternative outcomes is expected to exacerbate deprivation feelings (supposedly because it makes people more aware of the possibility that things could be different), Folger argues that currently unfavorable outcomes will seem more acceptable when future improvement seems imminent. The crucial difference between "feasibility of alternative outcomes" and "likelihood of amelioration" thus appears to lie in the estimated likelihood that change will indeed occur. To the extent that change mostly constitutes a hypothetical possibility, it seems reasonable to assume that this mainly serves to make people more acutely aware of their current unfavorable situation. By contrast, Folger seems to refer to cases in which change has already been initiated, and actual improvement is imminent. A recent experiment confirmed the differential consequences of these two forms of status instability for members of lower status groups (Doosje, Spears, & Ellemers, in press).

REFERENCES

Branscombe, N. R., & Ellemers, N. (1998). Use of individualistic and group strategies in response to perceived group-based discrimination. In J. Swim & C. Stangor (Eds.), *Prejudice: The target's perspective* (pp. 243–266). New York: Academic Press.

Branscombe, N., Ellemers, N., Spears, R., & Doosje, B. (1999). The context and content of social identity threat. In N. Ellemers, R. Spears, & B. Doosje (Eds.), *Social identity: Context, commitment, content* (pp. 35–58). Oxford: Basil Blackwell.

Brewer, M. B. (1991). The social self: On being the same and different at the same time. *Personality and Social Psychology Bulletin, 17*, 475–482.

Cook, T. D., Crosby, F., & Hennigan, K. M. (1977). The construct validity of relative deprivation. In J. M. Suls & R. L. Miller (Eds.), *Social comparison processes: Theoretical and empirical perspectives* (pp. 307–333). Washington, DC: Hemisphere.

Deaux, K., & Ethier, K. A. (1998). Negotiating social identity. In J. Swim & C. Stangor (Eds.), *Prejudice: The target's perspective* (pp. 302–324). New York: Academic Press.

Diehl, M. (1990). The minimal group paradigm: Theoretical explanations and empirical findings. *European Review of Social Psychology, 1*, 263–292.

Dion, K. L. (1986). Responses to perceived discrimination and relative deprivation. In J. M. Olson, C. P. Herman, & M. P. Zanna (Eds.). *Relative deprivation and social comparison: The Ontario symposium* (Vol. 4, pp. 159–179). Hillsdale, NJ: Lawrence Erlbaum.

Doosje, B., Ellemers, N., & Spears, R., (1995). Perceived intragroup variability as a function of group status and identification. *Journal of Experimental Social Psychology, 31*, 410–436.

Doosje, B., Spears, R., & Ellemers, N. (in press). The dynamic and determining nature of group identification: Responses to anticipated and actual changes in the intergroup status hierarchy. *British Journal of Social Psychology.*

Dubé, L., & Guimond, S. (1986). Relative deprivation and social protest: The personal-group issue. In J. M. Olson, C. P. Herman, & M. P. Zanna (Eds.). *Relative deprivation and social comparison: The Ontario symposium* (Vol. 4, pp. 201–216). Hillsdale, NJ: Lawrence Erlbaum.

Ellemers, N. (1991). *Identity management strategies: The influence of socio-structural variables on strategies of individual mobility and social change.* PhD Thesis, University of Groningen.

Ellemers, N. (1993a). The influence of socio-structural variables on identity enhancement strategies. *European Review of Social Psychology, 4,* 27–57.

Ellemers, N. (1993b). Sociale identiteit en sekse: Het dilemma van succesvolle vrouwen. [Social identity and gender: The dilemma of successful women.] *Tijdschrift voor Vrouwenstudies, 14,* 322–336.

Ellemers, N. (in press). Individual upward mobility and the perceived legitimacy of intergroup relations In J. T. Jost & B. Major (Eds.), *The psychology of legitimacy.* New York: Cambridge University Press.

Ellemers, N., Barreto, M., & Spears, R. (1999). Commitment and strategic responses to social context. In N. Ellemers, R. Spears, & B. Doosje (Eds.), *Social identity: Context, commitment, content* (pp. 127–146). Oxford: Basil Blackwell.

Ellemers, N., & Bos, A. (1998). Individual and group level responses to threat experienced by Dutch shopkeepers in East-Amsterdam. *Journal of Applied Social Psychology, 28,* 1987–2005.

Ellemers, N., Doosje, E. J., Van Knippenberg, A., & Wilke, H. (1992). Status protection in high status minorities. *European Journal of Social Psychology, 22,* 123–140.

Ellemers, N., Kortekaas, P., & Ouwerkerk, J. (1999). Self-categorization, commitment to the group and social self-esteem as related but distinct aspects of social identity. *European Journal of Social Psychology, 29,* 371–389.

Ellemers, N., Spears, R., & Doosje, B. (1997). Sticking together or falling apart: Group identification as a psychological determinant of group commitment versus individual mobility. *Journal of Personality and Social Psychology, 72,* 123–140.

Ellemers, N., Van Knippenberg, A., De Vries, N., & Wilke, H. (1988). Social identification and permeability of group boundaries. *European Journal of Social Psychology, 18,* 497–513.

Ellemers, N., Van Knippenberg, A., & Wilke, H. (1990). The influence of permeability of group boundaries and stability of group status on strategies of individual mobility and social change. *British Journal of Social Psychology, 29,* 233–246.

Ellemers, N., & Van Rijswijk, W. (1997). Identity needs versus social opportunities: The use of group-level and individual-level identity management strategies. *Social Psychology Quarterly, 60,* 52–65.

Ellemers, N., Van Rijswijk, W., Bruins, J., & De Gilder, D. (1998). Group commitment as a moderator of attributional and behavioural responses to power use. *European Journal of Social Psychology, 28,* 555–573.

Ellemers, N., Wilke, H., & Van Knippenberg, A. (1993). Effects of the legitimacy of low group or individual status on individual and collective identity enhancement strategies. *Journal of Personality and Social Psychology, 64,* 766–778.

Festinger, L. (1954). A theory of social comparison processes. *Human Relations, 7,* 117–140.

Folger, R. (1987). Reformulating the preconditions of resentment: A referent cognitions model. In J. C. Masters & W. P. Smith (Eds.), *Social comparison, social justice, and relative deprivation: Theoretical, empirical, and policy perspectives* (pp. 183–215). Hillsdale, NJ: Lawrence Erlbaum.

Guimond, S., & Dubé-Simard, L. (1983). Relative deprivation theory and the Quebec nationalist movement: The cognition-emotion distinction and the personal-group deprivation issue. *Journal of Personality and Social Psychology, 44,* 526–535.

Haslam, S. A., & Turner, J. C. (1992). Context-dependent variation in social stereotyping 2: The relationship between frame of reference, self-categorization, and accentuation. *European Journal of Social Psychology, 22,* 251–278.

Hinkle, S., & Brown, R. J. (1990). Intergroup comparisons and social identity: Some links and lacunae. In D. Abrams & M. A. Hogg (Eds.), *Social identity theory: Constructive and critical advances* (pp. 48–70). London: Harvester Wheatsheaf.

Hogg, M. A. (1996). Social identity, self-categorization, and the small group. In E. H. Witte & J. H. Davis (Eds.), *Understanding group behavior, Vol. 2: Small group processes and interpersonal relations* (pp. 227–253). Mahwah, NJ: Lawrence Erlbaum.

Jost, J. T., & Banaji, M. R. (1994). The role of stereotyping in system-justification and the production of false consciousness. *British Journal of Social Psychology, 33,* 1–27.

Kawakami, K., & Dion, K. L. (1995). Social identity and affect as determinants of collective action. *Theory and Psychology, 5,* 551–577.

Kelly, C., & Breinlinger, S. (1996). *The social psychology of collective action.* London: Taylor & Francis.

Klandermans, P. G. (1997). *The social psychology of protest.* Oxford: Basil Blackwell.

Lemaine, G. (1974). Social differentiation and social originality. *European Journal of Social Psychology, 4,* 17–52.

Levine, J. M., & Moreland, R. L. (1987). Social comparison and outcome evaluation in group contexts. In J. C. Masters & W. P. Smith (Eds.), *Social comparison, social justice, and relative deprivation* (pp. 105–127). Hillsdale, NJ: Lawrence Erlbaum.

Lind, E. A., & Tyler, T. R. (1988). *The social psychology of procedural justice.* New York: Plenum.

Luhtanen, R., & Crocker, J. (1991). Self-esteem and intergroup comparisons: Toward a theory of collective self-esteem. In J. Suls, & T. A. Wills (Eds.), *Social comparison: Contemporary theory and research* (pp. 211–234). Hillsdale, NJ: Lawrence Erlbaum.

Mackie, D. M., & Smith, E. R. (1998). Intergroup relations: Insights from a theoretically integrative approach. *Psychological Review, 105,* 499–529.

Major, B. (1994). From social inequality to personal entitlement: The role of social comparisons, legitimacy appraisals, and group membership. In M. P. Zanna (Ed.), *Advances in experimental social psychology* (Vol. 26, pp. 293–355). San Diego, CA: Academic Press.

Major, B., Testa, M., & Bylsma, W. H. (1991). Responses to upward and downward social comparisons: The impact of esteem-relevance and perceived control. In J. Suls & T. A. Wills (Eds.), *Social comparison: Contemporary theory and research* (pp. 237–260). Hillsdale, NJ: Lawrence Erlbaum.

Martin, J. (1981). Relative deprivation: A theory of distributive injustice for an era of shrinking resources. *Research in Organizational Behavior, 3,* 53–107.

Martin, J., Brickman, P., & Murray, A. (1984). Moral outrage and pragmatism: Explanations for collective action. *Journal of Experimental Social Psychology, 20,* 484–496.

Merton, R. K. (1965). *On the shoulders of giants: A shandean postscript.* New York: Harcourt Brace & World.

Messick, D. M., & Mackie, D. M. (1989). Intergroup relations. *Annual Review of Psychology, 40,* 45–81.

Mullen, B., Brown, R., & Smith, C. (1992). Ingroup bias as a function of salience, relevance, and status: An integration. *European Journal of Social Psychology, 22,* 103–122.

Oakes, P. J. (1987). The salience of social categories. In J. C. Turner, M. A. Hogg, P. J. Oakes, S. D. Reicher, & M. S. Whetherell (Eds.), *Rediscovering the social group: A self-categorization theory* (pp. 117–141). Oxford: Basil Blackwell.

Ouwerkerk, J., Ellemers, N., & de Gilder, D. (1999). Commitment and performance in an organizational context. In N. Ellemers, R. Spears, & B. Doosje (Eds.), *Social identity: Context, commitment, content* (pp. 184–204). Oxford: Basil Blackwell.

Ouwerkerk, J. Ellemers, N., Smith, H. J., & Van Knippenberg, A. (2000). *The swinging pendulum: Affective and motivational consequences of temporal intergroup comparisons.* Manuscript under review.

Pettigrew, T. F. (1967). Social evaluation theory: Convergences and applications. In D. Levine (Ed.), *Nebraska symposium on motivation* (Vol. 15, pp. 241–315). Lincoln: University of Nebraska Press.

Rabbie, J. M., & Bekkers, F. (1978). Threatened leadership and intergroup competition. *European Journal of Social Psychology, 8,* 9–20.

Reicher, S. D. (1987). Crowd behaviour as social action. In J. C. Turner, M. A. Hogg, P. J. Oakes, S. D. Reicher, & M. S. Wetherell (Eds.), *Rediscovering the social group: A self-categorization theory* (pp. 171–202). Oxford: Blackwell.

Roese, N. J., & Olson, J. M. (1995). Functions of counterfactual thinking. In N. J. Roese, & J. M. Olson (Eds.) *What might have been: The social psychology of counterfactual thinking* (pp. 169–198). Mahwah, NJ: Lawrence Erlbaum.

Rothgerber, H., & Worchel, S. (1997). The view from below: Intergroup relations from the perspective of the disadvantaged group. *Journal of Personality and Social Psychology, 73,* 1191–1205.

Runciman, W. (1966). *Relative deprivation and social justice.* London: Routledge and Kegan Paul.

Sidanius, J., & Pratto, F. (1993). The inevitability of oppression and the dynamics of social dominance. In P. M. Sniderman, P. E. Tetlock, & E. G. Carmines (Eds.), *Prejudice, politics, and the American dilemma* (pp. 173–211). Stanford, CA: Stanford University Press.

Simon, B. (1997). Self and group in modern society: Ten theses on the individual self and the collective self. In R. Spears, P. J. Oakes, N. Ellemers, & S. A.

Haslam (Eds.), *The social psychology of stereotyping and group life* (pp. 318–335). Oxford: Blackwell.

Simon, B., & Hamilton, D. L. (1994). Self-stereotyping and social context: The effects of relative in-group size and in-group status. *Journal of Personality and Social Psychology, 66,* 699–711.

Simon, B., Loewy, M., Stürmer, S., Weber, U., Freytag, P., Habig, C., Kaupmeier, C., & Spahlinger, D. (1998). Collective identification and social movement participation. *Journal of Personality and Social Psychology, 74,* 646–658.

Simon, B., Pantaleo, G., & Mummendey, A. (1995). Unique individual or interchangeable group member? The accentuation of intragroup differences versus similarities as an indicator of the individual self versus the collective self. *Journal of Personality and Social Psychology, 69,* 106–119.

Spears, R., Doosje, B., & Ellemers, N. (1997). Self-stereotyping in the face of threats to group status and distinctiveness: The role of group identification. *Personality and Social Psychology Bulletin, 23,* 538–553.

Tajfel, H. (1974). Social identity and intergroup behaviour. *Social Science Information, 13,* 65–93.

Tajfel, H. (1975). The exit of social mobility and the voice of social change. *Social Science Information, 14,* 111–118.

Tajfel, H. (1978). Interindividual behaviour and intergroup behaviour. In H. Tajfel (Ed.), *Differentiation between social groups: Studies in the social psychology of intergroup relations* (pp. 27–60). New York: Academic Press.

Tajfel, H., & Turner, J. C. (1979). An integrative theory of intergroup conflict. In W. G. Austin & S. Worchel (Eds.), *The social psychology of intergroup relations* (pp. 33–47). Monterey, CA: Brooks/Cole.

Taylor, D. M., & McKirnan, D. J. (1984). A five-stage model of intergroup relations. *British Journal of Social Psychology, 23,* 291–300.

Taylor, D. M., & Moghaddam, F. M. (1987). *Theories of intergroup relations: International social psychological perspectives.* New York: Praeger.

Tesser, A. (1988). Toward a self-evaluation maintenance model of social behavior. *Advances in experimental social psychology, 21,* 181–227.

Triandis, H. C. (1990). Cross-cultural studies of individualism and collectivism. In J. Berman (Ed.), *Nebraska symposium on motivation* (pp. 41–133). Lincoln: University of Nebraska Press.

Tripathi, R. C., & Shrivastava, R. (1981). Relative deprivation and intergroup attitudes. *European Journal of Social Psychology, 11,* 313–318.

Turner, J. C. (1987). A self-categorization theory. In J. C. Turner, M. A. Hogg, P. J. Oakes, S. D. Reicher, & M. S. Wetherell (Eds.), *Rediscovering the social group: A self-categorization theory* (pp. 42–67). Oxford: Blackwell.

Turner, J. C., Hogg, M. A., Turner, P. J., & Smith, P. M. (1984). Failure and defeat as determinants of group cohesiveness. *British Journal of Social Psychology, 23,* 97–111.

Tyler, T. R., Boeckmann, R. J., Smith, H. J., & Huo, Y. J. (1997). *Social justice in a diverse society.* Oxford: Westview Press.

Tyler, T. R., & Lind, A. E. (1992). A relational model of authority in groups. In M. P. Zanna (Ed.), *Advances in experimental social psychology* (Vol. 25, pp. 115–191). San Diego, CA: Academic Press.

Vanneman, R. D., & Pettigrew, T. F. (1972). Race and relative deprivation in the United States. *Race, 13*, 461–486.

Walker, I., & Mann, L. (1987). Unemployment, relative deprivation, and social protest. *Personality and Social Psychology Bulletin, 13*, 275–283.

Wann, D. L., & Branscombe, N. R. (1990). Die-hard and fair-wheather fans: Effects of identification on BIRGing and CORFing tendencies. *Journal of Sport and Social Issues, 14*, 103–117.

Wright, S. C. (1997). Ambiguity, social influence, and collective action: Generating collective protest in response to tokenism. *Personality and Social Psychology Bulletin, 23*, 1277–1290.

TWELVE

Relative Deprivation and Counterfactual Thinking

James M. Olson and Neal J. Roese

The specific phenomenon that has been the principal stimulant of research on *relative deprivation* is the frequent discontinuity between objective and subjective well-being. Individuals' objective conditions (wealth, health, etc.) are, at best, imperfect predictors of their subjective satisfaction with their lives or situations. The insight provided by the construct of relative deprivation is that people evaluate their outcomes in relation to standards; when their outcomes fall below the standards, they feel "deprived." Thus, feelings of deprivation are *relative*; that is, they imply a *comparison* with a standard.

Most sociologists and psychologists who have studied relative deprivation have focused on one particular type of comparison standard, namely, the outcomes of other people. That is, *social comparisons* have constituted the central mechanism hypothesized to underlie the occurrence of relative deprivation (see Olson, Herman, & Zanna, 1986). For example, in the most influential model of personal relative deprivation, Crosby (1976) proposed that one necessary precondition of relative deprivation is the perception that another person possesses a desired object.

Of course, other people's outcomes provide only one of many possible standards with which one's own outcomes could potentially be compared. For example, individuals could compare their current outcomes with their own outcomes in the past. Such *temporal comparisons* might yield dissatisfaction if past outcomes exceed current ones. Indeed, Gurr (1970) used the term *decremental deprivation* to refer to this situation, where decreasing outcomes over time yield anger.

A third possible standard is the focus of this chapter. Like Folger (1986), we believe that this third standard is, in fact, the necessary or critical one in relative deprivation, capable of encompassing the demonstrated effects of other standards like social and temporal comparisons. Specifically, we focus on *counterfactual comparisons* – comparisons of one's current outcomes with the outcomes that one *might have* obtained but did not (hence, the imagined outcomes are "counterfactual," i.e. counter to the facts). Counterfactual comparisons involve mental simulations of "possible worlds," wherein individuals imagine what their outcomes might have been if circumstances had been different. For example, individuals might imagine how their outcomes would have been different if only they had worked harder or been given a second chance.

In this chapter, we discuss how counterfactual thinking might influence relative deprivation. In the process, we review research and theory on counterfactual thinking in domains other than relative deprivation and consider how these findings might help us to understand the mechanisms underlying feelings of dissatisfaction. To illustrate the heuristic value of this perspective, we describe two of our recent studies that have tested relevant hypotheses. We then consider how several particular findings on counterfactual thinking by other researchers might be applied to relative deprivation. Finally, we identify some issues in the relative deprivation literature and discuss the relevance of our analysis of counterfactual thinking for these issues. To begin, though, we must define counterfactual thinking more precisely. We also need to describe Folger's (1986) referent cognitions theory, which initially drew the link between relative deprivation and mental simulation and therefore provided the foundation for our analysis.

DEFINITION OF COUNTERFACTUAL THINKING

Counterfactual thinking refers to thoughts about past events in which elements prior to an event are mentally mutated and possible changes to the outcome are considered (Kahneman & Miller, 1986). Often, these reconstructive thoughts take a conditional form, containing both an antecedent ("if") and a consequent ("then"). For example, a student might think, "If only I had not panicked during the exam, then I would have passed." As illustrated in this example, counterfactual thoughts can have causal implications: If the mutation of an antecedent (e.g., panicking to not panicking) changes the outcome (e.g., failing to passing), then the original, true antecedent (panicking) is implicated as a cause of the actual outcome (failing).

Cognitive and social psychologists have studied many aspects of counterfactual thinking (for reviews, see Miller, Turnbull, & McFarland, 1990; Roese & Olson, 1995a, 1997). For example, the factors that trigger counterfactual thinking have been examined, which include negative outcomes, unexpected outcomes, and "close calls" where something almost occurred or just missed occurring. The content of counterfactual thoughts has also been studied; for example, when perceivers think about how things might have been different, they tend to focus on salient and unusual antecedents to the event, changing them to be more routine or ordinary. Finally, the consequences of counterfactual thinking have received a great deal of attention, ranging from causal judgments to expectations for the future to affective states like regret. Later, we will review several topics from the counterfactual literature in more detail and articulate some general principles of counterfactual thinking that may have implications for relative deprivation.

FOLGER'S REFERENT COGNITIONS MODEL OF RELATIVE DEPRIVATION

Our analysis of how counterfactual thinking might influence relative deprivation rests on a model proposed more than a decade ago by Folger (1986). Folger's "referent cognitions" model took an explicitly cognitive approach to relative deprivation, which was quite different from the models that preceded it. Specifically, Folger proposed that people evaluate their current outcomes by comparing them with whatever alternative reconstructions of the past are most cognitively accessible. That is, he suggested that people's satisfaction or dissatisfaction with their current outcomes depends on the nature of their most accessible thoughts of "what might have been" (i.e., counterfactual thoughts).

Folger hypothesized that there are three preconditions of relative deprivation. First, individuals must be able to easily imagine how better outcomes might have occurred in the past. This precondition sets up the potential for resentment, because the current outcomes are worse than they might have been. Second, individuals must think that it is unlikely that they will obtain better outcomes in the near future. This precondition makes the deprivation seem relatively permanent and therefore changes the potential deprivation into actual deprivation. Third, the processes or events that could have produced better outcomes must seem fairer or more appropriate than the processes that led to the actual outcome. This precondition introduces the element of unfairness or injustice into the deprivation.

Folger has conducted several experiments to test predictions of the referent cognitions model. In these studies, some participants have been provided with information designed to make it easier to generate thoughts about how their outcomes could have been better (counterfactual thoughts), whereas others have not been provided with such information.

The prediction is that the former individuals should report more dissatisfaction with their outcomes than the latter, especially when they (the former individuals) are pessimistic about the future and/or when the conditions that led to the actual outcomes were unfair or arbitrary.

For example, Folger, Rosenfield, and Robinson (1983) had participants compete against one another for a desirable reward. A scoring rule for determining the winner was announced prior to the competition. Immediately after the competition, however, a change in the scoring rule was announced. All participants were told that they had lost the competition on the basis of the new rule. Some participants were told that they would have won the competition under the old rule, whereas others were told that they would have lost in either case. This manipulation was expected to determine whether or not participants could easily imagine how their outcomes could have been better. Further, some participants were given a good explanation for the change in rules, whereas others received a poor explanation that made the change seem arbitrary. This manipulation was expected to influence whether participants would see the procedures that determined their poor outcomes as fair or unfair. Participants then completed a questionnaire that included measures of resentment about the arrangements for assigning rewards in the experiment. As predicted by referent cognitions theory, participants reported the most relative deprivation when they could easily imagine how things could have been better (i.e., when they would have won the reward under the old rules) *and* when the procedures that determined the outcome were unfair (i.e., when the explanation given for the change was poor).

This study and a few others constitute the extant evidence for the referent cognitions model of relative deprivation (see Folger, 1986, 1987, 1993). These data provide good support for the basic elements of Folger's model (e.g., that counterfactual thoughts about how good outcomes could have been better are necessary for relative deprivation to occur), and we are rather surprised at the paucity of relevant studies in the last decade. Earlier, we suggested that comparisons with counterfactual alternatives might be the only necessary comparison in relative deprivation, capable of encompassing the effects of social and temporal comparisons. How can such an argument be feasible, given the evidence in support of the effects of social comparisons on relative deprivation (e.g., Bernstein & Crosby, 1980)? The answer is that social and temporal comparisons may influence resentment because they influence counterfactual comparisons. If so, then counterfactual comparisons may be the immediate psychological precursor of relative deprivation even when social or temporal comparison information is manipulated. For example, if many people possess a desired object, it is easier for deprived persons to imagine that they, too, might have possessed it. Similarly, if deprived individuals possessed a desired object in the past, they will probably find it easier to imagine how the object could still be in their possession than if the object had never been possessed. Thus, although social and temporal comparisons can influence relative deprivation, we agree with Folger (1986) that they do so via counterfactual thinking.

APPLICABILITY OF CONCLUSIONS ABOUT COUNTERFACTUAL THINKING TO RELATIVE DEPRIVATION

Although few researchers in the last decade have examined Folger's (1986) model of relative deprivation, there has been a great deal of research on counterfactual thinking in other domains. Indeed, since the appearance of Kahneman and Miller's (1986) norm theory, mental simulation (including counterfactual thinking) has become one of the most active topics in social psychology.

In this section, we discuss several points of potential overlap between counterfactual thinking and relative deprivation. Specifically, we identify several conclusions that researchers have drawn about counterfactual thinking that seem equally applicable to (or very compatible with) the construct of relative deprivation. These points culminate in a functional perspective that addresses the potential adaptive benefits of "if only" thoughts, which may also help us to understand *why* humans experience resentment about deprivation.

Outcome Valence

Counterfactual Thinking. An important trigger for counterfactual thinking is the valence of an outcome. Specifically, individuals are more likely to generate counterfactual thoughts spontaneously after a negative rather than a positive outcome (Roese & Olson, 1996, 1997; Sanna & Turley, 1996). For example, Roese and Olson (1997) asked participants to read a scenario in which a university student did either well or poorly on an exam. When asked to list the sorts of thoughts that might run through the student's head after learning the outcome, participants generated approximately three times as many counterfactual thoughts in the negative than in the positive outcome condition.

Applicability to Relative Deprivation. If lacking a desired object (deprivation) is considered a negative outcome (which seems sensible), then the findings just mentioned suggest that counterfactual thinking is likely to occur in deprived individuals. That is, when people become aware that they lack a desired object, they are likely to spontaneously generate thoughts about how their outcomes might have been different. Thus, deprivation will stimulate counterfactual thoughts.

Direction of Thoughts

Counterfactual Thinking. Counterfactual thoughts can be characterized in terms of the direction of the comparison between actual and possible outcomes. *Upward* counterfactual thoughts involve the consideration of how things might have turned out *better* than they actually did. Thus, the hypothetical outcome is more favorable than the actual outcome. For example, an individual might think, "If I had been driving slower, I wouldn't have had a car accident." *Downward* counterfactual thoughts involve the consideration of how things might have turned out *worse* than they did. Thus, the hypothetical outcome is less favorable than the actual outcome. For example, an individual might think, "If I hadn't been wearing my seatbelt, I might have been killed in the accident."

The effects of outcome valence described in the preceding section are particularly true for upward counterfactual thoughts. That is, when something bad happens, people tend to generate thoughts about how things could have turned out better. For example, Markman, Gavanski, Sherman, and McMullen (1993) had participants play a computerized blackjack game for real money. Participants received feedback that framed the outcome as a win, as a loss, or as neutral. Participants spontaneously generated more upward counterfactuals in the loss condition than in either of the other two conditions.

Applicability to Relative Deprivation. Folger proposed that people must be able to think about how their outcomes could have been *better*, not just *different*, in order for relative deprivation to occur. That is, he proposed that people must generate *upward* counterfactual thoughts to experience resentment. Given the results just described, if deprivation constitutes a negative outcome, it is likely to produce the upward counterfactual thoughts that are requisite for resentment.

Contrast Effects and Causal Inferences

Counterfactual Thinking. Researchers have been interested in counterfactual thoughts because such thoughts have consequences for individuals' psychological states and behaviors. For example, counterfactual thoughts have been implicated in attributions of responsibility (Wells & Gavanski, 1989), the intensity of suspicion (Miller, Turnbull, & McFarland, 1989), and the intensity of regret (Gilovich & Medvec, 1995; Landman, 1993; Miller & Taylor, 1995). We have argued (Roese & Olson, 1997) that virtually all of the observed consequences of counterfactual thinking derive from two mechanisms: contrast effects and causal inferences.

Counterfactual thoughts can produce psychological consequences by way of *contrast effects*. Contrast effects occur when a salient standard makes a judgment or state more extreme. For example, an outcome may seem more positive when salient alternative outcomes are worse, but more negative when salient alternative outcomes are better.

Most demonstrations of counterfactual contrast effects have focused on affective states. That is, emotions like regret, disappointment, and satisfaction have been shown to be intensified when a contrasting counterfactual comparison is salient. For example, in the previously mentioned study using computerized blackjack, Markman et al. (1993) showed that situational factors (e.g., a losing outcome) that induced upward counterfactual thoughts also produced heightened feelings of dissatisfaction.

Counterfactual thoughts can also produce psychological consequences by way of *causal inferences*. As noted earlier, if the mutation of an antecedent changes the outcome, then that antecedent is implicated as a cause of the outcome (Wells & Gavanski, 1989). Roese and Olson (1997) presented data showing that individuals made causal judgments about an event more quickly if they had previously answered a counterfactual question than if they had not; such facilitation suggests that the counterfactual judgment gave participants information relevant to causal reasoning.

The causal information provided by counterfactual thinking can also affect behavioral intentions. For example, Roese (1994) manipulated the direction of participants' counterfactual thoughts about a recent, disappointing exam performance by asking them to list thoughts about how this performance could have been either better or worse (upward vs. downward counterfactual thoughts). Subsequently, participants were asked to indicate their intentions to perform several success-facilitating behaviors in the future. Participants who were induced to list upward counterfactual thoughts expressed stronger intentions to perform the behaviors than did those in the downward counterfactual thoughts condition. Presumably, by thinking about how their test performance could have been better, participants in the upward counterfactual thoughts condition inferred that their performance *would* have been better if they had acted differently, which increased their intentions to perform success-facilitating behaviors.

Applicability to Relative Deprivation. We have already suggested that awareness of deprivation is likely to stimulate upward counterfactual thoughts about how outcomes could have been better. Based on the material just reviewed, such thoughts should have at least two consequences. First, via a contrast effect, the current outcome (the state of deprivation) will seem worse because the salient counterfactual alternative is hedonically superior. Consequently, the upward counterfactual will induce negative affect via a contrast effect. Of course, resentment about deprivation is itself a form of negative affect; thus, this prediction is very compatible with the concept of relative deprivation.

Second, counterfactual thoughts concerning deprivation will provide information about factors that caused the deprivation. That is, via causal reasoning, people who have thought about how they could have obtained the desired object will believe that certain antecedents were responsible for their deprivation. Thus, these persons may intend to perform corrective behaviors in the future.

A Functional Perspective

Counterfactual Thinking. Many of the preceding points about counterfactual thinking can be integrated within a functional perspective. Theorists (e.g., Johnson & Sherman, 1990; Roese, 1994; Roese & & Olson, 1995b, 1997) have suggested that counterfactual thinking can serve important functions for individuals. Perhaps most significant, a *preparative* function reflects that counterfactual thoughts can provide ideas to people about how to prevent negative outcomes in the future (Mandel & Lehman, 1996). This function is fulfilled primarily by upward counterfactual thoughts that, via causal inferences, identify behaviors that would have resulted in a better outcome.

It is also possible that, via contrast effects, upward counterfactual thoughts generate negative affect, which motivates individuals to follow through on the prescriptive behaviors that have been identified. This proposed benefit of negative affect is consistent with the idea that negative emotions, in general, serve as signals to the organism that something is wrong and needs to be changed (Schwarz, 1990; Taylor, 1991).

Applicability to Relative Deprivation. A functional perspective on relative deprivation asks: What adaptive value might relative deprivation have? Why have humans evolved to experience this negative affective state? Theorizing on counterfactual thinking may help us to answer this question. If relative deprivation results from counterfactual thoughts about how outcomes could have been better, then it may work toward improving outcomes by identifying ways that the desired outcome can be obtained in the future. Further, the negative affect inherent in relative deprivation will motivate the person to reduce the discrepancy between the actual and the hypothetical outcomes, presumably by attempting to obtain the desired object. Thus, upward counterfactual thoughts will both provide strategies for obtaining the object and motivate the individual to implement such strategies. This reasoning shows how relative deprivation might have survival value.

ILLUSTRATIVE STUDIES OF LINKS BETWEEN COUNTERFACTUAL THINKING AND RELATIVE DEPRIVATION

In this section, we briefly describe two of our studies that have tested the link between counterfactual thinking and relative deprivation. These studies illustrate how conclusions from research on counterfactual thinking can be heuristically valuable by suggesting possible studies of relative deprivation.

The fundamental assumption underlying our research is that, if relative deprivation is caused by upward counterfactual thoughts that compare current outcomes with hypothetically better outcomes, then factors that increase such thoughts should increase resentment about deprivation. Our first study tested this idea. Of course, direct manipulations of upward versus downward counterfactual thoughts should also impact on reported resentment in unfair situations. Our second study tested this hypothesis.

Outcome Closeness

Effects on Counterfactual Thinking. When outcomes *almost* occur, they constitute very salient counterfactual possibilities. For example, when a basketball team loses on the last shot, or when someone just barely makes a connection and catches a plane, winning the game or missing the plane are highly salient comparisons that intensify the resulting pain or relief (Kahneman & Tversky, 1982; Kahneman & Varey, 1990).

These effects may rest partly on the fact that when something almost occurred, less mutation of reality is necessary to imagine how it could have occurred. For example, it is easier to imagine how a two-point loss in basketball could have been avoided than a 20-point loss (and, indeed, the former loss *really is* closer to a win than the latter). But outcome closeness does not need to be rational for it to exert demonstrable effects. For example, Turnbull (1981) found that participants who failed to win a lottery prize were more disappointed when their ticket number was close to (rather than far from) the winning number, even though the closeness of the numbers on a ticket to the winning ticket says nothing about how close that ticket actually came to being selected. Kahneman and Varey (1990) found that losing a race was thought to be more disappointing when the competitor had been steadily moving up in the pack than when the competitor remained in a constant position throughout the race, even though the final placing was identical; the authors proposed that, in the former case, there was a *propensity* toward winning that made winning a more plausible and salient counterfactual alternative.

Application to Relative Deprivation. In a relative deprivation context, the outcome closeness factor suggests that when individuals *almost* obtained the desired object, they should feel more resentful about their deprivation than when they did not come close to obtaining the object. For example, if Turnbull's (1981) lottery experiment were adapted so that there was potential unfairness in the draw (e.g., some people received more tickets than they deserved), then rather than producing only disappointment, participants whose numbers were close to the winning number would also report more resentment and anger than participants whose numbers were more distant.

We recently tested the possible effects of outcome closeness on resentment about deprivation. Participants read two hypothetical scenarios that described situations of deprivation. Information in the scenarios manipulated whether or not the negative outcome (deprivation) almost did *not* occur (closeness of better outcome: close vs. distant) and the fairness of the outcome (fair vs. unfair). We expected that unfair negative outcomes would produce more resentment than fair negative outcomes, especially when the better outcome was close to occurring, because closeness would increase the frequency and/or vividness of upward counterfactual thoughts.

One scenario asked participants to imagine that they were the co-owner of a racehorse, in which they had invested several thousand dollars. One afternoon, the horse was being prepared for its first race, which had cost $200 to enter but would be profitable if the horse finished in one of the top three positions. Just as the horse was about to get a special nutritional supplement that would provide a burst of quick energy for 30 minutes, a race official came into the stables and confiscated the supplement. He said that the supplement was no longer allowed in this race jurisdiction. For some participants (*fair* condition), the scenario continued that the official had already made sure that none of the other horses would receive the supplement either. For other participants (*unfair* condition), someone in the stables complained that he had already seen other horses who were competing in the same race receive the supplement; the race official said that he could only stop those incidents that he witnessed personally. The outcome of the race was then described, including a manipulation of the closeness of a better outcome. Following Kahneman and Varey (1990), some participants (*close* condition) were told that the horse started near the back of the pack but slowly improved and moved up throughout the race, finishing in fourth place, just behind the third-place horse (thus, out of the money). Other participants (*distant* condition) were told that the horse remained steady in fourth position throughout the race.

Participants answered several questions on nine-point scales about how they would feel about this event. A composite measure was calculated by averaging three questions: "Would you think that it was unfair that you finished out of the money?"; "Would you feel like it was unjust that you finished out of the money?"; and "Would you feel like you'd been unfairly deprived of finishing in the top three positions?"

Table 12.1 presents the means for the closeness × fairness design. There was a strong main effect of fairness, with participants understandably reporting more relative deprivation when the outcome was determined by unfair procedures (selective application of the rules) than by fair procedures (uniform treatment of all horses). We expected that the effect of an unfair (vs. fair) outcome would be stronger when conditions facilitated upward counterfactual thoughts (the close condition); as predicted, the difference between the unfair and fair means was larger in the close condition than in the distant condition.

One problem with the racehorse scenario was that it evoked only minimal relative deprivation; the mean across all participants was only 3.59

Table 12.1. *Mean Relative Deprivation in the Race Horse Scenario*

	Counterfactual Closeness	
	Distant (Steady)	Close (Improve)
Fair (uniform treatment)	2.59	1.67
Unfair (selective application)	4.97	5.22

Note: Possible scores range from 1 to 9, with higher numbers reflecting more relative deprivation.

on a 9-point scale where 3 meant "a little." A second scenario, however, described a state of deprivation that was more intense. Specifically, participants imagined that they were living in a rented house with two friends. On returning from a store, they found their house on fire, with firefighters working to contain the flames. All their possessions were destroyed or damaged, with the loss in the thousands of dollars. Unfortunately, there was no insurance to cover the losses. Participants were told that they had forgotten to renew their fire insurance when the bill arrived in the mail. Those in the *close* condition were told that their policy and coverage lapsed only three days ago, whereas participants in the *distant* condition were told that their coverage lapsed eight months ago (this manipulation was borrowed from Meyers-Levy & Maheswaran, 1992). Participants also learned that the fire had been caused either by a lightning strike (*fair* condition) or by an arsonist who broke a basement window and set the inside curtains on fire (*unfair* condition). Participants answered several items about how they would feel, including three that paralleled the first scenario, which were averaged to form a composite score: "Would you think that your loss was unfair?"; "Would you feel like your loss was unjust?"; and "Would you feel like you'd been unfairly deprived of your possessions?"

The mean relative deprivation across all participants was substantially higher for this scenario, $M = 6.22$ on a 9-point scale where 7 meant "very." Table 12.2 presents the means for the closeness × fairness design. Once again, there was a substantial main effect for fairness, with participants reporting more relative deprivation following arson than a lightning strike. Inspection of the interaction means suggested a somewhat different outcome than expected. Specifically, *either* unfair causes *or* salient upward counterfactual thoughts were sufficient to produce relative deprivation. As expected, the least relative deprivation occurred in the condition when

Table 12.2. *Mean Relative Deprivation in the Fire Scenario*

	Counterfactual Closeness	
	Distant	**Close (Recent)**
Fair (lightning)	5.20	6.11
Unfair (arson)	7.05	6.49

Note: Possible scores range from 1 to 9, with higher numbers reflecting more relative deprivation.

the fire resulted from natural causes and the insurance policy lapsed months ago (fair–distant). When the fire resulted from arson, it did not matter whether the policy lapsed a few days or eight months before – participants reported that they would feel relatively deprived. Also, when the policy lapsed only a few days ago, participants reported that they would feel relatively deprived whether the fire resulted from unnatural or natural causes. Presumably, the latter condition (fair–recent) generated such vivid upward counterfactual thoughts that individuals imagined they would feel upset even though the processes were not unfair. Of course, it is possible that a lightning strike is not perceived as exactly "fair," though it is not patently unfair either. At any rate, closeness of outcome influenced reports of relative deprivation.

Direct Manipulation of Upward Counterfactual Thoughts

In the scenario study just described, counterfactual thoughts were not measured directly. Instead, the role of upward counterfactual thoughts was inferred from the impact of outcome closeness. A more direct test of the role of upward counterfactual thoughts in relative deprivation would involve the manipulation of participants' thoughts. In a recent experiment, we took this approach and moved away from a scenario methodology to focus on real experiences of participants.

Participants were asked to think of a negative event that they had experienced in the past year. Half of the participants were asked to think of an *unfair* negative event, and half a *fair* negative event. For each group, two, paragraph-long examples of the appropriate kind of negative event were given. In the unfair condition, the examples were a breakup of a romantic relationship where the partner secretly dated other people and, when confronted, denied having ever agreed to an exclusive relationship, and a poor test performance where students were misled about the content and form of the exam. In the fair condition, the examples were a breakup of a romantic relationship in which the individuals simply grew apart in interests and decided jointly that they should date other people, and a poor test performance when the student did not prepare adequately for the exam. Participants wrote a few sentences describing a negative event they had experienced in the past year that fit the appropriate category (all participants were able to do so).

After describing the negative event, participants were directed to list a specific kind of counterfactual thought, either upward or downward. In each condition, three examples of the relevant kind of counterfactual thought were provided to participants. For example, participants who were asked to generate *upward* counterfactual thoughts about a *fair* negative event were given the following example for the romantic relationship case: "If only the two of you had shared more interests, you might have stayed together." Participants who were asked to generate *downward* counterfactual thoughts about an *unfair* negative event were given the following example for the academic case: "If you had been drinking the night before, you would have done even worse on the exam."

After listing the requested kind of thoughts, participants answered four items on nine-point scales that were averaged to assess their relative deprivation, including "Are you resentful over the negative event that happened to you?" and "Do you feel angry about the negative event that you just described?"

Participants generated an average of 3.58 counterfactual thoughts. Inspection of the thoughts showed that virtually all represented the appropriate kind of thought that participants had been asked to generate.

Table 12.3 presents the mean relative deprivation scores for each cell in the fairness of negative event × direction of counterfactual thoughts design. A main effect of fairness showed that participants who thought about unfair negative events reported more resentment than those who thought about fair negative events. As predicted, however, this difference between fair and unfair events was much larger when participants generated upward counterfactual thoughts than when they generated downward counterfactual thoughts. Thus, an unfair situation produced more relative deprivation than a fair situation primarily when participants generated upward counterfactual thoughts. The fact that participants were thinking about real events that had occurred to them increases the external validity of the findings. Also, the fact that counterfactual thoughts were manipulated directly increases our confidence

Table 12.3. *Mean Relative Deprivation in the Negative Event Study*

	Direction of Counterfactual Thoughts	
	Downward	**Upward**
Fair negative event	4.25	4.50
Unfair negative event	5.20	6.03

Note: Possible scores range from 1 to 9, with higher numbers reflecting more relative deprivation.

that such thoughts played a causal role in determining the pattern of reported relative deprivation.

OTHER POSSIBLE LINKS BETWEEN COUNTERFACTUAL THINKING AND RELATIVE DEPRIVATION

The two studies described in the preceding section addressed only very limited aspects of the potential overlap between counterfactual thinking and relative deprivation. There are numerous other factors that have been shown to increase upward counterfactual thinking and that therefore should impact on resentment about deprivation. In this section, we identify three such factors.

Antecedent Normality

Effects on Counterfactual Thinking. Perhaps the most widely cited idea in the psychological literature on counterfactual thinking is that perceivers focus on exceptional or abnormal antecedents when constructing counterfactual thoughts. For example, Kahneman and Tversky (1982) had participants read about a man who was killed in an automobile accident on the way home from work. Some participants learned that he left work early but drove home via his usual route, whereas others learned that he left work at his usual time but took an unusual route home. When asked how the accident could have been avoided, the former participants mutated the departure time ("he would still be alive if he had left work at his usual time"), whereas the latter participants mutated the route home ("he would still be alive if he had taken his normal route"). Of course, either mutation was theoretically possible in either condition.

There is some debate about whether the presence of an exceptional antecedent produces *more* counterfactual thinking per se, or whether it simply influences the *content* of counterfactual thoughts, such that individuals are likely to select exceptional antecedents for mutation when present (cf. Kahneman & Miller, 1986; Roese & Olson, 1997). It is possible that both effects can occur, but the latter, content effect may be stronger than the former, activation effect.

Application to Relative Deprivation. If the presence of unusual or exceptional antecedents increases the number or vividness of counterfactual thoughts, then relative deprivation may be greater when deprivation follows an unusual event than when it follows a routine event. For example, if someone has a car accident caused by "unfair" means, such as a drunk driver, then resentment about the accident may be greater if the individual was driving home via an unusual route than if he or she was driving home via a typical route.

Outcome Expectedness

Effects on Counterfactual Thinking. Unexpected outcomes appear to stimulate more cognitive processing than expected outcomes (Olson, Roese, & Zanna, 1996), presumably because it is important for perceivers to understand events that were not predicted successfully (Taylor, 1991). In the counterfactual thinking literature, the effects of outcome expectancy on the generation of counterfactual thoughts have been a matter of debate (cf. Kahneman & Miller, 1986; Roese & Olson, 1997). Empirical tests have yielded some support, however, for the hypothesis that unexpected outcomes trigger counterfactual thinking. For example, Sanna and Turley (1996) surveyed students before and after an exam, with the post-exam measures including open-ended, nondirective questions tapping their thoughts about the exam. Spontaneous counterfactual thoughts were counted in these listings. Both the valence of the outcome (actual performance) *and* the unexpectedness of the outcome (the absolute difference between pre-exam expectancies and actual performance) independently predicted the total number of counterfactual thoughts, with worse outcomes and more unexpected outcomes producing more thoughts.

Application to Relative Deprivation. If unexpected events elicit more counterfactual thinking than expected events, then unfair negative events should produce more upward thoughts about how the outcome might have been better (which should produce more relative deprivation) when they are unexpected rather than expected. For example, if two individuals apply for a job but are not selected because of unfair or illegitimate reasons (e.g., the boss's nephew is hired, who had no relevant qualifications), then one individual who expected to obtain a job easily after graduation might feel more relatively deprived than another who expected to be unemployed for a period of time. Thus, the same deprivation might produce more resentment when it is unexpected rather than expected.

An existing finding in the relative deprivation literature may reflect this role of outcome expectedness. Specifically, relative deprivation researchers have found that individuals report more resentment when they feel entitled to, or deserving of, a desired outcome than when they feel less entitled (e.g., Crosby, 1976; Olson, Roese, Meen, & Robertson, 1995). Perhaps this finding reflects that perceptions of entitlement make failure to obtain an object (deprivation) more unexpected and more painful.

Expectancies for the Future

Effects on Counterfactual Thinking. We have previously noted that upward counterfactual thoughts produce negative affect. An interesting exception to this principle was documented by Boninger, Gleicher, and Strathman (1994), who showed that *when people expect the future to be better,* upward counterfactual thoughts do *not* unleash negative affect. That is, when counterfactual thoughts lead individuals to think that their outcomes *will* improve in the future, these thoughts do not evoke negative affect, even though present outcomes may be poor.

Application to Relative Deprivation. Recall that one of the prerequisites for relative deprivation, according to Folger's (1986) referent cognitions theory, is that people must think it is unlikely that their outcomes will improve in the near future. Thus, to the extent that counterfactual thoughts lead individuals to feel optimistic about the future, Folger would predict that they will experience little relative deprivation, just as Boninger et al. (1994) predicted that optimism defuses negative affect from upward counterfactual thoughts.

Olson and Ross (1984) found that possessing high qualifications increased resentment about deprivation when a resource was scarce, but decreased resentment about deprivation when a resource was abundant. This pattern of findings can be interpreted using the work on outcome expectedness and expectancies for the future articulated in this and the preceding section. Specifically, when people feel well qualified for an outcome, they become very angry if (1) they are currently deprived *and* (2) because the resource is scarce, the future also looks bleak. In this instance, individuals' qualifications originally led them to expect to obtain the outcome, which makes deprivation unexpected and painful, and they lack optimism to counteract their resentment. On the other hand, when people feel well qualified for an object that is abundant, their qualifications serve to make them optimistic about the future, which ameliorates their resentment (even though the current deprivation was unexpected). This reasoning illustrates how the counterfactual and relative deprivation literatures can be integrated.

ISSUES IN RELATIVE DEPRIVATION

In this final section, we briefly mention a few issues concerning relative deprivation that might be viewed from a different perspective using concepts from the counterfactual thinking literature.

Personal versus Group Relative Deprivation

An important distinction in the relative deprivation literature is between personal and group relative deprivation. Personal relative deprivation is resentment about one's own outcomes, whereas group relative deprivation is resentment about the outcomes of one's group (Runciman, 1966). Personal relative deprivation predicts symptoms and behaviors relevant to the self (e.g., stress, self-improvement), whereas group relative deprivation predicts group-directed attitudes and behaviors (e.g., support for and participation in collective behaviors like protest and revolt; see Hafer & Olson, 1993; Olson et al., 1995; Smith & Ortiz, this volume; Walker & Mann, 1987).

If personal relative deprivation occurs when one's own poor outcomes are highly mutable (i.e., when better outcomes for the self are easily imagined), then group relative deprivation should occur when one's group's poor outcomes are highly mutable. Thus, when it is easy to imagine how one's group's outcomes could have been better, group relative deprivation should occur. From this perspective, factors that influence group relative deprivation do so by making better outcomes for one's group more easily imagined. For example, exposure to information about positive outcomes being received by members of outgroups should serve to make thoughts about better outcomes for one's ingroup easier and more vivid.

Personal–Group Discrimination Discrepancy

One interesting finding that has arisen out of research on personal versus group relative deprivation is that individuals often report more group deprivation or discrimination than personal deprivation or discrimination; this tendency has been termed the "personal–group discrimination discrepancy" (Crosby, 1984; Olson & Hafer, 1996; Taylor, Wright, & Porter, 1994; see also Walker, Wong, & Kretzschmar, this volume). The most popular explanation for this phenomenon is that individuals are motivated to underestimate or deny personal experiences of discrimination to justify their inaction against perpetrators of disadvantage.

The counterfactual comparisons perspective on relative deprivation suggests another explanation for the personal–group discrimination discrepancy, not necessarily incompatible with the preceding one. Perhaps group outcomes are, in general, more cognitively mutable than personal outcomes. That is, it may be easier for people to imagine how their group could have obtained better outcomes than it is to imagine how they themselves could have obtained better outcomes. For example, perhaps the abstractness of the group context allows greater flexibility in imagined outcomes, or perhaps the detailed knowledge about situational determinants of personal outcomes engenders a sense of inevitability.

There is a second way to relate findings on the personal–group discrimination discrepancy to the counterfactual thinking literature. Norm theory (Kahneman & Miller, 1986) predicts that any event or stimulus that is a deviation from the norm automatically evokes thoughts of the norm, whereas the reverse is not true (i.e., normal events do not evoke thoughts of unusual events). If perceivers are making judgments about a minority group (a deviation from the norm), they should automatically think about the dominant group as the reference point. Thus, judgments by members of a disadvantaged group are likely to involve comparisons of their own group's outcomes with those of the majority group – an intergroup comparison that will yield the judgment that one's group has been discriminated against. In contrast, the self is the norm for judgments about oneself, so there is no clear, better-off referent for judgments of personal experiences of discrimination. These conditions would produce a personal–group discrimination discrepancy.

Improving Outcomes

One of the paradoxes of resentment is that improving outcomes can sometimes trigger discontent and assertive action. That is, individuals can become more intensely dissatisfied with their situation after a period of improvement than they would have been if no improvement had occurred (deCarufel, 1979; Gurr, 1970). The usual explanation for this phenomenon is rising expectations: The period of improvement leads people to expect and to feel entitled to further improvements, and strong dissatisfaction occurs if such improvements do not occur.

Again, the counterfactual comparisons perspective provides another, not necessarily incompatible, view of these findings. Perhaps improving outcomes increase the mutability of current outcomes. That is, by exposing individuals to increased outcomes, improvements make it easier to imagine alterations (especially upward changes) in current outcomes. If people have received constant outcomes over time, outcomes are likely to be perceived as static, inflexible, and unchanging. In contrast, improvements over time render current outcomes more cognitively mutable.

CONCLUSIONS

Because the topic of this book is relative deprivation, we have focused in this chapter on the implications of research on counterfactual thinking for understanding relative deprivation. The heuristic benefits of an integrative perspective can also flow in the opposite direction, of course. That is, the relative deprivation literature can inform work on counterfactual thinking. For example, counterfactual researchers have rarely addressed the behavioral consequences of counterfactual thinking, other than its potential impact on performance. In contrast, relative deprivation researchers have offered more specific behavioral predictions – for example, when legitimate avenues for change are cut off, resentment will lead to nonnormative actions (e.g., protest, sabotage; see Olson & Hafer, 1996; Walker & Mann, 1987). Thus, if participants in Roese's (1994) previously described study who generated thoughts about a recent exam performance had believed that their grades were illegitimately generated (e.g., the professor discriminated against them), relative deprivation theorists would predict assertive responses, potentially including illicit actions. More generally, work on relative deprivation adds to our understanding of the relation between counterfactual thoughts and affect. Whereas upward counterfactual thoughts can lead to a range of affective responses, specific elements in the thoughts steer emotions in particular directions; for example, judgments of unfairness must be coupled with upward counterfactual thoughts to produce resentment and anger. The concept of relative deprivation has proven to be a useful one for psychologists and sociologists interested in such topics as collective action and self-improvement. We hope that an integrative perspective that connects the concept to counterfactual thinking can provide an even fuller understanding of the emotional and behavioral consequences of perceived unfairness.

ACKNOWLEDGMENTS

The writing of this chapter, as well as the research by the authors described in it, was supported by a grant to James Olson from the Social Sciences and Humanities Research Council of Canada and by faculty startup funds provided to Neal Roese by Northwestern University.

REFERENCES

Bernstein, M., & Crosby, F. (1980). An empirical examination of relative deprivation theory. *Journal of Experimental Social Psychology, 16*, 442–456.
Boninger, D. S., Gleicher, F., & Strathman, A. (1994). Counterfactual thinking: From what might have been to what may be. *Journal of Personality and Social Psychology, 67*, 297–307.

Crosby, F. (1976). A model of egoistical relative deprivation. *Psychological Review, 83*, 85–113.

Crosby, F. (1984). The denial of personal discrimination. *American Behavioral Scientist, 27*, 371–386.

deCarufel, A. (1979). Factors affecting the evaluation of improvement: The role of normative standards and allocator resources. *Journal of Personality and Social Psychology, 37*, 847–857.

Folger, R. (1986). A referent cognitions theory of relative deprivation. In J. M. Olson, C. P. Herman, & M. P. Zanna (Eds.), *Relative deprivation and social comparison: The Ontario symposium* (Vol. 4, pp. 33–55). Hillsdale, NJ: Erlbaum.

Folger, R. (1987). Reformulating the preconditions of relative deprivation: A referent cognitions model. In J. C. Masters & W. P. Smith (Eds.), *Social comparison, justice, and relative deprivation* (pp. 183–215). Hillsdale, NJ: Erlbaum.

Folger, R. (1993). Reactions to mistreatment at work. In J. K. Murnighan (Ed.), *Social psychology in organizations* (pp. 161–183). Englewood Cliffs, NJ: Prentice-Hall.

Folger, R., Rosenfield, D., & Robinson, T. (1983). Relative deprivation and procedural justifications. *Journal of Personality and Social Psychology, 45*, 268–273.

Gilovich, T., & Medvec, V. H. (1995). The experience of regret: What, when, and why. *Psychological Review, 102*, 379–395.

Gurr, T. R. (1970). *Why men rebel*. Princeton, NJ: Princeton University Press.

Hafer, C. L., & Olson, J. M. (1993). Beliefs in a just world, discontent, and assertive actions by working women. *Personality and Social Psychology Bulletin, 19*, 30–38.

Johnson, M. K., & Sherman, S. J. (1990). Constructing and reconstructing the past and the future in the present. In E. T. Higgins & R. M. Sorrentino (Eds.), *Handbook of motivation and cognition: Foundations of social behavior* (Vol. 2, pp. 482–526). New York: Guilford.

Kahneman, D., & Miller, D. T. (1986). Norm theory: Comparing reality to its alternatives. *Psychological Review, 93*, 136–153.

Kahneman, D., & Tversky, A. (1982). The simulation heuristic. In D. Kahneman, P. Slovic, & A. Tversky (Eds.), *Judgement under uncertainty: Heuristics and biases* (pp. 201–208). New York: Cambridge University Press.

Kahneman, D., & Varey, C. A. (1990). Propensities and counterfactuals: The loser that almost won. *Journal of Personality and Social Psychology, 59*, 1101–1110.

Landman, J. (1993). *Regret: The persistence of the possible*. New York: Oxford University Press.

Mandel, D. R., & Lehman, D. R. (1996). Counterfactual thinking and ascriptions of cause and preventability. *Journal of Personality and Social Psychology, 71*, 450–463.

Markman, K. D., Gavanski, I., Sherman, S. J., & McMullen, M. N. (1993). The simulation of better and worse possible worlds. *Journal of Experimental Social Psychology, 29*, 87–109.

Meyers-Levy, J., & Maheswaran, D. (1992). When timing matters: The influence of temporal distance on consumers' affective and persuasive responses. *Journal of Consumer Research, 19*, 424–433.

Miller, D. T., & Taylor, B. R. (1995). Counterfactual thought, regret, and superstition: How to avoid kicking yourself. In N. J. Roese & J. M. Olson (Eds.), *What might have been: The social psychology of counterfactual thinking* (pp. 305–331). Mahwah, NJ: Erlbaum.

Miller, D. T., Turnbull, W., & McFarland, C. (1989). When a coincidence is suspicious: The role of mental simulation. *Journal of Personality and Social Psychology, 57*, 581–589.

Miller, D. T., Turnbull, W., & McFarland, C. (1990). Counterfactual thinking and social perception: Thinking about what might have been. In M. P. Zanna (Ed.), *Advances in experimental social psychology* (Vol. 23, pp. 305–331). New York: Academic Press.

Olson, J. M., & Hafer, C. L. (1996). Affect, motivation, and cognition in relative deprivation research. In R. M. Sorrentino & E. T. Higgins (Eds.), *Handbook of motivation and cognition: The interpersonal context* (Vol. 3, pp. 85–117). New York: Guilford.

Olson, J. M., Herman, C. P., & Zanna, M. P. (Eds.). (1986). *Relative deprivation and social comparison: The Ontario symposium* (Vol. 4). Hillsdale, NJ: Erlbaum.

Olson, J. M., Roese, N. J., Meen, J., & Robertson, D. J. (1995). The preconditions and consequences of relative deprivation: Two field studies. *Journal of Applied Social Psychology, 25*, 944–964.

Olson, J. M., Roese, N. R., & Zanna, M. P. (1996). Expectancies. In E. T. Higgins & A. W. Kruglanski (Eds.), *Handbook of social psychology: Basic principles* (pp. 211–238). New York: Guilford.

Olson, J. M., & Ross, M. (1984). Perceived qualifications, resource abundance, and resentment about deprivation. *Journal of Experimental Social Psychology, 20*, 425–444.

Roese, N. J. (1994). The functional basis of counterfactual thinking. *Journal of Personality and Social Psychology, 66*, 805–818.

Roese, N. J., & Olson, J. M. (1995a). Counterfactual thinking: A critical overview. In N. J. Roese & J. M. Olson (Eds.), *What might have been: The social psychology of counterfactual thinking*. Mahwah, NJ: Erlbaum.

Roese, N. J., & Olson, J. M. (1995b). Functions of counterfactual thinking. In N. J. Roese & J. M. Olson (Eds.), *What might have been: The social psychology of counterfactual thinking*. Mahwah, NJ: Erlbaum.

Roese, N. J., & Olson, J. M. (1996). Counterfactuals, causal attributions, and the hindsight bias: A conceptual integration. *Journal of Experimental Social Psychology, 32*, 197–227.

Roese, N. J., & Olson, J. M. (1997). Counterfactual thinking: The intersection of affect and function. In M. P. Zanna (Ed.), *Advances in experimental social psychology* (Vol. 29, pp. 1–59). San Diego, CA: Academic Press.

Runciman, W. G. (1966). *Relative deprivation and social justice: A study of attitudes to social inequality in twentieth century England*. Berkeley: University of California Press.

Sanna, L. J., & Turley, K. J. (1996). Antecedents to spontaneous counterfactual thinking: Effects of expectancy violation and outcome valence. *Personality and Social Psychology Bulletin, 22*, 906–919.

Schwarz, N. (1990). Feelings as information: Informational and motivational functions of affective states. In E. T. Higgins & R. M. Sorrentino (Eds.), *Handbook of motivation and cognition: Foundations of social behavior* (Vol. 2, pp. 527–561). New York: Guilford.

Taylor, D. M., Wright, S. C., & Porter, L. E. (1994). Dimensions of perceived discrimination: The personal/group discrimination discrepancy. In M. P. Zanna & J. M. Olson (Eds.), *The psychology of prejudice: The Ontario symposium* (Vol. 7, pp. 233–255). Hillsdale, NJ: Erlbaum.

Taylor, S. E. (1991). Asymmetrical effects of positive and negative events: The mobilization-minimization hypothesis. *Psychological Bulletin, 110,* 67–85.

Turnbull, W. (1981). Naive conceptions of free will and the deterministic paradox. *Canadian Journal of Behavioral Science, 13,* 1–13.

Walker, I., & Mann, L. (1987). Unemployment, relative deprivation, and social protest. *Personality and Social Psychology Bulletin, 13,* 275–283.

Wells, G. L., & Gavanski, I. (1989). Mental simulation of causality. *Journal of Personality and Social Psychology, 56,* 161–169.

THIRTEEN

Relative Deprivation and Attribution

From Grievance to Action

Iain Walker, Ngai Kin Wong, and Kerry Kretzschmar

Relative deprivation theory belongs to a family of *social evaluation* theories (Pettigrew, 1967) that have as their common bond a focus on the social comparative nature of social judgments. The core of the relative deprivation (RD) construct is that when people's expectations about the goods and conditions of life to which they believe they are entitled are thwarted, they become angry and are motivated to redress the perceived inequity. Judgments about entitlements can only be made relatively – people compare their current or anticipated outcomes with those of other individuals or groups. Unfortunately, as with most members of the family of social evaluation theories, when RD theory has been applied to major social issues, it has typically been in a post hoc manner. As a theory, it will only mature if it lends itself to prediction, rather than retrospection. This point has been made for several decades now.

One reason why RD theory has been applied retrospectively more than prospectively is the relative absence of testable models linking the perception of deprivation, through various mediators, to behavioral outcomes. In this chapter we attempt to specify such a model. The model we suggest integrates Folger's Referent Cognition Theory (RCT) of RD (Folger, 1984, 1986, 1987; Mark & Folger, 1984) and Weiner's version of attribution theory (1985, 1986, 1995). We begin by describing RCT, and claim that it is a general, useful, and parsimonious model of RD. This is followed by a brief description of Weiner's attributional model, and a consideration of how it can be integrated into RCT to provide a more adequate model of the links between RD and behavior. Finally, we present results from two studies testing some of our ideas.

FOLGER'S REFERENT COGNITIONS MODEL

Folger's (1984, 1986, 1987; Mark & Folger, 1984; Olson & Roese, this volume) RCT is built on the notion of *simulation heuristics,* which are related to the comparison of an existing state of affairs with an alternatively imaginable state of affairs. There are three elements in RCT. *Referent outcomes* provide a frame of reference for evaluation of outcomes in the form of mental simulations of alternatively imaginable outcomes that differ from existing outcomes. *Justification* refers to the perceived appropriateness or moral acceptability of the circumstances resulting in the current outcomes. *Likelihood of amelioration* corresponds to a projection about the level of future outcomes. According to RCT, RD occurs when an actual outcome is below the standard of the referent outcome (i.e., high referent outcome); when the procedure leading to the actual outcome is not justified (i.e., low in justification); and when there is little likelihood of amelioration of existing conditions (i.e., low likelihood).

As Folger (1987) points out, RCT has several advantages over alternative formulations. First, RCT is more parsimonious than models such as Crosby's (1976) influential formulation. Second, the shift of attention from specific sources of perceived discrepancies to the process of comparison between referent and actual outcomes enhances theoretical flexibility. Particularly, the sources of referent outcomes are not narrowly restricted to social or temporal comparisons, but can also accommodate hypothetical possibilities as well as personal or collective ideals.

Another benefit of RCT is that it provides the basis of a better account of the personal–group distinction. This distinction, originally made by Runciman (1966), is now well entrenched in the literature (e.g., Olson, Roese, Meen, & Robertson, 1995; Tyler & Smith, 1998). Traditionally, personal RD is seen to stem from intra- or interpersonal comparisons, and group RD from intergroup comparisons. Personal RD is related to individual-level outcomes, and group RD to group-level outcomes (Olson et al., 1995; Pettigrew, 1967; Smith & Ortiz, this volume; Tyler & Smith, 1998; Walker & Pettigrew, 1984). The distinction is not as neat as it first appears, though. For example, do self-outgroup comparisons (e.g., Vanneman & Pettigrew, 1972; our second study later) lead to personal or to group RD? And some comparison dimensions do not lend themselves easily to the personal–group distinction. For example, in our first study, we look at environmental activism. Outcomes here (e.g., environmental quality) affect everyone (more or less), whether they are in a privileged or a deprived group. Or perhaps, because the outcomes affect everyone equally, there is no sense in a distinction between ingroup and outgroup. Folger's RCT helps avoid these problems by recasting the RD process. Typically, the personal–group distinction rests on judgments based on overall patterns of outcome distribution. However, RCT defines RD more procedurally than distributively, hence the personal–group distinction is less important in this formulation of RD (see also Tyler & Lind, this volume).

A final and important benefit of the RCT approach to RD is that it is expandable to include propositions linking, more directly, the antecendents and consequences of RD. Indeed, Mark and Folger (1984) attempt to develop a conceptual framework relating RCT to the various responses to RD. They propose that responses to RD can be directed to the self, the object or outcome one is deprived of, or the system responsible for the distribution of outcomes (self-directed, object-directed, and system-directed responses, respectively). There are two dimensions for each set of responses: attitudinal and behavioral, and, thus, six categories of possible responses.

Mark and Folger (1984) also specify how certain antecedents of RD predispose particular responses. Low justification coupled with low likelihood is likely to result in negative system-directed responses (particularly negative attitudes). Although such attitudes may be associated with a tendency for negative system-directed behavior, actual manifestations of system-directed behavior depend on situational factors such as available resources to mobilize and opportunities to behave.

The latter point probably constitutes a weakness of the RCT approach, as it is not possible to account for these situational factors. In addition, Mark and Folger (1984) have noted that the RCT approach is essentially partial. Particularly, Mark (1985) has suggested that further development should expand on Weiner's attribution theory and examine the attributions people make about their conditions of RD. Despite the passage of a decade and a half, no such development has occurred.

To the extent that RD (according to the RCT model) is a result of perceived discrepancies between referent and actual outcomes, the concept of RD is related to the notion of non-attainment of goals. This is one of the antecedents of attributional search (Weiner, 1985). When the goals are important and non-attainment is associated with negative outcomes, attributional search is more likely. Thus, it is reasonable to propose that the antecedents of RD also direct attributional search.

CAUSAL ATTRIBUTION

Causal attribution is concerned with the processes by which people infer causes of observed behaviors or events. Weiner's work on causal attribution in achievement-related contexts has led to a systematic formulation of an attributional theory of motivation and emotion (Weiner,

1985, 1986, 1995). Causal attributions occur in the face of an unexpected, important, or negative outcome, and can be situated on three general dimensions – *locus* (is the cause internal or external to the person?), *stability* (is the cause relatively invariant with consistent effects or does it fluctuate?), and *controllability* (how much is the cause subject to the person's volitional control?). Given this three-dimensional taxonomy, causes can be theoretically classified within one of eight cells (2 locus × 2 stability × 2 controllability). Empirical studies of causal dimensions based on factor analysis, multidimensional scaling, and correlational procedures have been cited to support the proposed schema of causal structures (Weiner, 1985).

Weiner also postulates that causal dimensions of attribution exert specific influences on motivation and emotion, and hence subsequent behavior in achievement-related contexts. Specifically, the locus of the cause influences self-esteem: internal attributions for success will elicit pride, but will lower self-esteem following failure. The stability of the cause influences expectancy of future success and hence induces feelings of hopefulness or hopelessness. Lastly, controllability can determine emotions such as guilt (from failure attributed to a controllable cause) and shame (from failure attributable to an uncontrollable cause). The affects and expectancies follow from particular attributions and, in turn, influence behaviors. For instance, when a person has a low expectancy for future success and is feeling low self-esteem, hopeless, and ashamed, this individual will be more likely to exhibit withdrawal behavior than instrumental behavior.

Weiner's formulation is grounded in achievement-related contexts in which causes of success and failure are examined, but he is confident of the theoretical generality of his model. This generality is provided by two conceptual mechanisms. First, by conceptualizing achievement success and failure in more general terms as attainment or non-attainment of a goal or outcome, the theory can be, and has been, applied to other domains of social or personal failures such as alcoholism (McHugh, Meckman, & Frieze, 1979), crime (Carroll, 1978), depression (Abramson, Seligman, & Teasdale, 1978), and deprivation (Mark, 1985). Second, although the causal attributions examined vary widely both within and across domains, they can be readily classified according to their positions on the causal dimensions of locus, stability, and controllability.

At the level of group behavior, Ferree and Miller (1985) assert that the cognitive processes of attribution are crucial to the judgment of legitimacy, the definition of collective goals, and the creation of individual interest in collective goods. Hence, attributional processes are important in the decision to participate in social movements. Of particular importance are the

causal explanations of social events or outcomes. Ferree and Miller identify four types of attributions, based on location of causality (internal vs.
external) and stability (stable vs. unstable). When causes are judged to be
internal and stable, the result is an attribution made to some enduring,
often congenital, aspect of self. When the cause is internal but unstable, the
resulting attribution is to a controllable aspect of self. External, stable
causes lead to system-directed attributions; external, unstable causes produce attributions based on chance or fate. Ferree and Miller claim that self-
directed (internal) attributions account for the uncomplaining inaction of
those who suffer objective hardships. In contrast, external attributions for
negative social outcomes tend to "undercut the legitimacy of the system"
(Ferree & Miller, 1985, p. 44). However, chance attributions (external,
unstable) promote resignation to fate. Thus, only system-directed attributions (external, stable) can instigate social movement participation.

This formulation is consistent with the finding by Pandey, Sinha,
Prakash, and Tripathi (1982) that activists, regardless of their political orientation, tended to attribute more importance to system causes than to
personal causes of poverty. It is also consistent with findings regarding the
importance of system blame and the influence of powerful others in generating social movement participation (see Klandermans, 1983, for a
review of 31 such studies).

In considering the relative applicability of Ferree and Miller's attributional account and of Weiner's attributional theory to the context of
social movements, it is apparent that Ferree and Miller's account is
clearer and more explicit, but that Weiner's is fuller. There is also a
direct contradiction between the two formulations. Ferree and Miller
argue that external and stable attributions about negative social
outcomes predispose people toward social movement participation. In
contrast, Weiner's theory suggests that stable attributions for non-
attainment of a goal will result in a lowered expectancy for future success, a sense of hopelessness, and a tendency for withdrawal behavior.
A similar position is also put forward by Abramson, Metalsky, and
Alloy (1989) in explaining clinical depression, and by Seligman (1974) in
his earlier account of learned helplessness. The weight of evidence
would seem to favor Weiner rather than Ferree and Miller. However, the
evidence from Abramson et al. and Seligman pertains only to individual
functioning, not to broad patterns of social inequity. Also, crucial differences between the outcomes predicted by Ferree and Miller and by
Weiner would seem to depend on judgments of the *legitimacy* of the
external, stable causes of the negative outcomes, and on the possibility

of imagining alternative referent outcomes. These points are central to Social Identity Theory's account of the behavioral consequences of threats to social identity (see, e.g., Ellemers' chapter in this volume).

Integrating Relative Deprivation and Attribution Theories

Grievance interpretation involves the perception and evaluation of negative social outcomes, and, in turn, forms the basis of the potential for mobilization in social movements. Such perceptual and evaluative processes can be understood in terms of relative deprivation and causal attribution. RD is considered as an intervening state between social evaluation and responses to that evaluation. There are different types and components of RD, and different types of behavioral response to RD. Causal attribution is conceived of as a mediator of responses to RD. An understanding of the relationships between RD and causal attribution would further theoretical development and specification of the links between patterns of resource distribution, social evaluation, and consequent social behaviors.

We have already mentioned that RD, conceived of as the perceived discrepancy between referent and actual outcomes and the attendant affects, is related to the non-attainment of goals, and hence to attributional search. This is especially so when the goals are important and when non-attainment is associated with negative outcomes. Attributional search has affective and cognitive consequences that may enhance or reduce the feeling of RD. Low justification, for example, which is related to Crosby's (1976) notion of lack of self-blame, is likely to lead to an external rather than an internal attribution. Accordingly, low justification is likely to produce responses associated with external attributions, such as anger, rather than self-deprecation.

Another possible connection between RD and causal attribution is between the likelihood of amelioration and the stability of attribution. Specifically, low likelihood of amelioration corresponds to a stable attribution for the cause of an undesirable outcome. It has been postulated that low likelihood can lead to less striving for, or to devaluation of, the goal. This is consistent with Weiner's predictions about the effects of a stable attribution for the cause of non-attainment of a goal: a sense of hopelessness and lowered striving. Empirical studies manipulating the likelihood factor have produced conflicting results, though, suggesting the possibility of other attributional processes mediating the responses to RD.

The three attributional dimensions identified by Weiner – locus, stability, and controllability – provide clues to other likely mediating attributional processes. These three dimensions resemble the mediators of RD

responses proposed by Crosby in her 1976 model.[1] Specifically, her notion
of direction of blame (intro- vs. extrapunitiveness) for the undesirable outcome corresponds to Weiner's internal versus external causal dimension.
The degree of personal control is compatible with Weiner's notion of controllability. And, finally, the opportunity for change is related to the likelihood of amelioration and, by extension, the stability of attribution.
Identifying these points of correspondence between Crosby's model of
egoistic RD and Weiner's attribution theory is not merely a translation of
terminologies – it produces a net theoretical gain. Incorporating variables
from attribution theory into the RD model allows mediating processes to
be theoretically chosen rather than selected ad hoc. And the generality of
causal attribution theory allows for more than the four responses to RD
that are considered in Crosby's 1976 model.

Considering these interconnections between the different models of RD
and causal attribution theory, it is possible to state a more precise theory of
RD that explicitly accounts for the underlying social psychological
processes and bridges the gap between the experience of RD and
responses to RD. We do this by setting out a series of empirically testable
propositions.

Proposition 1. The sole precondition of cognitive RD[2] is a perceived
discrepancy between referent and actual outcomes. There are many possible sources of referent outcomes: past experience (a person thinks it feasible to have X); ideals (feels entitled to X); or another person, persons, or
groups (sees others have X).

Proposition 2. The referent and actual outcomes must be important to
the person. The person must want X. This represents the motivational
component of RD.

Proposition 3. A perceived discrepancy between referent and actual
outcomes important to the person will lead to attributions about the
causes of the discrepancy. These attributions can be ordered along three
dimensions: locus of causality (internal vs. external), controllability (controllable vs. uncontrollable), and stability (stable vs. unstable).

Proposition 4. The position of the causal attribution for the perceived
discrepancy on the three causal dimensions will affect the experience of
RD. The feeling of RD will be enhanced if the person makes an external
attribution for the cause of the undesirable outcome (cf., Crosby's notion

of lack of self-blame and Folger's low justification), or if the person makes a stable attribution for the cause of the undesirable outcome (cf., Folger's low likelihood of amelioration).

Proposition 5. There are three sets of possible responses to RD: self-directed, object-directed, and system-directed. Negative self-directed responses include self-deprecation, learned helplessness, and stress. Positive self-directed responses include self-striving and self-improvement. Object-directed responses include revaluation of the object or outcome, or their substitution. System-directed responses include actions aimed at changing the procedural or distributive system.

Proposition 6. The position of the attribution for the perceived discrepancy on the three causal dimensions will affect the choice of response to RD. Internal attributions will lead to self-directed responses, and external attributions will lead to system-directed responses. Stress or self-deprecation will follow an uncontrollable, stable attribution, and self-improvement will follow a controllable, stable attribution. Controllable attributions will lead to conventional social action, and uncontrollable attributions will lead to unconventional social action.[3] Social action will be more likely following an unstable than a stable attribution, and apathy will be the most likely response to a stable, uncontrollable attribution.

We turn now to a brief discussion of two studies that examine some of our ideas about the interplay between RD and attribution.

STUDY ONE: RD AND ENVIRONMENTAL ACTION

The broad aim of this study (see Wong & Walker, 2000) was to reintegrate the social psychology of grievance interpretation into a more general account of social movement participation, focusing in particular on predicting participation in the environmental movement (see also Klandermans, 1997; Kowalewski & Porter, 1992; Kriespi, Saris, & Wille, 1993; Tranter, 1999). We especially wanted to examine empirically the role of attributional processes in forming responses to RD. We use the common distinction between *conventional* and *unconventional* participation. Conventional action is generally associated with positive evaluation of the whole political system, and short-term dissatisfaction with performance of a particular government only increases conventional activities (Marsh, 1990). However, the basic evaluative source for unconventional action lies in dissatisfaction with the existing political system. Similarly, Sayles (1986)

has proposed that conventional activists differ from unconventional
activists in terms of the level of system-blame and political trust.

Our choice to examine participation in the environmental movement
poses peculiar theoretical problems for RD. Two in particular are discussed: the selection of relevant comparison dimensions, and the distinction between personal and group RD.

Discrepancies between referent and actual outcomes can occur on
many different comparison dimensions. Being able to predict which
dimensions are the important ones has always been one of the banes of RD
theory (and social evaluation theories, more generally). In relation to environmental action, though, the quality of environment is probably the most
pertinent comparison dimension. Nonetheless, environmental quality
may not be the only relevant comparison dimension. New class theorists
have argued that the discrepancy between aspired and actual *power status*
is responsible for inciting the new middle class to participate in various
social movements, including the environmental movement (see, e.g., Eckersley, 1989). Although RD researchers have typically assumed that *economic* RD leads to general dissatisfaction and hence to protest and
participation in social movements, postmaterialist theorists (e.g., Ingle-
hart, 1990; Opp, 1990; Rohrschneider, 1988, 1990) have argued that new
social movements, such as the environmental movement, are driven more
by postmaterial concerns and less by material or economic concerns.
Given these three possible comparison dimensions – environmental quality, power status, and economic condition – pertinent to participation in
the environmental movement, we decided to try to measure them all in
our attempt to predict participation in the environmental movement.

The second major problem we faced was how to deal with the personal–group RD distinction. Typically, personal RD is defined as arising
from social comparisons between self and some other individual, and
group RD is a consequence of social comparisons between an ingroup
and an outgroup. That is, personal and group RD are defined by the categories being compared. In adopting Folger's RCT approach, we focus
more on the comparison process itself rather than the comparison categories. We refer to personal RD as resulting from evaluations of outcomes for the individual, while group RD is related to evaluations of
outcomes for the group. Thus, the distinction is based on the types of
outcome evaluated rather than the sources of comparison. In this way,
the concept of group RD is not necessarily limited to ingroup-outgroup
comparisons, but can also accommodate other sources of comparison
referents (e.g., past experience, another person, ideals, values, etc) as

long as the outcome evaluated is concerned with the ingroup. Thus, the theoretical flexibility of the RCT model with regard to the sources of comparison is not compromised.

This theoretical flexibility is necessary for one main reason. In contrast to other social movements (e.g., civil rights movements, women's movements) that pit distinctive, dichotomous groups (Black vs. White, women vs. men) against one another, a distinctive ingroup-outgroup dichotomy is not apparent in the case of the environmental movement. It may be suggested that those who oppose the environmental movement constitute an outgroup for environmentalists, but environmentalists and their opponents experience the same environmental conditions (broadly, although the specific environmental conditions of environmentalists are often suburban and more affluent than those of non-environmentalists), regardless of group membership. Instead, it is more plausible that environmentalists have sources of comparison referents other than members of any outgroup. Particularly, alternative ideals based on certain values or ideologies can serve as referent outcomes. This argument may apply more to the comparison dimension involving environmental conditions than to the other comparison dimensions of income and power status.

In summary, we aimed in this study to examine the proposed mediating effects of causal attribution on RD responses. We tested the hypotheses that cognitive RD, affective RD, and the locus, controllability, and stability of attributions have interactive effects on conventional and unconventional environmental action. These hypotheses are examined for both personal and group RD on the comparison dimensions of income, power status, and environmental conditions.

Our data came from a mail survey of samples randomly drawn from two prominent environmental groups in Western Australia: the Australian Conservation Foundation and The Wilderness Society. We obtained 353 usable questionnaires, with a response rate of 63%.

The questionnaire contained measures of intention to participate in conventional and unconventional environmental action, RD, the three causal attribution dimensions, and a host of other variables. The RD measures were separated into cognitive and affective dimensions of personal and group RD, on each of three comparison dimensions (income, power status, environmental condtions). The causal attribution measures were adapted from the Causal Dimension Scale (Russell, 1982).

The respondents indicated that they had engaged in reasonable amounts of conventional activity, and that they intended to continue these activities. Reported participation in, or intention to engage in, unconventional activities (many of which were illegal and/or violent) was much lower.

To try to predict these self-reported activities, and intentions to engage in activities, we constructed a series of hierarchical regression equations. In these equations, effects due to the main effects of the RD variables and the attribution variables were entered on step one, the second-order interactions among the RD and attribution variables on step two, and the third-order interactions on step three. Fourth-order and fifth-order interactions were not examined, as we had reached the limits of the equations' (and our) tolerance. There were four dependent variables: past participation and planned participation in each of conventional and unconventional activities. Generally, the results were disappointing.

For the comparison dimensions of income and power status, none of the effects in the regressions was significant, indicating that RD on these dimensions was unrelated to past or future participation in conventional or unconventional environmental action. Nor did RD interact with any of the attribution measures to influence the environmental action scores.

However, when we examined the comparison dimension of environmental quality, we did find a significant effect for past participation in unconventional activities. Group RD was related to scores on this dimension, but personal RD was unrelated. (The group RD measure involved respondents selecting from a list of groups the one that is closest to them, and rating whether that group's current environmental conditions were better or worse than they deserved). The group RD effect was only apparent at the third step, though. That is, the first-order and second-order effects were not significant. The third-order effect was pursued by splitting (at the midpoint rather than the median) each of the independent variables and crossing them. The ANOVA indicated that only one of the third-order interaction effects was significant – involving group RD, locus, and controllability. This effect could be understood as follows. In the "no-RD" condition, increased controllability greatly reduced activism when the outcome was attributed to internal causes. Increased controllability, however, had the reverse effect of increasing activism when such outcomes were attributed to external causes. This pattern was reversed in the "RD" condition: Increased controllability increased activism when the RD was attributed to internal causes but suppressed activism when it was attributed to external causes.

The general absence of results was disappointing, and the one third-order effect we did obtain was not quite the one we had predicted. Our theoretical analysis suggested that high RD, coupled with external, uncontrollable, and variable attributions for the outcomes on the comparison dimension (in this case, the quality of the environment of the group closest to the respondent, relative to the quality of environment that group deserved) would be associated with participation in (unconventional) environmental activism. Unfortunately, our results do not clearly support this proposition. In fact, the third-order interaction suggested that the highest scores on the participation in unconventional action variable occurred in the *absence* of RD (!) condition, coupled with internal and uncontrollable attributions.

The absence of substantial results from this study is all the more striking when the statistical power of the study is considered. Given that our theoretical integration of RD and causal attribution is sensible and produces testable hypotheses, and given the size of effects typically reported in the literature examining social movement participation, we expected that the relationship between the combined RD/attribution variables and the criterion variables would have a moderate effect size. Following Cohen's (1988) procedure, the present regressions would have a power of .94 (at the 5% level) or .80 (at the 1%) level to detect a moderate sized effect. The implication of this power analysis must be either that the theoretical integration is deficient, that the theoretical propositions do not apply in the context of participation in the environmental movement, or that Nature's dice have rolled the wrong way. We opt for the second of the three – that participation in the environmental movement represents a boundary condition for RD theory – for reasons that already have been alluded to, and that we briefly recap here.

Most studies relating RD to social protest do so in the context of binary groups (e.g., men/women, Black/White). In these contexts, outcomes are often perceived to be distributed ipsatively – the more one group receives, the less the other receives. When the comparison dimension is environmental conditions, however, the outcomes are not zero-sum. A positive or negative outcome on the comparison dimension is not associated with one group to the exclusion of others. Instead, outcomes will be more or less similar for all people regardless of their memberships within any particular social categories. Closely related to this point is the fact that the comparison groups in the case of environmental conditions are less salient than in most research because they are not based on distinctive or historically opposed categories based on social class, gender, race, or ethnicity. Due to the nonexclusive nature of the outcomes on the comparison dimension of environmental conditions and the low salience of comparison groups, social comparisons or evaluations with regard to environmental conditions may be less likely to occur. Thus, the RD construct may not apply in the case of participation in the environmental movement. However, this does not preclude its utility in understanding other social movements in which the relevant comparison groups and comparison dimensions are more salient. So we turn now to a second study to examine some of the propositions derived from our integration of RD and attribution theories.

STUDY TWO: RELATIVE DEPRIVATION, WOMEN, AND WORK

It is now well established that people are often able to acknowledge that their ingroup is deprived or discriminated against, but then deny that they themselves are deprived or discriminated against (Crosby, 1982, 1984; Crosby, Pufall, Snyder, O'Connell, & Whalen, 1989; Jackson, 1989; Olson, 1986). For example, Crosby (1982) found that a sample of American working women felt aggrieved, dissatisfied, and pessimistic about the situation of working women generally, yet expressed little anger or dissatisfaction about their own personal working conditions – a phenomenon labeled the "paradox of the contented woman worker." This discrepancy applies more generally than to working women, though, having been demonstrated in samples of Francophone managers in Quebec (Guimond & Dube-Simard, 1983), Anglophone Quebecers (Taylor, Wong-Rieger, McKiernan, & Bercusson, 1982), gay men in England (Birt & Dion, 1987) and Haitian and Indian women immigrants in Montreal (Taylor, Wright, Moghaddam, & Lalonde, 1990) (see also the theoretical discussion provided by Wright & Tropp, this volume).

Studies of the disjunction between the perception of group deprivation and the failure to perceive personal deprivation often rely on RD theory as a framework. The "paradox of the contented woman worker," or the self-group discrepancy, can be recast more generally in terms of RD theory. Implicit in studies of the self-group discrepancy is the notion that it is not simultaneously possible for one's membership group to be deprived relative to some outgroup and for oneself not to be deprived relative to that same outgroup. Because one belongs to a deprived ingroup, one is also more likely to be deprived, when deprivation in both cases (ingroup and self) is assessed relative to the same comparison outgroup. In the case of studies of the working woman paradox, it has been assumed that "women" can be identified as a homogeneous social category, such that all members of that category must share equally any deprivation or discrimination directed at that category on a categorial basis. This is unlikely to be the case. In any organizational setting, women may be found at any and all levels within that organization, although to be sure they more sparsely populate the higher levels than a gender-free distribution would allow. Because social goods (pay, power, status, etc.) are not distributed evenly across all levels of an organization, there is an "objective" sense in which women at higher levels receive more – relative to women at lower levels, although probably not relative to men at the same level. When women respondents complete survey questions asking about the relative positions of women and men, they are forced to provide a single answer to represent all women. Regardless of whether they use a prototype- or exemplar-based heuristic, women at higher levels of an organization are likely to see themselves as "better-off" than "all women," and women at lower levels are likely to see themselves as "worse-off" than "all women." Thus, women's perceptions of personal RD and of group RD are likely to be affected by their position in the organizational structure. This suggests that women at all levels are equally likely to acknowledge that women, as a group, are deprived relative to men, but women at higher levels are less likely to acknowledge personal deprivation relative to men and hence are more likely to exhibit the paradox.

In Folger's RCT, RD ensues when an actual outcome is worse than a referent outcome (high referent outcome), when the procedure is not justified (low in justification), and when there is little likelihood of amelioration (low amelioration). Mark and Folger (1984) suggest that responses to RD can be directed to self, to the object one is deprived of, or to the system responsible for the outcome. Responses may be positive or negative, and they may be attitudinal or behavioral. The model allows for RD to produce compound responses, and for multiple sequenced responses. Different patterns of judgments about referent outcomes, justification, and likelihood of amelioration will lead to different responses. Thus, for example, low justification coupled with low likelihood (and assuming high referent outcome) will produce negative system-directed responses, especially negative attitudes.

In the case of working women, the judged positions of working women and of self as lower than that of working men can reasonably be taken to indicate high referent outcomes – working women perceive actual outcomes for themselves and for the group of working women that are worse than those of working men. Justification is likely to be low, since the circumstances leading to the actual outcomes (social and institutional gender inequity) are "morally inferior" (Mark & Folger, 1984, p. 195) to those imagined circumstances (equity) that produce the referent outcome. Finally, likelihood of amelioration is likely to vary among working women much more than either of the other two dimensions. Mark and Folger (1984, p. 196) predict that high likelihood is "a more appealing state than low likelihood and will lead to lower distress." Any links between Folger's three dimensions and behavioral outcomes thus will be driven mostly by variation among women in the extent to which they see the conditions as likely to change.

In the earlier part of this chapter, we indicated ways in which principles of causal attribution can be applied to RD to predict behavioral outcomes. The environmental movement study failed to provide much support for our speculations. Rather than test such an elaborate model of attributional linkages again, we decided it was perhaps more prudent to test a simpler model of how attributional patterns may mediate between RD and behavior. We turned to the notion of attributional style (see Kretzschmar & Walker, 1999, for a full account of this study).

Attributional style refers to the ways in which individuals differ in the tendency to attribute causes to events in a consistent manner (Abramson, Seligman, & Teasdale, 1978; Tiggeman, Winefield, Winefield, & Goldney, 1991). Individuals who habitually offer internal, stable, and global explanations for negative or bad events are referred to as having a depressive explanatory style (Peterson & Villanova, 1988) which puts them at risk of depression when such events occur. In contrast, the same attributions (internal, stable, and global) for positive events are seen as being a "healthy, positive" attributional style, and are associated in an occupational setting with job success, motivation, and satisfaction (Furnham, Sadka, & Brewin, 1992).

Causal attributions are likely to happen following an unexpected, important, or negative outcome (Weiner, 1985). Working women typically believe that their outcomes (both personal and group) at work are worse than those of men. Although this may not be an unexpected outcome, it is presumably an important and a negative one, and hence will lead to attributional search. Individual differences in the tendency to make particular sorts of attributions ought then to mediate between the perception of RD and the behavioral responses to that RD. In particular, stable, internal, and global attributions about negative outcomes such as being worse-off than men at work should lead to negative self-directed behaviors, and unstable, external, and global attributions should lead to negative system-directed behaviors.

A final issue we wish to address in this study is the specification and measurement of affective RD. In many studies (including our environmental movement study), RD is assessed using the self-anchoring striving scale (SASS) of Cantril (1965). Some researchers (e.g., Walker & Pettigrew, 1984) have argued that the SASS only measures a cognitive component of RD, and ignores the more potent affective component. A recent meta-analysis of the RD literature confirms this position (see Smith & Ortiz, this volume). Accordingly, we sought in this study to incorporate a measure of affective RD.

This study relied on a convenience sample of 102 women working in the state public service in Perth, Western Australia, and included administrative officers, research and project officers, secretaries, psychologists, managers, and directors.

Using a SASS, we obtained measures of *personal RD* (the difference between the positions of self and working women), *group RD* (the difference between working men and working women), and *self-outgroup RD* (the difference between self and working men). Affective RD was measured using an adjective check list instrument based on Crosby (1982). We also included measures of likelihood of amelioration, attributional style (based on a modified version of the Occupational Attributional Style Questionnaire (OASQ) of Furnham et al., 1992), and behavioral responses to RD (using a scale developed by us, based on the model of Mark & Folger, 1984).

Factor analysis of the *affective RD* measure produced two factors, one comprising positive emotions (joyous, elated, proud, happy, grateful), and the other negative emotions (angry, outraged, upset, annoyed, worried, bitter, disappointed, deprived). These factors were *independent* of one another, echoing results in an experimental setting (Walker, 1999). Two independent factors also emerged from factor analysis of the measure of behavioral responses to RD: one we labeled powerlessness, the other competitiveness. Finally, scores on the OASQ were summed separately for the description of positive events and for negative events. Higher scores indicate a greater tendency to make internal, stable, and global attributions across a variety of occupational settings.

We hypothesized that responses to perceived discrepancies between self and outgroup would be mediated by affective RD, attributional style, and likelihood of amelioration. Median splits applied to each of the two affective RD dimensions produced four groups: low positive/low negative (low affect group, $n = 12$), low positive/high negative (negative group, $n = 15$), high positive/low negative (positive group, $n = 15$), and high positive/high negative (high affect group, $n = 11$). Median splits were also applied to each of the positive events attributional style and negative events attributional style scales, producing a high and a low group on each scale. Finally, scores on the likelihood of amelioration scale were split at the median to produce a high and a low group.

We examined the relative rankings of self, working women, and working men for evidence of the paradox of working women. There was a clear hierarchy across the three categories: working men were rated highest ($M = 7.23$), self the next highest ($M = 5.94$), and working women the lowest ($M = 4.86$). All these differences were significant. It is interesting to note that not one respondent placed the position of women higher than that of men. Thus, working women in this sample believe that the group of working women is deprived relative to the group of working men. Although they believe they are better off than the group of working women, they also acknowledge that they, individually, are deprived relative to the group of working men. Hereafter, for reasons of space and clarity, we focus only on reactions to the relative positions of self and working men, and analyses only include those women who rated self lower than working men.

Scores on the cognitive RD measure (comparing self and men) were significantly correlated with both the affective RD dimensions, but to a different extent and in different directions ($r = .61$, $p < .01$, for resentment, and $r = -.46$, $p < .01$, for happiness), thus supporting the validity of the distinction between the two affective dimensions.

There were two independent dimensions of behavioral responses to perceived inequality between self and working men – competitiveness and powerlessness. Competitiveness scores were greater for women who tended to attribute positive events to stable, internal, and global factors than for women who tended to attribute otherwise. Women who scored high on the positive affect dimension and who thought the likelihood of amelioration was low gave significantly lower competitiveness scores than did either women who scored high on the positivity dimension who thought the likelihood of amelioration was high, or women who scored low on likelihood of amelioration and who were high on both the positivity and negativity dimensions.

Women who attributed negative events to stable, internal, and global factors scored significantly higher on the powerlessness dimension than did women who attributed otherwise. Powerlessness scores were also higher for women who scored high on the negative affect dimension than for those who scored low. Similarly, women who scored high on the negativity dimension, and women who scored low in likelihood of amelioration, gave significantly higher powerlessness scores than either women low on negativity or high on likelihood of amelioration.

The results of this study are illuminating in at least three ways: what they say about the paradox of the contented woman worker, the nature of responses to RD, and the attributional mediators between RD and behavioral responses. We discuss each of these briefly in turn.

The "paradox of the contented woman worker" suggests that working women fail to acknowledge that they are deprived relative to the group "working men," even though they readily acknowledge that the group to which they belong (working women) is, as a group, deprived relative to the group working men. Our study conflicts with this. Our sample of working women acknowledged that working women are deprived relative to working men, and also that they themselves are deprived relative to working men, but they do not rate themselves as being as deprived as working women generally.

The difference between our results and those in the literature may reflect differences due to time or culture. Neither of these explanations is particularly satisfying, but neither can be eliminated. Instead, we believe the difference in results can be largely attributed to an important aspect of the methods employed in our and others' studies.

In our study, respondents were explicitly instructed to provide ranked positions of self, working women, and working men. They were then asked to think about the relative positions of self and working men, and to describe various affective and behavioral reactions to those two positions. This method makes explicit the relative statuses of self, working women, and working men. In Crosby's seminal study in this area (Crosby, 1982), the measures were less direct. Working women and men were asked to rate their satisfaction with their situation, on several dimensions (e.g., "In view of your training and abilities, is your present job as good as it ought to be?"). The groups of working women and men were equally highly satisfied with their job. Both groups were matched on age, job status, and so on, yet the working women earned on average just 60% of the working men's salaries. Therefore, the discrimination evident in comparing women's and men's outcomes, having previously established that the two groups are equivalent in occupational inputs, is not translated into each woman's evaluation of her job and satisfaction with that job.

In another study, Crosby et al. (1989) surveyed a sample of lesbians, asking respondents about personal, local, and national discrimination against lesbians, with questions such as "Overall, are you discriminated against on the basis of sexual preference and not simply gender?" The lesbians in this study reported that discrimination was greatest at the national level, then at the local level, and least at the personal level. Taylor et al. (1990) adopted a similar measurement strategy to that of Crosby et al. (1989). Working with a sample of Indian and Haitian women in Montreal, they asked respondents if they "personally had been discriminated against because of their (a) race, (b) culture, (c) newcomer status to Canada, or (d) sex" (p. 257). These questions were followed by similar questions asking if Indian/Haitian women in general were discriminated against.

The questions posed by Crosby (1982), Crosby et al. (1989), and by Taylor et al. (1990) are all *indirect* ways of obtaining information about how respondents see the relative positions of self, ingroup, and outgroup. Respondents could answer these questions without necessarily comparing their own position with that of the outgroup.[4] Our questions, though, were explicit, and respondents could hardly avoid making direct, conscious, comparisons between self, ingroup, and outgroup.

It is interesting to note, also, that Crosby (1982), Crosby et al., (1989), and Taylor et al. (1990) all used Likert-type statements to assess the degree of deprivation or discrimination, whereas we used the SASS ranking technique. A second study reported by Crosby et al. (1989), of a sample of working-class respondents, used the SASS and found, as we did, that respondents readily acknowledged both personal and group discrimination.

We suggest that some measurement techniques, such as the SASS, make the relative positions of self, ingroup, and outgroup (and hence judgments about deprivation and discrimination) explicit and unavoidable. Other techniques, such as the use of Likert-type items to assess satisfaction with, or deprivation experienced by, just one referent (self, ingroup, or outgroup) may not make these social comparisons explicit, and respondents will not necessarily be aware of the relative positions of each of the referents being asked about (see also the importance of measurement in the meta-analysis reported in Smith & Ortiz, this volume). This implies, then, that the "paradox" is a product of the way questions are asked, and does not necessarily reflect a denial by members of disadvantaged groups of their personal experience of deprivation. These suggestions are, of course, conjectural, and require further investigation.

The second implication of our study concerns responses to RD. The RD literature distinguishes between cognitive and affective components of RD (Olson & Hafer, 1996; Walker & Pettigrew, 1984). Studies that measure the two together often assume the two are independent dimensions (e.g., Guimond & Dube-Simard, 1983; Petta & Walker, 1992). Instead of this, we used a measurement technique that required the affective component to *follow* the cognitive. So, respondents were asked to think about the difference between the nominated positions of self and working men, and then to rate how much each of a set of 24 adjectives described how they felt.

This study and another experimental study (Walker, 1999) are unique in attempting to describe the emotional reactions to the cognitive recognition of deprivation in this way, with both suggesting that emotional reactions can be organized into two independent dimensions, one positive and one negative. RD theory often assumes that resentment is the emotion that most clearly defines the experience of RD. However, our results suggest that resentment is not the only emotion that can follow the recognition of deprivation. Our label for the second dimension is not meant to imply that some women were happy when they thought about the relative positions of self and working men; only that a cluster of similar "positive" emotions (or a cluster of absences of similar positive emotions) co-occurred.

An adequate typology of behavioral responses is lacking in RD theory. Mark and Folger (1984) proposed a "preliminary, first-generation" model of responses in an attempt to stimulate theoretical development. We developed items to indicate each of the response alternatives captured in the model and asked respondents to indicate how likely they are to engage in each of the behaviors we indicated. Factor analysis of responses showed two clear independent dimensions, which we labeled powerlessness and competitiveness. As with the affective responses, this result suggests that there are several possible behavioral responses, not just one, to the recognition of deprivation. Thus, in response to the same recognition of self-outgroup deprivation, women in our sample could be motivated either to engage in competitive behaviors, ready to challenge the existing state of affairs, or to feel powerless to do anything to change matters. This is an important theoretical point, and indicates a promising area of development for RD theory.

If it is the case that some women respond to self-outgroup deprivation by engaging in competitive behaviors and others feel powerless to do anything, then the obvious theoretical question must be "What are the variables which mediate between the perception of deprivation and one or the other behavioral response?" This is the third implication of our study, concerning the mediation of behavioral responses to the experience of RD. We attempted in this study to examine the mediating effects of affective RD, likelihood of amelioration of the conditions that produce that RD, and attributional style.

Women who had a high attributional style score for positive work-related events (i.e., who attributed those events to stable, internal, and global factors) showed greater competitiveness than women who had a low attributional style score. Women who thought that the conditions producing the deprivation would ameliorate showed greater competitiveness than women who thought they would not. Of those women who thought the conditions would not ameliorate, those who were high on both positive and negative affect were more competitive than those who were high on positivity only.

Women who had a high attributional style score for negative work-related events felt more powerless than women with a low attributional style score. Women who reported negativity felt more powerless than those who did not. Women who thought the conditions that produced the deprivation were not likely to change felt more powerless than those who thought the conditions were likely to change.

Unfortunately, our sample size was too small to allow us to explore fully all the possible interactions between the different mediating variables. Nonetheless, our results provide support for Folger's (1984) model, which posits that likelihood of amelioration plays an important role in the translation of RD into action. Our results also highlight the importance of giving full sway in RD models to affective RD. Too often studies measure only cognitive RD. And our results point to the importance of attributional style in determining behavioral responses to RD.

CONCLUSIONS

In this chapter we have attempted to delineate a theoretical integration of principles from attribution theory into RD theory. In setting out a series of testable hypotheses, we hope to stimulate further research in this area. The two studies we presented lead us to three general conclusions. The first, from the environmental movement study, points to a limit in the applicability of RD theory, suggesting that the group RD construct may apply only in intergroup contexts featuring historically opposed (or at least paired) groups. In the absence of such opposition, it appears that people do not – perhaps cannot – evaluate outcomes in terms of ingroups and outgroups.

The second, following from both studies, is that the path from perceiving grievance to engaging in action covers familiar attributional territory. How people respond to perceived grievance depends on what emotions are stirred by such perception, and on their attributional analyses of the causes of the grievance. These attributional analyses can reflect stable, chronic individual differences in tendency to attribute to internal or external causes, and/or to more context-specific, ephemeral attributions.

And, third, further development of RD theory requires further theoretical and emprical work to develop a more adequate typology of behavioral responses to RD, and a fuller understanding of the complexities of the links between grievance and action.

ACKNOWLEDGMENTS

We thank the helpful comments on earlier drafts provided by Tom Pettigrew and Heather Smith. Iain Walker's contribution to this chapter was partly supported by grants from the Australian Research Council and Murdoch University.

NOTES

1. Although Crosby (1986) gave up on her 1976 model, and ultimately settled on just two preconditions of RD, the variables contained within her model remain as important mediators between RD and behavior.
2. Cognitive RD is the conscious recognition of being worse-off than some referent. Affective RD is the affective or motivational response to that recognition (see Olson & Hafer, 1996).
3. Conventional action is considered as normal or legitimate, whereas unconventional action involves extra-legal or illegitimate activities (e.g., Dalton, 1988; Sayles, 1986).
4. Indeed, results from a study by Klar and Giladi (1999) suggest that ratings about self and group are made through entirely different processes.

REFERENCES

Abramson, L. Y., Metalsky, G. L., & Alloy, L. B. (1889). Hopelessness depression: A theory-based subtype of depression. *Psychological Review, 96,* 358–372.

Abramson, L. Y., Seligman, M. E. P., & Teasdale, J. (1978). Learned helplessness in humans: Critique and reformulation. *Journal of Abnormal Psychology, 87,* 49–74.

Birt, C. M., & Dion, K. L. (1987). Relative deprivation theory and responses to discrimination in a gay male and lesbian sample. *British Journal of Social Psychology, 26,* 139–145.

Cantril, H. (1965). *The pattern of human concerns.* New York: Rutgers University Press.

Carroll, J. S. (1978). Causal attributions in expert parole decisions. *Journal of Personality and Social Psychology, 36,* 1501–1511.

Cohen, J. (1988). *Statistical power analysis for the behavioral sciences* (2nd ed.). Hillsdale, NJ: Lawrence Erlbaum.

Crosby, F. J. (1976). A model of egoistical relative deprivation. *Psychological Review, 83,* 85–113.

Crosby, F. J. (1982). *Relative deprivation and working women.* New York: Oxford University Press.

Crosby, F. J. (1984). The denial of personal discrimination. *American Behavioral Scientist, 27,* 371–386.

Crosby, F. J., Pufall, A., Snyder, R. C., O'Connell, M., & Whalen, P. (1989). The denial of personal disadvantage among you, me, and all the other ostriches. In M. Crawford & M. Gentry (Eds.), *Gender and thought: Psychological perspectives* (pp. 79–99). New York: Springer-Verlag.

Dalton, R. J. (1988). *Citizen politics in western democracies: Public opinion and political parties in the United States, Great Britain, West Germany, and France.* Chatham, NJ: Chatham House.

Eckersley, R. (1989). Green politics and the new middle class: Selfishness or virtue? *Political Studies, 39,* 205–223.

Ferree, M. M., & Miller, F. D. (1985). Mobilization and meaning: Toward an integration of social psychological and resource mobilization perspectives on social movements. *Sociological Inquiry, 55,* 38–51.

Folger, R. (1984). Perceived injustice, referent cognitions, and the concept of comparison level. *Representative Research in Social Psychology, 14,* 88–108.

Folger, R. (1986). A referent cognitions theory of relative deprivation. In J. M. Olson, C. P Herman, & M. P. Zanna (Eds.), *Relative deprivation and social comparison: The Ontario symposium* (Vol. 4, pp. 33–55). Hillsdale, NJ: Lawrence Erlbaum.

Folger, R. (1987). Reformulating the preconditions of resentment: A referent cognitions model. In J. C. Masters & W. Smith (Eds.), *Social comparison, social justice, and relative deprivation: Theoretical, empirical, and policy perspectives* (pp. 76–83). Hillsdale, NJ: Lawrence Erlbaum.

Furnham, A., Sadka, V., & Brewin, C. (1992). The development of an occupational style questionnaire. *Journal of Organizational Behavior, 13,* 27–39.

Guimond, S., & Dube-Simard, L. (1983). Relative deprivation theory and the Quebec Nationalist Movement: The cognitive-emotion distinction and the person-group deprivation issue. *Journal of Personality and Social Psychology, 44,* 526–535.

Ingelhart, R. (1990). *Culture shift in advanced industrial society.* Princeton, NJ: Princeton University Press.

Jackson, L. A. (1989). Relative deprivation and the gender wage gap. *Journal of Social Issues, 45,* 117–133.

Klandermans, B. G. (1983). Rotter's IE Scale and sociopolitical action-taking: The balance of 20 years of research. *European Journal of Social Psychology, 13,* 399–415.

Klandermans, B. G. (1997). *The social psychology of protest.* Oxford: Blackwell.

Klar, Y., & Giladi, E. E. (1999). Are most people happier than their peers, or are they just happy? *Personality and Social Psychology Bulletin, 25,* 585–594.

Kowalewski, D., & Porter, K. L. (1992). Ecoprotest: Alienation, deprivation, or resources? *Social Sciences Quarterly, 73,* 523–534.

Kriesi, H., Saris, W. E., & Wille, A. (1993). Mobilization potential for environmental protest. *European Sociological Review, 9,* 155–171.

Kretzschmar, K., & Walker, I. (1999). *Women at work: A study of relative deprivation in an organizational setting.* Unpublished manuscript. Murdoch University.

Mark, M. M. (1985). Expectations, procedural justice, and alternative reactions to being deprived of a desired outcome. *Journal of Experimental Social Psychology, 21,* 114–137.

Mark, M. M., & Folger, R. (1984). Responses to relative deprivation: A conceptual framework. *Review of Personality and Social Psychology, 5,* 192–218.

Marsh, A. (1990). *Political action in Europe and the USA*. London: Macmillan.

McHugh, M. C., Beckman, L., & Frieze, I. H. (1979). Analyzing alcoholism. In I. H. Frieze, D. Barstal, & J. S. Carroll (Eds.), *New approaches to social problems* (pp. 168–208). San Francisco: Jossey Bass.

Olson, J. M. (1986). Resentment about deprivation: Entitlement and hopefulness as mediators of the effects of qualifications. In J. Olson, C. P. Herman, & M. Zanna (Eds.), *Relative deprivation and social comparison: The Ontario symposium* (Vol. 4, pp. 57–77). Hillsdale, NJ: Lawrence Erlbaum.

Olson, J. M., & Hafer, C. L. (1996). Affect, motivation, and cognition in relative deprivation research. In R. M. Sorrentino & E. T. Higgins (Eds.), *Handbook of motivation and cognition. Vol. 3: The interpersonal context* (pp. 85–117). New York: Guilford Press.

Olson, J. M., Roese, N. J., Meen, J., & Robertson, D. J. (1995). The preconditions and consequences of deprivation: Two field studies. *Journal of Applied Social Psychology, 25,* 944–964.

Opp, K. D. (1990). Postmaterialism, collective action, and political protest. *American Journal of Political Science, 34,* 212–235.

Pandey, J., Sinha, Y., Prakash, A., & Tripathi, R. C. (1982). Right-left political ideologies and attributions of the causes of poverty. *European Journal of Social Psychology, 12,* 327–331.

Peterson, C., & Villanova, P. (1988). An expanded attributional style questionnaire. *Journal of Abnormal Psychology, 97,* 87–89.

Petta, G., & Walker, I. (1992). Relative deprivation and ethnic identity. *British Journal of Social Psychology, 31,* 285–293.

Pettigrew, T. F. (1967). Social evaluation theory. In D. Levine (Ed.), *Nebraska Symposium on Motivation* (Vol. 15, pp. 241–315). Lincoln: University of Nebraska Press.

Rohrschneider, R. (1988). Citizens' attitudes toward environmental issues: Selfish or selfless? *Comparative Political Studies, 21,* 347–367.

Rohrschneider, R. (1990). The roots of public opinion toward new social movements: An empirical test of competing explanation. *American Journal of Political Science, 34,* 1–30.

Runciman, W. G. (1966). *Relative deprivation and social justice: A study of attitudes to social inequality in twentieth-century England*. Berkeley: University of California Press.

Russell, D. W. (1982). The Causal Dimension Scale: A measure of how individuals perceive causes. *Journal of Personality and Social Psychology, 42,* 1137–1145.

Sayles, M. L. (1986). Assessing and synthesizing various social psychological approaches to political activism. *Cornell Journal of Social Relations, 18,* 41–68.

Seligman, M. E. P. (1974). Depression and learned helplessness. In R. J. Friedman & M. M. Katz (Eds.), *The psychology of depression: Contemporary theory and research*. Washington, DC: Winston-Wiley.

Taylor, D. M., Wong-Rieger, D., McKiernan, D. J., & Bercusson, T. (1982). Social comparison in a group context. *Journal of Social Psychology, 117,* 257–269.

Taylor, D. M., Wright, S. C., Moghaddam, F. M., & Lalonde, R. N. (1990). The personal/group discrimination discrepancy: Perceiving my group, but not myself, to be a target for discrimination. *Personality and Social Psychology Bulletin, 16,* 254–262.

Tranter, B. (1999). Environmentalism in Australia: Elites and the public. *Journal of Sociology, 35*, 331–350.

Tyler, T. R., & Smith, H. J. (1998). Social justice and social movements. In D. T. Gilbert, S. T. Fiske, & G. Lindzey (Eds.), *Handbook of social psychology* (4th ed., Vol. 2, pp. 595–629). New York: McGraw-Hill.

Tiggeman, M., Winefield, A., Winefield, H., & Goldney, R. (1991). The stability of attributional style and its relation to psychological stress. *British Journal of Clinical Psychology, 30*, 247–255.

Vanneman, R. D., & Pettigrew, T. F. (1972). Race and relative deprivation. *Race, 13*, 461–486.

Walker, I. (1999). Effects of personal and group relative deprivation on personal and collective self-esteem. *Group Processes and Intergroup Relations, 2*, 365–380.

Walker, I., & Pettigew, T. F. (1984). Relative deprivation theory: An overview and conceptual critique. *British Journal of Social Psychology, 23*, 301–310.

Weiner, B. (1985). An attributional theory of achievement motivation and emotion. *Psychological Review, 92*, 548–573.

Weiner, B. (1986). *An attributional theory of motivation and emotion.* New York: Springer-Verlag.

Weiner, B. (1995). Inferences of responsibility and social motivation. In M. P. Zanna (Ed.), *Advances in experimental social psychology* (Vol. 27, pp. 1–47). San Diego, CA: Academic Press.

Wong, N. K., & Walker, I. (2000). *Grievance interpretation and environmental activism: The interactive effects of relative deprivation and causal attribution on environmental action.* Unpublished manuscript. Murdoch University.

FOURTEEN

Spontaneous Temporal and Social Comparisons in Children's Conflict Narratives

Anne Wilson, Etsuko Hoshino-Browne, and Michael Ross

Theories of relative deprivation present an intriguing contradiction. On the one hand, their basic tenets (e.g., Crosby, 1976) are little more than common sense. Few people would be astonished to learn, for example, that individuals compare their own outcomes to those of others. Or that individuals feel deprived when they discover that someone else possesses an object that they crave and feel entitled to own. On the other hand, the concept of relative deprivation can help explain some quite surprising research findings. Researchers have reported that impoverished, elderly African American widows living in objectively deplorable conditions are highly satisfied with their lives, with an average rating above 9 on a 10-point satisfaction scale (Cairns & Cairns, 1994, pp. 148–150). Also, visually impaired and physically handicapped individuals are about as satisfied with their lives as nonhandicapped individuals (Cameron, Titus, Kostin, & Kostin, 1973). These findings can be explained in terms of the differing frames of reference people adopt to evaluate their lives. The data illustrate the importance of viewing deprivation as relative rather than absolute.

Deprivation may be relative, but to what standards do people compare their own outcomes? Several theorists have emphasized the distinction between personal (or egoistic) and group (or fraternalistic) relative deprivation (Pettigrew, 1967, 1978; Runciman, 1966; Walker & Pettigrew, 1984). Group relative deprivation results from comparing an ingroup's position (a group to which one belongs) to that of a better-off outgroup. Personal relative deprivation occurs when an individual compares his or her own conditions to those of others, either ingroup or outgroup members.

Theorists have argued that only group relative deprivation motivates group conflict, such as civil unrest or outgroup discrimination. Although comparisons with ingroup members are most frequent, perceptions of deprivation will not produce social conflict. If a man feels economically deprived relative to his co-workers, he could be motivated to effect individual change (e.g., quit his job, talk to his boss), but he probably will not attempt to incite an office revolt. In contrast, if he believes that both he and his co-workers are being mistreated relative to comparable other workers in the company, then he might attempt to mobilize his group to rectify the injustice. Researchers have found that, compared to personal deprivation, group relative deprivation is a better predictor of social behavior, from voting patterns to rioting (e.g., Caplan, 1970; Pettigrew, 1978). Dube and Guimond (1986) concluded that social activism may be unrelated to both objective and personal deprivation, but significantly related to perceptions of group deprivation.

The concept of relative deprivation is often used to explain significant, real-world phenomena, such as the origins of revolutions (Davies, 1962) and working women's reactions to pay inequities (Crosby, 1982). As a result, relative deprivation tends to be studied in surveys and with correlational data rather than in social psychology experiments. It is difficult to study revolution and social protest in the laboratory, although some researchers have ventured to do so (e.g., Ross, Thibaut, & Evenbeck, 1971; Wright, Taylor, & Moghaddam, 1990).

Like relative deprivation theories, Leon Festinger's (1954) social comparison theory emphasizes the importance of social standards in assessing outcomes. In its original form, social comparison theory was intended to explain how people evaluate the accuracy of their opinions or the level of their abilities. According to Festinger, people use social standards to make these judgments when objective standards are lacking. Compared to theories of relative deprivation, social comparison theory has typically inspired the study of less socially important questions; in addition, much of the research has occurred in social psychological laboratories with university students as participants. Social comparison researchers have studied such issues as: Whose additional test scores does a woman want to see after she, herself, has received either a low or high score on an anagrams test?

In developments subsequent to the original theorizing, researchers in both the relative deprivation and social comparison literatures introduced an additional standard of comparison – people's own earlier outcomes. Runciman (1966), a relative deprivation theorist, proposed that feelings of deprivation can be experienced relative to one's own past conditions as well as relative to outcomes obtained by other people. Crosby (1976, p. 85) illustrated this point by quoting Sorokin: "Poverty or wealth of a man is measured, not by what he has at present but by what he used to have before or by what others have." Similarly, Albert (1977) proposed that temporal comparisons – comparisons to one's own past outcomes and experiences – can function very much like social comparisons when people evaluate their opinions and abilities.

Some researchers and theorists have discussed the links between social comparison and relative deprivation theories. Davis (1959), the first to propose a formal theory of relative deprivation, recognized the related heritage of Festinger's (1954) social comparison theory. According to Davis, the two theories concern the same empirical phenomena, with these differences: relative deprivation theorists typically focus on consequences for the *group* when perceptions and evaluations are *unambiguous;* in contrast, social comparison theorists generally examine consequences for the *individual* when perceptions and evaluations are *ambiguous*. Thomas Pettigrew, in his classic integrative review and proposal of the broader "social evaluation theory" (1967), suggested that a general theory of social evaluation should answer questions about the referent others chosen for comparison, the attributes evaluated, and the motivational and cognitive consequences of the evaluations. Theories of social comparison and relative deprivation each answer some of these queries, but no one theory addresses all the relevant issues. More recently, Olson and Hazlewood (1986) explored the links between relative deprivation, social comparison, *and* temporal comparison. They identified four major areas of overlap between theories. First, people use an "other" (person, group, or past experience or outcome) to evaluate aspects of self, including abilities, opinions, status, and outcomes. Next, each perspective shares the assumption that people are motivated to seek this social or temporal information; it is actively pursued and attended to, not just accidentally noticed. Third, each position implies that comparisons will have affective consequences, which may include resentment, satisfaction, and gratification. Finally, people take into account the "related attributes" of potential comparison targets. When one's attributes (e.g., age, experience) do not match the "other's," the comparison is deemed irrelevant or uninformative. Thus, a teenager will not feel particularly deprived when comparing her wages to those of a 50 year old.

Over time, the boundaries between relative deprivation and social comparison theories have become fuzzier. Relative deprivation researchers now study the consequences of deprivation for the individual (e.g., Crosby, 1976) and social comparison researchers study group-level comparisons (e.g., Major, Sciacchitano & Crocker, 1993). Also, researchers interested in social comparison have extended their focus well beyond attitudes and abilities to include a host of additional traits and outcomes, including life satisfaction and self-perceptions of adjustment to breast cancer (for reviews see Wood, 1989, 1996). Researchers in both traditions explore the factors that influence people's selection of a comparison standard, as well as the effect of their choice on their feelings, decisions, and behaviors.

In our own research, we have studied relative deprivation and other kinds of comparisons in children's descriptions of their conflicts with their siblings. Conflict interactions between family members are of practical interest because the family plays a central role in determining the social, emotional, and physical well-being of its members (Emery, 1992). Conflict is practically inevitable in families. As family members typically spend a great deal of time together, their goals will almost certainly clash from time to time (e.g., "We cannot go to *both* restaurants for dinner") (Shantz & Hobart, 1987). Conflict is particularly common and intense among siblings. Estimates of the frequency of conflicts among young siblings range from 8 to 12 per hour (Dunn & Munn, 1985), and over 90% of school-aged siblings state that quarrels or other forms of negative interaction are important parts of their sibling relationships (Furman & Buhrmester, 1985).

Sibling relationships may also be a particularly fertile ground for the occurrence of relative deprivation and other comparisons. Siblings often grow up almost as "measuring sticks" of each other's successes and failures. Freud (1920/1935) emphasized the comparative and conflictual nature of the sibling relationship when he wrote, "there is probably no nursery without violent conflicts between its inmates. The motives for these are rivalry for parental love, competition for common possessions, even for the actual space in the room they occupy" (p. 205). The implication is that sibling relationships foster social comparisons and such comparisons may help explain the frequency of conflict among young brothers and sisters.

Theorists of relative deprivation have devoted little attention to its role in dyadic disputes. However, evidence that comparison processes are important in dyadic conflict can be found in a variety of literatures. According to equity theorists, individuals who believe that they are being treated unfairly are motivated to act to restore equity (Adams, 1965; Walster, Walster, & Bercheid, 1978). One way to reestablish equity is to oppose the individual who is perceived to be the cause of the deprivation. Rusbult (1983; Rusbult, Zembrodt, & Gunn, 1982) noted that interpersonal relationships involve the exchange of both material and psychological rewards, and that as rewards improve, people's satisfaction increases and they deal with conflict more constructively. Emery (1992) suggested that family conflicts can be "about" any number of issues, but that the deeper meaning underlying the disputes tends to be a perceived imbalance in one's level of power or intimacy in the relationship. Feelings of entitlement play an important role in children's conflicts; for example, more disputes occur over refusals to share a communal toy than over refusals to share a toy that is "owned" by a particular child (Eisenberg-Berg, Haake, & Bartlett, 1981). Finally, research on the role of social comparison processes in the regulation of self-esteem (e.g., Tesser, 1988) indicates that people are motivated to reduce the threat to their self-esteem caused by the superior performance of another individual. Esteem-maintenance strategies that could potentially lead to conflict include derogating superior individuals ("She's not really so talented, it was mostly luck") or hampering their performance (Tesser & Smith, 1980).

We examined comparisons that were *spontaneously generated* by young sibling disputants during interviews that occurred within a week of the conflict incidents. Our study differs from research on relative deprivation in which comparisons are assumed rather than measured. In *The American Soldier,* for example, Stouffer, Suchman, DeVinney, Star, and Williams (1949) invoked the concept of relative deprivation to explain several unexpected results, such as that soldiers in the air corps were more dissatisfied with opportunities for advancement than were soldiers in the military police, even though promotion rates in the air corps were more than double those in the military police. Stouffer et al. speculated that soldiers in the air corps must have been comparing their own situation to that of better-off others (e.g., people who were promoted particularly rapidly); whereas, soldiers in the military police must have been comparing their situation to similar or worse-off others (e.g., other failures to be promoted).

It seems reasonable to assume that the two groups of soldiers adopted different frames of reference, which led to different expectations for advancement. However, soldiers were not asked to explain their views on promotion or to indicate to whom they compared themselves. As a result, other interpretations of the findings are possible. For example, the air corps may have included more ambitious and upwardly mobile soldiers than the military police did; a difference in personnel along these lines would explain why soldiers in the air corps were less satisfied with their lot. Such alternative interpretations indicate the need to assess, not simply assume, comparisons and feelings of relative deprivation. Unfortunately, this tendency to invoke social comparisons and relative deprivation as explanatory concepts without actually measuring them is common in a variety of literatures, including studies of students' self concepts (e.g., Davis, 1966; Marsh & Parker, 1984) and research on self-esteem in minority and stigmatized groups (Crocker & Major, 1989).

Our investigation was motivated, in part, by the general lack of research on spontaneous comparisons by adults or children, especially in the context of conflict. In the typical study of social comparison, individuals are given a range of comparison options and expected to choose one. These studies may prompt the use of comparisons that people would not normally adopt (Brickman & Janoff-Bulman, 1977), as researchers rarely allow for the possibility that people may choose to compare to standards excluded from the prescribed list or even prefer not to compare at all (Ross, Eyman, & Kishchuk, 1986). In our study, children recounted their conflicts and we assessed their spontaneous expressions of comparison or relative deprivation.

We could locate only three studies of spontaneous comparisons in adults.[1] Wheeler and Miyake (1992) asked university students to record on a daily basis the details of their social comparisons in everyday life. Participants reported more same-level comparisons (comparisons to similar others) with their friends than for other individuals, and the number of same-level comparisons decreased linearly as the participant's relation with the comparison target became more distant. The number of upward (to better-off individuals) and downward (to worse-off individuals) comparisons varied rather unpredictably with target and comparison dimension. Wood, Taylor, and Lichtman (1985) interviewed breast cancer patients and coded their spontaneous social comparisons. Comparisons were not especially frequent, but those that did occur were most often with other women who were worse-off than the respondents. Ross et al. (1986) asked adult respondents to rate their life satisfaction and then to explain their ratings. Ross et al. coded participants' explanations for instances of social and temporal comparisons. Unexpectedly, such comparisons were extremely rare. Note that none of these studies of spontaneous comparison examined it in the context of conflict.

Spontaneous comparisons have also been investigated in children, usually in classroom or achievement settings. Generally, the frequency of social comparison increases with age, and social comparisons have a greater impact on the self-evaluations and decisions of older than of younger children (e.g., Frey & Ruble, 1985; Ruble, 1983; Ruble, Feldman, & Boggiano, 1976). The evidence suggests either that the ability to form, or the interest in making, social comparisons in achievement settings does not develop until at least the age of seven, and most studies did not include children five years or younger. Although Ruble and her colleagues repeatedly find little evidence of comparison in children under the age of seven or eight, they caution that children may use comparison information much earlier in familiar, naturalistic contexts as opposed to their typically novel laboratory settings (Ruble, Boggiano, Feldman, & Loebl, 1980).

The few studies examining comparisons in nonachievement settings suggest that even children as young as preschool age (three and up) make spontaneous social comparisons, most frequently about possessions and activities (Mosatche & Bragonier, 1981), and that they make comparisons to highlight both differences and similarities between themselves and their friends and acquaintances (Gottman & Parkhurst, 1980). In addition, Masters (1971) presented evidence from several studies that social comparisons motivate behavior (primarily self-reward) in preschool children. Masters' anecdotal example (p. 44) is familiar: He described the antagonistic behavior of a young child who makes her felt deprivation quite known at an older sibling's birthday party, when "rewards" are not distributed equally. Masters noted that, in such a situation, some families give token gifts to their youngest members to avoid the comparison-motivated behavior associated with an otherwise happy occasion.

We were unable to find any studies of spontaneous temporal comparison in children. A study by Ruble and Flett (1988) is relevant, however. These researchers provided second, fourth, and sixth graders with the opportunity to obtain both social and temporal comparisons while evaluating their arithmetic ability. Overall, children were more likely to seek social comparison information, although the oldest and highest ability children showed more interest in temporal information. Despite the lack of evidence for temporal comparison in young children, Suls (1986; Suls & Mullen, 1982) contends that temporal comparisons may be particularly important early in the life span. He presented a theory of comparison through the life span that suggests that children between the ages of three and eight years old should prefer temporal over social comparisons. The rapid development experienced by young children may make temporal comparison especially informative. In addition, at least until school age, their social contacts appropriate for comparisons may be limited.

In sum, there is very little research in the adult or child literatures on spontaneous comparisons, social or temporal. The research that does exist has not been conducted in the context of conflict. As well, with the exception of Wheeler and Miyake (1992) and Wood et al., (1985), researchers have not explicitly examined the direction of spontaneous comparisons.

We studied sibling pairs in which the younger child was between the ages of 3.5 and 5.3 years and the older child was between the ages of 5.5 and 8.9 years. We asked parents to provide daily reports of the conflicts that occurred between their two children. We then selected the incidents that parents rated as most important for their children, and interviewed both siblings about the same incidents. Thus, our data set consists of conflicts that are nominated by a third party, and are subsequently described separately by both siblings involved in the disputes. The interviewer did not ask specifically for any comparison information, but did follow a protocol that remained as consistent as possible across children. First, children were reminded, in a sentence or two, of the issue and setting of the conflict. They were then asked to describe what happened in their own words. After children provided their synopsis of the conflict, the interviewer asked four additional questions. Children were asked what they and their sibling had wanted and whether each of them got what they wanted; how they and their sibling felt during the conflict; whether they and their sibling thought the outcome was fair; and if they and their sibling were happy with the outcome or "ending" of the dispute.

CODING OF COMPARISON PROCESSES

Our coding system combines and extends concepts from relative deprivation and social comparison. We relied on the similarities and blurred the distinctions between theoretical perspectives. First, we identified all of the spontaneous comparisons made by the children in our study. We then coded whether the individuals making the comparisons saw themselves as worse-off, better-off, or similar to the "other." "Other" could be another person (social) or a reference to one's own past experiences or outcomes (temporal). There were no instances in which children compared themselves to a group, or compared their "ingroup" to some outgroup, so such comparisons will not be discussed further. Table 14.1 provides the coding scheme and examples of each type of code.

RESEARCH QUESTIONS AND HYPOTHESES

Because of the lack of research on children's comparisons in conflict settings, we considered our research to be preliminary and kept our questions simple.

1. *When children recount their version of conflicts they have experienced, do they spontaneously make comparisons?*

We expected that comparisons would be common because of the focus on interpersonal conflict, and because children would be describing a familiar incident (e.g., Ruble et al., 1980).

2. *If comparisons occur, are they social (with another person) or temporal (with previous experiences or outcomes)?*

Table 14.1. *Coding Scheme for Spontaneous Social and Temporal Comparisons*

Comparison Type	Comparison Direction	Example
Social	Upward (other better-off)	"It's her, not me, who gets her own way"
	Downward (other worse-off)	"I got to watch my movie and my brother didn't"
	Same-level (other equal)	"I felt sort of sad and I bet my sister felt sort of sad, too"
	Upward (past self better off)	"I used to get stickers on my report card, but I don't get them anymore"
Temporal	Downward (past self worse off)	"I was sad when he took it and was happy when he gave it back"
	Same-level (past self equal)	"I always let her beat me up the stairs"

We had no strong hypotheses regarding the relative frequency of temporal versus social comparisons, although we suspected that the interpersonal nature of the issues being discussed might make social comparison more relevant and thus more frequent.

3. *Do children compare themselves to a target who is better off (upward comparison), worse off (downward), or similar to themselves (same-level)?*

Conflict can emerge from feelings of relative deprivation. As a result, descriptions of the origins of conflict should include upward comparisons, at least from the aggrieved party (she has a toy that I want). Conflict can also spring from competition for scarce resources (both children want exclusive rights to play with the same toy that neither currently possesses). In this instance, social comparisons may be at the same level, as narrators focus on the similar goals of each protagonist. Comparisons may also occur when children describe the outcome of the conflict. In this case, the direction of the comparison should reflect the nature of the outcome. Satisfactory or happy outcomes should be associated with same-level or downward comparisons and unhappy outcomes with upward comparisons. Comparisons should also commonly occur in response to the fairness questions. The direction of comparison should reflect children's perceptions of the fairness of the outcome. Unfair outcomes should be most highly associated with upward comparisons and fair outcomes with same-level comparisons.

4. *Are there differences in the number or type of comparisons made by older versus younger siblings?*

If comparisons in a conflict context follow a similar (though earlier) developmental trajectory to that described by Ruble (1983), then younger children should make fewer comparisons than their older siblings.

FINDINGS

We present results based on 127 conflicts from 40 sibling dyads. Both siblings were interviewed separately about the same parent-nominated conflicts, resulting in 254 interviews with 80 children. Siblings were interviewed once a week for three weeks, about conflicts that had occurred within the past seven days. Because families reported on different numbers of sibling conflicts, the number of comparisons was controlled by the number of conflicts for each family in the statistical analyses.

We focused on the issues and events as reported by children. It may be that a fight over who sits in the front seat of the car is "really" about securing the territory closest to the parent – or maybe not. We limited our analysis to the issues and comparisons that the children presented to us. Sibling conflicts were reported about a variety of issues. Many of them (slightly over 50%) revolved around questions of competition (Who can run to the door first to greet mom?) and control over often-scarce resources (Who gets to choose the television channel, sit in the front seat of the car, or feed the fish?). Conflicts also commonly occurred (25%) over teasing, bothering, and "hurting sibling's feelings" (one sibling is "looking at" the other in an apparently irritating manner, older sibling won't let her younger brother join her game). Slightly over 10% of conflicts occurred over verbal or physical harm or control (one sister bosses the other, one pokes the other in the eye), and a final 10% over property damage and other broken rules (one child knocks over the other's Lego castle). Children generally recalled the conflicts once they were reminded of them, and even the youngest children were able to describe what happened. Overall, older children talked slightly but non-significantly more than their younger siblings. Although sibling pairs described the same events, the interpretation of the causes and justifications for conflict behaviors differed considerably between siblings (Wilson, Smith, Ross, & Ross, 1997). Both siblings tended to report more of their siblings' transgressions than their own, and to provide more justifications for their own actions.

Do Children Make Comparisons?

Overall, children do make comparisons, with the tendency varying individually and by age. Thirty-five of 40 older children made some kind of comparison, and 30 younger children compared at least once. Social comparisons were significantly more common than temporal comparisons among both older and younger siblings. Thirty-one older children made 211 social comparisons; whereas 28 of their younger siblings made 103 social comparisons. In contrast, only 16 older siblings made temporal comparisons 30 times; and a mere 6 younger children made a total of 12 temporal comparisons. Older children made more comparisons overall, although they were not more talkative.

Social comparisons were overwhelmingly between self and the opposing sibling. Only 1% of all social comparisons were not with sibling, and as a result the nonsibling category was dropped. It appears that when children do socially compare, they do so with the relevant, salient other. Because of the small number of temporal comparisons made by even fewer children, we will not describe them further.

What Is the Direction of Social Comparisons?

Both older and younger siblings were more likely to make same-level social comparisons than any other kind. Same-level were five times more prevalent than upward comparisons for older children, and at least twice as likely for younger siblings. Older children also made more same-level social comparisons than did their younger siblings. The remaining comparisons were about equally divided in direction – half were comparisons to their better-off sibling, and half to their sibling who was worse-off than themselves. Over all, only 14% of the comparisons were upward, suggesting that the children did not tend to focus on relative deprivation. When children did make upward comparisons, they were most commonly about their lack of a possession or right that their sibling enjoyed.

We were struck by the number of same-level comparisons made in the context of conflict. We had expected that because of the conditions that tend to lead to conflict, feelings of relative deprivation would be common. Gottman and Parkhurst (1980) found that children show a preference for comparisons emphasizing similarity, but in the very different context of developing friendships.

On reflection, we realized that there were a number of opportunities for same-level comparisons in our conflict interviews. First, a comparison was defined as same-level if the child identified his or her goals, feelings, or outcomes as similar or equivalent to their sibling's, or when the child reported that distribution of justice was equal for both children. Thus, in any conflict that occurred because of a scarce resource (e.g., only one child at a time can play a computer game), children might report having the same goals as their opponents (e.g., "I wanted to play with the computer game. My brother wanted to, too.") which would be coded as same-level comparisons. On closer examination of the types of same-level comparisons made, we found that 37% of them were of this sort. In addition, 18% of same-level comparisons occurred when children reported that their sibling felt the same emotions that they did ("I felt sort of sad and I bet my sister felt sort of sad, too"), and 38% occurred when children reported that outcomes were the same or equally fair to both children ("[it was fair because] we each got what we wanted"). Thus, there were many opportunities to report same-level comparisons, and children appear to show a preference for this kind of comparison.

Because we do not have data on the *actual* disputes, we cannot say whether the predominance of same-level comparisons is a reflection of reality (siblings really did have similar goals, feelings, and outcomes) or if children tend to selectively remember and report same-level as opposed to upward or downward contrasts. However, we can examine the direction of comparisons when children describe different aspects of the conflicts – specifically, the proportion of upward, downward, and same-level comparisons made when children consider their goals and feelings, or the fairness and nature of the conflict outcomes.

Comparisons for Questions about Goals, Feelings, Fairness, and Outcome

We found that both older and younger siblings made the most comparisons (44% of the total number) when describing their own and their siblings' conflict goals, and whether one or both of them obtained those goals during the dispute. Of those goal-related comparisons, almost 70% were same-level. Thus, children tended to frame their goals as being similar to their siblings' goals (e.g., "I wanted the pogo ball because it was my pogo ball, but my sister wanted it because she would like to play on the pogo ball, too"); they also focused on equality when relating how the goals were obtained (e.g., "So we each got the same amount of time"). The remaining goal-related comparisons were about equally divided between upward and downward comparisons. For example, one child reported deprivation relative to his sister because he "had to" let her win a race to stop her from crying ("I didn't [get what I wanted]. She got what she wanted. I had to go back there and let her beat me").

Children also tended to compare frequently when discussing the fairness of the dispute. This context followed goals in frequency of comparisons and yielded significantly more comparisons than were obtained when children discussed their feelings during the conflict and their satisfaction with the conflict outcomes. Children often judged fairness by contrasting their own outcomes to those of their siblings. Children might be less inclined to compare emotions spontaneously because their siblings' feelings during the conflict were not observable or salient. In the "heat of battle," combatants may focus primarily on their own hurt feelings and tend to ignore the emotions of their opponent (e.g., "anger-induced myopia," Holmes & Murray, 1996).

In each context, older children made predominantly same-level comparisons. They regarded their goals, feelings, and assessments of fairness as similar to their siblings'. Younger children showed the same preference for same-level comparisons about goals and emotions, but exhibited more variation in direction regarding fairness and outcome. Perhaps the weaker position of younger children in a sibling relationship sensitizes them to inequalities in fairness and outcome.

Comparisons for Happy and Unhappy Endings

Are children's social comparisons related to the way they perceive conflict outcomes? We expected that unhappy endings would be more strongly associated with upward comparisons than happy endings. Happy endings, in contrast, might be associated with a focus on equality, or same-level comparisons. We classified the ending of each of the conflict narratives as happy or unhappy on the basis of the child's response to the question, "Were you happy with how [the conflict] ended?" Both older and younger children reported that their disputes ended happily about 70% of the time. To analyze the number of comparisons made in conflicts with happy and unhappy endings, we controlled for the number of happy/unhappy endings reported by that individual.

Overall, siblings made more same-level comparisons for conflicts with happy than unhappy endings. Fifty-eight percent of all social comparisons made by older children were same-level comparisons about happy endings.

They compared at the same level significantly more than they made either upward or downward comparisons during these happy-ending disputes. In contrast, only 11% of their social comparisons were same-level comparisons about conflicts that ended unhappily. For unhappy endings, the number of upward, downward, and same-level comparisons did not differ.

Younger children made more same-level comparisons than upward and downward comparisons for both happy and unhappy endings. There were no significant differences between the proportions of same-level comparisons for disputes with happy endings than unhappy endings.

It may be that older siblings recognize that if the conflict conditions and outcomes were equal (e.g., "[I was happy because] we both got the same amount of money"), the resolution was most likely to be satisfactory. In contrast, they may perceive feelings of inequality or injustice (e.g., "'Cause she didn't have to make anything. She's lucky. She's the littlest. She doesn't have to do anything. I wish I was the littlest.") as more often associated with an unhappy conclusion to the dispute. Unlike their older siblings, younger children did not appear to associate their outcome satisfaction with the kinds of comparisons they made.

SUMMARY AND CONCLUSIONS

Our research successfully accomplished one of its major aims. We developed a procedure in which it was possible to study children's spontaneous comparisons. We discovered that comparisons occurred at much younger ages than would be predicted by research in achievement settings. At the same time, however, we obtained the expected developmental trajectory with comparisons occurring more often in the conflict narratives of older children. We also found that temporal comparisons were extremely rare. Children were much more likely to contrast their situation to that of their siblings than to their own previous outcomes or experiences. It is unclear whether this disparity reflects the context in which we studied comparisons, the ages of the children, or a more general scarcity of spontaneous temporal comparisons. We suspect that the relative proportion of social to temporal comparisons will vary with context, but that, from an actuarial standpoint, social comparisons may indeed be more frequent, at least in our culture. This would help explain why theorists and researchers have focused more on social than temporal comparisons and why there are apparently few previous studies of spontaneous temporal comparisons.

Even if rare, temporal comparisons may be psychologically meaningful. For example, Davies (1962) highlighted their significance in his theory of rev-

olution, Ross and Wilson (2000) discussed their importance to self-perceptions and the regulation of self-esteem, and various theorists have discussed
their contribution to older people's attempts to review their lives and put
events into perspective (e.g., Butler, 1963). There remains a dearth of
research, however, on the circumstances that prompt spontaneous temporal
comparisons, as well as the prevalence and consequences of such contrasts.

One of the more intriguing findings in the present study is that the children seemed quite happy about how their conflicts ended. We attempted
to select the major sibling conflict of the week and children remembered
the conflicts with considerable clarity. Nonetheless, they provided little
indication that they felt relatively deprived compared to their siblings.

Perhaps this level of contentment is partly due to the fact that children
narrated about the conflicts between a day and a week after their occurrence. There may be a tendency to forget the inequalities after a conflict has
been terminated and the initial feelings and frustrations have subsided. If
children were asked to describe their perspective *during* a dispute, or immediately after it transpired, inequalities that motivated, or were not relieved
by, the conflict would be much more salient. The parents reported that many
of these disputes were accompanied by crying, hitting, and other evidence
of emotional upset on the part of the siblings. Over time, children's conflict
narratives may shift emphasis to the similarity and equalities between disputants rather than the injustices they have suffered.

Moreover, when family members basically like each other, as was the
case with our sibling dyads,[2] they may be particularly inclined to deem-
phasize past inequalities. Along these lines, Murray and Holmes (1994)
demonstrated that happy couples often construct stories about their partners' earlier transgressions that downplay the seriousness of the episode.
Unhappy couples do not show the same level of forgiveness. Although
Murray and Holmes did not report longitudinal data, it is likely that the
happy partners' reactions to the transgressions were much more negative
at the time of their occurrence than in retrospect.

Our data suggest a need for longitudinal investigations in which disputants' reactions are assessed over time. The data also imply that it might
be misleading to use retrospective reports as a basis for studying people's
original reactions to conflict (see also, Ross, 1989, for a discussion of the
accuracy of autobiographical memories). Retrospective reports can provide a snapshot of what adults or children currently feel and believe. Such
reports may be less informative about what individuals felt or believed at
an earlier time. Nonetheless, it is important to emphasize the value of retrospective reports. People's present behavior and feelings toward their

interaction partners are more likely to be guided by their current beliefs and emotions than by earlier evaluations that they have now abandoned.

Finally, our data showing that children did not typically report feeling relatively deprived may illustrate a general principle of human social cognition. Almost anyone could select a comparison that would make him or her feel relatively deprived. For the most part, people don't seem to choose such contrasts spontaneously. Recall that past research reveals that individuals who are far more deprived in objective terms than the children in our study are quite satisfied with their outcomes in life (e.g., Cairns & Cairns, 1994). Perhaps people avoid focusing on relative deprivation unless they believe that they can act to relieve it. Even young children may possess the wisdom to realize that dwelling on irresolvable deprivations can cause irremediable distress.

NOTES

1. We refer here to explicit comparisons. There are many more studies in which comparisons are directly implied by participants' reactions. For example, Morse and Gergen (1970) showed that participants' self-esteem went down following exposure to an impeccably dressed and groomed individual. For this effect to have occurred, participants must have been comparing themselves to the other person.
2. Children's perceptions of their sibling relationship were assessed using the "Myself as a sibling questionnaire" (Ross, Woody, Smith, & Lollis, unpublished manuscript). Over 80% of children responded in the affirmative to the question, "Do you like your brother/sister?"

REFERENCES

Adams, J. S. (1965). Inequity in social exchange. In L. Berkowitz (Ed.), *Advances in experimental social psychology* (Vol. 2, pp. 267–299). New York: Academic Press.

Albert, S. (1977). Temporal comparison theory. *Psychological Review, 84,* 485–503.

Brickman, P., & Janoff-Bulman, R. (1977). Pleasure and pain in social comparison. In J. Suls & R. Miller (Eds.), *Social comparison processes: Theoretical and empirical perspectives* (pp. 149–186). Washington, DC: Hemisphere.

Butler, R. J. (1963). The life review: An interpretation of reminiscence in the aged. *Psychiatry, 26,* 65–76.

Cairns, R. B., & Cairns, B. D. (1994). *Lifelines and risks.* New York: Cambridge University Press.

Cameron, P., Titus, D. G., Kostin, J., & Kostin, M. (1973). The life satisfaction of nonnormal persons. *Journal of Counseling and Clinical Psychology, 41,* 207–214.

Caplan, N. (1970). The new ghetto man: A review of recent empirical studies. *Journal of Social Issues, 26,* 59–73.

Crosby, F. (1976). A model of egotistical relative deprivation. *Psychological Review, 83,* 85–113.

Crocker, J., & Major, B. (1989). Social stigma and self-esteem: The self-protective properties of stigma. *Psychological Review, 96,* 608–630.

Crosby, F. (1982). *Relative deprivation and working women.* Oxford: Oxford University Press.

Davies, J. (1962). Toward a theory of revolution. *American Sociological Review, 27,* 5–18.

Davis, J. A. (1959). A formal interpretation of the theory of relative deprivation. *Sociometry, 22,* 280–296.

Davis, J. A. (1966). The campus as a frog pond: An application of the theory of relative deprivation to career decisions of college men. *American Journal of Sociology, 72,* 17–31.

Dube, L., & Guimond, S. (1986). Relative deprivation and social protest: The personal-group issue. In J. M. Olson, C. P. Herman, & M. P. Zanna (Eds.), *Relative deprivation and social comparison: The Ontario symposium* (Vol. 4, pp. 201–216). Hillsdale, NJ: Lawrence Erlbaum.

Dunn, J., & Munn, P. (1985). Becoming a family member: Family conflict and the development of social understanding. *Child Development, 56,* 480–492.

Eisenberg-Berg, N., Haake, R. J., & Bartlett, K. (1981). The effects of possession and ownership on the sharing and proprietary behaviors of preschool children. *Merrill-Palmer Quarterly, 27,* 61–67.

Emery, R. E. (1992). Family conflicts and their developmental implications: A conceptual analysis of meaning for the structure of relationships. In C. U. Shantz & W. W. Hartup (Eds.), *Conflict in child and adolescent development* (pp. 270–298). New York: Cambridge University Press.

Festinger, L. (1954). A theory of social comparison processes. *Human Relations, 7,* 117–140.

Freud, S. (1920/1935). Introductory lectures to psychoanalysis. In Strachey, J. (Ed.), *The standard edition of the complete psychological works of Sigmund Freud.* London: The Hogarth Press. (Original work published 1917)

Frey, K. S. & Ruble, D. N. (1985). What children say when the teacher is not around: Conflicting goals in comparison and performance assessment in the classroom. *Journal of Personality and Social Psychology, 48(3),* 550–562.

Furman, W., & Buhrmester, D. (1985). Children's perceptions of the qualities of sibling relationships. *Child Development, 56,* 448–461.

Gottman, J., & Parkhurst, J. A. (1980). A developmental theory of friendship and acquaintanceship processes. In W. A. Collins (Ed.), *Minnesota symposium on child psychology* (Vol. 13, pp. 197–253). Hillsdale, NJ: Lawrence Erlbaum.

Holmes, J. G., & Murray, S. L. (1996). Conflict in close relationships. In E. T. Higgins & A. W. Kruglanski (Eds.), *Social psychology: Handbook of basic principles* (pp. 622–654). New York: Guilford Press.

Major, B., Sciacchitano, A. M., & Crocker, J. (1993). In-group versus out-group comparisons and self-esteem. *Personality and Social Psychology Bulletin, 19,* 711–721.

Marsh, H. W., & Parker, J. W. (1984). Determinants of student self-concept: Is it better to be a relatively large fish in a small pond even if you don't learn to swim as well? *Journal of Personality and Social Psychology, 47,* 213–231.

Masters, J. C. (1971). Social comparison by young children. *Young Children, 27,* 37–60.

Mosatche, H. S., & Bragonier, P. (1981). An observational study of social comparison in preschoolers. *Child Development, 52,* 376–378.

Morse, S., & Gergen, K. J. (1970). Social comparison, self-consistency, and the concept of self. *Journal of Personality and Social Psychology, 16,* 148–156.

Murray, S. L., & Holmes, J. G. (1994). Storytelling in close relationships: The construction of confidence. *Personality and Social Psychology Bulletin, 20,* 650–663.

Olson, J. M., & Hazlewood, J. D. (1986). Relative deprivation and social comparison: An integrative perspective. In J. M. Olson, C. P. Herman, & M. P. Zanna (Eds.), *Relative deprivation and social comparison: The Ontario symposium* (Vol. 4, pp. 1–15). Hillsdale, NJ: Lawrence Erlbaum.

Pettigrew, T. F. (1967). Social evaluation theory: Convergences and applications. In D. Levine (Ed.), *Nebraska symposium on motivation* (Vol. 15, pp. 241–311). Lincoln: University of Nebraska Press.

Pettigrew T. F. (1978). Three issues in ethnicity: Boundaries, deprivations, and perceptions. In J. M. Yinger & S. J. Cutler (Eds.), *Major social issues: A multidisciplinary view* (pp. 25–49). New York: Free Press.

Ross, H. S., Woody, E. Z., Smith, M. D., & Lollis, S. *Family appraisals of sibling relationships.* Unpublished manuscript. University of Waterloo.

Ross, M. (1989). The relation of implicit theories to the construction of personal histories. *Psychological Review, 96,* 341–357.

Ross, M., Eyman, A., & Kishchuk, N. (1986). Determinants of subjective well-being. In J. M. Olson, C. P. Herman, & M. P. Zanna (Eds.), *Relative deprivation and social comparison: The Ontario symposium,* (Vol. 4, pp. 79–93). Hillsdale, NJ: Lawrence Erlbaum.

Ross, M., Thibaut, J., & Evenbeck, S. (1971). Some determinants of social protest. *Journal of Experimental Social Psychology, 1,* 401–418.

Ross, M. & Wilson, A. E. (2000). Constructing and appraising past selves. In D. L. Schacter & E. Scarry (Eds.), *Memory, brain, and belief* (pp. 231–258). Cambridge: Harvard University Press.

Ruble, D. N. (1983). The development of social-comparison processes and their role in achievement-related self-socialization. In E. T. Higgins, D. N. Ruble, & W. W. Hartup (Eds.), *Social cognition and social development: A sociocultural perspective* (pp. 135–157). Cambridge: Cambridge University Press.

Ruble, D. N., Boggiano, A. K. Feldman, N. S., & Loebl, J. H. (1980). A developmental analysis of the role of social comparison in self-evaluation. *Developmental Psychology, 16,* 105–115.

Ruble, D. N., Feldman, N. S., & Boggiano, A. K. (1976). Social comparison between young children in achievement situations. *Developmental Psychology, 12,* 192–197.

Ruble, D. N., & Flett, G. L. (1988). Conflicting goals in self-evaluative information seeking: Developmental and ability level analyses. *Child Development, 59,* 97–106.

Runciman, W. G. (1966). *Relative deprivation and social justice: A study of attitudes to social inequality in twentieth century England.* Berkeley: University of California Press.

Rusbult, C. E. (1983). A longitudinal test of the investment model: The development (and deterioration) of satisfaction and commitment in heterosexual involvements. *Journal of Personality and Social Psychology, 45,* 101–117.

Rusbult, C. E., Zembrodt, I. M., & Gunn, L. K. (1982). Exit, voice, loyalty, and neglect: Responses to dissatisfaction in romantic involvements. *Journal of Personality and Social Psychology, 43*, 1230–1242.

Shantz, C. U., & Hobart, C. J. (1987). Social conflict and development: Peers and siblings. In T. J. Berndt & G. W. Ladd (Eds.), *Peer relationships in child development* (pp. 71–94). New York: John Wiley.

Stouffer, S. A., Suchman, E. A., DeVinney, L. C., Star, S. A., & Williams, R. M. Jr. (1949). *The American soldier: Adjustment during army life.* Princeton, NJ: Princeton University Press.

Suls, J. (1986). Social processes in relative deprivation: A life-span analysis. In J. M. Olson, C. P. Herman, & M. P. Zanna (Eds.), *Relative deprivation and social comparison: The Ontario symposium* (Vol. 4, pp. 95–116). Hillsdale, NJ: Lawrence Erlbaum.

Suls, J., & Mullen, B. (1982). From the cradle to the grave: Comparison and self-evaluation across the life-span. In J. Suls (Ed.), *Psychological perspectives on the self* (Vol. 1, pp. 97–125). Hillsdale, NJ: Lawrence Erlbaum.

Tesser, A. (1988). Toward a self-evaluation maintenance model of social behavior. In L. Berkowitz (Ed.), *Advances in experimental social psychology* (Vol. 21, pp. 181–227). New York: Academic Press.

Tesser, A., & Smith, J. (1980). Some effects of friendship and task relevance on helping: You don't always help the one you like. *Journal of Experimental Social Psychology, 16*, 582–590.

Walker, I., & Pettigrew, T. F. (1984). Relative deprivation theory: An overview and conceptual critique. *British Journal of Social Psychology, 23*, 301–310.

Walster, E., Walster, G. W., & Bercheid, E. (1978). *Equity: Theory and research.* Boston: Allyn and Bacon.

Wheeler, L., & Miyake, K. (1992). Social comparison in everyday life. *Journal of Personality and Social Psychology, 62*, 760–773.

Wilson, A. E., Smith, M. D., Ross, H., & Ross, M. (1997). *Multiple versions of reality: Family members' accounts of sibling disputes.* Poster presented at the American Psychological Association, August 1997 Convention, Chicago.

Wood, J. V. (1989). Theory and research concerning social comparisons of personal attributes. *Psychological Bulletin, 106*, 231–248.

Wood, J. V. (1996). What is social comparison and how should we study it? *Personality and Social Psychology Bulletin, 22*, 520–537.

Wood, J. V., Taylor, S. E., & Lichtman, R. R. (1985). Social comparison in adjustment to breast cancer. *Journal of Personality and Social Psychology, 49*, 1169–1183.

Wright, S. C., Taylor, D. M., & Moghaddam, F. M. (1990). Responding to membership in a disadvantaged group: From acceptance to collective protest. *Journal of Personality and Social Psychology, 58*, 994–1003.

FIFTEEN

Prejudice as Intergroup Emotion

Integrating Relative Deprivation and Social Comparison Explanations of Prejudice

Eliot R. Smith and Colin Ho

Since the term relative deprivation was coined by Stouffer in 1949, research on relative deprivation has progressed in many directions. One trend in recent research has been the application of relative deprivation concepts to the study of prejudice and intergroup relations. For example, relative deprivation concepts have been used to understand minority group members' emotional and behavioral reaction to perceived discrimination (Dion, 1986), and to understand when minority and subordinate groups will respond to their disadvantaged positions with political protest or violence (Dube & Guimond, 1986). These studies have typically examined a group (or fraternal) type of deprivation, as opposed to a personal (individual) type of deprivation (Abeles, 1976; Martin, 1981; Runciman, 1966). Closely associated with group deprivation, the concept of intergroup comparison has also been used to explain prejudice and intergroup relations (Goethals & Darley, 1987; Levine & Moreland, 1987; Tajfel & Turner, 1986). Tajfel and Turner's (1986) social identity theory, for example, assumes that people are motivated to maintain or enhance self-esteem through comparison, or the avoidance of comparison, with various other groups.

The primary purpose of this chapter is to describe Smith's (1993) conceptual framework of prejudice and to show that this conceptualization links both group relative deprivation and intergroup social comparisons to intergroup prejudice. After presenting an overview of Smith's (1993) model, we illustrate its utility by applying it to explaining prejudice toward Asian Americans.

PREJUDICE AS INTERGROUP EMOTION

As background for the new conceptualization of prejudice advanced by Smith (1993), consider the traditional approach, which places prejudice firmly within the framework of attitude theory. Within a standard attitude model like that of Fishbein and Ajzen (1975), a group stereotype is conceptualized as a set of beliefs about the positive or negative characteristics of the stereotyped group. Prejudice, in turn, is the evaluation of that group (i.e., the perceiver's attitude toward the group) based on the beliefs (Eagly & Mladinic, 1989). Finally, discrimination amounts to attitude-driven behavior. Instances of dissociation between expressed prejudice and behavioral discrimination (e.g., LaPiere, 1934) are analyzed as standard instances of attitude-behavior inconsistency (Fishbein & Ajzen, 1975).

This traditional conceptualization has numerous strengths, most important in bringing prejudice and the related phenomena of stereotypes and discrimination within a well-developed, intensively researched theoretical framework (see Eagly & Chaiken, 1994). By the same token, however, this conceptualization seemingly fails to account for some of the unique and special characteristics of intergroup relations. Viewed from the perspective of attitude theory, stereotypes, prejudice, and discrimination look just the same as beliefs, attitudes, and behaviors toward any other object – for example, a brand of automobile with a negative image regarding quality (stereotype), which buyers dislike for that reason (prejudice) and avoid buying (discrimination). This approach also makes it somewhat difficult to understand why prejudice sometimes becomes virulent and violent, rather than remaining at the level of mere dislike.

The alternative approach advanced by Smith (1993) analyzes prejudice with the tools of self-categorization theory (Turner, Hogg, Oakes, Reicher, & Wetherell, 1987) and emotion theory (e.g., Frijda, 1986) rather than attitude theory. The starting point is the idea that group membership can become a part of the psychological self, an idea that is shared by self-categorization theory and other versions of social identity theory (Tajfel, 1982). For this reason group membership, like any other self-relevant information, comes to possess affective and motivational significance. In turn, the emotional reactions that people experience based on self-relevant events are described by appraisal theories of emotion (e.g., Frijda, 1986; Roseman, 1984). Appraisal theories describe the dimensions that people use to assess events or situations and their implications for the self – such as the positive or negative nature of the event, its causation, expected stability or duration. They also predict what specific emotions people experience based on combinations of these appraisals, such as anger felt when a negative event was caused by another person in an unjustified manner. Appraisal theories have invariably assumed that emotions are responses to events that affect the individual self; for example, "To arouse an emotion, the object must be appraised as affecting me in some way, affecting me personally as an individual" (Arnold, 1960, p. 171). However, there is no inherent reason for this restriction, and much reason to suppose that emotions can arise with respect to collective as well as individual aspects of the self.

In this way, by combining self-categorization and emotion-appraisal theories, Smith (1993) proposed that stereotypes could be viewed as the emotion-relevant appraisals of an intergroup situation, prejudice as a "social emotion experienced with respect to one's social identity as a group member, with an outgroup as a target" (p. 304), and discrimination as emotion-driven behavior. This theoretical proposal, unlike attitude theory, distinguishes intergroup relations from other types of situations involving attitudes (such as avoiding a brand of automobile that has a poor reputation for quality) on the basis of the inherent links between group membership and the self, which are absent for most other types of attitude object. Further, this model offers insights into the fact that feelings and actions in intergroup situations can become extreme, heated, and violent. Potentially high levels of self-involvement and emotional arousal, not just mild feelings of like and dislike, are considered to be the basis for intergroup prejudice.

Approaching prejudice from an emotion perspective also has three more general advantages. First, by conceptualizing prejudice as social emotions, the assessment of prejudice toward social groups can be based on the measurement of negative emotions toward them. Although emotion theorists tend to disagree about a precise definition, most would acknowledge that emotions include cognitions, subjective feelings, facial expressions, physiological or behavioral action tendencies, and instrumental behaviors (Fischer, Shaver, & Carnohan, 1990). This multidimensional nature of emotion means that researchers can measure prejudice toward outgroups in a multitude of ways. Second, a growing number of studies show that emotions make a significant contribution to the prediction of intergroup attitudes, sometimes even exceeding the contribution of stereotypic beliefs (Dijker, 1987; Esses, Haddock, & Zanna, 1993; Jackson, Hodge, Gerard, Ingram, Ervin, & Sheppard, 1996; Stangor, Sullivan, & Ford, 1991). Stangor et al. (1991), for example, showed that emotional responses were a more consistent and stronger predictor of attitudes and social distance toward several social groups than social stereotypes were.

Finally, several theorists have proposed that the identification of specific emotions present in a particular intergroup relation allows us to (1) identify the particular features of the relationship that elicit those emotions, and (2) predict the behaviors that are likely to characterize the intergroup relation. This ability to identify emotion antecedents and predict behaviors via the identification of emotions present in an intergroup situation is possible because specific emotions are associated with a limited number of general antecedents and with specific emotional tendencies. An empirical demonstration of the link between emotions and action tendencies is provided by Dijker (1987). Dijker found four categories of emotions (positive mood, anxiety, irritation, and concern) that were strongly associated with native Dutch attitudes toward three minority groups in the Netherlands. The four categories of emotions were each found to relate to a specific kind of action tendencies. For example, irritation was associated with the tendency to aggress against the outgroup, while anxiety was associated with the tendency to avoid the outgroup.

Existing Evidence for Prejudice as Intergroup Emotion
Several types of already existing evidence support the model of prejudice as intergroup emotion. First, laboratory studies using typical social cognition research methods have demonstrated the overlap between mental representations of the self and the ingroup that is fundamental to this model (as well as to self-categorization and social identity theory in general). Smith and Henry (1996) used a method related to the logic of Stroop interference to examine the assumption that self- and ingroup representations can overlap. In the Stroop task, people are asked to name the color of ink in which various words are printed. If the words themselves are color words, specific patterns of facilitation and inhibition are found. If the ink color mismatches the word (e.g., the word "red" printed in blue ink), the response "blue" is slowed (inhibited). On the other hand, if the ink color and word match, the response is speeded (facilitated). The basic idea is that when people respond to one attribute of an object (the ink color), matches or mismatches from other salient attributes (the word meaning) will affect their response.

Building on research by Aron, Aron, Tudor, and Nelson, (1991), Smith and Henry (1996) had undergraduate students complete three questionnaires describing themselves, an ingroup of moderate salience (e.g., liberal arts or engineering majors), and the corresponding outgroup on 90 diverse traits. They then sat down at a computer and responded to the same 90 traits in terms of their self-descriptiveness. That is, as each trait word appeared on the computer screen, the participants pressed a "yes" or "no" key to indicate whether or not the word described them, under speed and accuracy instructions. Analyses of the response times indicated, as predicted, that traits on which the participant's view of the self matched the ingroup gave rise to faster responses, and traits involving self-ingroup mismatches to slower responses.

In another study, Smith, Coats, and Walling (1997) tested the hypothesis of self-ingroup representation overlap in a different way. They used the same general procedures, except that on the computer task participants assessed whether the traits described their ingroup (not the self). The hypothesis, based on the same logic as previously, is that even though the computer task in no way overtly involved the self, matches or mismatches between self- and ingroup representations would facilitate or inhibit responses. Results confirmed this hypothesis. Thus, these two studies converge on the conclusion that mental representations of self and ingroup overlap, with both representations becoming activated and influencing responses even when only one is relevant to the person's overt task.

Other recent laboratory-based research also illustrates the importance of group membership in affecting spontaneous reactions to social comparisons. Brewer and Weber (1994) told undergraduate research participants that they belonged to either a small or large social category on the basis of a bogus "perceptual estimation" task. The participants then viewed a videotape of another student who was identified as a member of the same or the other category. The taped student was interviewed and either gave a very impressive, positive performance or came across as generally negative and incompetent. Finally, the participant's own self-evaluation was assessed.

Results showed a striking pattern of effects of group membership on the participants' reactions to the social comparison target (the videotaped student). When the target supposedly belonged to the majority group, making group membership low in salience, all participants (regardless of their group membership) reacted in the usual manner to the comparison target, rating themselves higher when the target was incompetent and lower when the target was outstanding. In contrast, when the target belonged to the minority group, majority-group participants effectively ignored the minority target's performance – it had no impact on their self-ratings. Most important, participants who also belonged to the minority rated themselves in line with the target's performance, rather than showing contrast effects. This condition shows that the comparisons that are relevant for the participant's self-evaluation are intergroup (rather than interpersonal) in nature when the participant and target share an unusual and therefore salient group membership. In effect, participants feel good if the target's outstanding performance makes their distinctive ingroup look good, rather than feeling bad as a function of the negative interpersonal-level comparison.

Other studies showing the importance of emotional ties to group membership have taken place outside the laboratory, typically using survey research methods. Pettigrew (1997) analyzed group-based pride, or feelings of patriotism and glorification of an ingroup, as a predictor of prejudice against outgroups. Such a relationship would be expected on the basis of the Smith (1993) model; people who are most closely identified with the group should have the greatest tendency to display both positive ingroup emotions of pride and loyalty, and negative emotions directed at outgroups. Pettigrew analyzed data collected in four European nations and found in each case that pride in ingroup membership was related to prejudice against salient outgroups, even when other important causes of prejudice (such as age and general conservatism) are controlled. Similarly, Clore and Rahn (1997) found in a U.S. national sample that reports of feeling various emotions (such as hope, excitement, fear, or anger) on behalf of the United States as an ingroup were correlated with politically significant attitudes. These included trust in government, feelings of collective efficacy, and worry about group conflict. Thus, emotions experienced with respect to ingroup membership have been found to be important and consequential not only for intergroup prejudice but in other ways as well.

Linking Prejudice to Intergroup Comparisons and Relative Deprivation

If prejudice is conceptualized as an intergroup emotion in the way just outlined, strong linkages to social comparison and relative deprivation become evident. The key observation is that specific emotions can arise from upward social comparison, particularly frustration, envy, and resentment. In an intergroup context, these emotions may be directed at an outgroup, such as Asian Americans, who may be perceived as outdoing the perceiver's ingroup (white Americans). These social-comparison emotions seem to be frequent components of intergroup prejudice in real life, though a strong empirical basis for this claim is lacking because current measures of prejudice have not been designed to assess specific emotional reactions.

This interpretation thus makes emotional reactions to group-level relative deprivation a major potential contributor to prejudice. But as we have long known, social comparisons and feelings of relative deprivation can occur at either the individual (interpersonal) or intergroup levels. Only the intergroup level is relevant to this analysis of prejudice. Still, a great deal of evidence makes clear that under many realistic circumstances, intergroup comparisons and feelings of group relative deprivation are deeply significant to people.

First, a number of existing findings in the literature on "symbolic racism" point to the idea that symbolic racism is a stronger predictor of intergroup attitudes and behaviors than measures of individual self-interest (Kinder & Sears, 1981; McConahay, 1982). Importantly, Bobo (1983) and others have argued that "symbolic racism" is actually better viewed as perceived group-based interests. Therefore, these findings mean not that self-interest is unimportant, but that it operates at the group rather than the individual level.

Second, the relative deprivation literature includes many illustrations of the idea that group deprivation matters more than personal deprivation based on interpersonal comparisons (Runciman, 1966; Vanneman & Pettigrew, 1972). For example, whites' opposition to busing for school desegregation in Boston was related to perceptions that other groups were doing better than their own group, rather than to feelings of individual-level deprivation (Useem, 1980). Pettigrew (1997) meta-analyzed the relative deprivation literature and found that across numerous studies, the effects of group-level deprivation on prejudice average about twice as large as effects of individual-level deprivation. The largest effects of all are found for measures of group-based deprivation that include an affective component (rather than just a cognitive assessment of group differences), consistent with the model of prejudice as group-based emotion.

Finally, an interesting laboratory study complements these findings. H. J. Smith and Spears (1996) found that a salient group identity can induce people to make intergroup comparisons that may result in the recognition of disadvantage. Group identification also makes them less likely to rationalize or explain away such a disadvantage, as people often do when disadvantage is experienced at an individual level. Perceptions of collective disadvantage may therefore be important in motivating people to challenge an inequitable social distribution of rewards. These findings, along with those we reviewed earlier, therefore underscore the significance of group-level social comparisons and the experience of group relative deprivation. The model of prejudice as group-based emotion (Smith, 1993) conceptually links these concepts to intergroup prejudice.

PREJUDICE TOWARD ASIAN AMERICANS

There has been little theoretical and empirical work on prejudice toward Asian Americans – particularly in contrast to the extensive research on prejudice toward African Americans. Yet Asian Americans constitute a particularly interesting case for the traditional attitude-based model of prejudice. This is because the cultural stereotype of Asian Americans is largely positive, but they are still targets of hostility, resentment, and other negative and prejudicial reactions. How such negative attitudes could emerge on the basis of positive stereotypes is difficult to explain with traditional attitude theories.

The generally positive nature of the Asian-American stereotype has been well documented. (Indeed, the positive stereotype may be part of the reason that researchers concerned with stereotypes and prejudice have paid so little attention to Asian Americans.) At present, Asian Americans are thought of as intelligent, industrious, and successful (Hurh & Kim, 1989; Yee, 1992). In addition, Asian Americans have been saluted as a model minority (Kitano & Sue, 1973; Yee, 1992). In this view, Asian Americans are perceived to be upwardly mobile, economically successful, and free from social problems that afflict other minorities.

Despite the positive stereotypes and model minority image, however, negative attitudes toward Asian Americans clearly exist (Yee, 1992). Most notably, Asian Americans appear to be experiencing a backlash born of their perceived success. For example, there appears to be growing hostility and resentment over the perceived success of Asian Americans in higher education (Uba, 1994). It should be noted that prejudice toward Asian Americans is not new to Asian–white relationships. Fear of Asians as an economic threat has permeated negative attitudes toward Asians since the 1800s (e.g., Fredrickson, 1981; Miller, 1969; Portes & Manning, 1986). Fredrickson (1981), for example, found that economic competition was the root cause of white workers' mobilization against the Chinese in the nineteenth century. As previously noted, negative attitudes toward Asian Americans are difficult to explain with traditional attitude theories. Based on the predominantly positive stereotypic attributes that have been ascribed to Asian Americans (e.g., intelligent, industrious), traditional attitude theories would predict that attitudes toward Asian Americans would be positive. According to Smith's (1993) model, however, prejudice toward an outgroup is dependent not on the valence of the stereotypic attributes per se, but on people's appraisal of those stereotypic attributes: Do they have positive or negative implications for my ingroup?

The starting point for Smith's (1993) conceptualization of prejudice is the notion of self-categorization. With regards to prejudice toward Asian Americans, we propose that prejudice toward Asian Americans arises because American whites self-categorize themselves as Americans and, by non-inclusion, Asian Americans as foreigners. The exclusion of Asian Americans from the "Americans" category may stem from what sociologists have termed racial nativism – a belief about what America or Americans are or should be (Higham, 1963). Racial nativism, or what may be termed Anglo-Saxonism, began by defining the ingroup directly; outsiders were defined by non-inclusion. Anglo-Saxonism emerged as the dominant leitmotif of American society beginning in the late nineteenth century and was essentially an affirmation of the positive qualities of the Anglo-Saxon race (e.g., its supposed love of freedom and capacity for self-government). Equating Americanism with Anglo-Saxonism implies that all non-Anglo-Saxons are not "true" Americans. The continuing influx of Asian immigrants into the United States is likely to perpetuate the perception of Asian Americans as foreigners. In 1994, over 60% of Asian Americans were foreign born (with the exception of the Japanese), and most were recent immigrants (Sue, 1994).

To the extent that a self-categorization becomes salient as an element of social identity, it possesses affective and motivational significance. Smith (1993) proposes that stereotypic beliefs about an outgroup's attributes and their relation to one's own group form a type of appraisal that can trigger emotions. Individuals' beliefs about the positive stereotypic attributes of Asian Americans (e.g., intelligent, industrious, successful), and their relation to whites as a group, therefore, form appraisals that can trigger emotions toward Asians.

To generate predictions about the specific emotions that may be felt by whites toward Asian Americans, we build on the links described earlier between relative deprivation and intergroup comparison theories of prejudice and Smith's (1993) prejudice model. Relative deprivation research suggests that whites, a relatively successful social group, may nonetheless be resentful and dissatisfied if they perceive Asian Americans as having better outcomes (e.g., economic success). One study by Vanneman and Pettigrew (1972) indirectly supports this idea, though it investigated attitudes toward African Americans rather than Asian Americans. The study found that white respondents who felt group relative deprivation (i.e., thought their racial group had been deprived of recent gains relative to African Americans as a group) were the least willing to vote for African American mayoral candidates, and also had the most negative images of that group. These findings have implications for attitudes toward Asian Americans, who are much more likely than African Americans to be perceived as having outcomes that are superior to whites. In the past two decades, the mass media have published numerous success stories of Asian Americans. The headlines of some of these news articles alone would convince readers that Asian Americans are doing better than whites: "Success Story: Outwhiting the Whites" (*Newsweek*, 1971) and

"Why Asians are Going to the Head of the Class" (*New York Times*, 1986). In addition, many of these news articles emphasize the greater than average educational levels, occupational prestige, and incomes of Asian Americans. Thus, believing that Asian Americans are more economically successful than one's group is an appraisal that may lead to anger, resentment, and dissatisfaction.

Intergroup comparison theories of prejudice also make predictions about the type of emotions that are likely to be elicited by Asian Americans. To the extent that whites perceive Asian Americans as a "successful" group, comparisons with Asian Americans may often be upward comparisons. Several field studies have shown that upward comparison can result in negative affect (e.g., Hemphill & Lehman, 1991; Wheeler & Miyake, 1992). Although most studies have examined the effect of upward comparisons on broad undifferentiated mood states rather than on specific emotions, it seems reasonable to assume that specific emotions would accompany upward social comparisons. Salovey (1991) suggests that the emotions triggered by social comparisons are likely to include what Ortony, Clore, and Collins (1988) labeled the appreciation emotions (e.g., admiration, respect), the reproach emotions (e.g., contempt, disdain), and the resentment emotions (e.g., envy, jealousy).

In summary, we predict that individuals may feel different specific emotions regarding Asian Americans, depending on their appraisals of that target group and its specific relationship to the group with which the perceiver identifies (e.g., perceived competitive threat). Appraising Asian Americans as more economically successful than one's group may lead to anger, resentment, and dissatisfaction. The appraisal that Asian Americans are intelligent and industrious, and thus formidable competitors, may trigger hostility, fear, and threat. Of course, individuals may also have positive appraisals of Asian Americans (i.e., perceive no negative implications for their ingroup).

What factors influence perceivers' appraisals of an ethnic outgroup and therefore the positive or negative nature of their emotional reactions to the group? General discussion of important appraisals and their implications for emotions can be found in Smith (1993) and in works by emotion-appraisal theorists (e.g., Frijda, 1986). Specifically regarding appraisals of Asian Americans, existing research has not directly addressed this question, but we can offer speculative answers based on existing theory. Three factors may be important: the security of the perceiver's individual self-esteem or social identity, individual differences in orientation toward intergroup relations, and the way the perceiver thinks of group boundaries.

1. First, some research suggests that people with stable high individual self-esteem react less negatively than other people (or even positively) to upward social comparisons (Reis, Gerrard, & Gibbons, 1993; Wheeler & Miyake, 1992). Similarly, Jackson and Smith (1999) found that people with what they termed insecure social identity – those who saw the intergroup situation as threatening and unstable – tended to derogate outgroups. In contrast, secure social identity was associated with positive feelings about ingroups but not negative evaluations of outgroups. Findings such as these lead to the speculation that people whose individual or social self-esteem is stable and secure may be less inclined to appraise Asian Americans as a threat, compared to people whose self-esteem is low, variable, or insecure.

2. Individual differences in orientation toward intergroup relations, measured by scales such as Right-Wing Authoritarianism (Altemeyer, 1993) or Social Dominance Orientation (Sidanius, Feshbach, Levin, & Pratto, 1997), have been found in other contexts to relate to the favorability of attitudes toward outgroups. Certainly the same correlations are likely to be found with respect to white Americans' prejudice toward Asian Americans.

3. Finally, people will vary in the extent to which they perceive Asian Americans as an outgroup. Some may regard Asian Americans as Americans (ingroup members) whose attributes such as intelligence and hard work will benefit America and other Americans. Individuals who perceive Asian Americans in this manner are likely to experience positive instead of negative emotions (e.g., admiration, respect, inspiration). This suggestion is supported by research on the "common ingroup identity model" (Gaertner, Rust, Dovidio, Bachman, & Anastasio, 1994), which shows that when members of previously distinct groups are led to think of themselves as members of a superordinate category, positive regard for ingroup members is transferred to the new, more inclusive ingroup.

Empirical Evidence on Prejudice Toward Asian Americans

A recent study (Ho, 1997) provides evidence that supports some predictions of Smith's (1993) model concerning attitudes toward Asian Americans. In this study, a new measure, the Attitudes Towards Asian Americans Scale (ATA), was developed and validated. As part of the validation process, participants' emotions toward Asian Americans were measured and correlated with responses to the ATA, a semantic differential measure of general attitude toward Asian Americans, and a stereotyping measure. Research participants (non-Asian college students) reported a variety of emotions toward Asian Americans that are consistent with the predictions of Smith's (1993) model. Specifically, White participants reported negative emotions such as anger, frustration, hostility, resentment, and feeling threatened by Asian Americans. Positive emotions such as admiration, encouragement, inspired by, and respect for Asian Americans were also reported. These emotions were significantly correlated with attitudes toward Asian Americans. Negative emotions were correlated with negative attitudes toward Asian Americans, whereas positive emotions were correlated with positive attitudes toward Asian Americans.

Importantly, there was also some evidence that positive and negative emotions toward Asian Americans were triggered by different appraisals of the same stereotypic attributes (e.g., intelligent). Positive emotions toward Asian Americans, for example, were associated with beliefs that the intelligence and diligence of Asian Americans were beneficial to the United States as a whole. Negative emotions, in contrast, were associated with beliefs that the intelligence and diligence of Asian Americans made them untrustworthy and overly competitive. These findings are consistent with the postulate that it is the appraisal of the stereotypic attributes that determines prejudice toward Asian Americans and not the valence of the stereotypic attributes per se.

Consistent with our speculation that prejudice toward Asian Americans arises because Whites self-categorize themselves as "Americans," and by noninclusion, Asian Americans as foreigners, negative emotions toward Asian Americans were associated with perceptions of Asian Americans as non-Americans. For example, negative emotions were associated with the belief that Asian Americans were taking jobs that "rightfully belong to U.S. born Americans," that Asians should have stayed in their own countries where they belong, and that they were out to "drain American resources." Positive emotions toward Asian Americans, in contrast, were associated with beliefs that suggested the inclusion of Asian Americans in the category "Americans." This is consistent with the predictions of Gaertner's Common Ingroup Identity Model (Gaertner et al., 1994). As mentioned earlier, positive emotions were associated with beliefs that the intelligence of Asians benefits America.

Attitudes toward Asian Americans have often been observed to be polarized (Yee, 1992). Real-life examples of polarization include the very positive attitudes of American workers at Japanese automotive plants in Kentucky as compared to the anti-Japanese attitudes of workers and executives at U.S. owned plants in Michigan; and the Central Pacific executives in the nineteenth century who valued the Chinese rail workers, as compared to the Union Pacific workers who despised competition with Asians (Yee, 1992). The polarization of attitudes toward Asian Americans can be effectively explained by postulating different appraisals of Asian Americans and of the stereotypic attributes ascribed to them. Positive attitudes toward Asian Americans are likely to result from appraisals of Asians as nonthreatening and as productive co-workers or subordinates. Negative attitudes toward Asian Americans, in contrast, are likely to result from appraisals of Asian Americans as a threat to the well-being of one's ingroup. Viewing prejudice as social emotions also allows us to explain effectively the high levels of hostility and violence against Asian Americans. The U.S. Commission on Civil Rights (1992) reported that although Asian Americans constitute less than 4% of Philadelphia's population, Asian Americans constituted 20% of the hate crime victims in 1988. Strong negative emotions such as resentment, threat, hostility and frustration are likely to be the basis for aggression against Asian Americans.

Implications for Reducing Prejudice Toward Asians

It was hypothesized that prejudice toward Asian Americans arises from appraisals that Asian Americans are a threat to one's ingroup. Such appraisals often have a "kernel of truth" in realistic intergroup conflicts over resources. These appraisals will, therefore, be difficult to change. Although some theorists have suggested that prejudice can be reduced by making individuals aware that outgroups have admirable qualities, this approach may not work with Asian Americans. If the positive qualities of Asian Americans are in fact responsible for prejudice toward them, then making individuals aware of those qualities may only exacerbate prejudice.

Reducing the salience of the ingroup–outgroup distinction may perhaps be the best available option to reduce prejudice toward Asian Americans. One way to achieve this is to induce White individuals to categorize Asian Americans and themselves into one superordinate category (cf. Gaertner et al., 1994). As noted in the study by Ho (1997), participants who reported positive emotions toward Asian Americans appeared to categorize Asian Americans and themselves as members of a superordinate category (i.e., Americans), thus avoiding an ingroup–outgroup distinction between whites and Asian Americans. Reducing the salience of an ingroup–outgroup distinction between Whites and Asian Americans, however, will be difficult given that a number of factors encourage this distinction. For example, the physical differences of Asian Americans from Whites, the perception of Asian

Americans as possessing different attributes from Whites (e.g., quiet, obedient), and competitive relations between Whites and Asian Americans are factors that may increase the likelihood of Whites developing social identities that exclude Asian Americans.

CONCLUSIONS

Both relative deprivation and intergroup comparison concepts have been used to explain prejudice and intergroup relations. Although both approaches have proven fruitful, this chapter argues that Smith's (1993) conceptualization of prejudice provides a general formulation of the two related literatures and, in addition, yields unique predictions that cannot be derived from the relative deprivation and intergroup comparison literature. Smith's (1993) model, for example, predicts not only resentment and dissatisfaction but also other types of negative as well as positive emotions (e.g., envy, threat, anger, admiration, and respect). In addition, Smith's (1993) prejudice model accounts for the situational specificity of prejudice, an issue not addressed by either relative deprivation or intergroup comparison theories of prejudice.

The utility of the model of prejudice as intergroup emotion was illustrated by applying the model to explaining prejudice toward Asian Americans. The model allowed us to make the counterintuitive prediction that the positive stereotypic attributes of Asian Americans can lead to negative emotions toward them. These predictions were shown to be consistent with existing evidence on attitudes toward Asian Americans. The conceptualization of prejudice as social emotions (Smith, 1993) thus appears to be a viable approach that can be profitably applied to studying prejudice toward outgroups. We strongly recommend that future research on prejudice toward Asian Americans (as well as other groups) should include measures of emotional reactions to outgroups (such as admiration, resentment, fear, annoyance, or disgust) as well as ingroups (including pride, disappointment, or anxiety). Such measures will permit stronger tests of the notion of prejudice as intergroup emotion, and may offer important empirical insights into the processes underlying intergroup conflict.

ACKNOWLEDGMENTS

Preparation of this chapter was facilitated by NIMH Grants R01 MH46840 and K02 MH01178.

REFERENCES

Abeles, R. P. (1976). Relative deprivation, rising expectations, and black militancy. *Journal of Social Issues, 32*, 119–137.
Altemeyer, B. (1993). Reducing prejudice in right-wing authoritarians. In M. P. Zanna & J. M. Olson (Eds.), *The psychology of prejudice: The Ontario symposium* (Vol. 7, pp. 134–148). Hillsdale, NJ: Lawrence Erlbaum.
Arnold, M. B. (1960). *Emotion and personality: Vol. I. Psychological aspects.* New York: Columbia University Press.
Aron, A., Aron, E. N., Tudor, M., & Nelson, G. (1991). Close relationships as including other in the self. *Journal of Personality and Social Psychology, 60*, 241–253.
Bobo, L. (1983). Whites' opposition to busing: Symbolic racism or realistic group conflict? *Journal of Personality and Social Psychology, 45*, 1196–1210.
Brewer, M. B., & Weber, J. G. (1994). Self-evaluation effects of interpersonal versus intergroup social comparison. *Journal of Personality and Social Psychology, 66*, 268–275.
Clore, G., & Rahn, W. (1994). *American national identity, public mood, and political judgment: The informative function of social emotion.* Unpublished paper, Department of Psychology, University of Illinois.
Dijker, A. J. M. (1987). Emotional reactions to ethnic minorities. *European Journal of Social Psychology, 17*, 305–325.
Dion, K. L. (1986). Responses to perceived discrimination and relative deprivation. In J. M. Olson, C. P. Herman, & M. P. Zanna (Eds.), *Relative deprivation and social comparison: The Ontario symposium* (Vol. 4, pp. 159–179). Hillsdale, NJ: Lawrence Erlbaum.
Dube, L., & Guimond, S. (1986). Relative deprivation and social protest: The personal-group issue. In J. M. Olson, C. P. Herman, & M. P. Zanna (Eds.), *Relative deprivation and social comparison: The Ontario symposium* (Vol. 4, pp. 201–215). Hillsdale, NJ: Lawrence Erlbaum.
Eagly, A. H., & Chaiken, S. (1994). *The psychology of attitudes.* Fort Worth: Harcourt Brace Jovanovich.
Eagly, A. H., & Mladinic, A. (1989). Gender stereotypes and attitudes toward women and men. *Personality and Social Psychology Bulletin, 15*, 543–558.
Esses, V. M., Haddock, G., & Zanna, M. P. (1993). Values, stereotypes, and emotions as determinants of intergroup attitudes. In D. Mackie & D. Hamilton (Eds.), *Affect, cognition, and stereotyping* (pp. 137–166). San Diego, CA: Academic Press.
Fischer, H. W., Shaver, P. R., & Carnohan, P. (1990). How emotions develop and how they organize development. *Cognition and Emotion, 4*, 81–127.
Fishbein, M. P., & Ajzen, I. (1975). *Belief, attitude, intention, and behavior.* Reading, MA: Addison-Wesley.
Fredrickson, G. M. (1981). *White supremacy: A comparative study in African and South African History.* New York: Oxford University Press.
Frijda, N. H. (1986). *The emotions.* Cambridge, England: Cambridge University Press.
Gaertner, S. L., Rust, M., Dovidio, J. F., Bachman, B. A., & Anastasio, P. (1994). The contact hypothesis: The role of a common ingroup identity on reducing intergroup bias. *Small Groups Research, 25*, 224–249.

Goethals, G. R., & Darley, J. M. (1987). Social comparison theory: Self-evaluation and group life. In D. L. Hamilton (Ed.), *Cognitive processes in stereotyping and intergroup behavior* (pp. 333–353). Hillsdale, NJ: Lawrence Erlbaum.

Hemphill, K. J., & Lehman, D. R. (1991). Social comparisons and their affective consequences: The importance of comparison dimension and individual differences. *Journal of Social and Clinical Psychology, 10,* 372–394.

Higham, J. (1963). *Strangers in the land: Patterns of American nativism, 1860–1925.* New York: Atheneum.

Ho, C. P. (1997). *Attitudes towards Asian Americans.* Unpublished doctoral dissertation, Purdue University, West Lafayette, Indiana.

Hurh, W. M., & Kim, K. C. (1989). The success image of Asian Americans: Its validity, and its practical and theoretical implications. *Ethnic and Racial Studies, 12,* 512–538.

Jackson, J. W., & Smith, E. R. (1999). Conceptualizing social identity: A new framework and evidence for the impact of different dimensions. *Personality and Social Psychology Bulletin, 25,* 120–135.

Jackson, L. A., Hodge, C. N., Gerard, D. A., Ingram, J. M., Ervin, K. S., & Sheppard, L. A. (1996). Cognition, affect and behavior in the prediction of group attitudes. *Personality and Social Psychology Bulletin, 22,* 306–316.

Kinder, D. R., & Sears, D. O. (1981). Prejudice and politics: Symbolic racism versus racial threats to the good life. *Journal of Personality and Social Psychology, 40,* 414–431.

Kitano, H. H. L., & Sue, S. (1973). The model minorities. *Journal of Social Issues, 29,* 1–9.

LaPiere, R. T. (1934). Attitudes vs. actions. *Social Forces, 13,* 230–237.

Levine, J. M., & Moreland, R. L. (1987). Social comparison and outcome evaluation in group contexts. In J. C. Masters & W. P. Smith (Eds.), *Social comparison, social justice, and relative deprivation: Theoretical, empirical and policy perspectives* (pp. 105–127). Hillsdale, NJ: Lawrence Erlbaum.

Martin, J. (1981). Relative deprivation: A theory of distributive justice for an era of shrinking resources. In L. L. Cummings & B. M. Staw (Eds.), *Research in organizational behavior* (Vol 3, pp. 53–107). Greenwich, CT: JAI Press.

McConahay, J. B. (1982). Self-interest versus racial attitudes as correlates of anti-busing attitudes in Louisville: Is it the buses or the blacks? *Journal of Politics, 44,* 692–720.

Miller, S. C. (1969). *The American image of the Chinese, 1785–1882.* Berkeley: University of California Press.

Ortony, A., Clore, G. L., & Collins, A. (1988). *The cognitive structure of emotions.* New York: Cambridge University Press.

Pettigrew, T. F. (1997). The affective component of prejudice: Empirical support for the new view. In S. A. Tuch & J. K. Martin (Eds.), *Racial attitudes in the 1990s: Continuity and change* (pp. 76–90). Westport, CT: Praeger.

Portes, A., & Manning, R. D. (1986). The immigrant enclave: Theory and empirical examples. In S. Olzak & J. Nagel (Eds.), *Competitive ethnic relations* (pp. 47–68). Orlando, FL: Academic Press.

Reis, T. J., Gerrard, M., & Gibbons, F. X. (1993). Social comparison and the pill: Reactions to upward and downward comparison of contraceptive behavior. *Personality and Social Psychology Bulletin, 19,* 13–20.

Roseman, I. J. (1984). Cognitive determinants of emotion: A structural theory. In P. Shaver (Ed.), *Review of personality and social psychology* (Vol. 5). Beverly Hills, CA: Sage.

Runciman, W. G. (1966). *Relative deprivation and social justice.* Berkeley: University of California Press.

Salovey, P. (1991). Social comparison processes in envy and jealousy. In J. Suls & T. Wills (Eds.), *Social comparison: Contemporary theory and research* (pp. 261–285). Hillsdale, NJ: Lawrence Erlbaum.

Sidanius, J., Feshbach, S., Levin, S., & Pratto, F. (1997). The interface between ethnic and national attachment: Ethnic pluralism or ethnic dominance? *Public Opinion Quarterly, 61,* 102–133.

Smith, E. R. (1993). Social identity and social emotions: Towards new conceptualizations of prejudice. In D. Mackie & D. Hamilton (Eds.), *Affect, cognition and stereotyping* (pp. 297–315). San Diego, CA: Academic Press.

Smith, E. R., Coats, S., & Walling, D. (1997). *Overlapping mental representations of self, in-group, and partner: Further response time evidence.* Unpublished paper, Purdue University, Department of Psychological Sciences.

Smith, E. R., & Henry, S. (1996). An in-group becomes part of the self: Response time evidence. *Personality and Social Psychology Bulletin, 22,* 635–642.

Smith, H. J., & Spears, R. (1996). Ability and outcome evaluations as a function of personal and collective (dis)advantage: A group escape from individual bias. *Personality and Social Psychology Bulletin, 22,* 690–704.

Stangor, C., Sullivan, L. A., & Ford, T. E. (1991). Affective and cognitive determinants of prejudice. *Social Cognition, 9,* 359–380.

Sue, D. W. (1994). Asian American mental health and help seeking behavior: Comment on Solberg et al. (1994), Tata and Leong (1994), and Lin (1994). *Journal of Counseling Psychology, 41,* 292–295.

Tajfel, H. (1982). *Social identity and intergroup relations.* Cambridge, England: Cambridge University Press.

Tajfel, H., & Turner, J. C. (1986). The social identity theory of intergroup behavior. In W. G. Austin & S. Worchel (Eds.), *Psychology of intergroup relations* (pp. 7–24). Monterey, CA: Brooks/Cole.

Turner, J. C., Hogg, M. A., Oakes, P. J., Reicher, S. D., & Wetherell, M. S. (1987). *Rediscovering the social group: A self-categorization theory.* Oxford: Blackwell.

Uba, L. (1994). *Asian Americans: Personality patterns, identity, and mental health.* New York: Guilford Press.

Useem, M. (1980). Solidarity model, breakdown model, and the Boston anti-busing movement. *American Sociological Review, 45,* 357–369.

Vanneman, R. D., & Pettigrew, T. F. (1972). Race and relative deprivation in the urban United States. *Race, 13,* 461–486.

Wheeler, L., & Miyake, K. (1992). Social comparison in everyday life. *Journal of Personality and Social Psychology, 62,* 760–773.

Yee, A. H. (1992). Asians as stereotypes and students: Misperceptions that persist. *Educational Psychology Review, 4,* 95–131.

PART FOUR

CONCLUSION

SIXTEEN

Summing Up

Relative Deprivation as a Key Social Psychological Concept

Thomas F. Pettigrew

Theoretical ideas arise to solve puzzles. Not surprisingly, Samuel Stouffer devised the concept of relative deprivation (RD) as a post hoc explanation for the famous anomalies from his World War II *American Soldier* studies (Stouffer, 1962: Chapter 2; Stouffer, Suchman, DeVinney, Star, & Williams, 1949).

Recall how the military police were more satisfied with slow promotions than the air corpsmen with rapid promotions, and how African American soldiers in southern camps were more satisfied than those in northern camps. The apparent puzzles assumed the wrong referent comparisons. Immediate comparisons, Stouffer reasoned, were the salient referents: the military police compared their promotions with other military police, and the African American soldiers in the South with African American civilians in the South.

Stouffer, my principal research mentor, did not think of himself as a theorist.[1] His greatest achievement, together with his friend Paul Lazarsfeld of Columbia University, was the fashioning of the large probability survey into a major empirical instrument of the social sciences. He was a genius at analyzing survey data, skillfully controlling for relevant variables and making sense out of complex findings. To this day, his terse volume *Communism, Conformity, and Civil Liberties* (Stouffer, 1955) offers a model for precision in survey analysis. His favorite Shakespearian citation from *King Henry IV* has Glendower asserting that he could "call spirits from the vasty deep." But, Hotspur retorts, "Why, so can I, or so can any man; But will they come when you do call for them?" When Stouffer called for them from survey data, the answers always came.

Stouffer resisted sociology's penchant for "grand theory." He believed in close-to-the-data reasoning and middle-level concepts. RD is a prime example of this style. "Intervening opportunities," an equally useful demographic concept to account for migration flows, offers another example (Stouffer, 1940). Yet Stouffer did not make explicit the underpinnings of his concepts – a task of this volume.

A comparative approach to explain his *American Soldier* puzzles came readily to Stouffer. Between the world wars, cultural anthropology had firmly established a relativity perspective in the social sciences. Hyman (1942) was the first to reflect this emphasis in social psychology with his introduction of reference group theory. Following World War II, comparative ideas abounded in the "Golden Age" of American social science. In economics, for instance, another Harvard University professor introduced a similar concept in the same year Stouffer introduced relative deprivation. Duesenberry (1949; Dybvig, 1995) fashioned "the ratchet effect" to explain consumer behavior. And soon after in psychological social psychology, Festinger's (1954) social comparison theory emerged.

Theories in social psychology – such as authoritarianism, cognitive dissonance, and causal attribution – typically burn hot and then suddenly cool. But the family of social evaluation theories, including RD and social comparison, have simmered slowly on a back burner for half a century.

Every few years, an important work emerges to continue the steady progress these theories have enjoyed. Hence, soon after Stouffer introduced RD, Merton (1957; Merton & Kitt, 1950) enlarged the idea within a reference group framework. Other advances have trickled out over the years, each expanding the original concept and linking it with other concepts and phenomena. Runciman (1966) broadened the construct by carefully distinguishing between egoistic (individual) and fraternal (group) RD. This work led me to point out that RD was but one of a large family of concepts and mini-theories that employed relative comparisons in both sociological and psychological social psychology (Pettigrew, 1967). From sociology, this theoretical family embraces Hyman's (1942, 1960) and Merton's (1957) reference group theory, Lenski's (1954) concept of status crystallization, Blau's (1964) concept of fair exchange, and Homans' (1961) concept of distributive justice. From psychology, these social evaluation ideas include equity theory, social comparison theory, Thibaut and Kelley's (1959) concept of comparison level, and Centers' (1949) concept of subjective class identification. Advances in any of these areas sheds light on the others. Indeed, Tougas and Beaton in their chapter skillfully use equity theory to link group RD with RD on behalf of others.

During the 1970s, Suls and Miller (1977) edited a volume that offered a host of interconnections between these comparative concepts and such other disciplinary concerns as causal attributions. Crosby (1976) provided a detailed analysis of individual RD, while Albert (1977) focused on temporal comparisons in an influential article. The following decade witnessed further advances. Mark and Folger (1984) introduced their referent cognitions model of RD that several chapters in this volume employ. And a major work edited by Olson, Herman, and Zanna (1986) offered additional bonds between social comparison theory and RD.

RD lends itself easily to such steady development and bridging to other social psychological ideas. It is a key construct that can link different levels of analysis rather than being a fully developed theory itself. It is a model social psychological concept, for it postulates a subjective state that shapes emotions and cognitions and influences behavior. As such, RD melds easily with other social psychological processes to provide more integrative theory – a prime disciplinary need (Pettigrew, 1991a). The book's chapters have successfully interwoven RD with attribution, social identity, self-categorization, and equity theories as well as procedural justice and counterfactual thinking processes.

This volume continues in this tradition of steady progress. The editors have effectively organized the volume in terms of specification, development, and integration of the concept. My chapter attempts to integrate basic themes that emerge from the book's diverse analyses. Eight focal issues are considered: (1) expanding the concept to the advantaged; (2) temporal comparisons; (3) the pivotal role of affect; (4) the RD process and its integration with other areas; (5) generalization of the RD phenomenon; (6) the importance of the social context; (7) linking individual RD with group RD; and (8) the consequences of RD. We shall note that many of these issues are basic concerns for social psychological theory generally – not just RD. In addition, the chapter will offer new analyses that test further many of these fundamental issues.

Expanding the Concept to the Advantaged

Like other social sciences, social psychology focuses much of its attention on the problematic side of social life – stigma, prejudice, intergroup conflict. In addition, economic market and rational choice models have strongly influenced social psychological thinking. Despite research findings on pro-social behavior, the discipline in the last half of the twentieth century has focused increasingly on the individual and on self-enhancing motivations.

Gartrell, in his chapter, reminds us that terms prefaced by "self" – such as Tesser's (1988) self-evaluation maintenance theory (SEM) – typically view behavior through a severely individualistic lens that assumes competitiveness. His student subjects revealed that nurturing social relationships was also an important motivation that often proved stronger than the motives considered by SEM. Similarly, relative deprivation has been studied for half a century but not its reverse – relative gratification. What are the consequences of making comparisons for yourself and your group that reveal your advantaged position? Two chapters specifically consider this seldom asked question.

In their innovative contribution, Leach, Snider, and Iyer consider three main classes of response. (1) The relatively gratified can simply take their privileged position for granted. Hence, there is no perceived need for change; the dominant norms support their advantages as an appropriate entitlement. (2) There also can be a "strategic modesty." Here the relatively gratified minimize their advantage to limit claims and guilt. This response reveals some minimal awareness of advantage, however, and potential conversion to the third type – (3) the full acknowledgment of their advantages. Ellemers warns us, however, that the opposite reaction is also common. Awareness of advantage can elicit strategic behavior to protect privilege. For example, Tyler and Lind point out that the privileged can stress that procedural justice exists and thus draw attention away from differential outcomes.

The most interesting response by the relatively gratified is the acknowledgment of privilege. Leach and his colleagues note that this requires downward comparisons with at least four dimensions: a self-other focus as well as perceived control, stability, and legitimacy. This analysis fits snugly with other chapters. Temporal comparisons are implicit in much of this process. And the emphasis on perceived legitimacy and fairness is a recurrent theme throughout the book. Once people regard group differentials as illegitimate, justice norms are invoked and the differentials are subject to question and change.

Beaton and Tougas consider the same phenomenon. They show that "RD on behalf of others" directly relates to altruistic attitudes and behavior (see also Veilleux & Tougas, 1989). This finding suggests that future work on relative gratification should exploit both the altruistic and empathy literatures. In recent years there has been a renewed interest in these long-neglected areas. McFarland (1999) has found, for example, those scoring high in empathy are less prejudiced controlling for both authoritarianism and social dominance orientation. And Batson et al. (1997) found that experimentally induced empathy reduces prejudice.

Social psychologists must pay more attention in the future to relative gratification and RD on behalf of others. Any general theory of social evaluation must be able to explain reactions of both the deprived and nondeprived. Moreover, RD on behalf of others is a widely observed phenomenon of social life – from the thousands of White Americans who participated in the Civil Rights Movement of the 1960s to the many men who support equal rights for women.

Temporal Comparisons
Longitudinal research designs are rare in the discipline. Social psychologists are fond of citing Sherif's (Sherif, Harvey, White, Hood, & Sherif, 1961) famous Robbers' Cave field experiment. Yet this classic study obtained its striking findings only because it was longitudinal and repeatedly measured its dependent variables (Pettigrew, 1991b). Such studies remain rare, and dependent variables are typically not repeatedly measured over time. RD research is no exception. RD writings have long stressed temporal comparisons (Davies, 1962; Pettigrew, 1967; Runciman, 1966; Walker & Pettigrew, 1984), but RD research seldom tests such comparisons with adequate overtime designs.

Nonetheless, this volume emphasizes throughout the special significance of temporal comparisons. Thus, Gartrell needs such comparisons for his network applications. Tougas and Beaton show their importance for individual RD (IRD), group RD (GRD), and RD on behalf of others. And while Wilson and her colleagues find temporal comparisons rare among children, they point out that temporal comparisons require longitudinal research designs. Retrospective recollections are framed by the present and usually systematically distorted accordingly. The Wilson chapter also raises two broad questions for future research. What are "the circumstances that prompt spontaneous temporal comparisons, as well as the prevalence and consequences of such contrasts"? And do "people avoid focusing on RD unless they believe that they can act to relieve it"?

This last question suggests the routine measurement in RD research of subjects' perceived efficacy in changing the perceived deprivation. Such a variable would aid in combining RD and resource mobilization ideas. Thus, it has been argued that the U.S. Civil Rights Movement of the 1960s burst forth in that decade and not before precisely because African

Americans at that point had both aroused group RD and an awareness that racial change was possible (Pettigrew, 1964).

The Pivotal Role of Affect

As part of psychology's cognitive revolution during the 1960s and 1970s, social cognition virtually ignored emotion. RD research reflected this trend. Stouffer held that dissatisfaction with the perceived comparative difference was an essential element in RD. Yet many researchers simply used the Cantril ladder and other measures of perceived discrepancies without asking respondents how they *felt* about the discrepancies. As Figure 16.1 makes clear, meta-analytic results show that RD measures with affect obtain significantly larger mean effect sizes for prejudice measures than those using only cognitive indicators (from Smith & Pettigrew, 2001). These and other results underscore the correctness of Stouffer's position: Affect is a core ingredient of RD, not simply a mediator of RD's effects.

Both the Smith-Ortiz and Wright-Tropp chapters underscore the importance of RD affect for collective behavior. Earlier workers in this area had prematurely abandoned RD considerations in part because they ignored the role of affect (e.g., McPhail, 1971). Yet such emotions as dissatisfaction and feelings of unfairness are critical for group RD's effects on collective action (Grant & Brown, 1995). Consistent with this point, Taylor notes that affective RD draws the concept especially close to such other theories of prejudice as group position and racial resentment.

The affective component of RD also proves important for a range of effects. Only affective RD has causal implications for prejudice in the

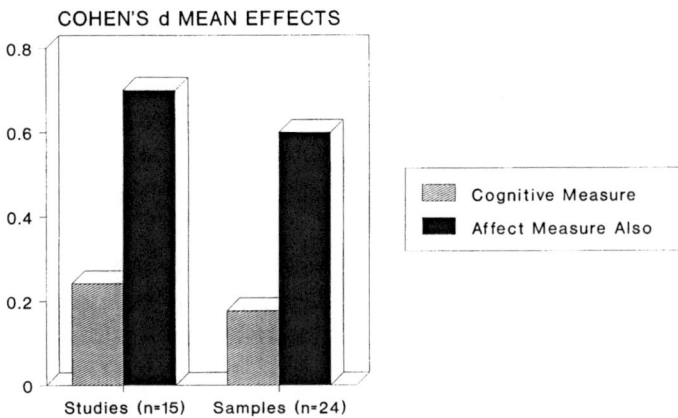

Figure 16.1. Group relative deprivation and prejudice: the role of affect.

Duckitt and Mphuthing study. Walker (1999) found induced RD had effects on self-esteem when affect had been aroused. And only affective group RD relates significantly to nationalism among the Quebecois (Guimond & Dube-Simard, 1983).

This and other research led Eliot Smith (1993) to take the next step and define prejudice as an intergroup emotion. In their chapter, Smith and Ho review this new approach and integrate it with RD as a correlate of prejudice. Combining insights from various theories of emotion and cognition, they define prejudice as a social emotion experienced with respect to one's social identity as a group member, with an outgroup as a target. Note that they, like other chapter writers, lean heavily on social identity and self-categorization theory as well as appraisal theories of emotion. Prejudice becomes primarily an emotion toward outgroups that is shaped by a person's identity with their ingroup.

This fresh look at prejudice has several interesting implications for RD. It stresses the greater importance of a group than an individual focus in prejudice – a point consistent with RD research. It also emphasizes that prejudice is generally quite specific to the intergroup situation with particular emotions elicited. Hence, RD should trigger a narrow range of "resentment" emotions concerned with unfairness and legitimacy – as many chapters have underscored. Smith and Ho also show how RD can help explain an apparent paradox in the prejudice literature – namely, how seemingly positive stereotypes can accompany prejudice against such minorities as Asian Americans.

The RD Process and Its Integration with Other Areas

To borrow Kelley's (1983) analogy, social psychologists dig deeply like mining engineers but seldom generalize across phenomena like geologists. The discipline too often gives cute new labels to specific phenomena without relating them to broader middle-range theory. So basic integrative work that broadens RD ideas is especially welcome. Varied chapters of this book have made precisely this needed progress. They have done so by integrating the RD process with other social psychological processes – social identity, procedural justice, and counterfactual thinking.

Social identity is an integral component of the RD process. And comparison processes are central to social identification theory (SIT). Hence, links between RD and SIT have often been sought (Kawakami & Dion, 1995; Walker & Pettigrew, 1984). And several chapters carry forward this idea by showing the critical role in the group RD process played by social identity. Thus, Ellemers demonstrates how social identity shapes comparison referents. Smith and Ortiz find it critical in understanding the differential effects of IRD and GRD. Tougas and Beaton show how social identity, self-esteem, and RD together form an integrative model. Smith and Ho view ingroup identity as basic to their approach to inter-group prejudice as an emotion. For Wright and Tropp, ingroup identity is an essential precondition for collective action in two ways. Self-categorization as a group member is obviously required to initiate the process. And strong identification with the group relates to greater group RD and support for collective action.

It remained for Ellemers to provide in her chapter an integrative model connecting the antecedents of social identification with its consequences. From SIT, she predicted that the combination of low ingroup status and access to a higher status group would have major effects: less ingroup identification, increased perception of intragroup heterogeneity, self-presentation as an atypical group member, and even discrimination against former ingroup members. Both her experimental and field data supported these predictions. Ellemer's intriguing study with the tiny group of female professors in the Netherlands should be repeated in nations where female professors are far more common.[2] With normative pressures to be masculine in style reduced, SIT's predictions should find less support.

Procedural justice issues also are fundamental to both IRD and GRD processes. Tyler and Lind extend RD thinking beyond relative outcomes to include how these outcomes are distributed. This extension, especially to group RD, is valuable on several counts. Procedural considerations help embed the micro-level phenomena of RD within a structural context. As their chapter's examples reveal, structural issues of the justice system and other institutions become relevant for RD.

Moreover, a focus on procedural issues joins easily with other major contentions of this volume. Perceptions of procedural treatment are directly tied to the causal attributions that Walker, Wong, and Kretzschmar emphasize in their model. They also are intimately entwined with the judgments of legitimacy and fairness that the volume has stressed throughout. And procedural considerations may help to explain the tokenism phenomenon discussed by Wright and Tropp. Tokenism – the entrance of a few members of a previously excluded outgroup into high-status ranks – may well trigger a sense of procedural fairness out of proportion to its structural importance. Similarly, Stouffer's (1962) famous example of the surprisingly satisfied military police may have involved their sense of procedural fairness in their slow promotion system.

Counterfactual thinking also advances our understanding of the RD process. RD requires comparison. Like Mark and Folger (1984) earlier, Olson and Roese bring this perspective and research literature to bear on this crucial component of RD. Counterfactual thoughts, they reveal, can mediate both social and temporal comparisons. Integrating the two research areas leads to new explanations for established phenomena.

A case in point concerns the personal-group discrimination discrepancy. Olson and Roese offer two new reasons why people are more likely to perceive discrimination against their ingroup than against themselves personally. First, the group context is more abstract and flexible than the detailed knowledge held about one's personal situation. Hence, judgments about group outcomes are likely to be "more cognitively mutable" than personal outcomes. Second, ratings of a minority group's outcomes evoke those of the majority group as the comparison. But there is no such clear comparison referent for individual judgments.

Generalization of the Relative Deprivation Phenomenon

Social psychology all too often lacks concern about the universality of its phenomena. The discipline usually assumes universality from testing college students in Western nations (Sears, 1986). For example, does the just-world hypothesis operate in non-Western cultures as it does in prosperous, industrial cultures? Recalling my time among Zulus in South Africa years ago, I have serious doubts. Many Zulus see the world as capricious – neither just nor unjust. And they often find it uproariously comical when negative events shock Westerners.

Consequently, it is reassuring to have chapters in this book show that RD operates among a variety of groups – children and adults as well as college students, in Australia, Japan, the Netherlands, and South Africa as well as in North America. Indeed, the meta-analytic data cited by Smith and Ortiz (and also used in this chapter) draws results from studies conducted in more than a dozen varied nations from all the world's continents. Generalization of the phenomenon is also enhanced by the diversity of group comparisons employed throughout the book – racial and gender groups, majorities and minorities, and so on. Moreover, a great variety of methods – from laboratory experiments to national probability surveys – yield confirming evidence.

Several chapters, however, specify cautionary limitations. The results of Walker and his co-authors suggest that group RD may apply only in intergroup contexts in which there are salient, historically opposed groups. Without such salience and opposition, people may not evaluate outcomes in ingroup and outgroup terms. Similarly, Wright and Tropp suggest that RD is strongest when there exists a clearly advantaged outgroup that is perceived to be responsible for the ingroup's disadvantage. These conditional factors remind us that the social context is critical in the RD process.

The Importance of Social Context

RD links the micro-individual level of analysis with the meso- and macro-group levels. Like many social psychological concepts, RD mediates the effects of broad social variables on the individual. As such, the phenomenon is perforce sensitive to the social context. We have seen many such instances in this volume. For instance, Crosby, Ozawa, and Crosby note that Japanese men and women are more accepting of gender discrimination than their American college counterparts. And this difference in both norms and perceptions has implications for how RD operates in the two nations. In accord with the contentions of both the Walker, Wong, and Kretzschmar and the Wright and Tropp chapters, the Japanese case demonstrates that often actual group RD in a society is viewed as acceptable and unremarkable.

Duckitt and Mphuthing provide another telling example of social context in their South African results. They found systematic differences in the African RD data according to whether the referent comparison consisted of Afrikaner or English South Africans. These differences reflect the historical realities of that strife-torn land. Although the English largely followed paternalistic policies toward Africans in the past, it was Afrikaners, once they seized power in 1948, who constructed a blatantly racist police state. The 1994 election symbolized the end of apartheid repression. Thus, it is hardly surprising that the larger RD shifts occurred for the Afrikaner referent.

Gartrell's chapter explicitly focuses on the social context. His network research "socializes" RD judgments. He rejects the prevalent view that individuals make such judgments in social isolation. Drawing on his sociological expertise in network theory, he provides a compelling demonstration that comparisons are often made among friends. His Canadian University students made reciprocal comparisons of their grades. And such comparisons were simply part of the everyday flow of their dyadic interactions. Hence, reciprocal comparisons increased as a direct function of the frequency, strength, and closeness of the relationships.

Group RD, in particular, requires consideration of an even larger societal context. Taylor presents a close reading of three theories and research literatures that rarely influence each other. From her sociological perspective, she finds group RD, Blumer's collective threat, and the many versions of racial resentment to be similar and overlapping. An interdisciplinary linking of the three conceptual areas promises gains for all three. For group RD, the other areas supply a societal frame. Blumer (1958) stresses the intergroup history and stratification system that defines group interests; Kinder and Sanders (1996) provide the political and mass media contributions to intergroup perceptions. Such larger social contexts shape both the group referents for comparison and the group comparisons themselves. That is, social contexts typically make particular comparisons focal while also influencing how the comparisons will be made. In return, group RD offers one direct indicator for key contentions of the group position, collective threat and symbolic racism theories.

Linking Individual and Group Relative Deprivation

Runciman's distinction between IRD and GRD has influenced research on the subject ever since it appeared a third of a century ago. Yet the link between them remains an unsettled issue. Indeed, as work continues, it turns out the distinction is not as simple as it first appeared. As Smith and Ortiz point out, an intermediate type is quite common – individuals who compare themselves with outgroup individuals. Indeed, the meta-analytic data of Smith and Pettigrew (2001) reveal that mean effect sizes for this third RD type differ from either individual or group RD.

The effect sizes for the two principal forms of RD vary markedly as a function of the type of dependent variable (Smith & Pettigrew, 2001). Individual RD has personal consequences – such as stress and personal effort. It tends not to have direct group consequences – such as intergroup prejudice. By contrast, group RD has group-level effects. In short, the two RD forms map on to dependent variables as a function of the appropriate level of analysis. But this difference in direct consequences does not mean that IRD and GRD are unrelated. The point at issue is *how* they are linked. Three primary possibilities have all been advanced: (1) IRD and GRD interact; (2) they are not related at all; or (3) GRD mediates the effects of IRD on group-level variables.

1. Foster and Matheson (1995) proposed an interactive model to connect the two RD types. Their hierarchical regression results show that the interaction between the forms added to the prediction of reported collective action beyond that of the main effects of individual and group RD. Hence, they held "double deprivation" to be a potent motivator of collective action. But their empirical demonstration is limited. The data are from a college sample of convenience of politically inactive Canadian females, and their RD measures tapped only the cognitive dimension. Whether

their simple interactive model operates depends on the dependent variables in question. Not surprisingly, more extensive research using large
probability adult samples, more adequate indicators of RD, and an array
of diverse dependent variables do not support the interactive model
(Pettigrew & Meertens, 1999; Taylor, 1980; Vanneman & Pettigrew, 1972).

2. Two chapters address the link between Runciman's two RD types.
Ellemers asserts "that there is no logical or self-evident connection between
the two forms of deprivation." She notes that considerable research has
shown that it is common for people to be satisfied with their personal situation though they express considerable group RD (Crosby et al., 1989; Major,
1994; Martin, 1981; Taylor, Wright, Moghaddam, & Lalonde, 1990).

3. Tougas and Beaton, however, show there is often a spillover effect
from high levels of individual RD to group RD. Clearly, IRD is not a necessary condition for GRD, but it can be a major contributing factor. In a
series of studies, Tougas and her colleagues have shown that IRD does not
directly predict such responses as support or resistance to affirmative
action employment programs (Beaton & Tougas, 1997; Tougas & Veilleux,
1991). But in path analyses, it indirectly relates to such responses through
its influence on GRD. In this indirect sense, then, Tougas and Beaton conclude in their chapter "the personal is political."

Notice, however, that Tougas and Beaton are using a special sense of
IRD – what Smith and Ortiz show is an intermediate RD type. That is, the
spillover effect they demonstrate occurs when people compare themselves
to an *outgroup* member. But does this interesting resolution of the issue
also occur for the classic definition of IRD involving comparison with an
ingroup member?

I employ two methods to answer this question – a small meta-analysis
of research that used the classic definition of IRD and new analyses. Each
test supports the Tougas-Beaton contentions. Both experimental and survey research have found individual and group RD to be positively and
significantly related. Although the effect sizes from 12 independent samples with 4,574 respondents are not homogeneous, the mean correlation
weighted for sample size is highly significant, +.33 (Cohen's $d = +.69$;
$p < .001$), with a range between +.10 and +.80.[3]

To explore this issue further, consider the results from one of the largest
probability studies of prejudice ever conducted – the 1988 Eurobarometer
Survey (Reif & Melich, 1991). Seven national probability surveys asked
3,806 British, Dutch, French, and German respondents an array of prejudice
measures together with indicators of individual and group RD.[4] Similar to
other studies, individual RD correlates with group RD +.335 ($p < .001$).

Moreover, the two RD forms share four social location variables that account for 30% of their shared variance. Rural, poorly educated people with low family incomes who regard themselves as having low social status are more likely to rank high on both individual and group RD.[5] Yet, even after controlling for these variables, the two RD types still correlate +.28 ($p < .001$). The two RD forms differ, however, on one major social variable – age. Elderly Europeans reveal greater individual RD but not greater group RD.

Table 16.1 offers strong support for the Tougas and Beaton model for three diverse scales of prejudice against new immigrant groups in Europe.[6] As typically found, group RD is a stronger correlate of prejudice before any controls are applied. Once group RD is controlled, individual RD's relationships with prejudice are sharply reduced. And once the four social variables are also controlled, these relationships disappear. By contrast, the group RD correlations remain significant with all controls applied and diminish only slightly when individual RD alone is partialled out. Thus, as Tougas and Beaton hold, individual RD's influence on intergroup prejudice is mediated through its contribution to group RD.

Table 16.1 *Relative Deprivation Correlations with Three Types of Prejudice*[a]

	Blatant Prejudice[b]	Subtle Prejudice	Ethnocentrism
Individual relative deprivation	+.115**	+.061**	+.085**
With controls for:			
Group RD	+.040*	+.019	+.033
Group RD and four			
social variables[c]	+.011	−.002	+.011
Group relative deprivation	+.230**	+.131**	+.161**
With controls for:			
Individual RD	+.204**	+.117**	+.141**
Individual RD and			
four social variables	+.146**	+.075**	+.095**

[a] The data are from the Eurobarometer 30 of 1988. See Reif and Melich (1991) and Pettigrew and Meertens (1995) for details.

[b] Described in the notes, the full scales are provided in Pettigrew and Meertens (1995).

[c] As described in the text, the four control variables are education, family income, subjective social class ratings, and size of the respondent's community – each of which correlates significantly with both individual RD and group RD.

* = $p < .01$ ** = $p < .001$

The Consequences of Relative Deprivation

We noted that the RD effects are shaped by whether it is the individual or group form of RD. The book's chapters extend further our understanding of RD's consequences. They also show the wide range of RD's effects – collective action (Smith & Ortiz, Wright & Tropp), support for particular policies and programs (Tougas & Beaton, Tyler & Lind), reactions to conflict (Wilson et al.), and prejudice (Smith & Ho, Taylor, Duckitt & Mphuthing).

Early RD research asked if rising RD makes collective action more likely. And does RD predispose people to participate in social action? Two chapters address these possible RD effects. Smith and Ortiz answer a qualified "yes" to both queries. Disputing prior claims that RD is unrelated to collective action, they maintain that when properly measured RD is indeed related to collective action. Smith and Ortiz show that group RD with affect directly measured does have important implications for collective action. In addition, they join Tyler and Lind in demonstrating that procedural issues, not just outcomes, can be critically important in determining RD.

In their contribution, Wright and Tropp push the analysis of RD and collective action further. In agreement with Smith and Ortiz, they find group RD and affect to be important. Also in close accord with other chapters, Wright and Tropp propose that strong ingroup identification and a perception that the ingroup's disadvantage is both illegitimate and subject to change are critical for RD to lead to collective action. They add to this list an additional condition – the rejection of individual upward mobility. Taking up where Martin (1986) left off, Wright and Tropp's many conditions help explain why gross intergroup inequalities so often fail to result in collective action.

But is RD truly causal? Or is it merely related to these outcomes – perhaps a consequence of these outcomes? For example, does group RD increase as a result of participating in collective action? Or does group RD lead to participation? Or could both causal paths be operating – a nonrecursive relationship?

The findings of Duckitt and Mphuthing address these crucial queries about the causal sequence. They found that the historic South African election of 1994 did occasion sharp reductions in RD. Yet, for cognitive RD and illegitimacy RD, these reductions did not presage changes in prejudice. Their cross-lag analyses, however, did suggest interesting causal relationships with affective RD for African subjects. Affective RD shifts related to changes in prejudice against Afrikaners, while prejudice shifts related to affective RD concerning English South Africans.

From these results, Duckitt and Mphuthing call into question the role of RD as a basic cause of prejudice. But their conclusion is premature. Experimental studies have shown that reduced group RD, properly induced and measured, does lead to declines in prejudice (e.g., Grant & Brown, 1995). Moreover, their findings appear to relate to their measurement. Affective RD is the most adequately measured and produces causal results. Both their cognitive RD and illegitimacy RD measures involve difference scores. And Smith and Ortiz and the Smith and Pettigrew (2001) meta-analysis make clear that this is an inadequate means of tapping RD. Difference scores are always suspect, because the same number can represent meaningfully different responses. Such scores are even more inappropriate for RD indices. Because respondents do not directly make the comparison, it is only the investigator's inference that the respondents are making comparative judgments. Smith and Pettigrew (2001) believe this is why RD effects in their meta-analysis are significantly lower in studies with Cantril Ladder difference scores. One also can question the adequacy of the study's unrepresentative samples of convenience, its 70% dropout rate, and the use of cross-lag analyses to detect cause. Moreover, it could well be that cognitive RD changes require more time to influence prejudice than allowed by this research. Hence, longer lag times might have detected prejudice reduction driven by the RD decline.

Nevertheless, Duckitt and Mphuthing boast longitudinal data – a design all too rare in RD research. So the causal sequence issue they raise deserves further attention by RD researchers using longitudinal designs. Many of the RD correlations of the literature may well not represent simple effects of RD on dependent variables. These associations may often represent effects on RD itself or, more likely, complex nonrecursive relationships.

Walker and his colleagues point out that we lack both an adequate typology of RD responses as well as a testable model of RD effects. Their chapter addresses both needs. First, they offer a tentative response typology consisting of both positive and negative emotions as well as powerlessness and competitiveness dimensions. Then they propose a model that melds Folger's referent cognitions theory (RCT) with Weiner's attribution theory. Their model's central contention is that causal attributions serve as important mediators of RD's effects.

I made a rough test of these contentions with the same 1988 European survey data used previously. To mediate between group RD and three prejudice scales, Table 16.2 employs the following item: *There is a great deal of discrimination against [West Indians] living here today that limits their chances to get ahead* (with agree strongly to disagree strongly responses).

Table 16.2. *Attribution Effects on Group Relative Deprivation Correlations with Three Types of Prejudice*[a]

	Blatant Prejudice[b]	Subtle Prejudice	Ethnocentrism
Group relative deprivation	+.230**	+.131**	+.161**
With control for:			
Denial of discrimination	+.167**	+.090**	+.114**

[a] The data are from the Eurobarometer 30 of 1988. See Reif and Melich (1991) and Pettigrew and Meertens (1995) for details.
[b] Described in the notes, the full scales are provided in Pettigrew and Meertens (1995).
** = $p < .001$

Reversing the scoring produces a measure of the denial of discrimination. Through the eyes of these majority respondents, such denial attributes intergroup problems to the minority itself. And, just as Walker et al. predict, control for this single item significantly reduces the group RD and prejudice association for each measure of prejudice ($p < .01$).

An Illustrative Path Model
Both to test and illustrate several of these critical conclusions, I developed the eight-variable path model predicting blatant prejudice shown in Figure 16.2. In particular, we test the volume's contentions concerning generalization, social context, the IRD-GRD relationship, and the role of causal attributions in RD's effects. Once again, this model is based on the 3,806 European respondents of the 1988 prejudice survey. The model produces a good fit, and all of its standardized path coefficients are statistically significant ($p < .001$.)

RD's generality is supported in that this model combines data from four different western European nations using six diverse target immigrant outgroups. Note, too, that the model is embedded in a social context. It employs four social variables – age, family income, subjective social class ratings, and education. No direct effects on prejudice of family income or subjective social class remain after mediation by the two RD predictors. Age and education, however, have direct as well as indirect effects on blatant prejudice.

The path model also incorporates the insights of the Tougas-Beaton and Walker-Wong-Kretzschmar chapters. Individual RD influences prejudice only indirectly through group RD. And part of the group RD effect on prejudice is mediated through the attribution item involving the denial of discrimination.

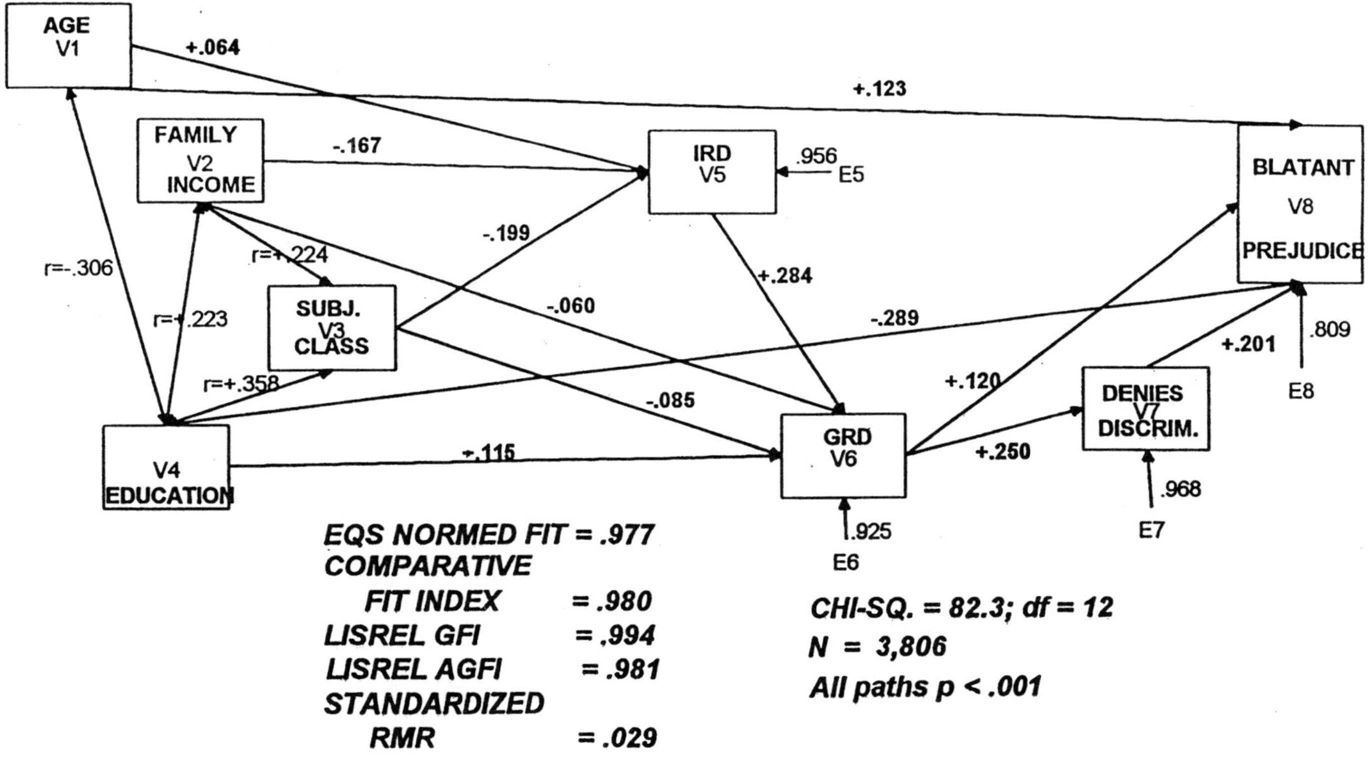
AGE
V1
FAMILY
V2
INCOME
SUBJ.
V3
CLASS
V4
EDUCATION
IRD
V5
GRD
V6
DENIES
V7
DISCRIM.
BLATANT
V8
PREJUDICE
+.064
+.123
-.167
.956
E5
r=-.306
r=+.224
r=+.223
r=+.358
-.199
+.284
-.060
-.289
-.085
+.115
+.120
+.250
+.201
.809
E8
.968
E7
.925
E6
EQS NORMED FIT = .977
COMPARATIVE
FIT INDEX = .980
LISREL GFI = .994
LISREL AGFI = .981
STANDARDIZED
RMR = .029
CHI-SQ. = 82.3; df = 12
N = 3,806
All paths p < .001

Figure 16.2. Illustrative path analysis.

LESSONS LEARNED

What have we learned in this volume? I believe that there are at least six valuable lessons to be gleaned from these pages.

1. RD appears to be a universal human phenomenon of importance. It is conditioned by the social context in which it occurs. In turn, RD, like many social psychological processes, mediates the effects of broad social factors on individuals. Individual RD relates to age and social class such that elderly and lower status respondents reveal high levels. Group RD is also greater among lower status individuals, particularly among the poorly educated. These relationships mean that the broad effects of such macro-variables as age, social class, and education – so central to sociological and political science theory – are in part mediated by RD for a range of important dependent variables (e.g., collective violence, prejudice).

2. Individual RD predicts a range of individual-level effects, such as stress. Group RD predicts a range of group-level effects, such as prejudice. But, following Tougas and Beaton, individual RD links with group-level effects indirectly by influencing group RD (see Table 16.1 and Figure 16.2). In repeated studies, the two RD types are consistently, positively, and moderately correlated.

3. Causal attributions mediate at least part of RD's effects. Walker and his co-authors supplied laboratory evidence, and the Eurobarometer supplied survey evidence for this contention (see Table 16.2 and Figure 16.2).

4. The effects of RD are widespread and varied. Yet we have seen how complex these effects can be. They appear strongest when RD is adequately measured; such measurement requires attention to both the cognitive and affective components of RD. People must not only perceive differences, but they must also regard these differences as unfair and resent them. In addition, the causal paths between RD and other variables may well be reciprocal. Simple recursive relationships cannot be casually assumed, and future research must routinely check for nonrecursive patterns.

5. Expanding the RD concept to the advantaged is clearly indicated. RD perceived and felt for others is apparently a common phenomenon. Future research on this topic, following the leads provided by several of the book's chapters, should prove valuable. And it could profitably be coupled with the existing theory and research on empathy, altruism, and pro-social behavior.

6. The more we learn about the RD process itself, the more intricate it appears. Two components of group RD are firmly established: Social identity is central to the process and complex social comparison processes are involved. For example, the process often entails temporal as well as con-

temporary comparisons – especially for the elderly. Counterfactual thinking is often implicated. In addition, the comparisons may not simply consist of differential outcomes. The distributional system of outcomes itself may be deeply embedded in the comparisons. Procedural justice – how fair and legitimate the distributional arrangements are – also can be a paramount factor in RD.

As often occurs in science, this volume supplies the foundation for a host of new questions and promising research directions for the future.

ACKNOWLEDGMENTS

For unusually helpful comments and critiques, I am indebted to Faye Crosby, Colin Leach, Heather Smith, Linda Tropp, and Stephen Wright.

NOTES

1. "I'll never be regarded as a great sociologist," joked Stouffer repeatedly. "I am not a theorist, and everyone can understand every word I write!"
2. I served for several years on an affirmative action committee at the University of Amsterdam. Most of the committee's cases involved gender discrimination in faculty hiring. Despite the nation's deserved reputation for racial tolerance (Pettigrew & Meertens, 1996), I found gender discrimination during the late 1980s at the professorial level to be surprisingly intense.
3. When trimmed of outliers to attain homogeneity, the mean r (+.39) remains essentially the same. The six studies with the 12 samples are: Foster & Matheson (1995), Guimond & Dube-Simard (1983), Kawakami & Dion (1992), Kelly & Kelly (1994), Kooman & Frankel (1992), and Pettigrew & Meertens (1999).
4. The IRD item reads: *"Would you say that over the last five years you have been economically a lot better off, better off, the same, worse off, or a lot worse off than other [British] people like yourself?"* The GRD reads: *"Would you say that over the last five years people like yourself in [Britain] have been economically a lot better off, better off, the same, worse off, or a lot worse off than most [West Indians] living here?"* Although these RD measures are limited to economic concerns and do not explicitly tap affect, they provided strong results – especially the GRD item with blatant prejudice (Pettigrew & Meertens, 1995, 1999). The explicit use of immigrant groups in the GRD item assures that affect is involved given the intense debates surrounding the issue in western Europe.
5. These variables have a multiple R of .30 with individual RD and .27 with group RD.
6. *"West Indians have jobs that the British should have"* is a sample from the 10-item Blatant Scale. Not ever feeling sympathy or admiration for the outgroup are two items from the 10-item Subtle Scale. The Ethnocentrism measure consists of reversing the 1–100 favorability ratings for three diverse groups: Black

Africans, Jews, and southern Europeans. The full scales are provided in Pettigrew and Meertens (1995, 1996).

REFERENCES

Albert, S. (1977). Temporal comparison theory. *Psychological Review, 84,* 485–503.

Batson, C. D., Polycarpou, M. P., Harmon-Jones, E., Imhoff, H. J., Mitchener, E. C., Bednar, L. L., Klein, T. R., & Highberger, L. (1997). Empathy and attitudes: Can feeling for a member of a stigmatized group improve feelings toward the group? *Journal of Personality and Social Psychology, 72,* 105–118.

Beaton, A. M., & Tougas, F. (1997). The representation of women in management: The more, the merrier? *Personality and Social Psychology Bulletin, 23,* 773–782.

Blau, P. M. (1964). *Exchange and power in social life.* New York: John Wiley.

Blumer, H. (1958). Race prejudice as a sense of group position. *Pacific Sociological Review, 1,* 3–7.

Centers, R. (1949). *The psychology of social classes.* Princeton, NJ: Princeton University Press.

Crosby, F. J. (1976). A model of egoistical relative deprivation. *Psychological Review, 83,* 85–113.

Crosby, F. J., Pufall, A., Snyder, R. C., O'Connell, & Whalen, P. (1989). The denial of personal disadvantage among you, me, and all other ostriches. In M. Crawford & M. Gentry (Eds.), *Gender and thought: Psychological perspectives.* New York: Springer-Verlag.

Davies, J. (1962). Toward a theory of revolution. *American Sociological Review, 27,* 5–18.

Duesenberry, J. S. (1949). *Income, saving, and the theory of consumer behavior.* Cambridge: Harvard University Press.

Dybvig, P. H. (1995). Duesenberry's ratcheting of consumption: Optimal dynamic consumption and investment given intolerance for any decline in standard of living. *Review of Economic Studies, 63,* 287–313.

Festinger, L. A. (1954). A theory of social comparison processes. *Human Relations, 7,* 117–140.

Foster, M. D., & Matheson, K. (1995). Double relative deprivation: Combining the personal and political. *Personality and Social Psychology Bulletin, 21,* 1167–1177.

Grant, P. R., & Brown, R. (1995). From ethnocentrism to collective protest: Responses to relative deprivation and threats to the identity. *Social Psychology Quarterly, 58,* 195–212.

Guimond, S., & Dube-Simard, L. (1983). Relative deprivation theory and the Quebec Nationalist Movement: The cognition-emotion distinction and the personal-group deprivation issue. *Journal of Personality and Social Psychology, 44,* 526–535.

Homans, G. C. (1961). *Social behavior: Its elementary forms.* New York: Harcourt, Brace & World.

Hyman, H. H. (1942). The psychology of status. *Archives of Psychology,* No. 269.

Hyman, H. H. (1960). Reflections on reference groups. *Public Opinion Quarterly, 24,* 383–396.

Kawakami, K., & Dion, K. L. (1993). The impact of salient self-identities on relative deprivation and action intentions. *European Journal of Social Psychology, 23,* 525–540.

Kawakami, K., & Dion, K. L. (1995). Social identity and affect as determinants of collective action: Toward an integration of relative deprivation and social identity theories. *Theory and Psychology, 5,* 551–577.

Kelley, H. H. (1983). The situational origins of human tendencies: A further reason for the formal analysis of structures. *Personality and Social Psychology Bulletin, 9,* 8–30.

Kelly, C., & Kelly, J. (1994). Who gets involved in collective action?: Social psychological determinants of individual participation in trade unions. *Human Relations, 47,* 63–88.

Kinder, D. R., & Sanders, L. M. (1996). *Divided by color: Racial politics and democratic ideals.* Chicago: University of Chicago Press.

Kooman, W., & Frankel, E. G. (1992). Effects of experienced discrimination and different forms of relative deprivation among Surinamese, a Dutch ethnic minority group. *Journal of Community and Applied Social Psychology, 2,* 63–72.

Lenski, G. E. (1954). Status crystallization: A non-vertical dimension of social status. *American Sociological Review, 19,* 405–413.

Major, B. (1994). From social inequality to personal entitlement: The role of social comparisons, legitimacy appraisals, and group membership. *Advances in Experimental Social Psychology, 26,* 293–355.

Mark, M. M., & Folger, R. (1984). Responses to relative deprivation: A conceptual framework. *Review of Personality and Social Psychology, 5,* 182–218.

Martin, J. (1981). Relative deprivation: A theory of distributive justice for an era of shrinking resources. *Research in Organizational Behavior, 3,* 57–107.

Martin, J. (1986). The psychology of injustice. In J. Olson, C. P. Herman, & M. Zanna (Eds.). *Relative deprivation and social comparison: The Ontario symposium* (Vol. 4, pp. 217–242). Hillsdale, NJ: Lawrence Erlbaum.

McFarland, S. (1999). Is authoritarianism sufficient to explain individual differences in prejudice? Unpublished paper presented at the meeting of the European Association of Experimental Social Psychology, Oxford, U.K.

McPhail, C. (1971). Civil disorder participation: A critical examination of recent research. *American Sociological Review, 36,* 1058–1073.

Merton, R. K. (1957). *Social theory and social structure* (rev. ed.). Glencoe, IL: Free Press.

Merton, R. K., & Kitt, A. S. (1950). Contributions to the theory of reference group behavior. In R. K. Merton & P. F. Lazarsfeld (Eds.), *Continuities in social research: Studies in the scope and method of "The American Soldier."* Glencoe, IL: Free Press.

Olson, J. M., Herman, C. P., & Zanna, M. P. (Eds.) (1986). *Relative deprivation and social comparison: The Ontario symposium* (Vol. 4). Hillsdale, NJ: Lawrence Erlbaum.

Pettigrew, T. F. (1964). *A profile of the Negro American.* New York: Van Nostrand.

Pettigrew, T. F. (1967). Social evaluation theory: Convergencies and applications. In D. Levine (Ed.), *Nebraska symposium on motivation, 1967.* Lincoln: University of Nebraska Press.

Pettigrew, T. F. (1991a). Toward unity and bold theory: Popperian suggestions for two persistent problems of social psychology. In C. Stephan, W. Stephan, & T. F. Pettigrew (Eds.), _The future of social psychology_. New York: Springer-Verlag.

Pettigrew, T. F. (1991b). The importance of cumulative effects: A neglected emphasis of Sherif's work. In D. Granberg & G. Sarup (Eds.), _Social judgment and intergroup relations: Essays in honor of Muzafer Sherif_. New York: Springer-Verlag.

Pettigrew, T. F., & Meertens, R. W. (1995). Subtle and blatant prejudice in western Europe. _European Journal of Social Psychology, 57_, 57–75.

Pettigrew, T. F., & Meertens, R. W. (1996). The _verzuiling_ puzzle: Understanding Dutch intergroup relations. _Current Psychology, 15_, 3–13.

Pettigrew, T. F., & Meertens, R. W. (1999). Relative deprivation, intergroup prejudice, and attitudes toward immigration policy in Europe. Unpublished paper. Department of Psychology, University of California, Santa Cruz.

Reif, K., & Melich, A. (1991). _Euro-barometer 30: Immigrants and out-groups in Western Europe, October–November 1988_. (ICPSR 9321). Ann Arbor, MI: Inter-university Consortium for Political and Social Research.

Runciman, W. G. (1966). _Relative deprivation and social justice_. London: Routledge & Kegan Paul.

Sears, D. O. (1986). College sophomores in the laboratory: Influences of a narrow data base on social psychology's view of human nature. _Journal of Personality and Social Psychology, 51_, 515–530.

Sherif, M., Harvey, O. J., White, B. J., Hood, W. R., & Sherif, C. (1961). _Intergroup conflict and cooperation: The Robbers Cave Experiment_. Norman, OK: Institute of Group Relations.

Smith, E. R. (1993). Social identity and social emotions: Toward new conceptions of prejudice. In D. M. Mackie & D. L. Hamilton (Eds.), _Affect, cognition, and stereotyping: Interactive processes in group perception_. San Diego, CA: Academic Press.

Smith, H., & Pettigrew, T. F. (2001). Relative deprivation: A conceptual critique and meta-analysis. Unpublished paper. Department of Psychology, University of California, Santa Cruz.

Stouffer, S. A. (1940). Intervening opportunities: A theory relating mobility and distance. _American Sociological Review, 5_, 845–867.

Stouffer, S. A. (1955). _Communism, conformity and civil liberties_. New York: Doubleday.

Stouffer, S. A. (1962). _Social research to test ideas_. New York: Free Press.

Stouffer, S. A., Suchman, E. A., DeVinney, L. C., Star, S. A., & Williams, R. M., Jr. (1949). _The American soldier: Vol. 1. Adjustment during army life_. Princeton, NJ: Princeton University Press.

Suls, J. M., & Miller, R. L. (Eds.) (1977). _Social comparison processes: Theoretical and empirical perspectives_. New York: Halsted Press.

Taylor, D. M., Wright, S. C., Moghaddam, F. M., & Lalonde, R. N. (1990). The personal/group discrimination: Perceiving my group, but not myself, to be a target for discrimination. _Personality and Social Psychology Bulletin, 16_, 254–263.

Taylor, M. C. (1980). Fraternal deprivation and competitive racism: A second look. _Sociology and Social Research, 65_, 37–55.

Tesser, A. (1988). Toward a self-evaluation maintenance model of social behavior. _Advances in Experimental Social Psychology, 21_, 181–227.

Thibaut, J. W., & Kelley, H. H. (1959). *The social psychology of groups.* New York: John Wiley.

Tougas, F., & Veilleux, F. (1991). Les reactions des hommes a l'action positive: Un equestion d'interet personnel or d'onsatisfaction face aux iniquites de sexe? *Revue Canadienne des Sciences Administratives, 8,* 37–42.

Vanneman, R. D., & Pettigrew, T. F. (1972). Race and relative deprivation in the urban United States. *Race, 13,* 461–486.

Veilleux, F., & Tougas, F. (1989). Male acceptance of men to affirmative action strategies for women: The result of altruistic or egoistical motives? *International Journal of Psychology, 24,* 59–70.

Walker, I. (1999). Effects of personal and group relative deprivation on personal and collective self-esteem. *Group Processes and Intergroup Relations, 2,* 365–380.

Walker, I., & Pettigrew, T. F. (1984). Relative deprivation theory: An overview and conceptual critique. *British Journal of Social Psychology, 23,* 301–310.

Index

comparisons *(continued)*
  intergroup, 16–7, 46, 53–7, 86–8, 91–3,
    96–105, 121, 138, 204, 208–16,
    242–5, 247, 252–255, 289, 313–4,
    332, 336, 338
  interpersonal, 46, 91–3, 96–105, 138,
    144, 208–16, 289, 313–4, 336, 338
  similar, 168–71, 172–3, 176–9
  temporal, 119, 122–3, 126–8, 243, 265,
    268–9, 289, 314–5, 319, 327, 354–6,
    368
common ingroup identity model, 342,
  343
communal orientation, 179
contextual analysis, 21, 30, 39
counterfactual thinking, 240, 266–7, 289,
  359, 369
Crocker, J., 102, 109, 129–30, 206
Crosby, F. 2, 14–15, 18, 192–3, 265, 289,
  293–4, 300, 305–6, 309 n1, 314, 353

Davies, J., 194, 326
Davis, J.A., 315
depersonalization, 205
deprivation
  affective, 14–5, 71–2, 77–84, 94,
    97–103, 120, 213–6, 309 n2, 356–7,
    365, 368
  cognitive, 27–8, 71–2, 77–84, 120,
    213–6, 294, 297, 303, 306, 309 n2,
    365, 368
  decremental, 265
  double, 125, 361, 368
  group, 3, 15–6, 27–30, 45–52, 71,
    120–4, 194, 208–17, 243, 255–6, 282,
    296, 298, 303, 332, 337–9, 340, 351,
    358, 360–3
  individual, 3, 15–6, 46, 70, 91–2,
    120–4, 194, 208–16, 243, 255–6, 282,
    296, 298, 303, 332, 337–9, 340, 351,
    358, 360–3
  on behalf of others, 16, 95, 124–6, 354,
    355
  self-outgroup, 93, 104–5, 120, 303–7,
    361–3

deserving, 2, 52–6, 192–3, 280
Dijker, A.J.M., 335
disadvantaged comparisons, *see*
  upward comparisons
discrimination, 63–4, 109–10, 257,
    332–3, 343–4
  denial of, 24, 282, 300, 366
  economic, 51–7, 69–70
  sex, 5, 153–4, 186–90, 360
disdain, 148–9, 341
distributive justice, 47, 52–6, 64–6, 201,
    351
distributive norms, 185–6
Doosje, B., 104, 146, 207–8, 252–3
Dube, L. 14, 18, 51, 72, 121, 194
Dunk, T., 149–50

efficacy
  personal, 147
  collective, 221, 337
egoistic relative deprivation, *see*
  individual relative deprivation
Ellemers, N., 104, 146, 207–8, 252–3
Emery, R.E., 316
emotion-appraisal theory, 333, 341
entitlement, 14, 17, 44, 192–3, 217, 220,
    245, 280, 288, 317
equality, 16, 27, 193, 324
equity, 139, 186, 204, 288, 301
equity theory, 120, 124, 201, 351
Erikson, B.H., 170–1, 179
ethnic identification, *see* ingroup
  identification
ethnocentrism, *see* ingroup favoritism

feasibility, 14, 192–3, 243–4, 258–9 n,
    267, 281
Ferree, M.M., 291–2
Festinger, L., 138, 165, 314–5, 351
Fishbein, M.P., 333
five stage model of intergroup
  relations, 219
Folger, R., 126, 243, 258 n, 265–9,
    270, 281, 288–90, 297, 301–2, 353,
    365

Lightning Source UK Ltd.
Milton Keynes UK
08 February 2011

167130UK00007B/125/P

9 780521 180696